Fodor's 5th Edition

# Turkey

Fodor's Travel Publications • New York, Toronto, London, Sydney, Auckland
www.fodors.com

# CONTENTS

# MAPS

Circled letters in text correspond to letters on the photographs. For more information on the sights pictured, turn to the indicated page number Ⓐ⟩ on each photograph.

# DESTINATION TURKEY

Turkey is exotic to Western eyes. Its domed mosques, their minarets reaching for heaven; the packed bazaars agleam with copper and brass and piled high with carpets; the ancient ruins and medieval palaces and fortresses—all are the stuff of legend come to life. These sights alone, to say nothing of Turkey's great natural beauty, would be enough to keep you coming back. But there is so much more to experience here than glorious architecture, stunning coasts and mountains, and the monumental legacies of great civilizations past. In Turkey, without expecting it and with a lightness of spirit, you will begin to feel untethered from the ways of the Western world. Formally, through pacts and protocols, the country seeks to join itself to Europe. Happily, in its soul, where it really counts, Turkey will always be a land apart. And for that very reason, you may find it hard to visit only once.

# ISTANBUL

Ⓐ❯42

Istanbul can fascinate, frustrate, and enchant you—all at once. Europe and Asia, the old ways and the modern, mix here in tight quarters, yielding bewitchingly out-of-sync images. Imagine an Armani-clad driver in a Lexus, shouting into a cell phone—and in the next lane, a donkey hitched to a cart, taking the daily gridlock philosophically. Picture young women in designer jeans lined up for a new Western flick and, passing by them, matrons robed to the ankles, bound for evening prayer. You'll find scenes like this all over the city. Much of what you've come to see—great mosques and palaces—is packed into the ancient heart of town, Old Stamboul. This is where Ⓐ⒟**Topkapı Sarayı,** a stunning palace steeped in lore, expanded over the centuries, serially embellished by rulers like Ahmet III (who built a grand street fountain here). Peewee pashas, their parents, and visitors alike are all attracted by the

Ⓑ❯37

priceless gems of the Treasury and the mysterious fascination of the palace's famous harem. Sinners have sought mercy, rather than material accomplishments, in the light-filled ©**Blue Mosque** and in ®**Aya Sofya**. The Byzantine Empire echoes in the mosaics of the latter, now a museum. Classical music echoes through the world's most handsome cistern, ©**Yerebatan Sarnıcı,** where water, precious in Istanbul to this day, was stored as siege insurance. While you're in the neighborhood, visit the Arkeoloji Müzesi (Archaeology Museum) for its extraordinary Greek and Roman antiquities; the Ibrahim Paşa Sarayı, for its Museum of Turkish and Islamic Arts; and the Mosaik Müzesi, to see glorious Byzantine mosaics of idyllic rural scenes. Stroll a few more blocks and you're at Sokollu Mehmet Paşa Cami, a masterwork designed by the 16th-century architect Sinan, the genius behind much of Istanbul's beauty. The mosque is intimate in scale, but no one ever said that size made a diamond perfect.

©42

©44

7

# ISTANBUL

Ⓕ▷ 58 Ⓖ▷ 36

Even after you've been dazzled by the great palaces, mosques, and museums of this endlessly intriguing city, you'll still have plenty to see. The texture of life in Istanbul is an attraction in itself. You won't find anything like it in Europe—or in the *rest* of Europe, as many locals would be quick to remind you. Outside of Beyoğlu, the new town, where lawyers bill by the minute and bankers lunch at their laptops, informality is the rule. At Ⓕ**Rumeli Café Restaurant**—or in a sommelier's nightmare—wine waits in a fountain. Why not? And why not beat the heat with a glass of cherry juice, deftly poured by costumed hawkers in ⒼⒽ**Old Stamboul**? Be advised: this stuff can be tart. Old-timers convene at places around town for tea, camaraderie, and a few hits on a water pipe. (If you can't take the smoke, stay out of the teahouse.) If you

think you're a born shopper, prove it while searching for carpets, copper, or fashions from slippers to handbags in the winding, covered lanes of the Ⓘ**Grand Bazaar.** To haggle is obligatory here; it's culturally thick not to. The first

Ⓗ▷ 36

price you'll hear will be absurd. Make an equally absurd counteroffer and then work slowly toward reason. Avoid jovial handshakes while talking dollars and cents. Shake hands and enjoy a glass of tea, and you've sealed the deal. Unless you crave coriander, your bankroll is safer in the ③**Egyptian Bazaar,**

where spices are a major item, as well as fruit and nuts. Treat your nose to a visit. Then please your taste buds with a fish pita at the Eminönü docks, five minutes away. You'll get today's catch plus added local flavor. The frenetic street vendors at Eminönü can make the Grand Bazaar seem like Sears. Now cross the Galata Bridge to the new town; the view from the bridge is inspiring, and the new town is worth a look for contrast alone. And save a day for a long boat ride, to view Istanbul from the Bosporus or to explore the bucolic Princes Islands, 20 kilometers (12 miles)—or is it light-years?—from the bustle of town.

The cultural winds of Europe can blow briskly in parts of Istanbul, but in southern Marmara, just south of the city, you'll barely feel them as breezes. You've got both feet in Asia now, and in a part of Turkey rich in history. In ⒶⒷ**İznik,** lakeside restaurants and hotels offer tranquil views, while timeless beauty

# SOUTHERN MARMARA

Ⓐ 86

Ⓑ 86

graces world-renowned İznik tiles, as lovely today as 500 years ago, when they were the rage of the Islamic universe. Older yet in İznik is Ⓓ **Sancta Sophia,** where great church councils shaped Christian doctrine. At Yeşil Cami, the Green Mosque, you can admire the Seljuk style, simpler than the Ottoman, and to Islamic holy buildings what Romanesque is to Gothic. Bearing the same name, Ⓒ**Yeşil Cami** in Bursa is an Ottoman masterpiece. İznik tiles help make it so, just as they make the inside of Ⓔ**Yeşil Türbe,** a sultan's mausoleum, a glory to behold. Don't miss the covered bazaar

YESIL CAMII
1412 - 1419

87

in Bursa—if Istanbul's Grand Bazaar taught you Haggling 101, here you're in graduate school. The local specialty, by the way, is luxurious Turkish towels. Close by, Uludağ has good skiing and a fine, hikable national park. Kuşcenneti National Park, west of Bursa, has superb bird-watching in the marshlands and forests near Lake Kuş. For things to see, do, and eat, Bursa ranks tops in the region, but try to squeeze in İznik and Termal, a splendid ancient spa where weary Turks, from the Ottomans to Istanbul cabbies, have long taken the waters. Visit the baths, and you may be inclined to hop in, too.

86

88

# AEGEAN COAST

Ⓐ▷ 126

The ancient Greeks, who knew a thing or two about living well, loved this white-sand coast and its turquoise waters, settling here as early as 1000 BC. The ancient Romans, who knew quite a bit about stealing good ideas from the Greeks, continued developing the area. The result today is a wealth of classical ruins, those same enticing beaches and waters, lodgings for all budgets, and excellent seafood. Pergamum, with its great Hellenistic acropolis, is magnificent, as is the Temple of Apollo in Ⓐ**Didyma,** where a massive head of Medusa stands guard. The Great Theater, also Greek-built, is the grandest ruin at Ⓑ**Miletus,** while the columns of Ⓒ **Hierapolis** are a legacy of imperial Rome. Aphrodisias holds the remains of the city of the goddess of love, but the centerpiece of antiquities is Ⓓ**Ephesus,** with its two-story Library of Celsus and splendidly preserved theater and temples. The place has great meaning for Christians: Paul preached here to hostile crowds, but managed to found a congregation. And nearby is Meryemana, the

Ⓑ▷ 125

house where Jesus's mother is believed to have spent her final years. Be ready for local guides claiming inside knowledge of where Mary did her laundry and sat on a rock. They're just trying to make a living, and she probably wouldn't mind.

# AEGEAN COAST

Life goes on, of course, amid ancient ruins, all along along the Aegean Coast, in quiet villages and high-voltage resorts. Local women make their own pita bread the old-fashioned way; the men make a living from the sea in boats no bigger than the craft of two millennia ago. You can watch them in pretty fishing villages like Ⓔ**Foça,** typical in most ways except for its jumbo-size Club Med. Offshore lie the Ⓗ**Siren Islets,** where Odysseus and his crew flirted with madness, a few succumbing to the sirens' irresistible song. The lure of the modern islets lies in their excellent beaches. You

F> 122

can pick up a Turkish tea set in the myriad curio shops of F**Kuşadası,** but tranquil ambience is a tougher find. This no-longer-sleepy port hums with seaside holiday energy— and British pub singing. If you like things boisterous after dark, Kuşadası is for you. If you prefer low-key evenings, it may not be, although its proximity to Ephesus is a huge plus. The nightlife in G**Bodrum** is more refined, more sophisticated—and more expensive. Most things are in this upscale resort, long beloved by Turks who've made good, and more recently by visitors who've caught on. With its flower-covered buildings and crescent-shape bays, Bodrum is beautiful, glitzy, and inevitably getting bigger. If it intrigues you, catch it now, before it gets any more popular.

G> 126

H> 108

# MEDITERRANEAN COAST

**Ⓐ⟩142**

Turkey's southern shoreline, say its fans a bit smugly, can match the Aegean Coast in everything but tour buses. You'll find the gamut of attractions here: unspoiled fishing villages, worldly resorts, bazaars, antiquities, exquisite beaches like İstuzu and Ⓓ**Kapitaş,** and opportunities for sailing and for scuba diving amid underwater ruins. Along the Turkish Riviera—as this lovely coast has regrettably been labeled—residents are inclined to see you as a true guest. The ancient sites here take a backseat to none. Spectacular rock tombs, a specialty of the Carians, are carved into cliffs near the fishing village of Ⓐ**Dalyan.** The Roman theater in ©**Aspendos** gives the Colosseum a run

**Ⓑ⟩150**

for its money, and you can catch a concert or performance here. At romantic Phaselis, the ruined streets descend into the clear sea. If you're camped in the resort of Ⓔ**Antalya,** near the east-ern end of the Mediterranean Coast, a day-trip to the spectacular ruins of Termessos is mandatory. This lofty fortress city in the mountains was never taken, not even by Alexander the Great. As Antalya helps anchor the coast's eastern reaches, the fashionable, sprawling resort of Marmaris anchors the western end. Close to it, the laid-back market town of Ⓕ**Köyceğiz** is a gateway to great bird-watching, as well as to Dalyan's monumental tombs. But for many the finest gems of the entire coast are along Ⓑ**Kekova Sound,** including pretty

Ⓔ▷155

Kale on Kekova Island. It's hard to resist taking a swim in the sound's crystalline waters. The area is famous for its great natural beauty, submerged Greek and Roman ruins, and centuries-old way of life.

Ⓕ▷142

When Kemal Atatürk, the father of Turkish independence, chose Ankara as his seat of government in 1923, he had a vision of building something unprecedented in Turkey—a modern, secular city like the national capitals of the West. Ankara was a provincial backwater, virtually a clean slate for city planning. Today its broad boulevards and refreshing green spaces, such as Ⓐ**Gençlik Parkı,** create an urban roominess unique in the land. An honor guard is always at Ⓑ**Anıt Kabir,** Atatürk's mausoleum. Though statues of Atatürk are everywhere in Turkey, you'll gain a deeper sense here of the reverence

# ANKARA AND CENTRAL ANATOLIA

Ⓐ 185

Ⓑ 186

Turks feel for the man. Pride of nationhood is also strong at the treasure-filled Anadolu Medeniyetleri Müzesi, where there are artifacts of Anatolian civilizations from Assyrian to Hittite to Roman. Paintings

and sculptures by modern Turkish artists fill the ⒺResim ve Heykel Müzezi, a stroll away. Also of this century is the © Kocatepe Cami, Ankara's largest mosque. While Turkey is at its most contemporary in Ankara, nowhere is it more ancient than in surrounding Central Anatolia. The capital makes an ideal base for day-trips to the Hittite ruins at ⒹYazılıkaya, Hatuşaş, and Alacahöyük. As you admire these great temples and palaces remember this: they stood here long before there was an Athens or a Rome.

# ANKARA AND
# CENTRAL ANATOLIA

Southeast of Ankara lies terrain that might have been dreamed up by a set designer. Yielding easily to wind, rain, and oxidation, the volcanic rocks of Ⓕ**Cappadocia** have taken on improbable shapes and hues, delightful for viewing from muleback or hot-air balloon. When human hands embellished on nature's work, cave dwellings like those near Ⓗ**Zelve** emerged. For the most part, these were the cells of early Christian monks, who also built churches in the rock, many now preserved in Ⓘ**Göreme.** Close to Cappadocia's monastic caves, Ürgüp is a popular base, while in smaller villages here you'll see horse-drawn carts and folkways that haven't changed much for centuries. Cappadocia aboveground is fascinating enough, but another amazing feature lies below: underground cities that reached 20 stories beneath the surface and could hold up to 20,000 people. Under pressure from Arab raiders, Christians took refuge in these

Ⓕ▷ 191

Ⓖ▷ 201

marvels of engineering. At Kaymaklı, climb in yourself for a sense of life inside these hidden fortresses. Aksaray, with a minaret on one mosque that's a match for Pisa's errant tower, is worth a stop as you head

southwest for ⓖ**Konya,** home to treasures of Seljuk architecture   and to the mystics called whirling dervishes. The Mevlâna Müzesi and Türbesi is a museum and tomb dedicated to the founder of the Mevlevi dervishes. Their graceful, ecstatic dance is as beautiful as any act of devotion in the world.

# BLACK SEA COAST

Ⓐ⟩ 212

Wild and remote in many places, this scenic coast is worlds apart from Turkey's other beach areas. The stunning scenery, pretty villages with old Ottoman houses, and good bazaars can take at least a week to explore. You can start in ⒶⒻ**Şile,** whose striped lighthouse and picturesque harbor, complete with castle ruin, are familiar sights to Istanbulites needing a break by the sea. You'll find plenty of nightlife here. Enjoy it; you may not see it again for a while. Moving east, turn south at the walled city of Amasra and head for Safranbolu, where the lure is the well-preserved old town with its Ottoman houses. Also inland, medieval Kastamonu casts a spell with its historic castle and its this-is-the-real-thing bazaar. Back on the water, Sinop is the oldest city on the Black Sea Coast—old enough to have been founded, supposedly, by an Amazon queen—and full of reminders of its Greek and Byzantine, and Seljuk past. Press on to Samsun and head inland for ⒸⒹ**Amasya,** supposedly founded by *another* Amazon queen, and steeped in history reaching back to Alexander's

Ⓑ⟩ 220

Ⓒ⟩ 215

⧉ 215

time. Amasya was an intellectual training ground for Ottoman princes and a home to 18 seminaries. Carved into the cliff above the Ottoman houses of the town are the Kings' Rock Tombs, dating to the 4th century BC. Also in the area, Zile and Tokat are worth a stop for their old mosques and fortress ruins. It's downhill from here to Ünye on the coast, a nice little town with beaches. The last days of your journey take you to Tirebolu and its Genoese fortress, one of three in the vicinity; Bedrama is the best. Press on to Trabzon, with its mosques, its venerable bazaar, and especially ⑧**Aya Sofya,** a former church and mosque that is now a museum preserving Byzantine mosaics and frescoes. More Byzantine glory awaits in Sumela, where an energetic hike leads to the cliffside Monastery of the Virgin. In ⑤**Rize,** you've come to the end of the road. Climb up to the ruins of the Genoese castle and look westward. Yes, it's been a long haul. But you'd do it again.

Ⓔ⟩ 222

Ⓕ⟩ 212

237

# THE FAR EAST

Ⓑ 241

Harsh and beautiful, a land of sparsely settled plains, deserts, and austere black mountains, this is country for the adventurous—all the more so because of clashes between the Turkish army and Kurdish separatists going back to 1984; check the State Department's latest advisory before venturing in. Turkey's Far East is vast, and you may pick your pleasures depending on whether you enter through Erzurum or Diyarbakır. The sights in Erzu-rum include ancient mosques, seminaries, and a bazaar, but it's mainly a launch point for trips to the ruins at Ani, seat of a medieval Armenian kingdom in an awesome mountain setting. Also relatively nearby is majestic Mt. Ararat, where some say Noah's ark came to rest. From Diyarbakır, a truly ancient walled city with a fine medieval bazaar, you can strike out for Ⓑ**Mt. Nimrod,** where the Head of Heracles is just one of five great stone noggins in a grand temple complex. You can find creature comforts in Ⓒ**Mardin,** along

Ⓒ 243

with views of venerable mosques and a fantastic medieval citadel, against which Tamerlane batted one for two. In ⒹⒻ**Şanlıurfa,** reputed birthplace of Abraham, you can satisfy physical needs and more spiritual interests. The Hasan Paşa Mosque is said to watch over the very spot of the patriarch's birth. The area around Lake Van makes a long journey worthwhile, with its gloriously sited fortress, Ⓐ**Hoşap Kalesı;** the barren but beautiful landscape around the lake itself; and the university town of Van. The Ⓔ**Van Müzesi** houses Urartian artifacts from pots to jewelry, some 3,000 years old but looking spiffy enough for *Antiques Roadshow.*

# GREAT ITINERARIES

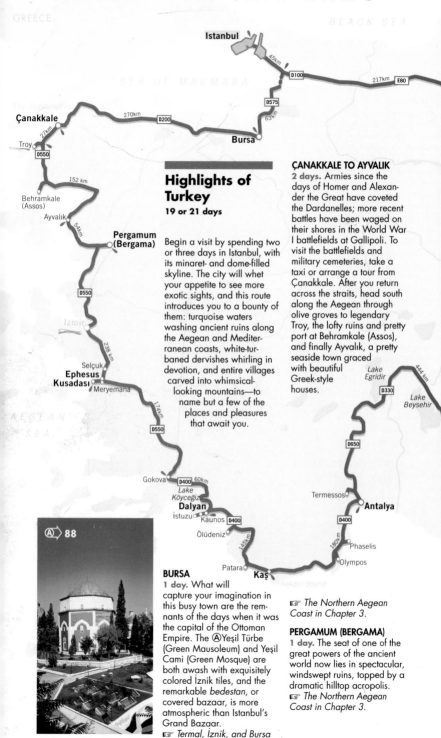

**GREECE**

**BLACK SEA**

**SEA OF MARMARA**

Istanbul

45km

D100

217km · E80

Çanakkale

270km · D200

27km

Troy · D550

D575

63km

**Bursa**

152 km

Behramkale (Assos)

Ayvalık

54km

Pergamum (Bergama)

D550

İzmir

238 km

Selçuk

**Ephesus**
**Kuşadası** · Meryemana

174km

D550

**AEGEAN SEA**

Lake Egridir

444 km

D330

Lake Beyşehir

D650

Gokova · D400 · 60km
Lake Köyceğiz

İstuzu

**Dalyan**

Kaunos · D400

Ölüdeniz

145km

Patara

**Kaş**

Gökova Sound

Termessos

**Antalya**

D400

180 km

Phaselis

Olympos

**MEDITERRANEAN SEA**

## Highlights of Turkey
### 19 or 21 days

Begin a visit by spending two or three days in Istanbul, with its minaret- and dome-filled skyline. The city will whet your appetite to see more exotic sights, and this route introduces you to a bounty of them: turquoise waters washing ancient ruins along the Aegean and Mediterranean coasts, white-turbaned dervishes whirling in devotion, and entire villages carved into whimsical-looking mountains—to name but a few of the places and pleasures that await you.

### ÇANAKKALE TO AYVALIK
**2 days.** Armies since the days of Homer and Alexander the Great have coveted the Dardanelles; more recent battles have been waged on their shores in the World War I battlefields at Gallipoli. To visit the battlefields and military cemeteries, take a taxi or arrange a tour from Çanakkale. After you return across the straits, head south along the Aegean through olive groves to legendary Troy, the lofty ruins and pretty port at Behramkale (Assos), and finally Ayvalık, a pretty seaside town graced with beautiful Greek-style houses.

### BURSA
**1 day.** What will capture your imagination in this busy town are the remnants of the days when it was the capital of the Ottoman Empire. The Ⓐ Yeşil Türbe (Green Mausoleum) and Yeşil Cami (Green Mosque) are both awash with exquisitely colored İznik tiles, and the remarkable *bedestan*, or covered bazaar, is more atmospheric than Istanbul's Grand Bazaar.
☞ *Termal, İznik, and Bursa in Chapter 2.*

☞ *The Northern Aegean Coast in Chapter 3.*

### PERGAMUM (BERGAMA)
**1 day.** The seat of one of the great powers of the ancient world now lies in spectacular, windswept ruins, topped by a dramatic hilltop acropolis.
☞ *The Northern Aegean Coast in Chapter 3.*

Ⓐ ▷ 88

Köyceğiz, a pleasant cruise upstream, is the center of a nature preserve. Take a relaxing soak in the sulfurous hot springs near the lakeshore.
☞ *The Turquoise Coast in Chapter 4.*

## THE TURQUOISE COAST AND KAŞ

**2 days.** Lycian and Roman ruins litter this part of the Mediterranean, one of the world's most beautiful coastlines. Pleasant stops on the

trip east from Dalyan are Ölüdeniz, rated by many as the most beautiful beach in Turkey, and Patara, where ruins of the Roman city are strung along another spectacular beach. Kaş is a fine place to laze by the sea and linger in a cafe. On nearby Kekova Sound, you can cruise over Greek and Roman ruins that lie just beneath the turquoise waters.
☞ *The Turquoise Coast in Chapter 4.*

## ANTALYA

**2 days.** Continuing east, combine a ramble through the ruins at Olympos and Phaselis with a dip in the sea. In Antalya, the picturesque harbor is surrounded by narrow lanes that lead to hilltop tea gardens where the brew comes from old-fashioned samovars. The ancient artifacts in the Antalya Müzesi (Antalya Museum) set the mood for a climb through the splendid mountaintop ruins at Termessos.
☞ *Antalya to Alanya in Chapter 4.*

## KUŞADASI AND EPHESUS

**2 days.** Kuşadası is a popular resort, but the draw is nearby Ephesus, one of the best-preserved and most evocative ancient cities anywhere. Adjacent Meryemana is said to be the place where the Virgin Mary ascended to heaven, and nearby Selçuk is a charming town huddled around a Byzantine fortress.
☞ *The Southern Aegean Coast in Chapter 3.*

## DALYAN

**2 days.** Cliffs etched with Carian tombs loom over this quiet fishing town on the Dalyan River. The first stop on a boat trip down the river is the ancient site of Kaunos, immortalized by Ovid in the *Metamorphoses;* then it's on to beautiful İstuzu beach, a nesting ground for *Caretta caretta* sea turtles. Lake

## KONYA

**1 day.** This city in the midst of an oasis is best known as home of the whirling dervishes. If you visit in December, you can catch the dancers in action; at other times you will encounter them in spirit at the magnificent Mevlâna Müzesi and Türbesi (Mevlâna Museum and Tomb of Mevlâna Celaleddin).
☞ *Cappadocia and Konya in Chapter 5.*

## CAPPADOCIA

**3 days.** You don't have to be a troglodyte to fall under the spell of this otherworldly region where houses, churches, and entire cities are carved into fantastically shaped rocky outcroppings. Ürgüp, Göreme, or one of the even smaller villages are the best bases from which to explore these wonders; all provide unique accommodation in cave dwellings.
☞ *Cappadocia and Konya in Chapter 5.*

## ANKARA

**2 days.** You'll encounter modern Turkey on the broad boulevards of its young capital, though the superb Ankara Anadolu Medeniyetleri Müzesi (Museum of Anatolian Civilizations) sweeps you into the past; so do the nearby Bronze Age cities of Hattuşaş and Alacahöyük.
☞ *Ankara and the Hittite Cities in Chapter 5.*

**By Public Transportation** All of the stops on this itinerary are well connected by bus service, though this will slow you down considerably. You can speed back to Istanbul from Ankara by plane or express train.

# Classical Civilizations

**14 days**

From the plains of Troy through the streets of Ephesus to the soaring peaks of Pergamum and Termessos and the enchanting groves of Phaselis and Harbiye, Turkey is littered with hundreds of ancient Roman and Greek ruins. Still proudly commanding their sublime natural settings along the Aegean and Mediterranean coasts, these ancient places evoke all the splendor of past civilizations.

## ISTANBUL

**2 days.** Although you won't want to devote your explorations of this fascinating city only to its ancient treasures, the Arkeoloji Müzesi (Archeological Museum) should be one of your first stops. Since most of treasures in the Greek and Roman collections come from Turkish sites, you will get a good idea of what belongs in all those empty niches you observe on your travels.
☞ *Chapter 1.*

## TROY AND NEARBY SITES

**1 day.** Çanakkale is a good base from which to explore the city whose capture more than 3,000 years ago launched Homer's timeless epics. Then turn south to visit the overgrown ruins of the once great city of Alexandria Troas, the scant remains of the Apollo Smintheon, and the lofty ruins of Behramkale (Assos).
☞ *The Northern Aegean Coast in Chapter 3.*

## PERGAMUM (BERGAMA)

**1 day.** At this once-magnificent architectural and artistic center, now one of Turkey's most spectacular ruins, parchment was invented for the famous library and the Asklepion was the world's first full-service health clinic.
☞ *The Northern Aegean Coast in Chapter 3.*

## EPHESUS

**2 days.** Easily visited from a base in Kuşadası or Selçuk, Ephesus is one of the best-preserved and most evocative ancient cities anywhere. Two other once-great cities, Priene and Miletus, as well as the seaside ⓑTemple of Apollo at Didyma, are within easy reach.
☞ *The Southern Aegean Coast in Chapter 3.*

## APHRODISIAS

**1 day.** The city built in honor of the goddess of love is one of the country's largest and best-preserved archeological sites—and a rewarding spot to break the day-long journey south to the Turquoise Coast.
☞ *The Southern Aegean Coast in Chapter 3.*

## KAŞ

**2 days.** This pleasant resort is an excellent base from which to explore a string of beautifully situated ancient cities: Pinara, romantically backed by high cliffs; Patara, where the seaside ruins are scattered among sand dunes; and Letoön, with its three temples. The most unusual settings, though, are those of the Lycian tombs and submerged Roman and Greek towns you'll see on a boat trip through Kekova Sound.
☞ *The Turquoise Coast in Chapter 4.*

## ANTALYA

**3 days.** The seaside ruins at Olympos and Phaselis are tempting detours as you travel east along the coast, but plan to be in Antalya in time for a sunset stroll around the harbor and old quarter. After studying the Greek and

ⓑ▷126

Roman artifacts in the Antalya Müzesi (Antalya Museum) and lingering beneath Hadrian's Gate, you can climb through ruins that cling to nearby mountainsides—Termessos, Perge, and Aspendos.
☞ *Antalya to Alanya in Chapter 4.*

## ANTAKYA (ANTIOCH)
**2 days.** It will take a full day to travel to the eastern edge of the Turkish coast, but you can take a break at Silifke, with its Roman theater, stadium, and Temple of Zeus. Antakya's Hatay Müzesi (Hatay Museum) houses mosaics considered to be among the highest achievements of Roman art; they come from nearby Harbiye, a beautiful gorge once sprinkled with Roman villas.
☞ *East of Alanya in Chapter 4.*

**By Public Transportation**
While you can reach all these main cities by bus, and the archeological sites by taxi, the easiest way to cover this itinerary is by car. If you become road weary, drop the car in Adana, the closest airport to Antakya, and fly back to Istanbul.

# Crossroads of Faith
### 8 days

Turkey is rich in sites that bear testimony to powerful Christian and Muslim empires. Whether you are in the primitive cave churches of Cappadocia or the imposing ©Blue Mosque in Istanbul, these places poignantly convey spirituality.

© 40

## ISTANBUL
**2 days.** Most notable of the religious monuments here are Aya Sofya, which has served as both church and mosque, and the great mosques: the Blue Mosque, Aya Sofya, Sokollu Mehmet Paşa Cami, and Süleymaniye Cami. You will also want to seek out lesser known sites, such as Eyüp Cami, the mosque complex that houses the tomb of the Prophet Muhammad's standard-bearer, and Divan Edebiyatı Müzesi (Divan Literature Museum), with memorabilia honoring Sufi mystics.
☞ *Chapter 1.*

## KONYA
**1 day.** The magnificent Mevlâna Müzesi and Türbesi (Mevlâna Museum and Tomb of Mevlâna Celaleddin) complex is dedicated to the 13th-century poet and philosopher who founded the mystic order of the Mevlevi dervishes. Several other religious sites grace the city, among them the Alaaddin Cami.
☞ *Cappadocia and Konya in Chapter 5.*

## CAPPADOCIA
**3 days.** Perhaps inspired by this mystical landscape of eroded rock, early inhabitants embraced Christianity with zeal, carving churches and monasteries into cliff faces. You can visit a large grouping of these haunting sanctuaries at the Göreme Açık Hava Müzesi (Göreme Open-Air Museum). The Ihlara Valley, at the southern edge of the region, is also riddled with churches.
☞ *Cappadocia and Konya in Chapter 5.*

## ANTAKYA (ANTIOCH)
**1 day.** The Sempier Kilisesi (Church of St. Peter), where the apostle preached to his converts, is darkened by 2,000 years of candle smoke.
☞ *East of Alanya in Chapter 4.*

## ŞANLIURFA
**1 day.** This eastern city is the birthplace of the biblical patriarch Abraham, revered by Muslims as the Prophet İbrahim.
☞ *Southeastern Turkey in Chapter 7.*

**By Public Transportation**
Fly or take the train from Istanbul to Ankara, and rent a car there to continue the itinerary. Return the car in Diyarbakir or Adana, near Sfianliurfa, and fly back to Istanbul.

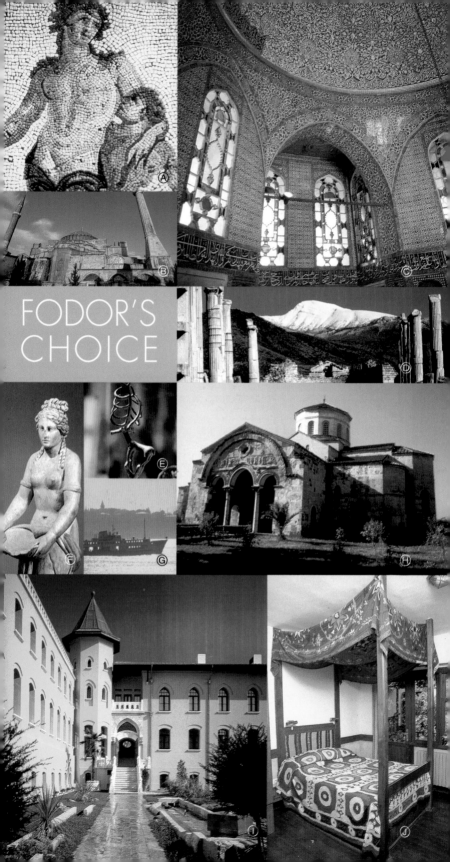

FODOR'S
CHOICE

*Even with so many special places in Turkey, Fodor's writers and editors have their favorites. Here are a few that stand out.*

### CLASSICAL SITES

Ⓓ **Aphrodisias.** The beauty of the city of Aphrodite, the goddess of love, is in its details—in statues, columns, decorative friezes. ☞ p. 120

**Theater at Aspendos.** Built during the reign of Emperor Marcus Aurelius, it's striking for its broad curve of seats, perfectly proportioned porticoes, and rich decoration. ☞ p. 162

**Ephesus.** This Aegean city of ruined temples, theaters, and colonnaded streets is one of the finest archaeological sites in the world. ☞ p. 114

**Pergamum.** The remains of one of the ancient world's leading architectural and artistic centers sprawl across a windswept mountain next to the Aegean. ☞ p. 106

**Termessos.** Behind Antalya, the ruins include a gymnasium and bath complex, a 5,000-seat theater, and a vast necropolis. ☞ p. 161

### BYZANTINE SITES

Ⓑ **Aya Sofya, Istanbul.** The most important church in Christendom for 900 years is one of the finest buildings ever constructed. ☞ p. 37

Ⓗ **Aya Sofya, Trabzon.** Stunning Byzantine frescoes and mosaics fill this ruined church overlooking the Black Sea. ☞ p. 220

**Monastery of the Virgin, Sumela.** The monks who founded this 4th-century retreat carved a labyrinth of cells, courtyards, corridors, and chapels from sheer rock. ☞ p. 221

**Yerebatan Sarnıcı, Istanbul.** The 336 marble columns lend a haunting, almost cathedral-like beauty to this underground cistern that is part of the Byzantine network of waterways built to supply the city. ☞ p. 44

### OTTOMAN SITES

**Blue Mosque, Istanbul.** Officially known as Sultan Ahmet Cami, this mosque is renowned for shimmering blue İznik tiles. ☞ p. 40

**Selimiye Cami, Edirne.** The great Ottoman architect Sinan considered this mosque his masterpiece. ☞ p. 77

**Süleymaniye Cami, Istanbul.** The grandest and most famous creation of the architect Sinan still dominates the Istanbul skyline. ☞ p. 47

Ⓒ **Topkapı Sarayı, Istanbul.** The sultans' imperial palace commands the Golden Horn, housing priceless jewels, porcelain, paintings, costumes, holy relics. ☞ p. 42

**Yeşil Cami, Bursa.** The beauty of this mosque extends from its carved-marble entrance to the lovely İznik tiles inside. ☞ p. 87

### MUSEUMS

Ⓔ **Ankara Anadolu Medeniyetleri Müzesi, Ankara.** A 15th-century bazaar and inn houses masterpieces from many eras, including fine Hatti and Hittite arts and crafts. ☞ p. 182

Ⓕ **Arkeoloji Müzesi, Istanbul.** Greek and Roman artifacts from throughout Turkey form the heart of this museum. ☞ p. 37

Ⓐ **Hatay Müzesi, Antakya.** Experts consider the exceptional mosaics to be among the highest achievements of Roman art. ☞ p. 173

### SPECIAL MOMENTS

Ⓖ **A ferry trip up the Bosporus.** Boats zigzag between Europe and Asia and stop at old-fashioned villages with castles and waterside restaurants near Istanbul. ☞ p. 52

**Call to prayer at sunset, Istanbul.** Listen to the chants of dozens of muezzins echoing throughout the city as you stand on the Galata Bridge and watch the sun slip behind a skyline of mosques and palaces. ☞ p. 48

**Cruising the Mediterranean Coast in a gulet.** Crusader castles, ancient ruins, and coves and inlets with crystal-clear water are just part of the experience aboard these traditional wooden boats. ☞ p. 143

**Cappadocia at sunrise.** The fantastic chimneylike rock formations, stunning from any vantage point, are most magical when seen from a hot-air balloon. ☞ p. 191

### DINING

**Amisos, Ankara.** Grab a table in the garden of this mansion-turned-restaurant which handles both Turkish and international specialties with aplomb. $$ ☞ p. 187

**Canlı Balık, Ayvalık.** Boats sway a few feet away from this romantic fish restaurant. $$ ☞ p. 105

**Dört Mevsim, Istanbul.** Turkish and French cuisine are served at this fine restaurant in a Victorian building. $$ ☞ p. 58

**Sumela Ciftlik Restaurant.** Seated on the stone terrace, you can dine on fresh trout as the river rushes by. $ ☞ p. 222

### LODGING

**Esbelli Evi, Ürgüp.** What is perhaps the most charming small inn in Turkey occupies beautifully restored cave houses. $$$ ☞ p. 194

Ⓘ **Four Seasons, Istanbul.** A beautifully renovated former prison in the old city is one of Istanbul's premier hotels. $$$$ ☞ p. 61

**Kismet, Kuşadası.** This small seaside hotel feels almost like a private Mediterranean villa. $$$ ☞ p. 123

**Marina Hotel, Antalya.** Three Ottoman houses provide comfortable, atmospheric lodging near the port in the old town. $$$ ☞ p. 158

**Yeşil Ev, Istanbul.** This restored mansion is done in Ottoman style and has a lovely garden. ☞ p. 64

Ⓙ **Hotel Empress Zoë, Istanbul.** The bar has great city views in this friendly small hotel in Sultanahmet. $ ☞ p. 66

# 1 ISTANBUL

*0 1190-212 (t november)*

Day and night, Istanbul is a city of many facets. At dawn, when the muezzin's call to prayer rebounds from ancient minarets, a few hearty revelers make their way home from the nightclubs and bars while other residents kneel on their prayer rugs, facing Mecca. Women in jeans or elegant designer outfits pass others wearing long skirts and head coverings. Donkey-drawn carts vie with old Chevrolets and shiny BMWs for dominance of the noisy, narrow streets. And the seductive bazaar competes with Western-style boutiques: The objects may be modern, but the song of the shopkeeper and the ritual bargaining are as old as the city itself.

Revised and
Updated by
Gareth Jenkins

**T**HOUGH IT IS OFTEN REMARKED THAT TURKEY straddles Europe and Asia, it is really Istanbul that does the straddling: The vast bulk of the country resides comfortably on the Asian side. European Istanbul is separated from its Asian suburbs by the Bosporus, the narrow channel that connects the Black Sea, north of the city, to the Sea of Marmara, to the south. (From there it is only a short sail to that superhighway of the ancient world, the Aegean.) The European side of Istanbul is itself divided by a body of water, the Golden Horn, an 8-km-long (5-mi-long) inlet that separates Old Stamboul, also called Old Istanbul, from the "new town," known as Beyoğlu. The Byzantines once stretched an enormous chain across the mouth of the Golden Horn in hopes of protecting their capital city from naval attack. The tactic worked for a time but ultimately failed, after the young Ottoman sultan Mehmet II (ruled 1451–81) had his ships dragged overland from the Bosporus and dropped in behind the chain.

To be sure, more than a mere accident of geography destined Istanbul for greatness. Much of the city's character and fame was created by the sheer force of will of four men. The town of Byzantium was already 1,000 years old when, in AD 326, Emperor Constantine the Great began to enlarge and rebuild it as the new capital of the Roman Empire. On May 11, 330, the city was officially renamed "New Rome," although it soon became better known as Constantinople, the city of Constantine. The new Byzantine empire in the East survived long after the Roman Empire had crumbled in the West. Under the Byzantine emperor Justinian (ruled 527–65), Constantine's capital flourished. Justinian ordered the construction of the magnificent Hagia Sophia (known as the Aya Sofya in Turkish and referred to throughout this book as such) in 532, on the site of a church originally built for Constantine. This awe-inspiring architectural wonder, which still dominates Istanbul's skyline, spawned untold imitators: Its form is copied by many mosques in the city and elsewhere in Turkey, most notably the Blue Mosque, which sits across Sultanahmet Square like a massive bookend. Under the Byzantines, Constantinople grew to become the largest metropolis the Western world had ever seen. Contemporaries often referred to it simply as the City.

The Ottoman sultan Mehmet II, known as Fatih (the Conqueror), is the man responsible for the fact that the Hagia Sophia clones are mosques and not churches. It was Mehmet who conquered the long-neglected, nearly ruined Constantinople in 1453, rebuilt it, and made it once again the capital of a great empire. In time it became known as Istanbul (from the Greek *eis tin polin,* meaning "to the city"). In 1468 Mehmet II began building a palace on the picturesque hill at the tip of the city where the Golden Horn meets the Bosporus. Later sultans embellished and extended the building until it grew into the fabulous Topkapı Palace, which can still be seen today. But most of the finest Ottoman buildings in Istanbul date from the time of Süleyman the Magnificent (ruled 1520–1566), who led the Ottoman Empire to its highest achievements in art and architecture, literature, and law. Süleyman commissioned the brilliant architect Sinan (1489–1587) to design buildings that are now recognized as some of the greatest examples of Islamic architecture in the world, including mosques such as the magnificent Süleymaniye, the intimate Sokollu Mehmet Paşa, and the exquisitely tiled Rüstem Paşa. The monuments built by these titans, or in their honor, dominate and define the city and lead you into the arms of the past at every turn.

Istanbul has its modern side, too, with all the concomitant traffic jams, air pollution, overdevelopment, and brash concrete-and-glass hotels and office towers creeping up behind its historic old palaces. But the city is more than grime and noise. Paradoxically, its beauty in part lies in the seemingly random juxtaposition of the ancient and the contemporary. Some of the perks that come with modernity are international casinos, designer clothing stores, and Western-style department stores.

## Pleasures and Pastimes

### Dining and Lodging

Istanbul has a range of restaurants—and prices to match. Most major hotels serve standard international cuisine, so it's more rewarding to eat in Turkish restaurants. In addition to the ubiquitous kebabs, Istanbul is also famous for its fish, although it is wise to check prices and ask what is in season before ordering. Beer, wine, the local spirit rakı, and sometimes cocktails are widely available, particularly in more up-market restaurants, despite Muslim proscriptions against alcohol. Dress is casual unless otherwise noted.

Almost everything that you probably want to see in Istanbul is in the older part of town, but the big modern hotels are mainly around Taksim Square in the new town and along the Bosporus, a 15- or 20-minute cab ride away. The Aksaray, Laleli, Sultanahmet, and Beyazıt areas have more modest hotels, as well as family-run *pansiyons* (guest houses) and the popular government run pansiyons. The trade-off for the simpler quarters is convenience: Staying here makes it easy to return to your hotel at midday or to change before dinner. No matter where you stay, plan ahead: Istanbul has a chronic shortage of beds.

For a chart that explains the cost of meals at the restaurants listed below, *see* Dining and Lodging Price Categories at the back of this book.

### Marketplaces

Atatürk moved the political capital to Ankara, but Turkey's commercial heart still beats in Istanbul. The city is a hive of free enterprise. Wherever you look, something is being traded: stocks or shares on Turkey's stock exchange; rugs; leather and jewelry in the 4,000 shops of the ancient Grand Bazaar; spices and dried fruit in the Egyptian Bazaar; fruit, vegetables, flowers, household utensils, and clothing in the city's numerous open markets and in countless street barrows or just on sheets of tarpaulin laid on the pavement; and the many wares that children hawk as they weave through rush-hour traffic.

### Museums

Until the early 1980s, Istanbul, with its crumbling ancient buildings, was its own best museum. Most artifacts of the city's past were locked away in storage areas or poorly displayed in dusty, badly lighted rooms. But in recent years Istanbul's museums have been transformed. Topkapı Palace, which for 400 years was the palace of the Ottoman sultans, contains a glittering array of jewels, ceramics, miniature paintings, and holy relics. The Archaeological Museum houses one of the most important collections of classical artifacts anywhere in the world. The Museum of Turkish and Islamic Arts holds superb examples of artistry and craftsmanship. The mosaics in the former church at Kariye are believed by many to be the finest surviving Byzantine artworks.

# EXPLORING ISTANBUL

How do you find your bearings in such an unpredictable place? Head for the Galata Bridge, which spans the mouth of the Haliç (Golden Horn). Look to the north, and you will see the new town, modern Beyoğlu, and Taksim Square. From the square, high-rise hotels and smart shops radiate out on all sides. Beyond Taksim lie the fashionable modern shopping districts of Şişli and Nişantaşı. The residential suburbs of Arnavutköy, Bebek, Yeniköy, Tarabya, and Sarıyer line the European shore of the Bosporus. Look southeast, across the Bosporus, and you can see the Asian suburbs of Kadıköy and Üsküdar. To the south, across the Galata Bridge from the new town, lies the old walled city of Stamboul and Sultanahmet (after the sultan who built the Blue Mosque), with Aya Sofya and Topkapı Palace at its heart. Turn to look up the Golden Horn, and you should be able to make out two more bridges, the Atatürk, favored by cab drivers hoping to avoid the Galata Bridge, and the Fatih, out at the city's northwestern edge.

## Great Itineraries

If you like monuments in a pristine state, you'll be sorely disappointed in this noisy and chaotic city. The Turks seem to take the mayhem in good spirits, though, and you should, too. The twisty, crowded, old city streets exude an infectious energy. See the sights, dodge the cars, eat heartily. Like strong Turkish coffee, Istanbul can be gritty, but its rich flavor is bracing.

### IF YOU HAVE 2 DAYS

Make your first stop Topkapı Sarayı, the palace at the heart of the Ottoman Empire for more than 400 years. You could easily spend your whole two days here, but at least see the Treasure Room, the Harem, and the Porcelain Collection. After a late lunch at one of the many restaurants lining Divan Yolu in Alemdar, visit the Blue Mosque and the Museum of Turkish and Islamic Arts inside the Ibrahim Paşa Sarayı, and stroll by the Hippodrome. Spend the next day exploring Aya Sofya and Yerebatan Sarayı, before heading to the 4,000 shops of the Grand Bazaar.

### IF YOU HAVE 7 DAYS

Start with a visit to Aya Sofya and Yerebatan Sarayı. Eat lunch on Divan Yolu, pass by the Hippodrome, and then visit the Blue Mosque and the Museum of Turkish and Islamic Arts. Spend day two at Topkapı Sarayı and stroll through nearby Gülhane Park before dinner. On the third day take a day's cruise up the Bosporus. Visit the Arkeoloji Müzesi on the morning of your fourth day, and take a taxi to Dolmabahçe Sarayı in the afternoon. On day five, explore Süleymaniye Cami, take a taxi to the Kariye Müzesi, and then take another to the Grand Bazaar. On the sixth day, take a taxi to the Rahmi Koç Industrial Museum, then one back to the Galata Kulesi (Galata Tower). After surveying the panoramic views from here, either take a taxi or walk to Tünel Square and the Divan Edebiyatı Müzesi (where the dervishes whirl). From here you can either take the trolley or walk along İstiklal Caddesi to Taksim Square. If you still have time, take a taxi to Yıldız Parkı. On the final day, take a side trip to the entrancing Princes Islands.

## Old Stamboul

Old Stamboul isn't large, but it can be overwhelming, for it spans vast epochs of history and contains an incredible concentration of art and architecture. The best way to get around is on foot.

### A Good Walk

*Numbers in the text correspond to numbers in the margin and on the Istanbul and Bosporus maps.*

Begin from **Topkapı Sarayı** ①. Walk back past **Aya Irini**, a smaller-scale version of Aya Sofya. The **Arkeoloji Müzesi** ② is just north of Aya Irini. A small square surrounding a fountain built by Sultan Ahmet III lies just outside the Topkapı Palace gate. Take a right down Soğukçeşme Sokak, a beautiful cobbled street lined with restored wooden Ottoman houses. At the bottom of Soğukçeşme Sokak, just before the entrance to Gülhane Park, take a left up Alemdar Caddesi to **Aya Sofya** ③ and **Yerebatan Sarnıcı** ④. Cross to the far left-hand corner of the small park between Aya Sofya and the **Blue Mosque** ⑤ to Kabasakal Caddesi. Approximately 325 ft along Kabasakal Caddesi is the **Mozaik Müzesi** ⑥, which is believed once to have been the imperial palace of the Byzantine emperors. Backtracking around the southern face of the Blue Mosque, you can see the foundation of the **Hippodrome** ⑦, a Byzantine stadium, stretching northeast for three blocks to Divan Yolu. West of the Hippodrome is **Ibrahim Paşa Sarayı** ⑧; walk to the southwest down Mehmet Paşa Yokuşu to get to **Sokollu Mehmet Paşa Cami** ⑨.

TIMING

Allow approximately 45 minutes to an hour to walk this route, two or more days to take in all its sights. Topkapı Sarayı and the Arkeoloji Müzesi are open daily. The Blue Mosque is also open daily, but the Carpet and Kilim museums within it are closed weekends. Aya Sofya and the Ibrahim Paşa Palace are closed Monday, the Mosaic Museum on Tuesday, and the Kariye Museum on Wednesday. It's best not to visit mosques during midday prayers on Friday.

## Sights to See

★ ☾ ❷ **Arkeoloji Müzesi** (Archaeology Museum). A fine collection of Greek and Roman antiquities—including pieces from Ephesus and Troy, along with a magnificent tomb believed by some to have belonged to Alexander the Great—is among the museum's highlights. Since most of the pieces have been removed from the archaeological sites of Turkey's ancient cities, touring the museum can help you visualize what belongs in the empty niches as you tour the country. Among the museum's sections is one for children, complete with a replica of the Trojan Horse; a special exhibit on Istanbul through the ages; and one on the different settlements at Troy. Because the children's wing is primarily intended for Turkish schoolchildren, the captions there are in Turkish. There are plans to open other special sections, but at press time (fall 2000), these have been hindered by a shortage of staff, which occasionally leads to existing sections being temporarily closed. Outside the museum is a small garden planted with bits of statuary and tombstones. In summer a small café is open.

Admission to the Arkeoloji Müzesi is also good for entry to the nearby **Eski Şark Eserleri Müzesi** (Museum of the Ancient Orient) and **Çinili Köşkü** (Tiled Pavilion). The first museum is something of a disappointment despite its Sumerian, Babylonian, and Hittite treasures. The place needs a fresh coat of paint, the displays are unimaginative, and the descriptions of what you see are terse at best. The Tiled Pavilion has ceramics from the early Seljuk and Ottoman empires and tiles from İznik, which produced perhaps the finest ceramics in the world during the 17th and 18th centuries. Covered in a bright profusion of colored tiles, the building itself is part of the exhibit. ⊠ *Gülhane Park, adjacent to Topkapı Palace,* ☎ *212/520–7740.* ☞ *$3 (total) for the 3 museums.* ☉ *Archaeology Museum: Tues.–Sun. 9:30–4:30; Tiled Pavilion: Tues.–Sun. 9:30–noon; Museum of the Ancient Orient: Tues.–Sun. 1–5.*

★ ❸ **Aya Sofya** (Hagia Sophia). The magnificent dome of Aya Sofya, more commonly known as Hagia Sophia (Church of the Holy Wisdom), was the world's largest church from its completion in 537 until St. Peter's Basilica was built in Rome 1,000 years later. Nothing like the dome's construction had ever been attempted before—new architectural rules had to be made up as the builders went along. Perhaps the greatest work of Byzantine architecture, the cathedral was Christendom's most important church for 900 years. It survived earthquakes, looting crusaders, and the city's conquest by Mehmet the Conqueror in 1453. The church

**38**

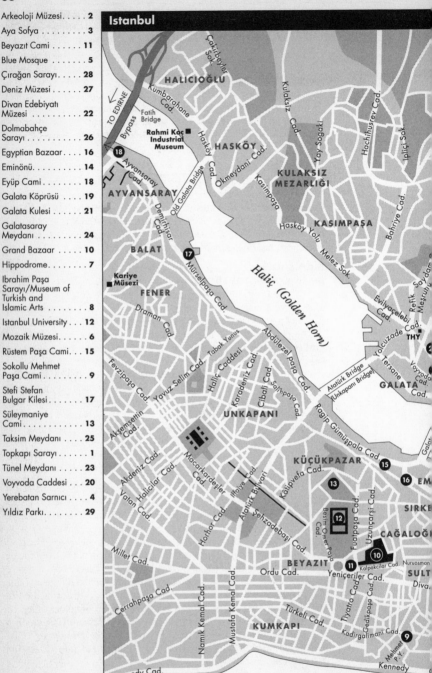

Istanbul

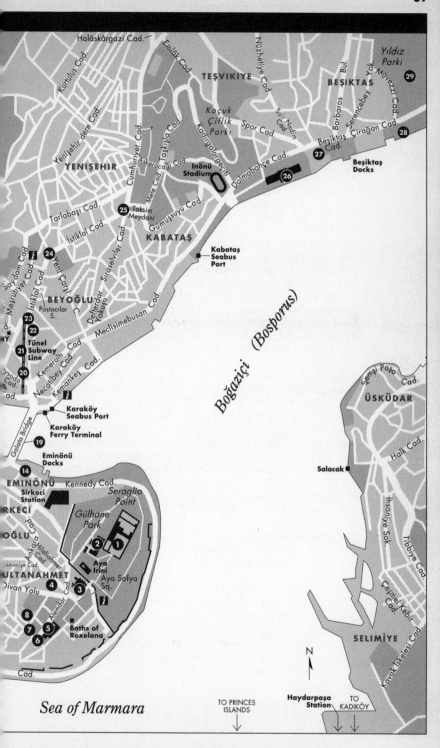

Halâskârgazi Cad.

Kurtuluş Cad.

Emlâk Cad.

Nüzhetiye Cad.

Yıldız Parkı

**TEŞVIKIYE**

**BEŞIKTAŞ**

Bul.

Barbaros

Müvezzi Cad.

Yol.

(29)

Koçuk Çiflik Parkı

Spor Cad.

Şair Nedim Cad.

Şerencebey

Beşiktaş Cad.

Çirağan Cad.

(28)

Yenişehir dere Cad.

Cumhuriyet Cad.

Askerocağı Cad.

Taşkışla Cad.

Kadırgalargeçit

Dolmabahçe Cad.

(27)

Beşiktaş Docks

**YENIŞEHIR**

Inönü Stadium

(26)

Tarlabaşı Cad.

Mete Cad.

Gümüşsuyu Cad.

Sıraselviler Cad.

Taksim Meydanı

(25)

**KABATAŞ**

Kabataş Seabus Port

İstiklal Cad.

Şaydam Cad.

Meşrutiyet Cad.

İstiklal Cad.

Yeni Çarşı

(24)

**BEYOĞLU**

Postacılar S.

Defterdar Yokuşu

Meclisimebusan Cad.

**Boğaziçi (Bosporus)**

Y.

(23)

(22)

**Tünel Subway Line**

Kemeraltı Cad.

Necatibey Cad.

Kemankeş Cad.

(21)

oyoğa Cad.

(20)

Karaköy Seabus Port

Karaköy Ferry Terminal

Şemşi Paşa Cad.

**ÜSKÜDAR**

Eminönü Docks

Galata Bridge

(19)

Halk Cad.

İhsaniye Sok.

(14)

**EMINÖNÜ**

Kennedy Cad.

Sirkeci Station

Seraglio Point

Salacak

**RKECI**

Gülhane Park

**OĞLU**

Ankara Cad.

Hilaliahmer Cad.

osmaniye Cad.

(2) (1)

Aya Irini

Aya Sofya Sq.

**ULTANAHMET**

(4)

(3)

Divan Yolu

Alemdar Cad.

(8)

(7) (5)

(6)

Baths of Roxelana

Tıbbiye Cad.

Çeşmei Kebir Cad.

Kavak İskelesi Cad.

**SELIMIYE**

Cad.

N

*Sea of Marmara*

TO PRINCES ISLANDS
↓

**Haydarpaşa Station**

TO KADIKÖY
↓

was then converted into a mosque; its four minarets were added by succeeding sultans.

The church's Byzantine mosaics were plastered over in the 16th century at the behest of Süleyman the Magnificent in accordance with the Islamic proscription against the portrayal of the human figure in a place of worship. In 1936, Atatürk made Aya Sofya into a museum. Shortly thereafter, American archaeologists rediscovered the mosaics, which were restored and are now on display. Above where the altar once stood is a giant portrait of a somber Virgin Mary with the infant Jesus, and alongside are severe-looking depictions of archangels Michael and Gabriel.

Ascend to the gallery above, and you will find the best of the remaining mosaics, executed in the 13th century. There is a group with Emperor John Comnenus, the Empress Zoë and her husband (actually, her third husband; his face was added atop his predecessors'), and Jesus with Mary, and another of John the Baptist. According to legend, the marble-and-brass **Sacred Column** in the north aisle of the mosque weeps water that can work miracles. Over the centuries believers have worn a hole through the column with their constant caresses. Today, visitors of many faiths stick their fingers in the hole and make a wish; nobody will mind if you do so as well. In recent years there has been growing pressure for Aya Sofya to be reopened for Muslim worship. Some people often gather to pray at the museum at midday on Friday. As with mosques, it is best not to try to visit then. ⊠ *Aya Sofya Sq.*, ☎ *212/522–1750.* ⊠ *$4.50.* ☉ *Tues.–Sun. 9:30–4:30.*

---

**NEED A BREAK?**   For a real treat, spend an hour in a Turkish bath. One of the best is **Cağaloğlu Hamamı** (⊠ Prof. Kazı Gürkan Cad. 34, Cağaloğlu, ☎ 212/522–2424), in a magnificent 18th-century building near Aya Sofya. Florence Nightingale and Kaiser Wilhelm II once soaked here; the clientele today remains generally upscale (Turks of lesser means head for plainer, less costly baths). You are given a cubicle in which to strip down—and a towel to cover yourself with—and are then escorted into a steamy, marble-clad temple to cleanliness. Self-service baths cost just $10; an extra $5–$10 buys you that time-honored, punishing-yet-relaxing pummeling known as Turkish massage. The baths are open daily 8–8 for women and until 10 PM for men.

---

★ ❺ **Blue Mosque** (Sultan Ahmet Cami). This massive structure, officially called Sultan Ahmet Cami (Mosque of Sultan Ahmet), is studded with mini- and semidomes and surrounded by six minarets. This number briefly linked it with the Elharam Mosque in Mecca, until Sultan Ahmet I (ruled 1603–17) was forced to send his architect down to the Holy City to build a seventh minaret and reestablish Elharam's eminence. Press through the throng of people selling things, and enter the mosque at the side entrance that faces Aya Sofya. You must remove your shoes and leave them at the entrance. Immodest clothing is not allowed, but an attendant at the door will lend you a robe if he feels you are not dressed appropriately. Women should cover their heads.

Only after you enter the Blue Mosque do you understand why it is so named. Inside it is decorated with 20,000 shimmering blue İznik tiles interspersed with 260 stained-glass windows; an airy arabesque pattern is painted on the ceiling. After the dark corners and stern, sour faces of the Byzantine mosaics in Aya Sofya, this light-filled mosque is positively uplifting. Architect Mehmet Aga, known as Sedefkar (Worker of Mother-of-Pearl), spent eight years getting the mosque just right, beginning in 1609. His goal, set by Sultan Ahmet, was to surpass Justinian's masterpiece, Aya Sofya—completed nearly 1,100 years earlier—and many believe he succeeded.

The **Hünkar Kasrı** (Carpet and Kilim museums), two good places to prepare yourself for dueling with modern-day carpet dealers, are in the stone-vaulted cellars of the Blue Mosque and upstairs at the end of a stone ramp, where the sultans rested before and after their prayers. Here rugs are treated as works of art and displayed in a suitably grand setting. ⊠ *Sultanahmet Sq.,* ☎ *212/518–1330 for museum information only.* ☒ *Mosque free; museums $1.50.* ⊙ *Blue Mosque: daily 9–5, access restricted during prayer times, particularly at midday on Fri.; museums: weekdays 8:30–noon and 1–3:30.*

**❼ Hippodrome.** Once a Byzantine stadium with seating for 100,000, the Hippodrome was the center for public entertainments such as chariot races and circuses. Disputes between rival groups of supporters of chariot teams often degenerated into violence. Thirty thousand people died here in what came to be known as the Nike riots of AD 531. The original shape of the Hippodrome is still clearly visible. The monuments that can be seen today on the grassy open space opposite the Blue Mosque—the **Egyptian Obelisk** (Dikilitaş) from the 15th century BC, the **Column of Constantinos** (Örme Sütün), and the **Serpentine Column** (Yılanlı Sütun), taken from the Temple of Apollo at Delphi in Greece—formed part of the central barrier around which the chariots raced. The Hippodrome was originally adorned with a life-size bronze sculpture of four horses. That piece was taken by the Venetians and can now be seen at the entrance to the Cathedral of San Marco in Venice. In this area you'll encounter hundreds of peddlers selling postcards, nuts, and souvenirs. ⊠ *Atmeydanı, Sultanahmet.* ☒ *Free.* ⊙ *Accessible at all hrs.*

★ **❽ Ibrahim Paşa Sarayı** (Ibrahim Paşa Palace). The grandiose residence of the son-in-law and grand vizier of Süleyman the Magnificent was built circa 1524. The striated stone mansion was outfitted by Süleyman to be the finest private residence in Istanbul, but Ibrahim Paşa didn't have long to enjoy it: He was executed when he became too powerful for the liking of Süleyman's power-crazed wife, Roxelana. The palace now houses the **Türk Ve Islâm Eserleri Müzesi** (Museum of Turkish and Islamic Arts), where you can learn about the lifestyles of Turks at every level of society, from the 8th century to the present. ⊠ *Atmeydanı 46, Sultanahmet,* ☎ *212/518–1385.* ☒ *$2.* ⊙ *Tues.–Sun. 9–4:30.*

**❻ Mozaik Müzesi** (Mosaic Museum). Tucked away behind the Blue Mosque, the often-overlooked Mosaic Museum is actually the ruins of the Great Palace of Byzantium, the imperial residence of the Byzantine emperors when they ruled lands stretching from Iran to Italy. The mosaics that give the museum its name lay hidden beneath the earth for 1,000 years before being uncovered by archaeologists in 1935. Scenes of animals, flowers, and trees in many of the mosaics depict rural idylls far removed from the pomp and elaborate ritual of the imperial court. ⊠ *Arasta Çarşısı, Kabasakal Cad., Sultanahmet,* ☎ *212/518–1205.* ☒ *$1.50.* ⊙ *Wed.–Mon. 9–4.*

**❾ Sokollu Mehmet Paşa Cami** (Mosque of Mehmet Paşa). This small mosque, built in 1571, is generally regarded as one of the most beautifully realized projects of the master architect Sinan, who designed more than 350 other buildings and monuments under the direction of Süleyman the Magnificent. Rather than dazzle with size, he integrated all the parts into a harmonious whole, from the courtyard and porticoes outside to the delicately carved *mimber* (pulpit) and well-preserved İznik tiles set off by pure white walls and floral-motif stained-glass win-

Imperial Gate . . . . . . . 1

Court of the Janissaries . . . 2

Aya Irini . . . . 3

Bab-ı-Selam . . 4

Second Courtyard . . . 5

Divan -ı-Humayun . . . 6

Harem . . . . . . 7

Third Courtyard . . 8

Bab -ı-Saadet . . . . 9

Treasury . . . . 10

Fourth Courtyard . . 11

Rivan Köskü . . . . . 12

Sünnet Odası . . . . . 13

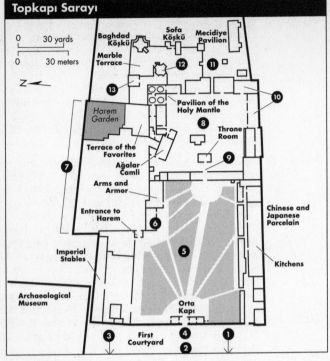

**Topkapı Sarayı**

dows inside. ⊠ *Mehmet Paşa Cad. at Özbekler Sok., Küçük Ayasofya,* ☎ *no phone.* 🎫 *Free.* ☉ *Daily sunrise–sunset, except during prayer times.*

★ ❶ **Topkapı Sarayı** (Topkapı Palace). Istanbul's number-one attraction sits on Seraglio Point, where the Bosporus meets the Golden Horn. The vast palace was the residence of sultans and their harems until 1868, when Sultan Abdül Mecit I (ruled 1839–61) moved to the European-style Dolmabahçe Palace farther up the Bosporus. The palace gates open at 9; plan to spend several hours and go early before the bus-tour crowds pour in. If you go by taxi, be sure to tell the driver you want the Topkapı Sarayı in Sultanahmet, or you could end up at the Topkapı bus terminal on the outskirts of town.

Sultan Mehmet II built the original palace during the 1450s, shortly after his conquest of Constantinople. Over the centuries sultan after sultan added ever more elaborate architectural frills and fantasies, until the palace had acquired four courtyards and quarters for some 5,000 full-time residents, including slaves, concubines, and eunuchs. The initial approach to the palace does little to evoke the many tales of intrigue, bloodshed, and drama attached to the structure. The first entrance, or Imperial Gate, leads to the **Court of the Janissaries**, also known as the First Courtyard, an area the size of a football field that now serves as a parking lot. As you walk ahead to the ticket office, look to your left, where you will see the **Aya Irini** (Church of St. Irene, Hagia Eirene in Greek). This unadorned redbrick building, now used for concerts, dates to the earliest days of Byzantium.

Formed in the 14th century as the sultan's corps of elite guards, the Janissaries were taken as young boys from non-Muslim families in Ottoman-controlled territories in the Balkans, taught Turkish, and instructed in Islam. Though theoretically the sultan's vassals, these professional soldiers quickly became a power in their own right, and more than once their protests culminated in the murder of the reigning sultan. During the rule of Sultan Mahmut II (ruled 1808–39), the tables were finally turned, and the Janissaries were massacred in what came to be known as the Auspicious Event.

Next to the ticket office is the **Bab-ı-Selam** (Gate of Salutation), built in 1524 by Süleyman the Magnificent, who was the only person allowed to pass through it on horseback; others had to dismount and enter on foot. Prisoners were kept in the towers on either side before their execution next to the nearby fountain. Once you pass this gate, you begin to experience the grandeur of the palace.

The **Second Courtyard,** just slightly smaller than the first, is planted with rose gardens and ornamental trees and filled with a series of ornate *köşks,* pavilions once used for both the business of state and for more mundane matters, like feeding the hordes of servants. To the right are the palace's immense kitchens, which now display one of the world's best collections of Chinese porcelain, including 10th-century T'ang, Yuan celadon, and Ming blue-and-white pieces dating from the 18th century, when the Chinese produced pieces to order for the palace. Straight ahead is the **Divan-ı-Humayun** (Assembly Room of the Council of State), once presided over by the grand vizier. When the mood struck him, the sultan would sit behind a latticed window, hidden by a curtain, so no one would know when he was listening, although occasionally he would pull the curtain aside to comment.

One of the most popular sections of Topkapı is the **Harem,** a maze of 400 halls, terraces, rooms, wings, and apartments grouped around the sultan's private quarters to the west of the Second Courtyard. Only 40 rooms, all meticulously restored, are open to the public; they can be visited only on tours, which leave every half hour (and cost $1.50). These rooms illustrate both the opulence and the regimentation of harem life. Only a few of the resident concubines qualified for presentation to the sultan; of those, only the chosen walked the Golden Way, by which the favorite of the night entered the sultan's private quarters. The first areas you see, which housed the palace eunuchs and about 200 lesser concubines, resemble a monastery; the tiny cubicles are as cramped and uncomfortable as the Harem's main rooms are large and opulent. Private apartments around a shared courtyard housed the chief wives (Islamic law permitted up to four); the *valide* sultan (queen mother), the absolute ruler of the Harem, had quite a bit of space as well as her own courtyard and marble bath. The sultan's private rooms are a riot of brocades, murals, colored marble, wildly ornate furniture, gold leaf, and fine carving. Fountains, also much in evidence, were not only decorative—they made it hard to eavesdrop on royal conversations. All told, it is a memorable, worthy backdrop to the rise and fall of princes and pretenders.

You exit the Harem into the somewhat smaller **Third Courtyard.** To see it to best advantage, make your way to its main gate, the **Bab-ı-Saadet** (Gate of Felicity), then exit and reenter. Shaded by regal old trees, the Third Courtyard is dotted by some of the most ornate of the palace's pavilions. Foreign ambassadors once groveled just past the gate in the **Arz Odası** (Audience Chamber), but access to the courtyard was highly restricted, in part because it housed the **Treasury,** four rooms filled with jewels, including two uncut emeralds, each weighing about 8 pounds, that once hung from the ceiling. Here, too, are the dazzling emerald dagger used in the movie *Topkapi* and the 84-carat Spoonmaker diamond, which, according to legend, was found by a pauper and traded for three wooden spoons. Not surprisingly, this is one of the most popular sections of the palace, and it can get quite crowded. Also within this courtyard you can view a collection of thousands of Turkish and Persian miniatures, relics of the prophet Muhammad, and the rich costumes of the Imperial Wardrobe. Imperial fashion (male, of course) evolves slowly in the magnificent display of sultans' robes from the first to the last ruler. Some robes are bloodstained and torn from assassins' daggers; garments are stiff with gold and silver thread, tooled leather, and gold, silver, and jewels.

The **Fourth Courtyard,** the last, contains small, elegant summer houses, mosques, fountains, and reflecting pools scattered amid the gardens. Here you will find the cruciform **Rivan Köşkü,** built by Murat IV in 1636 to commemorate a military victory. In another pavilion, the **İftariye** (Golden Cage), the closest relatives of the reigning sultan lived in strict confinement under what amounted to house arrest, ostensibly to help keep the peace, although it meant that heirs had no opportunity to prepare themselves for the formidable task of ruling a great empire. The custom began during the 1800s, superseding an older practice of murdering all possible rivals to the throne. Just off the open terrace with the wishing well is the lavishly tiled **Sünnet Odası** (Circumcision Room), where little princes would be taken for ritual circumcision during their 9th or 10th year. ✉ *Topkapı Palace, Gülhane Park, near Sultanahmet Sq.*, ☎ *212/512–0480.* 🖃 *$4, plus $2 for harem tour.* ☉ *Wed.– Mon. 9:30–4:30.*

---

**NEED A BREAK?**  Just past the Topkapı Palace's Treasury, on the right side of the courtyard, are steps leading to the 19th-century rococo-style Mecidiye Pavilion, also known as the Köşk of Sultan Abdül Mecit I (ruled 1839–61), for whom it was built. It now houses the **Konyalı Restaurant** (☎ 212/513–9696), which serves traditional Turkish dishes (albeit with a mass-produced flavor) and has magnificent views. On a terrace below is an outdoor café with an even better view. Go early to beat the tour-group crush. The restaurant and the café are open for lunch only.

---

★ ❹ **Yerebatan Sarnıcı** (Sunken Cistern). Also known as the Basilica Cistern, Yerebatan Sarnıcı is the most impressive part of an underground network of waterways said to have been created at the behest of Emperor Constantine in the 4th century and expanded by Justinian in the 6th century (most of the present structure dates from the Justinian era). The cistern was always kept full as a precaution against long sieges. Today it is an atmospheric space, with 336 marble columns rising 26 ft to support Byzantine arches and domes. Piped-in classical music accompanies the sound of endlessly dripping water. ✉ *Yerebatan Cad. at Divan Yolu*, ☎ *212/522–1259.* 🖃 *$3.* ☉ *Daily 9–4:30.*

---

**OFF THE BEATEN PATH**  **KARIYE MÜZESI** – Often passed over because of its inconvenient location at Istanbul's western edge, near the remnants of the city's Byzantine walls, the Kariye Museum occupies what was once the Church of the Holy Savior in Chora, erected in the 5th century under the aegis of Justinian and rebuilt several times since. You come to see the dazzling 14th-century mosaics and frescoes depicting biblical scenes from Adam to the life of Christ; they are considered among the finest Byzantine works in the world. The historic Ottoman buildings around the museum have been restored as well. A tea shop on the garden terrace serves light fare. Just west of the Chora are the Constantinian Walls, built by Emperor Theodosius II in AD 413. The massive walls, several stories high and from 10 ft to 20 ft thick in spots, protected Constantinople from onslaught after onslaught by Huns, Bulgarians, Russians, Arabs, Goths, and Turks. The walls were breached only twice: by the crusaders in the 1200s and by Mehmet the Conqueror in 1453. ⊠ *1 block north of Fevzipaşa Cad., by Edirne Gate in city's outer walls,* ☎ *212/631– 9241.* ☞ *$2.* ☉ *Thurs.–Tues. 9:30–4.*

# Grand Bazaar to Eminönü

This walk leads you through several markets, including two of Istanbul's largest, and takes you to two of the city's most beautiful mosques.

## A Good Walk

After a visit to the **Grand Bazaar** ⑩, exit through the front entrance on Yeniçeriler Caddesi and head west to that street's junction with Çadırcı Camii Caddesi. You'll see **Beyazıt Cami** ⑪ as you turn right onto Çadırcı Camii Caddesi, which runs into Fuatpaşa Caddesi. Follow Fuatpaşa Caddesi along the eastern side of the grounds of **Istanbul University** ⑫. Continue along Fuatpaşa Caddesi, keeping the grounds of the university on your left, until the junction with Prof. Sıddık Sami Ona Caddesi and Ismetiye Caddesi. Turn left along Prof. Sıddık Sami Ona Caddesi to **Süleymaniye Cami** ⑬. After visiting this mosque, retrace your steps along Prof. Sıddık Sami Ona Caddesi, continue straight across into Ismetiye Caddesi, and then turn left down Çarsı Caddesi. Along the narrow road leading downhill is a thriving market lined with stalls and small shops selling mostly cheap clothing. Continue down the hill to Hasırcılar Caddesi to head into the **Eminönü** ⑭ neighborhood. The **Rüstem Paşa Cami** ⑮ is at the western edge of this neighborhood. After visiting this mosque, continue along Hasırcılar Caddesi to the **Egyptian Bazaar** ⑯.

TIMING

Not counting the time you can spend exploring the Grand Bazaar, it takes about an hour to complete this walk. If you spend a brief amount of time in each of the mosques and bazaars and stop for lunch, then it will take you about four or five hours. The Grand and Egyptian bazaars are closed Sunday, though the small Arasta Bazaar, in the Sultanahmet neighborhood, is open. The Beyazıt, Rüstem Paşa, and Süleymaniye mosques are open daily.

## Sights to See

**⓫ Beyazıt Cami.** This domed mosque, inspired by Aya Sofya, dates from 1504 and is the oldest of the Ottoman imperial mosques still standing in the city. ⊠ *Beyazıt Meyd., Beyazıt,* ☎ *no phone.* ☞ *Free.* ☉ *Daily sunrise to sunset; usually closed during prayer times.*

★ **⓰ Egyptian Bazaar** (Mısır Çarşısı). Also known as the Spice Market, the Egyptian Bazaar is much smaller than the Grand Bazaar but is still lively and colorful. It was built in the 17th century to generate rental income to pay for the upkeep of the **Yeni Cami** (New Mosque), next door. Once a vast pharmacy filled with burlap bags overflowing with herbs and spices, the bazaar today is chockablock with white sacks of spices, as well as bags full of fruit, nuts, and royal jelly from the beehives of the Aegean Sea. ⊠ *Hamidiye Cad., across from Galata Bridge,* ☎ *no phone.* ☉ *Mon.–Sat. 8–7.*

NEED A
BREAK?

The **Pandelli**, up two flights of stairs over the arched gateway to the Egyptian Bazaar, is a frenetic Old Istanbul restaurant with impressive tile work. A lunch of typical Turkish fare is served; especially good are the eggplant *börek* (pastry) and the sea bass cooked in paper. ⊠ *Mısır Çarşısı 1, Eminönü,* ☎ *212/527–3909. AE, MC, V.*

⑭ **Eminönü.** The main transportation hub of Old Stamboul, Eminönü, is a neighborhood at the south end of the Galata Bridge. It has quays for hydrofoil sea buses, the more traditional Bosporus ferries (including those for the daylong Bosporus cruises), and the Sirkeci train station and tramway terminal. The main coastal road around the peninsula of the old city also traverses Eminönü. Thousands of people and vehicles rush through the bustling area, and numerous street traders here sell everything from candles to live animals.

⑱ **Eyüp Cami.** The mosque complex at Eyüp on the Golden Horn houses the tomb of Eyüp Ensari, the Prophet Muhammad's standard-bearer, who was killed during the first Arab siege, AD 674–78, of what was then Constantinople. Most of the original complex was built in the 15th century by Sultan Mehmet the Conqueror. It was added to by his successors and numerous Ottoman dignitaries, many of whom, including several sultans' wives, had their own tombs built close by. Today Eyüp is the holiest Islamic shrine in Turkey and attracts Muslim pilgrims from all over the world. Despite the numbers, particularly at Friday midday prayer, the plane-tree-shaded courtyards and hundreds of fluttering pigeons imbue it with a sense of peace and religious devotion not found anywhere else in this often frenetic city. The tomb itself is small and covered with brightly decorated ceramic tiles. Non-Muslims are welcome to join the hushed pilgrims who go to pray at the tomb but should remember to remove their shoes beforehand; women must be modestly dressed and must cover their heads before entering. ✉ *Camii Kebir Caddesi, Eyüp,* ☎ *no phone.* ☉ *Daily.*

★ ⑩ **Grand Bazaar** (Kapalı Çarşı). This early version of a shopping mall, also known as the Covered Bazaar, consists of a maze of 65 winding, covered streets crammed with 4,000 tiny shops, cafés, and restaurants. It reputedly has the largest number of stores under one roof anywhere in the world. Originally built by Mehmet II (the Conqueror) in the 1450s, it was ravaged in modern times by two fires—one in 1954 that nearly destroyed it, and a smaller one in 1974. In both cases, the bazaar was quickly rebuilt into something resembling the original style, with arched passageways and brass-and-tile fountains at regular intervals.

The Grand Bazaar is filled with thousands of items—fabric, clothing (including counterfeit brand names), brass candelabra, furniture, and jewelry. A sizable share of junk tailored for the tourist trade is sold as well. A separate section for antiques at the very center of the bazaar, called the *bedestan,* always has worthwhile offerings. Outside the western gate to the bazaar, through a doorway, is the **Sahaflar Çarşısı,** the Old Book Bazaar, where you can buy both new editions and antique volumes in Turkish and other languages. The best way to explore the bazaar is to take a deep breath and plunge on in. And remember: The best prices are those called out to you when the would-be seller thinks you are about to slip away. ✉ *Yeniçeriler Cad. and Fuatpaşa Cad.* ☎ *Free.* ☉ *Apr.– Oct., Mon.–Sat. 8:30–7; Nov.–Mar., Mon.–Sat. 8:30–6:30.*

⑫ **Istanbul University.** The university's magnificent gateway faces Beyazıt Square. The campus, with its long greensward and giant plane trees, originally served as the Ottoman war ministry, which helps explain the grandiose, martial style of the portal and the main buildings. In the garden stands the white-marble 200-ft **Beyazıt Tower,** the tallest structure in Old Stamboul, built in 1823 by Mahmut II (ruled 1808–39) as a fire-watch station. ✉ *Fuat Paşa Cad., Beyazıt.*

⑮ **Rüstem Paşa Cami** (Rüstem Paşa Mosque). This small and often overlooked mosque is another Sinan masterpiece. Tucked away in the backstreets to the north of the Egyptian Bazaar, it was built in the 1550s for Süleyman's grand vizier. Though unassuming from the outside, its interior is decorated with İznik tiles in an array of colors and patterns. ⊠ *Hasırcılar Cad., south of Sobacılar Cad.,* ☎ *no phone.* ☉ *Daily.*

**⑰ Stefi Stefan Bulgar Kilesi** (Bulgarian Church of St. Stefan), a neo-Gothic church, is one of the most remarkable structures in Istanbul. Both the exterior and all the interior decor, including what look to be carvings, are made entirely of cast iron. The church was prefabricated in Vienna, shipped down the Danube, and erected on the western shore of the Golden Horn in 1871 by the then-flourishing Bulgarian Orthodox community in Istanbul, which was anxious to have an impressive church of its own to back its demand for independence from the Greek Orthodox patriarchate. Despite the dwindling numbers of the Bulgarian community, which means that there is not always someone on hand to unlock the interior, the church has been recently restored and repainted and is set in neatly tended gardens. ⊠ *Mürsel Paşa Caddesi, Balat,* ☎ *no phone.* ☉ *Daily.*

**⑱ Süleymaniye Cami** (Mosque of Süleyman). The grandest and most famous creation of its designer, Sinan, this mosque houses his tomb and that of his patron, Süleyman the Magnificent. Its enormous dome is supported by four square columns and arches, and exterior walls buttress smaller domes on either side. The result is a soaring space that gives the impression the dome is held up principally by divine cooperation. This is the city's largest mosque, and it is both less ornate and more spiritual in tone than other imperial mosques. Note the İznik tiles in the *mihrab* (prayer niche). ⊠ *Süleymaniye Cad., near Istanbul University's north gate,* ☎ *no phone.* ☉ *Daily.*

## Galata to Taksim

This walk covers the heart of the new town, where the first thing you'll learn is that *new* is a relative term. Much of what you'll see dates from the 19th century—except for the shops and imported American movies, which are all strictly contemporary. You can take the tiny subway up Karaköy to Tünel Square; only 90 seconds long, the trip spares you a stiff walk.

### A Good Walk

Cross over the **Galata Köprüsü** ⑲, stopping on the bridge to take in one of the world's great city views. Continue due north up Karaköy Caddesi and then up some steps near the junction with **Voyvoda Caddesi** ⑳. Go straight up the appropriately named Yüksek Kaldırım Caddesi (Steep Rise Street), lined with shops selling electronics equipment. Halfway up the hill is **Galata Kulesi** ㉑; the views from the top of the tower (there is an elevator) will take away any breath that you may have left after your steep climb. From Galata Kulesi, continue up the same road, which is now called Galip Dede Caddesi. Head up to the **Divan Edebiyatı Müzesi** ㉒, the museum where you can see the dervishes whirl, and into **Tünel Meydanı** ㉓, the northern terminus of the minisubway from Karaköy. From the square a trolley runs along **İstiklal Caddesi** through **Galatasaray Meydanı** ㉔ to **Taksim Meydanı** ㉕, but it's more fun to walk. Stop along the way to have a look at the Üç Horan Armenian Church, marvel at the many splendid old buildings lining the street (some now house Western consulates), and browse in the lively flower and fish markets.

#### TIMING

The time needed for the walk will depend as much on your stamina as on how long you spend at the sights along the route. If you are reasonably fit and walk the whole way, allow from three to four hours. The Galata Kulesi is open daily. The Divan Edebiyatı Müzesi is closed Monday.

## Sights to See

**㉒ Divan Edebiyatı Müzesi** (Divan Literature Museum). Also called the Galata Mevlevihane, this museum contains costumes, instruments, and memorabilia used by the Sufi mystics known in the West as the whirling dervishes. On the last Sunday of each month dance performances and Sufi music concerts are held at 3. ⊠ *Galip Dede Cad. 15, southeast of Tünel Sq., off İstiklal Cad., Beyoğlu,* ☎ *212/245–4141.* ✆ *$2.* ☉ *Tues.–Sun. 9:30–4:30.*

★ **⑲ Galata Köprüsü** (Galata Bridge). The bridge that joins Istanbul's older, European districts to the new town yields one of the world's great city views. In Old Stamboul, behind you as you cross the bridge toward Karaköy, look for such landmarks as Topkapı Palace, the domes and minarets of Aya Sofya and the Blue Mosque, and the Süleymaniye and Yeni mosques. Ferries chug out on the Bosporus, and Galata Tower rises high on the Beyoğlu side of the Golden Horn, beyond Karaköy. The drawbridge that you're standing on opened in 1993, when it replaced the old pontoon bridge that had been around since 1910, in the days when horse-, ox-, or mule-drawn carriages rattled across it for a fee. ⊠ *Sobacılar Cad., in Eminönü, to Rıhtım Cad., in Karaköy.*

**㉑ Galata Kulesi** (Galata Tower). The Genoese built this tower as part of their fortifications in 1349, when they controlled the northern shore of the Golden Horn. In this century, the rocket-shaped tower served as a fire lookout until 1960. Today it houses a restaurant and nightclub (☞ Nightclubs *in* Nightlife and the Arts, *below*) and a viewing tower (accessible by elevator) that is open during the day. The area around the Galata Tower was a thriving Italian settlement both before and after the fall of Constantinople. In 1492, when the Spanish Inquisition drove Sephardic Jews from Spain and Portugal, many refugees settled here. For centuries after, a large Jewish population lived in Galata. Today, 16 active synagogues, one of which dates from the Byzantine period, serve a Jewish community of 25,000. The **Neve Shalom Synagogue**, on Büyük Hendek Sokak near the Galata Tower, was where 22 Sabbath worshipers were shot by Arabic-speaking gunmen in September 1986. A visit to the now high-security location requires a show of identification. Some older Turkish Jews still speak a dialect of medieval Spanish called Ladino, or Judeo-Spanish. ⊠ *Galata Tower: Büyük Hendek Cad.,* ☎ *212/245–1160.* ✆ *$1.* ☉ *Daily 9–8.*

**㉔ Galatasaray Meydanı** (Galatasaray Square). This square is in the heart of the Beyoğlu district. The impressive building behind the massive iron gates on the square is a high school, established in 1868 and for a time the most prestigious in the Ottoman Empire.

Across İstiklal Caddesi, at Number 51, is the entrance to the **Çiçek Pasajı** (Flower Arcade), a lively warren of flower stalls, tiny restaurants, and bars. Street musicians often entertain here. Curmudgeons swear the passage is a pale shadow of its former self—its original neobaroque home collapsed with a thundering crash one night in 1978, and its redone facade and interior feel too much like a reproduction—but you can still get a feel for its bohemian past. Behind the Flower Arcade is the **Balık Pazarı** (Fish Market), a bustling labyrinth of stands peddling fish, fruits, vegetables, and spices—with a couple of pastry shops thrown in—all of which makes for great street theater. The fish market is open from Monday through Saturday during daylight hours. At the end of the market, at Meşrutiyet Caddesi, is the **Üç Horan Armenian Church** (⊠ İstiklal Cad. 288). With its crosses and haloed Christs, the church is an unexpected sight in Muslim Istanbul.

**İstiklal Caddesi** (Independence Street). One of European Istanbul's main thoroughfares heads north and east to Taksim Square from Tünel Square. Consulates in ornate turn-of-the-century buildings and 19th-century apartments line the route, along with bookstores, boutiques, kebab shops, and movie theaters. To appreciate the architecture, look toward the upper stories of what was once the most fashionable street in the entire region. Return your gaze to eye level, and you will see every element of modern Istanbul's vibrant cultural melting pot. A trolley runs along İstiklal every 10 minutes or so, all the way to Taksim Square. The fare is about 50¢. If you have the time and energy, walk one way and take the trolley back.

**㉕ Taksim Meydanı** (Taksim Square). This square at the north end of İstiklal Caddesi is in the not particularly handsome center of the new town, especially since municipal subway digging has recently turned its belly into a deep concrete crevasse. It's basically a chaotic traffic circle with a bit of grass and the **Monument to the Republic and Independence,** featuring Atatürk and his revolutionary cohorts. Around the square are Istanbul's main concert hall, **Atatürk Kültür Merkezi** (Atatürk Cultural Center), the high-rise Marmara Hotel, and, on a grassy promenade, the 23-story Ceylan Inter-Continental (☞ Lodging, *below*). On **Cumhuriyet Caddesi,** the main street heading north from the square, are shops selling carpets and leather goods. Also here are the entrances to the Hyatt, Divan, and Istanbul Hilton hotels; several travel agencies and airline ticket offices; and a few nightclubs. Cumhuriyet turns into Halâskârgazi Caddesi. When this street meets Rumeli Caddesi, you enter the city's high-fashion district, where Turkey's top designers sell their wares.

NEED A
BREAK?

The **Patisserie Café Marmara,** in the Marmara Hotel on Taksim Square, serves hot and cold drinks and snacks, ice cream, and excellent home-made cakes. Despite the turbulence and often downright chaos of Taksim Square itself, the café retains an air of unhurried calm. A duo usually plays soothing classical music in the late afternoon and early evening. In summer the shaded terrace is a good place to observe the bustle of the square. ⊠ *Marmara Istanbul, Taksim Sq.,* ☎ *212/251–4696. AE, DC, MC, V.*

**㉓ Tünel Meydanı** (Tünel Square). The northern terminus of the city's mini-subway is at this square on the south end of İstiklal Caddesi. Nearby is the **Pera Palace,** one of the most famous of Istanbul's hotels, where Agatha Christie wrote *Murder on the Orient Express* and where Mata Hari threw back a few at the bar.

**㉗ Voyvoda Caddesi.** Considering all the romance that surrounds the 15th-century *voyvode* (prince) of Transylvania, Vlad the Impaler—better known as Count Dracula—it's a tad ironic that the street named after him is a nondescript commercial strip. As a child, Vlad was sent to the Ottoman sultan as ransom, and though he was finally released, he grew up despising the Turks. He devised elaborate tortures for his enemies and at length drove the Turks from Romania. Killed near Bucharest in 1476, his head was sent to Constantinople, where Mehmet II the Conqueror displayed it on a stake to prove to all that the hated Vlad was finally dead. Some say the street is the site of his grave.

OFF THE
BEATEN PATH

**RAHMİ KOÇ SANAYI MÜZESİ.** A restored foundry once used to cast anchors for the Ottoman fleet now houses this industrial museum tracing the development of technology. Exhibits include medieval telescopes and some well-crafted maritime instruments. A special section devoted to transportation includes planes, bicycles, motorbikes and the great engines that powered the Bosporus ferries. ⊠ *27 Hasköy Cad., Hasköy,* ☎ *212/256–7153 or 212/256–7154,* 𝔽𝔸𝕏 *212/256–7156.* ▤ *$1.50.* ☉ *Tues.–Sun. 10–4:30.*

# Beşiktaş

The shore of the Bosporus became the favorite residence of the later Ottoman sultans as they sought to escape overcrowded Old Stamboul. They remained here until the end of the empire when eventually they, too, were engulfed by the ever-expanding city and, one could argue, by history as well.

## A Good Walk

Start at the extravagant 19th-century **Dolmabahçe Sarayı** ㉖, the palace where the last sultans of the Ottoman Empire resided and where Atatürk lived. Exiting the palace, continue northeast along tree-lined Dolmabahçe Caddesi onto Beşiktaş Caddesi, site of the **Deniz Müzesi** ㉗, to get a sense of the Ottoman Empire's former naval power. From here, follow the main coast road past the Beşiktaş ferry terminal into Çırağan Caddesi and the **Çırağan Sarayı** ㉘, former home of the Sultan Abdül Aziz and now a luxury hotel. Directly opposite the hotel's main door is the entrance to the wooded slopes of **Yıldız Parkı** ㉙, probably the most romantic spot in Istanbul. Follow the road up the hill through the park and take a right at the top of the slope to get to Yıldız Şale, the chalet of the last of the Ottoman sultans.

### TIMING

Allow approximately two hours for the walk from Dolmabahçe Sarayı to the entrance to Yıldız Parkı, including 45 minutes in the Deniz Müzesi (Naval Museum) and 30 minutes in the Çırağan Sarayı. Allow another two to three hours to walk through Yıldız Parkı—it has numerous trails—and include 45 minutes to an hour to visit Yıldız Şale. Dolmabahçe Sarayı is closed Monday and Thursday, and the Naval Museum Monday and Thursday. Yıldız Parkı is open daily, but Yıldız Şale is closed Monday and Tuesday.

## Sights to See

㉘ **Çırağan Sarayı** (Çırağan Palace). Istanbul's most luxurious hotel (☞ Lodging, *below*) was built by Abdül Mecit's brother and successor, Sultan Abdül Aziz (ruled 1861–76), in 1863. That the palace is about a third the size of Dolmabahçe and much less ornate says a good deal about the declining state of the Ottoman Empire's coffers. The vacuous Abdül Aziz was as extravagant as his brother and was soon attempting to emulate the splendors he had seen on travels in England and France. Today the restored grounds, with a splendid swimming pool at the edge of the Bosporus, are worth a look, and the hotel bar provides a plush, cool respite with a view. You won't find much from the original palace, as a major fire gutted the place; the lobby renovations were done with a nod to the palace's original 19th-century design, though the color scheme is decidedly gaudier. ⊠ *Çırağan Cad. 84, Beşiktaş,* ☎ *212/258–3377.*

㉗ **Deniz Müzesi** (Naval Museum). The Ottoman Empire was the 16th century's leading sea power. The flashiest displays here are the sultan's barges, the long, slim boats that served as the primary mode of royal transportation for several hundred years. The museum's cannon collection includes a 23-ton blaster built for Sultan Selim the Grim. An early Ottoman map of the New World, cribbed from Columbus, dates from 1513. ⊠ *Beşiktaş Cad.,* ☎ *212/261–0040 or 212/261–0130.* ▤ *$1.* ☉ *Wed.–Sun. 9–12:30 and 1:30–5:30.*

㉖ **Dolmabahçe Sarayı** (Dolmabahçe Palace). The last sultans of the Ottoman Empire resided at this palace, erected in 1853. After the establishment of the modern republic in 1923, it became the home of Atatürk, who died here in 1938. The name, which means "filled-in garden," predates the palace; Sultan Ahmet I (ruled 1603–17) had an imperial garden planted here in the 17th century. The palace is an extraordinary mixture of Hindu, Turkish, and European styles of architecture and interior design. Abdül Mecit, whose free-spending lifestyle (his main distinction) eventually bankrupted his empire, intended the structure to be a symbol of Turkey's march away from its past and toward the European mainstream. He gave his Armenian architect, Balian, complete freedom and an unlimited budget. His only demand was that the palace "surpass any other palace of any other potentate anywhere in the world."

The result was a riot of rococo—marble, vast mirrors, stately towers, and formal gardens along a facade stretching nearly ½ km (⅓ mi). His bed is solid silver; the tub and basins in his marble-paved bathroom are carved of translucent alabaster. Europe's royalty contributed to the splendor: Queen Victoria sent a chandelier weighing 4½ tons, Czar Nicholas I of Russia provided polar-bear rugs. The result is as gaudy and showy as a palace should be, all gilt and crystal and silk, and every bit as garish as Versailles. The nearby **Dolmabahçe Cami** (Dolmabahçe Mosque) was founded in 1853 by Abdül Mecit's mother. You must join a guided tour—one takes about 80 minutes, and another, which omits the harem, takes about 45 minutes. ⊠ *Dolmabahçe Cad.*, ☎ *212/258-5544.* ☞ *$10 for long tour, $5.50 for short tour.* ☉ *Tues.–Wed. and Fri.–Sun. 9–4.*

㉙ **Yıldız Parkı.** The wooded slopes of Yıldız Park once formed part of the great forest that covered the European shore of the Bosporus from the Golden Horn to the Black Sea. During the reign of Abdül Aziz, the park was his private garden, and the women of the harem would occasionally be allowed to visit. First the gardeners would be removed, then the eunuchs would lead the women across the wooden bridge from the palace and along the avenue to the upper gardens. Secluded from prying eyes, they would sit in the shade or wander through the acacias, maples, and cypresses, filling their baskets with flowers and figs. Today the park is still hauntingly beautiful, particularly in spring and fall.

**Yıldız Şale** (Yıldız Chalet), at the top of the park, is yet another palace of Sultan Abdül Hamit II (ruled 1876–1909). Visiting dignitaries from Kaiser Wilhelm to Charles de Gaulle and Margaret Thatcher have stayed here. The chalet is often blissfully empty of other tourists, which makes a visit all the more pleasurable. Forgotten is the turmoil of the era when the palace was occupied by the last rulers of the once-great Ottoman Empire. All were deposed: free-spending Abdül Aziz; his unfortunate nephew, Murad (who, having spent most of his life in the Harem, was none too sound of mind); and Abdül Hamid, who distinguished himself as the last despot of the Ottoman Empire. ⊠ *Çırağan Cad.*, ☎ *212/261–8460 for park; 212/259–4570 for chalet.* ☞ *Park: 25¢ pedestrians, $1.50 cars; chalet: $1.50.* ☉ *Park: daily 9–9; chalet: Wed.–Sun. 9–4.*

★ The **Askeri Müze** (Military Museum), in the northwestern corner of the park, contains a fascinating collection of military memorabilia from the 15th century to the present. In addition to costumes, flags, and weapons—from swords and pistols to mighty cannons—the museum also houses some beautifully embroidered silk tents used by the Ottoman sultans on campaigns, personal artifacts belonging to Atatürk from the 1915 Gallipoli campaign, and even fragments of the great chain that the last Byzantine rulers of the Istanbul stretched across the Golden

Horn in a vain attempt to prevent the Turks from gaining access to the city by sea. A *Mehter* (Janissary) military band performs 17th- and 18th-century Ottoman military music in full period costume on the grounds of the museum at 3 Wed–Sun during the summer. ⊠ *Valikonağı Caddesi, Harbiye,* ☎ *212/233–2720.* 🖭 *$2.* ☉ *Wed-Sun 9–5.*

## The Bosporus

Though there are good roads along both the Asian and the European shores, the most pleasant way to explore the Bosporus is by ferry from the Eminönü docks in the old town (☞ Getting Around *in* Istanbul A to Z, *below*). Along the way you will see wooded hills, villages large and small, modern and old-fashioned, and the old wooden summer homes called *yalıs* (waterside houses) that were built for the city's wealthier residents in the Ottoman era. When looking at ferry schedules, remember that Rumeli refers to the European side, Anadolu to the Asian.

## A Good Ferry Tour     CA  6 HRS.

There are two ways to take a ferry tour of the Bosporus. One is to take one of the cruises that depart daily from Eminönü. These leave from Quay 3 (look for the sign BOĞAZ HATTI) at 10:35 and 1:35 (times are subject to change, so check first). The round-trip should cost about $2. The boats zigzag up the Bosporus, stop for a couple of hours near the Black Sea for lunch, then zigzag back down to Eminönü. The other way is to fashion your own tour, hopping on one of the regular Bosporus commuter ferries, stopping wherever you fancy, and then continuing your journey on the next ferry going your way. (Buy a ferry timetable—a *vapur tarifesi*—to figure out your itinerary.) The advantage of the latter is more freedom; the disadvantage is that you will probably end up spending considerable extra time waiting for the next ferry. Note, too, that not all ferries stop at every quay along the Bosporus, and during the middle of the day schedules can be erratic.

After departing from Eminönü, the ferry heads north out of the Golden Horn and past the Dolmabahçe and Çırağan palaces on the European shore. As you approach the first Bosporus bridge you pass Ortaköy Cami (Ortaköy Mosque) on the European shore, and just past the bridge on the Asian shore, the **Beylerbeyi Sarayı** ㉚. Back on the European side is the village of **Arnavutköy** ㉛, followed by the stylish suburb of **Bebek** ㉜. Just before the second Bosporus bridge (officially known as Fatih Sultan Mehmet Bridge) are two fortresses, **Anadolu Hisarı** ㉝, on the Asian side, and **Rumeli Hisarı** ㉞, on the European side. North of Fatih Sultan Mehmet Bridge, on the Asian side, lies the village of **Kanlıca** ㉟. Across the water are the wooded slopes of **Emirgan** ㊱. Still farther north on the European side are the fashionable resort area of Tarabya and the waterfront village of Sarıyer, the ferry stop for the **Sadberk Hanım Müzesi** ㊲, with its collection of Islamic and Turkish arts and Anatolian archaeological finds. Organized cruises from Eminönü usually stop at either Rumeli Kavağı or Anadolu Kavağı, two fishing villages, for a couple of hours. Anadolu Kavağı is particularly fun; its sidewalk vendors sell deep-fried mussels and sweet waffles. The ferries begin their return trips to Istanbul from Rumeli Kavağı and Anadolu Kavağı.

TIMING

Whether you take a Bosporus cruise or make your own way by ferry, you should allow a whole day. The cruises usually take about six hours. If you don't opt for a cruise, add at least an extra hour (if not longer) waiting for ferries, in addition to the time spent at stops along the way. Rumeli Hisarı is closed Monday. Beylerbeyi Sarayı is closed Monday and Thursday. Sadberk Hanım Müzesi is closed Wednesday.

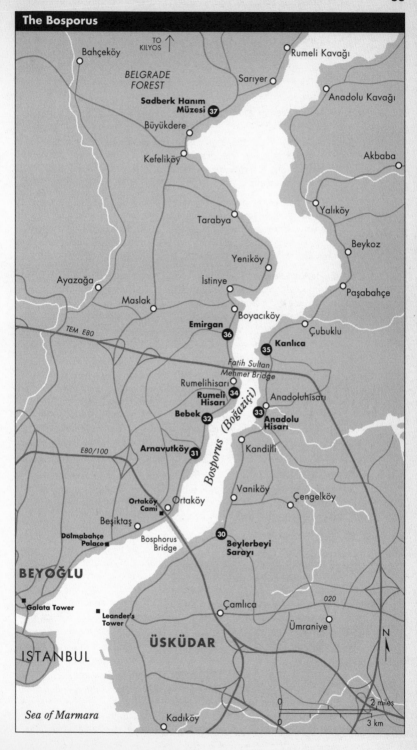

## Sights to See

**③③ Anadolu Hisarı** (Anatolian Castle). Sultan Beyazıt I built this fortress in 1393 to cut off Constantinople's access to the Black Sea. At the mouth of the Göksu stream, known in Ottoman times as one of the "Sweet Waters of Asia," the castle is a romantic sight (especially at sunset). Its golden stone blends into the surrounding forest, and tiny boats bob beneath its walls (some of which are crumbling, so be careful if walking on them. An unmarked path leads up to the castle ruins; there's no admission fee.

**③① Arnavutköy.** This village on the European side of the Bosporus has a row of 19th-century wooden houses at the water's edge. Up the hill from the water, narrow streets contain more old wooden houses, some of them with trailing vines.

**③② Bebek.** One of the most fashionable suburbs of Istanbul, particularly with an affluent expatriate community, Bebek has a shaded park on the waterfront next to the mosque, good restaurants and open-air cafés, and a jazz club. Small rowing boats and even sizable cutters with crew can be rented for trips around Bebek Bay.

**③⓪ Beylerbeyi Sarayı** (Beylerbeyi Palace). Built for Sultan Abdül Aziz in 1865, Beylerbeyi is a mini-Dolmabahçe, filled with marble and marquetry and gold-encrusted furniture. The central hall has a white-marble fountain and a stairway wide enough for a regiment. You must join a tour to see the palace. ⊠ *Çayıbaşı Durağı, Beylerbeyi,* ☎ *216/321–9320.* ⌑ *$3.* ☉ *Tues.–Wed. and Fri.–Sun. 9:30–5.*

**③⑥ Emirgan.** This town on the European shore of the Bosporus was named after a 17th-century Persian prince to whom Sultan Murat IV (ruled 1623–40) presented a palace here. The woods above are part of a park with flower gardens and a number of restored Ottoman pavilions. In late April the town stages a Tulip Festival. These flowers take their name from the Turkish *tulbend* (turban); the flowers were originally brought from Mongolia, and after their cultivation was refined by the Dutch, they were great favorites of the Ottoman sultans.

**③⑤ Kanlıca.** White 19th-century wooden villas line the waterfront of this village on the Asian shore. Kanlıca has been famous for its delicious yogurt for at least 300 years; it's served in little restaurants around the plane tree in the square by the quay.

**③④ Rumeli Hisarı** (Thracian Castle). Mehmet the Conqueror built this eccentric-looking fortress in 1452, a year before his siege of Constantinople finally succeeded. Its crenellated walls and round towers are popular with photographers, though what you view from the water is about all there is to see. In summer Rumeli Hisarı is sometimes used for Shakespeare performances (usually in Turkish) and music and folk dancing. ⊠ *Rumeli Hisarı Cad.,* ☎ *no phone.* ⌑ *$1.* ☉ *Tues.–Sun. 9:30–5.*

**③⑦ Sadberk Hanım Müzesi** (Sadberk Hanım Museum). An old waterfront mansion houses this museum named for the deceased wife of the late billionaire businessman Vehbi Koç. Though small, it houses an enviable collection of high-quality pieces. Half the museum is dedicated to Islamic and Turkish arts (from İznik tiles to Ottoman embroidery and calligraphy), and half to Anatolian archaeology (Hittite pottery and cuneiform tablets). ⊠ *Piyasa Cad. 27–29, Büyükdere,* ☎ *212/242–3813.* ⌑ *$2.* ☉ *Apr.–Oct., Thurs.–Tues. 10:30–6; Nov.–Mar., Thurs.–Tues. 10–5.*

# DINING

## Asian Shore

**$$$$** ✗ **Reşat Paşa Konağı.** A chic atmosphere prevails inside this pink-and-white gingerbread-style villa. It's a little out of the way, on the Asian side, but the delicious Ottoman and Turkish dishes are well worth the trip (which you can make with a taxi driver instructed by someone at your hotel). Order à la carte and sample the mixed seafood cooked in a clay pot, or let the waiter tempt you with the Paşa Sofrasi, a fixed-priced menu that includes 20 cold and hot appetizers, shish kebab as a main course, and lemon *helva* (halvah) for dessert, all accompanied by unlimited domestic drinks. A band plays *fasil* (traditional Turkish music) on weekends. ✉ *Sinan Ercan Cad. 34/1, Kozyatağı Mah., Erenköy,* ☎ *216/361–3411 or 216/361–3487. AE, DC, V. Closed Mon. No lunch.*

## South of the Golden Horn

**$$$** ✗ **Develi Restaurant.** One of the oldest and best kebab restaurants in
★ Istanbul also has great views across the Sea of Marmara. The specialty is dishes from southeast Anatolia, which are traditionally more spicy than those in the west of the country. Try the *patlıcan kebap* (kebab with eggplant) or the *fıstıklı kebap* (kebab with pistachios). ✉ *Balıkpazarı, Gümüşyüzük Sok. 7, Samatya,* ☎ *212/585–1189 or 212/529–0833. AE, MC, V.*

**$$$** ✗ **Gelik.** In a two-story 19th-century villa, this restaurant is usually packed with people savoring its delicious specialty: all types of meat roasted in deep cooking wells to produce rich, unusual stews. ✉ *Sahilyolu 68–70,* ☎ *212/560–7284. AE, DC, MC, V.*

**$$$** ✗ **Sarniç.** It's not often you get to dine deep down in an old Roman cistern. Candlelight reflects off the arched yellow-brick walls, and a large fireplace provides warmth in chilly weather. The service is fairly formal, and the fare is a mix of Turkish and Continental, ranging from duck à l'orange to *döner kebap* (meat roasted on a spit). ✉ *Sogukçesme Sok., Sultanahmet,* ☎ *212/512–4291. AE, MC, V.*

**$$** ✗ **Beyti.** One of the oldest and most famous meat restaurants in the
★ city, Beyti has grown over the last 55 years from a couple of chairs and a table to its current location close to the airport, its 500-person capacity spread over a terrace and a dozen ornately decorated rooms, the latter of which have ensured that Beyti has never lost its sense of intimacy. Photographs of famous, and sometimes infamous, former guests line the walls of the entrance. Although the starters and main courses are of an invariably high standard, the restaurant is most famous for the dish to which it gave its name, spicy meatballs wrapped in thin pastry—*beyti kebabı.* ✉ *Orman Sokak 8, Florya,* ☎ *212/663–2992. MC, V. Closed Mon.*

**$$** ✗ **Borsa Lokantasi.** This unpretentious spot with functional furnish-
★ ings is filled with a hungry crowd that comes to eat some great, reasonably priced food. The baked lamb in eggplant puree and the stuffed artichokes are especially good. ✉ *Yalıköşkü Cad., Yalıköşkü Han 60–62, Eminönü,* ☎ *212/522–4173. MC, V.*

**$$** ✗ **Darülziyafe.** This eatery in the Süleymaniye Mosque complex was
★ opened to preserve Ottoman cuisine. House specialties include Süleymaniye soup and Teşrifettin Naim Efendi stew. There is live classical Ottoman music (*fasil*) on Saturday evening. ✉ *Şifahane Cad. 6, Süleymaniye,* ☎ *212/511–8414. MC, V.*

**$$** ✗ **Fırat.** At this hopping Kumkapı fish house, you barely have time to settle in before food starts coming at you: salads, a savory baked liver

**56**

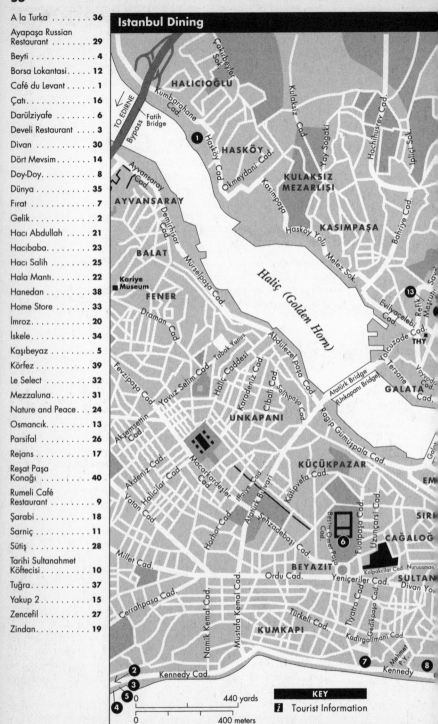

## Istanbul Dining

KEY

*i* Tourist Information

0      440 yards

0      400 meters

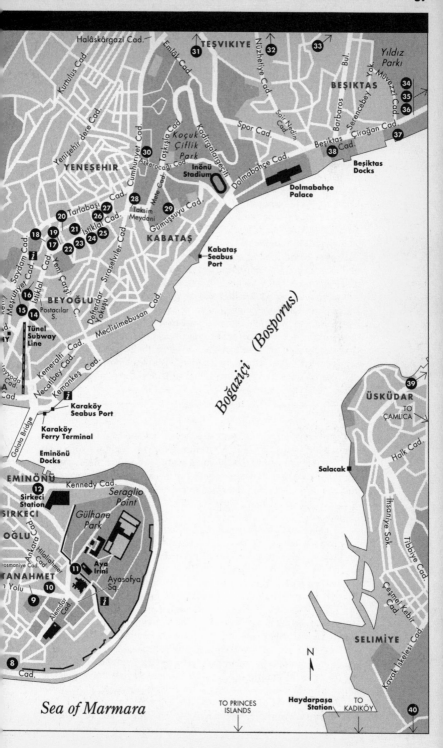

dish, shrimp with garlic. In addition to the usual grilled presentations, fish here is baked in a light cream- or tomato-based sauce to great effect. Just point at what you want, but try to save room for dessert. ⊠ *Çakmaktaş Sok. 11, Kumkapı,* ☎ *212/517–2308. AE, MC, V.*

$$ ✕ **Kaşıbeyaz.** This large meat restaurant close to the airport was
★ among the first in Istanbul to introduce spicy dishes from eastern Turkey. The house specialty is the pistachio kebab (*fıstıklı kebabı*), although the eggplant with browned ground beef (*patlıcanlı kebabı*) and meat patties on eggplant with garlic yogurt and parsley (*alenazik*)are also excellent. ⊠ *Çatal Sokak 10, Florya,* ☎ *212/633–2890. Reservations essential on weekends. MC, V.*

$ ✕ **Doy-Doy.** *Doy-doy* is a Turkish expression for "full," and you can indeed fill up here for a reasonable sum. Kebabs, *pide* (Turkish pizza), and mezes are served. If you're a vegetarian, the meatless pizzas and salad are good options. Service is friendly, and the menu's prices are unambiguous (sometimes a problem in Istanbul). ⊠ *Şifa Hamamı Sok. 13, Sultanahmet,* ☎ *212/517–1588. No credit cards.*

$$ ✕ **Rumeli Café Restaurant.** This little eatery in the heart of the main tourist
★ area offers good food at reasonable prices, including a range of salads and meat dishes. In summer you can sit outside at tables on the sidewalk. ⊠ *Ticarethane Cad. 8, Sultanahmet,* ☎ *212/512–0008. No credit cards.*

$ ✕ **Tarihi Sultanahmet Köftecisi.** Although a number of branches exist across the city, this one is the original home of Sultanahmet *köfte* (meatballs). This restaurant has built a small empire from a combination of bare, almost austere decor and an even simpler menu, which has remained virtually unchanged for more than 75 years—meatballs, *piyaz* (boiled white beans in olive oil), and salad. Its location, a couple of minutes' walk from the Blue Mosque and Aya Sofya, makes it ideal for a quick lunch. ⊠ *Divan Yolu 12, Sultanahmet,* ☎ *212/513–1438. No credit cards.*

## Beyoğlu Area

$$ ✕ **Çatı.** This restaurant on a side street serves hot and cold Turkish dishes and a good buffet. It's on the seventh floor, which allows you to appreciate the architectural splendors of İstiklal Caddesi. Before perusing the menu, ask the waiter about the day's specials. It's open late, and live music is often performed in the evening. ⊠ *Orhan Apaydın Sok. 20/7, İstiklal Cad., Beyoğlu,* ☎ *212/251–0000. AE, MC, V. Closed Sun.*

$$ ✕ **Dört Mevsim** (Four Seasons). A handsome Victorian building on the
★ new town's main drag houses this restaurant, noted for its blend of Turkish and French cuisine. It was opened in 1965 by an Anglo-Turkish couple, Gay and Musa, and you'll still find them in the kitchen overseeing the preparation of such delights as shrimp in cognac sauce and baked marinated lamb. ⊠ *İstiklal Cad. 509, Beyoğlu,* ☎ *212/293–3941 or 212/243–6320. AE, DC, MC, V. Closed Sun.*

$$ ✕ **İmroz.** One of the few remaining Greek tavernas in Istanbul, albeit with a Turkish menu, the İmroz is tucked away in a side street, serving meat and fresh fish as well as a range of appetizers, including the spicy cured-meat pastry *pastırmalı böreği,* and the fried cheese dish called *kaşarlı pane.* In summer all the local restaurants have tables outside, which gives the street an almost carnival atmosphere. ⊠ *Nevizade Sokak 24, Beyoğlu,* ☎ *212/249–9073. No credit cards.*

$$ ✕ **Osmancık.** On the 23rd floor of the Mercure Hotel, this Turkish restaurant has a 360-degree view of the Bosporus, the Golden Horn, and the rest of Istanbul. The fixed-price menu includes appetizers such as *osmancık boreği* (cheese-filled pastries topped with a yogurt sauce) and grills and all the domestic liquors you want to drink. Entertainment, which starts after 9 PM, comes in the form of traditional Turk-

ish music, followed by a belly dancer. ⊠ *Meşrutiyet Cad., Tepebası,* ☎ *212/251–5074. AE, DC, MC, V.*

**$$** ✕ **Parsifal.** Despite a preponderance of vegetarian dishes, as a concession to carnivores the menu also offers chicken. Small and intimate, with homely hardwood furniture, Parsifal serves specialties that include quiche, fried soybean patties, and banana crepes. ⊠ *Kurabiye Sokak 13, İstiklal Cad., Beyoğlu,* ☎ *212/245–2588. MC, V.*

**$$** ✕ **Rejans.** Established by Russian émigrés who fled the Bolshevik revolution, the restaurant is now run by their widows. In the 1930s and 1940s it was one of Istanbul's premiere restaurants. Plaques on the wall bear witness to the famous and infamous who once dined here, from statesmen to World War II spies and diplomats. The decor has remained basically unchanged since the restaurant's heyday, and live Russian music from an accordion-led trio is performed on the balcony Thursday–Saturday. The excellent range of appetizers includes piroshki and borscht, and main courses highlight beef Stroganoff, chicken Kiev, and pork chops. ⊠ *Emir Nevrut Sok. 17, İstiklal Cad., Beyoğlu,* ☎ *212/244–1610. Reservations essential Fri.–Sat. MC, V. Closed Sun.*

**$$** ✕ **Şarabi.** This three-story eatery has become famous for offering the largest range of Turkish wines in Istanbul. But it also serves high-quality Mediterranean food, such as steaks, salads and pasta dishes, all at very reasonable prices. ⊠ *İstiklal Cad. 174, Beyoğlu,* ☎ *212/244–4609. AE, MC, V.*

**$$** ✕ **Zindan.** Two hundred years ago this Ottoman *meyhane* was a prison. Today it is a popular haunt of Turkish intellectuals and businesspeople, drawn by superb Turkish cuisine and the atmosphere, created by live *fasıl* (Turkish classical music). ⊠ *İstiklal Cad., Olivai Han Geçidi 13, Galatasaray,* ☎ *212/252–7340. No credit cards.*

**$** ✕ **Hacı Abdullah.** Authentic, inexpensive traditional Ottoman and Turkish cuisine has made this a favorite for locals wishing to enjoy good food in a relaxed atmosphere. The restaurant is famous for its appetizers, grilled meats, and seemingly inexhaustible range of pickles and homemade fruit compotes. ⊠ *Ağa Camii Sakızağacı Cad. 17, Beyoğlu,* ☎ *212/293–8561. AE, MC, V.*

**$** ✕ **Hacıbaba.** The menu at this large, cheerful place runs the gamut of Turkish specialties; the lamb kebabs are good, and there are so many mezes that you may never get around to ordering main courses. The shady terrace overlooks a Greek Orthodox churchyard. ⊠ *İstiklal Cad. 49, Taksim,* ☎ *212/244–1886 or 212/245–4377. AE, MC, V.*

**$** ✕ **Hacı Salih.** You may have to line up for lunch at this tiny, family-★ run restaurant—it has only 10 tables. But the traditional Turkish fare is worth the wait. Lamb and vegetable dishes are specialties, and though alcohol is not served, you are welcome to bring your own. ⊠ *Anadolu Han 201/1–2, off Alyon Sok. (off İstiklal Cad.),* ☎ *212/243–4528. MC, V. Closed Sun. No dinner.*

**$** ✕ **Hala Mantı.** As its name suggests, this eatery on busy İstiklal Cad-★ desi specializes in *mantı,* Turkish ravioli. But it also serves excellent *gözleme,* which are thin pastry shells filled with such ingredients as cheese and spinach and then cooked on huge hot plates as you watch. ⊠ *İstiklal Cad. 211, Beyoğlu,* ☎ *212/292–7004. No credit cards.*

**$** ✕ **Nature and Peace.** One of the increasing number of health food restaurants opening in Istanbul, this small eatery serves a range of vegetarian and healthy dishes in a nostalgic, turn-of-the-century atmosphere. ⊠ *Büyükparmakkapı Sokak 21, Beyoğlu,* ☎ *212/252–8609. MC, V.*

**$** ✕ **Yakup 2.** This cheery hole-in-the-wall is smoky and filled with locals rather than tourists. It can get loud, especially if there is a soccer match on the television. From the stuffed peppers to the octopus salad, the mezes are several notches above average. ⊠ *Asmalı Mescit Cad. 35–37,* ☎ *212/249–2925. AE, V.*

$       ✕ **Zencefil.** The menu at this pioneering vegetarian restaurant, one of
the first to open in Istanbul, changes daily. But it usually includes the
house specialty, mushrooms with potatoes, as well as excellent home-
made breads and salads. The atmosphere is intimate and cafélike. ✉ *Kura-
biye Sok. 3, Beyoğlu,* ☎ *212/244–4082. No credit cards. Closed Sun.*

## Hasköy

$$$$    ✕ **Café du Levant.** Black-and-white floor tiles and turn-of-the century
European furnishings give this café next to the Rahmi Koç Industrial
Museum the feel of a Paris bistro. Chefs Giles and Cyril make superb
French cuisine, including fillet of turbot with zucchini and tomatoes.
For dessert try the crème brûlée or the orange cake with ice cream. ✉
*27 Hasköy Cad., Hasköy,* ☎ *212/235–6328. Reservations essential.
AE, DC, MC, V. Closed Mon.*

## Taksim Square Area

$$$     ✕ **Divan.** The Divan, in the hotel of the same name, provides an ex-
ception to the unwritten rule that you should avoid hotel restaurants.
The menu is a thoughtful blend of Turkish and French cuisine, the
surroundings are elegant, and the service is excellent. ✉ *In Divan
Hotel, Cumhuriyet Cad. 2, Beyoğlu,* ☎ *212/231–4100. AE, DC, MC.
Closed Sun.*

$$      ✕ **Ayaspaşa Russian Restaurant.** Once run by Russians and now by
Turks, the menu and ambience at this restaurant leave little doubt as
to its origins. Tapes of Russian folk songs play in the background, and
borscht, lemon vodka, and chicken Kiev are served. The beef Stroganoff
is also excellent, as are the consistently tasty pork chops. ✉ *İnönü Cad.
77/A, Gümüşuyu, Taksim,* ☎ *212/243–4892. MC, V.*

$$      ✕ **Mezzaluna.** This place arguably serves the best Italian cuisine in the
city. Set in one of Istanbul's most chic neighborhoods, this is a favorite
quick lunch venue for those working in the nearby offices. House spe-
cialties include linguine, seafood pappardelie and spaghetti vongole.
✉ *Abdi İpekçi Caddesi 38/1, Nişantaşı,* ☎ *212/231–3142. Reserva-
tions essential for dinner. AE, MC, V.*

$       ✕ **Sütiş.** This unpretentious spot on the edge of Taksim Square never
seems to close. Its cramped frontage opens into a spacious two-tiered
interior where the clientele changes with the hours, from office work-
ers eating cheese- or ground-beef-filled börek before work to shoppers
and students chatting over tea or a light lunch to bleary-eyed, late-night
revelers enjoying Turkish coffee and milk pudding before beginning the
journey home. ✉ *Sıraselviler Cad. 9/4, Taksim,* ☎ *212/252–9204. No
credit cards.*

## Etiler

$$$     ✕ **Home Store.** On the ground floor of the Akmerkez shopping mall,
in the shop of the same name, Home Store doubles as a bar for the
Turkish yuppies spilling out of the offices in the surrounding business
district. But the food—whether you come for lunch or an early dinner
(it closes at 10 PM)—is very good. The menu includes a range of salads, meat and vegetable dishes, superb soups, and desserts. ✉ *Home
Store, Akmerkez, Etiler,* ☎ *212/282–0253. MC, V.*

## Bosporus

$$$$    ✕ **Körfez.** Call ahead and this restaurant in the picturesque Asian village of Kanlıca can arrange to have you ferried across the Bosporus
from Rumeli Hisar. The look is nautical, and the seafood fresh and su-
perbly cooked to order; sample such dishes as flying-fish chowder and

sea bass cooked in salt. ⊠ *Körfez Cad. 78, Kanlıca,* ☎ *216/413–4314. Reservations essential. AE, DC, MC, V. Closed Mon.*

$$$$ ✗ **Tuğra.** In the Çırağan Palace, this spacious and luxurious restaurant serves the most delectable of long-lost and savored Ottoman recipes, including stuffed bluefish and Circassian chicken. Cookbooks from the Ottoman palace were used to re-create some of the dishes. But that's not all: The Bosporus view is flanked by the palace's marble columns, and ornate glass chandeliers hover above, making you feel like royalty. ⊠ *Çırağan Cad. 84,* ☎ *212/258–3377. Reservations essential. Jacket required. AE, DC, MC, V. No lunch.*

$$$$ ✗ **Le Select.** In an elegant villa in the upmarket Levent neighborhood, Le Select lives up to its name by offering a sumptuous selection of Turkish, French, and Russian cuisine. House specialties include marinated salmon, sea bass with thyme, and steak in wine sauce. ⊠ *Manolya Sokak 21, Levent,* ☎ *212/268–2120. Reservations essential. AE, MC, V.*

$$$ ✗ **İskele.** Situated on a restored quay on the Bosporus, İskele's romantic setting is more than matched by a fine range of seafood. Ask the waiter for a recommendation for what is in season. Phone ahead for a table by the window or outside on the terrace in warmer weather. ⊠ *Yahya Kemal Caddesi 1, Rumelihisarı,* ☎ *212/263–2997. Reservations essential. AE, MC, V.*

$$ ✗ **A la Turka.** This cozy little restaurant in the Bohemian quarter of Ortaköy serves excellent *mantı* (Turkish ravioli), *gözleme* (meat-, cheese-, or spinach-stuffed phyllo pastry), köfte, and a large range of salads, but no alcohol. In summer, outdoor seating is available. ⊠ *Hazine Sok. 8, Ortaköy,* ☎ *212/258–7924. MC, V.*

$$ ✗ **Dünya.** Right on the Bosporus in bustling Ortaköy, this restaurant has a view of the Bosporus Bridge, the Ortaköy Mosque, and many a passing boat. But as wonderful as these sights are, the food, such as fresh and delicious appetizers of eggplant or octopus salad, is even better. Ask for a table on the terrace as close to the water as possible. ⊠ *Salhane Sok. 10, Ortaköy,* ☎ *212/258–6385. MC, V.*

$$ ✗ **Hanedan.** The emphasis here is on kebabs—all kinds, all of them excellent. The mezes—tabbouleh, hummus, and the flaky pastries known as *böreks*—are tastier than elsewhere. Crisp white linens set off the cool, dark decor. Tables by the front windows offer the advantage of a view of the lively Beşiktaş Ferry terminal. ⊠ *Çiğdem Sok. 27, Beşiktaş,* ☎ *212/260–4854. AE, MC, V.*

# LODGING

## South of the Golden Horn

$$$$ 🏨 **Armada Hotel.** Only 10 minutes' walk from Istanbul's main tourist
★ sites, the Armada offers spacious, comfortable rooms that have either sea or old city views. One of the hotel's best views is from the terrace of its Ahırkapı restaurant at night. ⊠ *Ahırkapı, 34400,* ☎ *212/638–1370,* FAX *212/518–5060. 110 rooms with bath. 3 restaurants, bar, room service. AE, MC, V.* ✎

$$$$ 🏨 **Four Seasons Hotel.** A former prison, this elegant hotel became one
★ of Istanbul's premier accommodations the instant it opened in 1996. This neoclassical building is only steps from Topkapı Palace and the Aya Sofya. Rooms and suites overlook either the Sea of Marmara or an interior courtyard and are luxuriously outfitted with reading chairs, original works of art, and tile bathrooms with deep tubs. The glass-enclosed courtyard restaurant serves both international cuisine and local specialties. Service is exceptional. ⊠ *Tevkifhane Sok. 1, Sultanahmet, 34490,* ☎ *212/638–8200,* FAX *212/638–8530. 65 rooms with bath. Restaurant, bar, room service, health club, business services. AE, DC, MC, V.* ✎

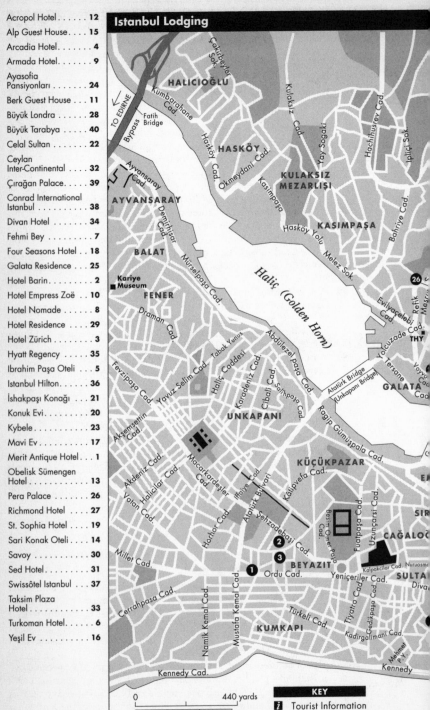

**Istanbul Lodging**

KEY

🛈 Tourist Information

0   440 yards

0   400 meters

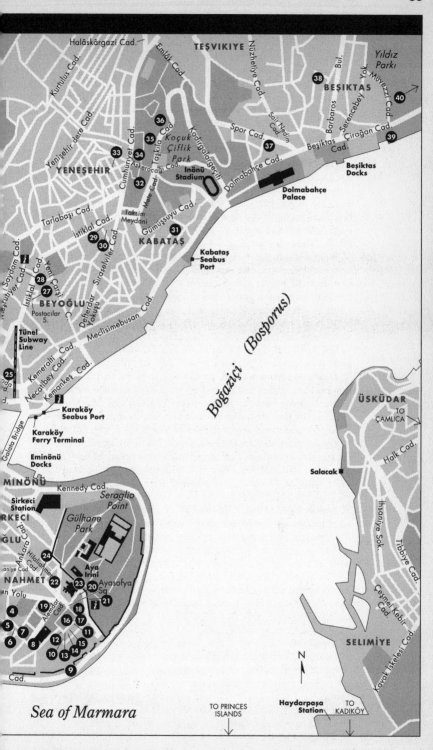

Halâskârgazi Cad.

Kurtuluş Cad.

**TEŞVIKIYE**

Nüzhetiye Cad.

Emlâk Cad.

Bul.

*Yıldız Parkı*

38

**BEŞIKTAŞ**

Müvezzi Cad.

40

Yenişehir dere Cad.

Şair Nedim Cad.

Barbaros

Serencebey Yok.

Çırağan Cad.

39

Cumhuriyet Cad.

36

Koçuk Çiflik Park

Kadırgalargeçiti

Spor Cad.

Beşiktaş Cad.

**Beşiktaş Docks**

33

35

34

Taşkla Cad.

Askerocağı Cad.

37

**YENEŞEHIR**

32

İnönü Stadium

Dolmabahçe Cad.

**Dolmabahçe Palace**

Tarlabaşı Cad.

Meşe Cad.

Gümüşsuyu Cad.

*Taksim Meydanı*

İstiklâl Cad.

29

30

31

**KABATAŞ**

**Kabataş Seabus Port**

Sıraselviler Cad.

**BEYOĞLU**

28

27

Yeni Çarşı

İstiklâl Cad.

*i*

Meşrutiyet Soydam Cad.

Postacılar S.

Defterdar Yokuşu

Meclisimebusan Cad.

**Tünel Subway Line**

Kemeraltı Cad.

Necatibey Cad.

Kemankeş Cad.

25

*Boğaziçi (Bosporus)*

*i*

**Karaköy Seabus Port**

Galata Bridge

**Karaköy Ferry Terminal**

**Eminönü Docks**

**ÜSKÜDAR**

TO ÇAMLICA

**MINÖNÜ**

Kennedy Cad.

*Seraglio Point*

**Sirkeci Station**

*Gülhane Park*

Halk Cad.

**RKECI**

**ĞLU**

Ankara Cad.

Hilaliahmer Cad.

İhsaniye Sok.

**Salacak**

24

**NAHMET**

22

**Aya Irini**

Ayasofya Sq.

İhsaniye Cad.

23

20

Çeşmei Kebir Cad.

an Yolu

21

*i*

19

18

4

Alemdar Cad.

5

16

17

**SELIMIYE**

7

6

11

8

12

15

10

13

14

Kavak İskelesi Cad.

9

Tıbbiye Cad.

Cad.

**N**

*Sea of Marmara*

TO PRINCES ISLANDS

**Haydarpaşa Station**

TO KADIKÖY

**$$$**   🏨 **Ayasofia Pansiyonları.** These guest houses are part of a project undertaken by Turkey's Touring and Automobile Club to restore a little street of 19th-century wooden houses along the outer wall of Topkapı Palace. One house has been converted into a library and the rest into pansiyons, furnished in late Ottoman style with Turkish carpets and kilims, brass beds, and big armoires. Front rooms have a view of Aya Sofya, but the rest do not, so if you want a view, specify when you reserve. In summer, tea and refreshments are served in the small courtyard. ⊠ *Soğukçeşme Sok., Sultanahmet, 34400,* ☎ *212/513–3660,* FAX *212/513–3669. 57 rooms with bath. Restaurant, bar, café, Turkish bath. AE, MC, V.* 🐾

**$$$**   🏨 **Mavi Ev** (Blue House Hotel). In the heart of the old city, this hotel has an eccentric blue wood facade and clean but slightly dowdily decorated rooms with a 1950s feel. Its rooftop terrace restaurant offers a stunning panorama across the Bosporus and Sea of Marmara and a breathtaking nighttime view of the floodlighted Blue Mosque. ⊠ *Dalbastı Sok. 14, Sultanahmet, 34490,* ☎ *212/638–9010,* FAX *212/638–9017. 27 rooms with bath. 3 restaurants, 2 bars. AE, MC, V.* 🐾

**$$$**   🏨 **Merit Antique Hotel.** Four turn-of-the-century apartment buildings were combined to create this hotel. Rooms are generic and unimpressive, but the public spaces couldn't be grander, with arched-glass canopies and reproduction furnishings in turn-of-the-century style. There's even a small stream stocked with goldfish running through the lobby. The only drawback is the neighborhood, on the old-town side, which is mostly full of cheap hotels and restaurants. ⊠ *Ordu Cad. 226, Laleli, 34470,* ☎ *212/513–9300,* FAX *212/512–6390. 247 rooms with bath. 4 restaurants, bar, pool, health club. AE, MC, V.* 🐾

**$$$**   🏨 **Obelisk Sümengen Hotel.** As its name suggests, this converted Ottoman house with a yellow-and-white-painted wooden facade is just a stone's throw from the obelisks in the Hippodrome. Most rooms are functionally furnished with parquet floors, although some have brass bedsteads and views across the Sea of Marmara. If you fail to locate one of the latter, you can always enjoy the breathtaking panorama from the terrace, where meals are served in warm weather. ⊠ *Amiral Tafdil Sokak 21, Mimar Mehmet Ağa Cad., Sultanahmet, 34490,* ☎ *212/517–7173,* FAX *212/517–6861. 71 rooms with bath. 2 restaurants, bar, Turkish bath. AE, MC, V.* 🐾

**$$$**   🏨 **Yeşil Ev** (Green House). Another Touring and Automobile Club proj-
★   ect, this lovely old house is on the edge of a small park between the Blue Mosque and Aya Sofya. The hotel is decorated in Ottoman style, with lace curtains and latticed shutters; rooms have brass beds and carved wooden furniture upholstered in velvet or silk (but they're small, with smallish baths and no phones or televisions). The hotel also has a delightful small garden, built around a marble fountain, where you can have breakfast in the warmer weather. ⊠ *Kabasakal Cad. 5, Sultanahmet, 34400,* ☎ *212/517–6786,* FAX *212/517–6780. 19 rooms with bath. Restaurant. AE, MC, V.*

**$$**   🏨 **Arcadia Hotel.** Tucked away in one of the quieter streets in Sultanahmet, this modern hotel has tastefully furnished rooms equipped with a full range of amenities. But its standout feature is its rooftop terrace with a stunning panoramic view, from the Sea of Marmara to the Blue Mosque and Aya Sofya, which is simply entrancing at night. ⊠ *Dr. İmran Öktem Cad. 1, Sultanahmet, 34400,* ☎ *212/516–9696,* FAX *212/516–6118. 42 rooms with bath, 6 suites. Restaurant. AE, MC, V.*

**$$**   🏨 **Acropol Hotel.** Another restored Ottoman house, in the quaintly named "White Mustache Street" offers rooms that combine rather cumbersome imitation period furniture with modern conveniences. Few, except for the suites, have much of a view, although the rooftop restaurant more than compensates. ⊠ *Akbıyık Cad. 25, Sultanahmet, 34400,*

☎ *212/638–9021*, 🅵🅰🆇 *212/518–3031. 24 rooms with bath, 2 suites. Restaurant. AE, MC, V.* ✎

**$$** 🏨 **Celal Sultan.** A restored town house, which opened as a hotel in 1996, the Celal Sultan has hardwood floors and kilims that give rooms a sense of warmth and quiet sophistication. From the rooftop terrace you can enjoy a fine view of the Blue Mosque and the Sea of Marmara. Unusual for Istanbul, the water in the hotel is filtered. The proprietor, Mr. Selami, and his wife are full of good sightseeing and shopping tips. ✉ *Salkımsöğüt Sok. 16, Yerebatan Cad., Sultanahmet, 34410,* ☎ *212/520–9323,* 🅵🅰🆇 *212/522–9724. 30 rooms with bath, 2 suites. Restaurant. AE, MC, V.* ✎

**$$** 🏨 **Fehmi Bey.** In a beautifully restored and refurbished old town house just off the Hippodrome, this hotel is adorned with owner Fehmi Bey's antiques and kilims. After a long day of sightseeing, the sauna and rooftop terrace bar with views of the old city relax and restore both body and soul. ✉ *Üçler Sok. 15, Sultanahmet, 34440,* ☎ *212/638–9083,* 🅵🅰🆇 *212/518–1264. 34 rooms with bath. Sauna. AE, MC, V.*

**$$** 🏨 **Hotel Barin.** Modern, clean, and comfortable, this hotel makes up for in convenience, functionality, and a friendly staff what it lacks in atmosphere. It attracts a large number of business travelers as well as tourists. ✉ *Fevziye Cad. 7, Şehzadebaşı, 34470,* ☎ *212/513–9100,* 🅵🅰🆇 *212/526–4440. 65 rooms with bath. Restaurant. AE, MC, V.* ✎

**$$** 🏨 **Hotel Zürich.** This 10-story hotel is efficient, well run, and one of the choicer options in the Laleli neighborhood (most other choices are rather shabby). The lobby is highly polished, and rooms are bright and carpeted and have little balconies. Ask for one of the higher floors; they're quieter. ✉ *Harikzadeler Sok. 37, Laleli, 34470,* ☎ *212/512–2350,* 🅵🅰🆇 *212/526–9731. 132 rooms with bath. Restaurant, 2 bars, nightclub, pool. MC, V.* ✎

**$$** 🏨 **Ibrahim Paşa Oteli.** This French-owned hotel in an exquisitely renovated Ottoman house in the historic Sultanahmet neighborhood has a rooftop terrace with glorious views of the Blue Mosque. Though rooms are small and simple, the lobby and bar downstairs, where you can have a wonderful breakfast, are warmly decorated and comfortable. The personable staff ensures a relaxing atmosphere. ✉ *Terzihane Sok. 5, Sultanahmet, 34400,* ☎ *212/518–0394 or 212/518–0395,* 🅵🅰🆇 *212/518–4457. 19 rooms with bath. Bar. AE, MC, V.* ✎

**$$** 🏨 **Konuk Evi.** Under the same management as its larger neighbor Ayasofia Pansiyonları, with which it shares contact details, this former Ottoman mansion has been restored with period furnishings, from the large brass mirrors and crystal chandeliers in the lobby to brass bedsteads and velvet curtains in the high-ceilinged rooms. In the summer meals are served in a delightful little garden. ✉ *Soğukçeşme Sok., Sultanahmet, 34400,* ☎ *212/513–3660,* 🅵🅰🆇 *212/513–3669. 10 rooms with bath, 2 suites. Restaurant, bar. AE, MC, V.* ✎

**$$** 🏨 **Kybele.** Named after an ancient Anatolian fertility goddess, the Kybele has numerous fascinating features, including a lobby lighted by 1,002 lamps, antique furniture, kilims, and calligraphic plates. Rooms have dark-wood furniture and bare walls, and some have kilims. ✉ *Yerebatan Cad. 35, Sultanahmet, 34410,* ☎ *212/511–7766,* 🅵🅰🆇 *212/513–4393. 16 rooms with bath. Bar. AE, MC, V.* ✎

**$$** 🏨 **St. Sophia Hotel.** This member of the Best Western International chain combines comfortable, tastefully decorated rooms with a full range of modern facilities and a very helpful staff. ✉ *Alemdar Caddesi 2, Sultanahmet, 34400,* ☎ *212/528–0974,* 🅵🅰🆇 *212/511–5491. 25 rooms with bath, 2 suites. Restaurant, bar. AE, MC, V.* ✎

**$$** 🏨 **Sari Konak Oteli.** This small, family-run hotel in an Ottoman-style building provides a very comfortable stay. The decor throughout is modern, but with Turkish tilework accents and an old, intricately paneled door at the front desk. From your room's tiny balcony with lattice shutters, lean out to hear the call to prayer echoing in Sultanahmet. If you don't want twin beds, and prefer a bathtub to a shower, say so when making reservations. On the rooftop terrace, you can sip a glass of rakı and contemplate either the Marmara Sea or the nearby Blue Mosque's spires. A treat in the morning is the delicious mix of yogurt, cereal, and dried fruits that's part of the Continental buffet.⊠ *Mimar Mehmet Aga Cad. 42–46, Sultanahmet,34400,* ☎ *212/638–6258,*⊠ *212/517–8635. 17 rooms. Breakfast room, air-conditioning (some), fans, in-room safes, minibars, non-smoking rooms, room service, laundry services, travel services. AE, MC, V. CP.* ✎

**$$**   ☷ **Turkoman Hotel.** This restored Ottoman house has a spacious lobby and simple, clean rooms with brass beds, old carpets and attractive wooden furniture. Ask for a room looking out over Aya Sofya. The terrace, where breakfast is served in summer, has a fine view over the Sea of Marmara. ⊠ *Asmalı Çeşme Sok. 2, Sultanahmet, 34400,* ☎ *212/516–2956,* ⊠ *212/516–2957. 20 rooms with bath. Bar AE, MC, V.* ✎

**$**   ☷ **Alp Guest House.** This small, clean hotel is in the heart of the old city and has comfortable, simply furnished rooms. The terrace offers fine views of the Blue Mosque and the Sea of Marmara. Airport pickup service is available on request. ⊠ *Adliye Sok. 4, Akbıyık Cad., Sultanahmet, 34490,* ☎ *212/517–9570,* ⊠ *212/638–3922. 12 rooms with bath. MC, V.* ✎

**$**   ☷ **Berk Guest House.** Cheerful Güngör and Nevin Evrensel run this clean, comfortable pansiyon in a converted private home. There are a small lounge inside and a terrace with beautiful views across the Sea of Marmara. Two of the rooms also have balconies overlooking a garden. ⊠ *Kutluğün Sok. 27, Sultanahmet, 34400,* ☎ *212/516–9671,* ⊠ *212/517–7715. 9 rooms with bath. AE, V.* ✎

**$**   ☷ **Hotel Empress Zoë.** This small, unusual hotel with a friendly staff
★ is near the sights in Sultanahmet. Named for the 11th-century empress who was one of the few women to rule Byzantium, it is decorated in the style of that period. The terrace bar offers fine panoramic views of the old city, and breakfast is served in the garden or indoors. Rooms are accented with colorful textiles; a couple have terraces, and some are very small. Note that to get up to rooms you must climb a spiral staircase. The American owner, Ann Nevans, can help you with your itinerary. ⊠ *Akbıyık Cad., Adliye Sok. 10, Sultanahmet, 34400,* ☎ *212/518–4360,* ⊠ *212/518–5699. 14 rooms with bath, 2 suites, 1 penthouse. MC, V.* ✎

**$**   ☷ **Hotel Nomade.** The service is personal, the beds comfortable, and the
★ prices low at this Sultanahmet pansiyon. The building is a restored five-story Ottoman house decorated with kilims and folk crafts. Rooms are small but the roof-garden bar and terrace have views of Sultanahmet. ⊠ *Ticarethane Sok. 15, Sultanahmet, 34400,* ☎ *212/511–1296 or 212/513–8172,* ⊠ *212/513–2404. 15 rooms with bath. AE, MC, V.* ✎

**$**   ☷ **İshakpaşı Konağı.** This little timber-face pansiyon has small, clean,
★ simply furnished rooms and looks out toward the walls of Topkapı Palace. In warm weather, breakfast is served in a pleasant garden. ⊠ *İakpaşı 15, Sultanahmet, 34400,* ☎ *212/638–6267 or 212/638–6027,* ⊠ *212/638–1870. 19 rooms with bath. AE, MC, V.*

## Beyoğlu Area

**$$$**   ☷ **Galata Residence.** This hotel is in the oldest apartment building in Istanbul, built in 1881 for the Camondos, one of the leading banking families of the late Ottoman Empire. Rooms have been carefully furnished with period furniture, supplemented discreetly with modern conveniences such as bathtubs and air-conditioning. Prices of the one- and two-bedroom apartments, which come with kitchenettes, compare very favorably with rooms at Istanbul's upscale hotels, many of which have only a fraction of the Galata's character. Apartments on the upper floors and the top-floor restaurant have excellent views across the Golden Horn to the old city. ⊠ *Felek Sok. 2, Bankalar Cad., Galata, 80020,* ☎ *212/292–4841,* FAX *212/244–2323. 15 apartments. Restaurant, café, air-conditioning, kitchenettes. AE, DC, MC, V.* ❧

$$$ 🛏 **Pera Palace.** Built in 1892 to accommodate guests arriving on the *Orient Express,* this hotel is full of atmosphere. Everyone who was any-one in the late 19th and early 20th centuries stayed here, from Mata Hari to numerous heads of state. The rooms once occupied by Kemal Atatürk and Agatha Christie have been turned into museums. The elevator looks like a gilded bird cage, the main stairway is white mar-ble, and the lobby surrounding it has 20-ft-high coral-marble walls. Unfortunately, though the hotel has been modernized, its facilities and rooms are not in the greatest shape, making it a favorite of romantics rather than those who need a full range of modern amenities. ⊠ *Meşru-tiyet Cad. 98, Tepebaşı, 80050,* ☎ *212/251–4560,* FAX *212/251–4089. 145 rooms with bath. Restaurant, bar, café. AE, DC, MC, V.* ❧

$$ 🛏 **Büyük Londra.** This six-story structure, built in the 1850s as the home of a wealthy Italian family, has grown old gracefully. Rooms are small and comfortably worn, and the current layout has the feel of an old apartment building. The dark woods and velvet drapes used in the high-ceiling lobby and dining room exude an aura of the Ottoman Victo-rian era. ⊠ *Meşrutiyet Cad. 117, Tepebaşı, 80050,* ☎ *212/293–1619,* FAX *212/245–0671. 54 rooms with bath. Restaurant. AE, MC, V.*

$$ 🛏 **Richmond Hotel.** On pedestrian İstiklal Caddesi, very close to the con-sulates, this hotel occupies a turn-of-the-century building. Rooms are plush and clean; some have views of the Bosporus. The sidewalk patis-serie Lebon at the entrance is a remake of the original. ⊠ *İstiklal Cad. 445, 80070,* ☎ *212/252–5460 or 212/252–9852,* FAX *212/252–9707. 109 rooms with bath. Restaurant, bar, café, meeting room. AE, V.* ❧

$ 🛏 **Hotel Residence.** On bustling İstiklal Caddesi, the rooms here are simple, comfortable, and clean, if a little lacking in character. Ask for room at the back, as those overlooking the street tend to be noisy very late into the night. ⊠ *Alışık Sok. 19, İstiklal Caddesi, 80070,* ☎ *212/ 252–7685,* FAX *212/243–0084. 52 rooms with bath. Bar. MC, V.*

## Taksim Square

$$$$ 🛏 **Ceylan Inter-Continental.** Until the mid-1990s, when its lease ran out, this hotel was the Istanbul Sheraton. Extensively refurbished into a plush luxury hotel under its new owners, the Inter-Continental has rapidly become one of Turkey's premier accommodations, with a broad range of top-class facilities. Rooms on the Bosporus side have excellent views. ⊠ *Askerocağı Cad. 1, Taksim, 80200,* ☎ *212/231– 2121, 800/327–0200 in the U.S., 0345/581–444 in the U.K.;* FAX *212/ 231–2180. 390 rooms, 55 suites with bath. 3 restaurants, 3 bars, pool, health club. AE, DC, MC, V.* ❧

$$$$ 🛏 **Hyatt Regency.** This massive but tastefully designed pink building recalls Ottoman splendor. So does the interior, with its plush carpet-ing and earthy tones. Rooms have views of the Bosporus and the Tak-sim district. ⊠ *Taşkıla Cad., Taksim, 80900,* ☎ *212/225–7000; 800/ 228–9000 in the U.S.;* FAX *212/225–7007. 360 rooms with bath. 3 restau-rants, 3 bars, café, pool, beauty salon, Turkish bath, health club, busi-ness services, baby-sitting. AE, DC, MC, V.* ❧

$$$$ 🛏 **Istanbul Hilton.** Lavishly decorated with white marble, Turkish rugs, and large brass urns, this is one of the best Hiltons in the chain. The extensive grounds, filled with rosebushes, make the hotel a restful

haven in a bustling city. Rooms are Hilton standard, with plush carpeting and pastel decor; ask for one with a view of the Bosporus. ⊠ *Cumhuriyet Cad., Harbiye, 80200,* ☎ *212/231–4650; 800/445–8667 in the U.S.;* FAX *212/240–4165. 501 rooms with bath. 4 restaurants, 2 bars, indoor pool, pool, spa, Turkish bath, 3 tennis courts, health club, squash, shops. AE, DC, MC, V.* ☜

$$$ 🏨 **Divan Hotel.** The staff at this quiet, modern hotel is thoroughly professional. The restaurant is excellent, and the public spaces and good-size rooms are comfortable if a little dowdy. ⊠ *Cumhuriyet Cad. 2, Taksim, 80200,* ☎ *212/231–4100,* FAX *212/248–8527. 180 rooms with bath. 2 restaurants, bar, tea shop, pool. AE, DC, MC.* ☜

$$$ 🏨 **Taksim Plaza Hotel.** This upmarket hotel in the center of Taksim is a favorite with visiting executives. Its rooms are modern and plushly furnished, and it has an elegant lobby and restaurant. ⊠ *Topçu Cad. 8, Taksim, 80090,* ☎ *212/238–9220,* FAX *212/238–9238. 142 rooms with bath. Restaurant, bar, sauna. AE, MC, V.*

$$ 🏨 **Savoy.** This modern 10-story hotel is centrally located in the heart of the new town, with comfortably furnished rooms and marble-lined bathrooms. Rooms at the front look out over Taksim Square, which can be lively into the early hours, while those on upper floors at the back have views across the Bosporus. ⊠ *Sıraselviler Cad. 29, Taksim, 80060,* ☎ *212/252–9326,* FAX *212/243–2010. 80 rooms with bath, 10 suites. Restaurant, bar. AE, MC, V.* ☜

## Bosporus

$$$$ 🏨 **Çırağan Palace.** This 19th-century Ottoman palace (pronounced *Shi-*
★ *rahn*) is the city's most luxurious hotel. The setting is exceptional, right on the Bosporus; the outdoor pool is on the water's edge. The public spaces are all done up in cool marble and rich tones. Rooms have Ottoman-inspired wood furnishings and textiles in warm colors (ask for a renovated one); views are exceptional. Most rooms are in the new wing, though there are 12 suites in the palace. ⊠ *Çırağan Cad. 84, Beşiktaş, 80700,* ☎ *212/258–3377,* FAX *212/259–6686. 287 rooms, 28 suites with bath. 4 restaurants, bar, indoor pool, pool, Turkish bath, health club. AE, DC, MC, V.* ☜

$$$$ 🏨 **Conrad International Istanbul.** This modern 14-story tower, catering primarily to business travelers, has spectacular views of the Bosporus and terraced gardens. Rooms are tastefully furnished with all the amenities expected of an international hotel. The staff is congenial and efficient. ⊠ *Barbaros Bul. 46, Beşiktaş, 80700,* ☎ *212/227–3000,* FAX *212/259–6667. 620 rooms with bath. 3 restaurants, 2 bars, indoor pool, pool, 2 tennis courts, health club, shops, business services. AE, DC, MC, V.* ☜

$$$$ 🏨 **Swissôtel Istanbul.** In a superb spot just above Dolmabahçe Palace,
★ this hotel was controversial—nobody liked the idea of such a big, modern structure towering over the palace. But you'll appreciate its views—all the way to Topkapı Palace across the Golden Horn. The vast, high-ceiling lobby is usually filled with the sound of a tinkling piano. The occasional Swiss-village mural strikes a jarring note in Istanbul, but service is crisp and efficient. Rooms, done in muted greens, have contemporary if undistinguished furnishings. ⊠ *Bayıldım Cad. 2, Maçka, 80680,* ☎ *212/326–1100,* FAX *212/326–1122. 600 rooms with bath. 7 restaurants, 3 bars, indoor pool, pool, health club, business services. AE, DC, MC, V.* ☜

$$$ 🏨 **Büyük Tarabya.** This summer resort, less than an hour's drive up the Bosporus from the center of Istanbul, is popular with more affluent locals. Though it has been around for years, it is well maintained and perfectly modern, with bright white walls and plenty of cool mar-

ble. It has a private beach. ⊠ *Kefeliköy Cad., Tarabya,* ☏ *212/262–1000,* ℻ *212/262–2260. 267 rooms with bath. Restaurant, bar, indoor pool, pool, health club, beach. AE, MC, V.*

**$$** 🏨 **Sed Hotel.** Tucked away on a side street, halfway down the hill from Taksim Square to Kabataş, the Sed makes up for being slightly off the tourist track by providing superb Bosporus views from many of its rooms at half the price of a five-star hotel. It also has a good restaurant. Insist on a room with a view. ⊠ *Beşaret Sok. 14, Ayapaşa, 80040,* ☏ *212/252–2710,* ℻ *212/252–4274. 50 rooms with bath. Restaurant, bar. MC, V.*

# NIGHTLIFE AND THE ARTS

For upcoming events, reviews, and other information, pick up a copy of *The Guide,* a reliable bimonthly English-language publication that has listings of hotels, bars, restaurants, and events, as well as features about Istanbul. The English-language *Turkish Daily News* is another good resource both for listings and for keeping abreast of what is happening in Turkish and international politics.

## Nightlife

### Bars and Lounges

With views of the Bosporus and a top-notch restaurant next door, **Bebek Bar** (⊠ Bebek Ambassadeurs Hotel, Cevdet Paşa Cad. 113, Bebek, ☏ 212/263–3000) attracts a dressed-up crowd. **Beyoğlu Pub** (⊠ İstiklal Cad. 140/17, Beyoğlu, ☏ 212/252–3842), in a pleasant garden in summer and indoors in winter, draws moviegoers from nearby theaters and expatriates. At the opposite end of İstiklal Caddesi from Taksim Square, **Café Gramofon** (⊠ Tünel Meyd. 3, Tünel, ☏ 212/293–0786), a café during the day, becomes a jazz bar evenings Tuesday–Saturday. The latest music and spicy Asian food have made **Buddha Bar** (⊠ Kuruçeşme Caddesi 22–24, Etiler, ☏ 212/265–9016) a firm favorite with the Istanbul jet set.

**Hayal Kahvesi** (⊠ Büyükparmakkapı Sok. 19, Beyoğlu, ☏ 212/224–2558) is a smoky, crowded late-night hangout for a mostly young crowd that likes live (and loud) rock and blues. **Harry's Jazz Bar** (⊠ Hyatt Regency Hotel, Takışla, Taksim, ☏ 212/225–7000) is a popular hangout for foreign and Turkish professionals, drawn by its avant-garde decor, its live music, which is often blues or rock rather than jazz, and its potent cocktails. The Irish pub **James Joyce** (⊠ Zambak Sokak 6, İstiklal Cad., Beyoğlu, ☏ 212/244–0241) offers a wide selection of imported beers and spirits, including the Irish staple, Guinness, and a fine range of malt whiskeys. There is live music every night and Irish music on weekends.

The **Orient Express Bar** (⊠ Pera Palace Hotel, Meşrutiyet Cad. 98, ☏ 212/251–4560) is hard to beat for its turn-of-the-century atmosphere; you can't help but sense the ghosts of the various kings, queens, and Hollywood stars who have passed through its doors. **Roxy** (⊠ Arslanyatağı Sok. 9, Sıraselviler, Taksim, ☏ 212/245–6539) is a popular bar with a spirited, young crowd and live music; it also serves a good range of foods to snack on between drinks and music. If you are looking to sample the latest in Turkish music, then **Kehribar** (⊠ Divan Hotel, Cumhuriyet Cad. 2, Taksim, ☏ 212/231–4100) has live pop and jazz. Zihni, which is only open in summer, is on a terrace on the shore of the Bosporus, with idyllic views; it can become crowded on weekends (⊠ Muallim Naci Cad. 19, Ortaköy, ☏ 212/258–1154).

## Dance Clubs

Dance clubs get rolling by about 10 and usually keep going until 3 or
4 in the morning. **Club 14** (✉ Abdülhakhamit Cad. 63, Talimhane, ☎
212/256–2121) is, as its hours—11 PM–4 AM—suggest, a lively late-
night spot. The classy **Club 29** (✉ Paşabahçe Yolu, Çubuklu, ☎ 216/
322–2829) holds forth in a faux-Roman villa by the Bosporus on the
Asian side from mid-June through September. **Havana** (✉ Fargo İş
Merkezi, Büyükdere Cad., Esentepe, ☎ 212/213–0136) is the place to
be seen for young socialites. It opens at 7 for dinner, but the dancing
really gets going after 10. In the summer it relocates to Muallim Naci
Caddesi, in Ortaköy, (☎ 212/259–5919), where it has become the city's
leading open-air dance spot. **Switch** (✉ Muammer Karaca Çıkmazı 3,
İstiklal Cad., Beyoğlu, ☎ 212/292–7458) is Istanbul's newest and
most up-to-date underground club, with guest Turkish and foreign DJs
on weekends.

## Nightclubs

Probably a good deal tamer than you might have expected to find in
Istanbul, the city's nightclub shows include everything from folk
dancers to jugglers, acrobats, belly dancers, and singers. Some routines
are fairly touristy but still fun. Typically, dinner is served after 8, and
floor shows start around 10. Be aware that these are not inexpensive
once you've totaled up drink, food, and cover. Reservations are a good
idea; be sure to specify whether you're coming for dinner as well as
the show or just for drinks.

Note that at the seedy striptease places off İstiklal Caddesi, the goal is
to get customers to pay outrageous drink prices for questionable com-
panionship. Those unwary enough to enter such places have reported
being physically intimidated when questioning a drinks bill that has
run into the hundreds of dollars.

**Galata Tower** (✉ Kuledibi, ☎ 212/245–1160) is high atop the new town
in a round room sheathed in windows; the ambience is strictly hotel
lounge, and the Turkish dishes are only average. The fixed prices are
around $70 for the show and dinner and $40 for the show and a drink.
Comfortable, well-established **Kervansaray** (✉ Cumhuriyet Cad. 30,
☎ 212/247–1630) hosts a varied floor show, including two belly
dancers, regional folk dances, and medleys of songs from around the
world; it serves a variety of Turkish dishes and costs about $70 for the
show and dinner, $50 for the show and a drink. **Orient House** (✉ Tiy-
atro Cad. 27, Eminönü, ☎ 212/517–6163 or 212/517–3488) presents
a floor show with belly dancers and Turkish folk dancing, along with
good traditional Turkish food. It's about $75 for the show and dinner
and $50 for the show and a drink.

# The Arts

The **Istanbul International Festival,** held from late June through mid-
July, attracts renowned artists performing modern and classical music,
ballet, opera, and theater. Shows occur throughout the city in historic
buildings, such as Aya Irini and Rumeli Hisar. To order tickets in advance, apply to the Istanbul Foundation for Culture and Arts (✉
Kültür ve Sanat Concer Vakfi, İstiklal Cad. 146, Beyoğlu, 80070, ☎
212/293–3133).

In May, Istanbul hosts an **International Theater Festival,** which attracts
major stage talent from eastern and western Europe. Because there is
no central ticket agency, ask your hotel to help you get tickets or in-
quire at the box office or local tourist offices.

## Concerts

The **Aksanat Cultural Center** (✉ Akbank Bldg., İstiklal Cad., Beyoğlu, ☎ 212/252–3500) shows classical and jazz concerts on a large laser-disc screen, presents films, and hosts exhibitions.

Istanbul's main concert hall is **Atatürk Kültür Merkezi** (☎ 212/251–5600), in Taksim Square. The Istanbul State Symphony performs here from October through May, and ballet and dance companies do shows year-round.

The **Cemal Reşit Rey Concert Hall** (✉ Gümüş Sok., Harbiye, ☎ 212/231–5498), close to the Istanbul Hilton, hosts recitals and chamber and symphonic music, modern dance, rock, folk, and jazz concerts performed by international talent. Tickets are often less than half the price they might be in the United States or Europe.

## Film

Some theaters on the strip of İstiklal Caddesi between Taksim and Galatasaray show the latest from Hollywood, with a few current European or Turkish movies thrown in. There are also plush, modern theaters at the Istanbul Princess Hotel, in Maslak, and Akmerkez shopping center, in Levent. It's a good idea to purchase tickets in advance for the latter, particularly on weekends. Most foreign films are shown with their original soundtrack and Turkish subtitles, although many children's films are dubbed into Turkish. Look for the words *Ingilizce* (English) or *orijinal* (original language). Films in languages other than English will have subtitles in Turkish. When in doubt, ask at the ticket office whether the film is dubbed (*dublaj* in Turkish) or subtitled (*altyazılı* in Turkish).

The annual **Istanbul International Film Festival,** which is held in the first two weeks of April, presents films from around the world; ask for a schedule at any box office and make sure to purchase tickets in advance. Seats are reserved.

# OUTDOOR ACTIVITIES AND SPORTS

## Beaches

Even though local boys playfully dive into the sea even in the heart of the city, swimming is not recommended. The European shore of the Sea of Marmara is muddy and unpleasant, the Bosporus is famous for its dangerously strong currents, and either way, the water is pretty cold and heavily polluted. Stick with the hotel pool. If you must, your best bet is to make the hour-long drive to the area's nicest beach, at **Kilyos** on the Black Sea. Avoid the municipal beaches at Florya, a suburb on the European side, where bacteria have dangerously contaminated the waters.

## Golf

Istanbul is not a noted golfing destination; you won't find Sawgrass or Pebble Beach, but the courses are perfectly fine if you need a fix. Itinerant players are welcomed at the **Istanbul Golf Club** (✉ Büyükdere Cad., Ayazağa, ☎ 212/264–0742). The **Kemer Golf & Country Club** (✉ Kemerburgaz in the Belgrade Forest, 25 mins from Istanbul, ☎ 212/239–7913) has a nine-hole course. A little farther afield, the **Klassis Country and Golf Clubb** (✉ Kemer Köyü, 45 mins from Istanbul, ☎ 212/748–4600) has a good standard 18-hole, par 72 course and often hosts international tournaments.

## Jogging and Walking

If exploring the city's streets still leaves you wanting more exercise, try one of its parks. The wooded slopes of **Yıldız Park,** just north of the

Çirağan Palace, are usually blissfully uncrowded. **Belgrade Forest** has enticing wooded paths and a 6.5-km (4-mi) walking and jogging track around the shores of old reservoirs. **Emirgân Park** is noted for its flower gardens and Bosporus views. **Gülhane Park** is conveniently located right alongside Topkapı Palace.

### Soccer

Soccer is Turkey's passion, and **Turkish Division One** is the country's major league. Matches take place from September through May at İnönü Stadium, Fenerbahçe Stadium, and Ali Sami Yen Stadium. You can get tickets at the stadiums or ask at your hotel for help. If you prefer comfort to atmosphere, ask someone at your hotel—almost everyone is a passionate fan of one of the city's teams—for the schedule of televised games.

# SHOPPING

It's almost impossible to leave Istanbul without buying something. Whether you're looking for trinkets and souvenirs, kilims and carpets, brass and silverware, leather, old books, prints and maps, or furnishings and clothes (Turkish textiles are among the best in the world), you can find them in Istanbul. Shopping in the city also provides a snapshot of its contrasts and contradictions, from migrants from eastern Turkey selling their wares on the streets to the leisurely, time-honored haggling over endless glasses of tea in bazaars and back alleys to the credit cards and bar codes of the plush, upscale Western-style department stores.

## Markets

The **Grand Bazaar** (☞ Exploring Istanbul, *above*) is a neighborhood unto itself and a trove of all things Turkish—carpets, brass, copper, jewelry, textiles, and leather goods. The fashions are not bad either—though not quite up to Italian style, they're dramatically less expensive. **Nuruosmaniye Caddesi,** one of the major streets leading to the Grand Bazaar, is lined with some of Istanbul's most stylish shops, with an emphasis on fine carpets, jewelry, and made-in-Turkey fashions. A flea market is held in **Beyazıt Square,** near the Grand Bazaar, every Sunday. In recent years it has become a favorite with street traders from the former Eastern Bloc, who sell everything from cheap vodka and electronic goods to cast-off Red Army uniforms. The **Arasta Bazaar,** in Sultanahmet, is one of few markets open on Sunday; you can get a lot of the same items here as at the Grand Bazaar, and the atmosphere is a lot calmer.

Definitely worth seeing is the **Egyptian Bazaar** (☞ Exploring Istanbul, *above*), also known as the Spice Market. The **Balıkpazarı** (Fish Market) sells, despite its name, everything connected with food, from picnic supplies to exotic spices and teas; it's on Beyoğlu Caddesi off İstiklal Caddesi. **Sahaflar Çarşışı** is home to a bustling book market, with old and new editions; most are in Turkish, but English and other languages are represented. The market is open daily, though Sunday has the most vendors. Along the Bosporus in the **Ortaköy** neighborhood is a Sunday crafts market with street entertainment.

## Shopping Areas

**İstiklal Caddesi** is a street with everything from stores selling old books and Levis to the Vakko department store to a less stylish Turkish version of Saks Fifth Avenue. The **high-fashion district** centers on Halâskârgazi Caddesi and Rumeli Caddesi in Nişantaşı, 1 km (½ mi) north of İstiklal Caddesi. Here you will find the best efforts of Turkish fashion designers. **Bağdat Caddesi, Bahariye Caddesi,** and the **Carrefoursa** mall, all on the Asian side, are the places to find more suburban shopping venues. The **Galleria** mall, in Ataköy near the airport, has more than 100 stores selling foreign and local brand-name clothing. **Akmerkez,** in the Etiler district, is a large and luxurious mall whose stores stock recognized trademarks. The center has a movie theater, a restaurant, a fast-food court, and cafés.

## Specialty Stores

### Antiques

These are a surprisingly rare commodity in this antique land, perhaps because the government, to ensure that Turkish culture is not sold off to richer nations, has made it illegal to export most categories of antiques more than 100 years old.

**Sofa** (⌧ Nuruosmaniye Cad. 42), an exception, stocks a fascinating collection of old maps and prints, original İznik and Kütahya ceramics, vintage jewelry, and assorted other treasures. **Çığır Kitabevi** (⌧ Sahaflar Çarşışı 17) has an impressive collection of old books, many of them illustrated. **Ory & Ady** (⌧ Serifagu Sok. 7–8, in the bedestan section of the Grand Bazaar) specializes in Ottoman miniatures, illustrations, and prints. If you know old books, you can pick up bargains from the dozen or so shops at the **Kasımpaşa** flea market (⌧ Kulaksız Cad. 5, Büyük Çarşı, Kasımpaşa); the **Horhor** flea market, in Aksaray (⌧ Kırık Tulumba Sok. 13–22, Aksaray); or, on the Asian side of the city, the **Kadıköy** flea market (⌧ Çakıroğlu İşhanı, Tellalzade Sok., Moda Cad., Kadıköy).

### Carpets and Kilims

You can find carpet shops at nearly every turn, all stocking rugs for a variety of prices. Each shop has slightly different pieces, so it's best to look at several to get a feel for the market. On the other hand, there's nothing wrong with buying from the first shop you go into if you find something you love. For the best buys, look outside Istanbul.

Some of the better shops in Istanbul include: **Adnan Hassan** (⌧ Halıcılar Cad. 90); **Al-Dor** (⌧ Faruk Ayanoğlu Cad. 5–8); **Celletin Senghor** (⌧ Grand Bazaar); and **Ensar** (⌧ Arasta Bazaar 109). Also try the shops along Nuruosmaniye Caddesi, particularly **Çınar,** at No. 6.

### Clothing

**Angel Leather** (⌧ Nuruosmaniye Cad. 67) has kidskin suede and leather skirts and jackets; the best of Turkish leather is on a par with Italian leather quality wise, though the designs are not as stylish. Fashionable **Beymen** (⌧ Halaskargazi Cad. 230) is Istanbul's version of Bloomingdale's. **Beymen Club** (⌧ Rumeli Cad. 81 and Akmerkez shopping mall, in Etiler) sells casual Polo-style clothing. **Silk and Cashmere** (⌧ Akmerkez shopping mall, in Etiler, or Galleria shopping mall, in Ataköy, or on the Asian side, the Carrefour shopping mall, in Kozyatağı) carries a fine selection of high-quality, affordable silk and cashmere menswear and women's wear.

**Sube** (⌧ Arasta Bazaar 131) has handmade kilim slippers with leather soles and kilim boots for a fraction of their prices in the United States. **Vakko** (⌧ İstiklal Cad. 123–125, Beyoğlu or Akmerkez shopping mall, in Etiler, or on the Asian side, Bağdat Cad. 422, in Suadiye) is one of Turkey's oldest and most elegant fashion houses, with an excellent fabric department. Former president Bill Clinton could occasionally be seen sporting one of the Vakko ties presented to him by visiting Turkish delegates. Turkish designer **Zeki Triko** (⌧ Valikonağı Cad.) sells his own bathing suits, completely up-to-date, at his eponymous boutiques.

### English-Language Bookstores

Many larger hotels and souvenir shops in the old city stock some English-language newspapers and books, mostly guides to the more famous sights. Although it is sometimes possible to find U.S. daily newspapers, most cost $10 or more. A more comprehensive range can be found at specialty stores in Beyoğlu and the fashionable shopping districts of Nişantaşı and Levent. Books originally published outside Turkey are marked up 15%–75%.

Some of the larger bookstores carrying English-language books include: **Homer** (⊠ Yeni Çarşı Cad. 28A, Galatasaray, Beyoğlu, ☎ 212/249–5902); **Galeri Kayseri** (⊠ Divanyolu 58, Sultanahmet 34410, ☎ 212/512–0456); **Pandora** (⊠ Büyük Parmakkapı Sok. 3, Beyoğlu, ☎ 212/243–3503); **Remzi Kitabevi** (⊠ Akmerkez shopping mall, basement floor, No. 121, Levent, ☎ 212/282–0245; ⊠ Rumeli Cad. 44, Nişantaşı, ☎ 212/234–5475); and **Robinson Crusoe** (⊠ İstiklal Cad. 389, Tünel, Beyoğlu, ☎ 212/293–6968).

A number of stores specialize in secondhand books, many in English, from dog-eared thrillers to rare old texts about the city. These include: **Aslıhan Sahaflar Çarsısı** (⊠ Galatasaray Balık Pazarı, Beyoğlu); **Librairie de Pera** (⊠ Galip Dede Sok. 22, Tünel, ☎ 212/245–4998); and a cluster of antiquarian booksellers in the **Sahaflar Çarsısı** (⊠ Sahaflar Çarsı Sok., Beyazıt).

### Jewelry

The most common type of jewelry you'll see are amber necklaces and ethnic Turkish silver jewelry threaded with coral and lapis lazuli. **Georges Basoğlu** (⊠ Cevahir Bedestan 36–37) and **Venus** (⊠ Kalpakcılar Cad. 160) sell distinctive and original pieces. **Nasit** (⊠ Arasta Bazaar 111) often carries vintage silver jewelry as well as new items. **Urart** (⊠ Abdi İpekçi Cad. 181) has chic interpretations of ancient Anatolian designs.

# SIDE TRIPS

## Princes Islands

*20 km (12 mi) off the coast of Istanbul from Sultanahmet.*

The nine islands in the Sea of Marmara have proven a useful amenity for Istanbul. In the days when the city was known as Constantinople, religious undesirables sought refuge here; in the time of the sultans, the islands provided a convenient place to exile untrustworthy hangers-on. By the turn of the last century, well-heeled businessmen had staked their claim and built many of the Victorian gingerbread–style houses that lend the islands their charm. But the islands remained a place of refuge. In the 1930s, Büyükada, the largest of the islands, was the home for several years of the exiled Leon Trotsky.

Today the islands provide a leafy retreat from Istanbul. Restrictions on development and a ban on automobiles maintain the old-fashioned peace and quiet—transportation is by horse-drawn carriage or bicycle. Though there are no real sights and populations swell significantly on summer weekends, the Princes Islands are perfect for relaxed outings. Of the nine islands, only four have regular ferry service, and only the two largest, Büyükada and Heybeli, are of real interest. Both are hilly and wooded, and the fresh breeze is gently pine scented.

### Büyükada

To the left as you leave the ferry, you will see a handful of restaurants with names like Monte Carlo, Capri, and Milano. They are pleasant dives, though somewhat overpriced, and there's little difference among them. **Yörük Ali Plaj,** the public beach on the west side of the island, is an easy walk from the harbor and also has a little restaurant.

To see the island's splendid old Victorian houses, walk to the clock tower and bear right. Carriages are available at the clock tower square. The carriage tour winds up hilly lanes lined with gardens filled with jasmine, mimosa, and imported palm trees. After all of Istanbul's mosques and palaces, the frilly pastel houses come as something of a surprise, but it's quite easy to imagine men in panama hats and women with parasols having picnics out in the garden. You can have your buggy driver wait while you make the 20-minute hike up Yücetepe Hill to the **Greek Monastery of St. George,** where there are three chapels and a sacred fountain believed to have healing waters. As you walk up the path, notice the pieces of cloth, string, and paper that visitors have tied to the bushes and trees in hope of a wish coming true. This is a popular Orthodox Christian pilgrimage site, especially at Greek Easter, when hundreds make the hike barefoot. If you're lucky, the outdoor restaurant next to the monastery will be serving its homemade wine.

### DINING AND LODGING

There is little difference from one spot on Büyükada's restaurant row to the next. The best bet is to look at a menu and ask to see the dishes on display. If a place is crowded with Turks, it is usually good.

**$$$** ⊞ **Splendid Hotel.** For character, it's hard to beat this wooden turn-of-the-century hotel, with its old-fashioned furniture, large rooms, and Ottoman Victorian styling. The building is topped by twin white domes, copies of those at the Hotel Negresco in Nice. It's difficult to get a room on summer weekends unless you book ahead. ⊠ *23 Nisan Cad. 71, Büyükada, 81330,* ☎ *216/382–6950,* FAX *216/382–6775. 70 rooms with bath. Restaurant, pool. MC, V. Closed Oct.–Apr.*

## Heybeli

The big building to the left of the dock, the **Deniz Kuvvetler** (Turkish Naval Academy), is open to visitors every day except Sunday, though there's not really that much to see. To the right of Heybeli's dock are teahouses and cafés stretching along the waterfront. You can take a leisurely carriage ride, stopping, if the mood strikes, at one of the island's several small, sandy, and rarely crowded beaches—the best are on the north shore at the foot of **Değirmen Burnu** (Windmill Point) and **Değirmen Tepesi** (Windmill Hill). You can rent a rowboat for a few dollars at these beaches for the trip out to one of the other Princes Islands across the way. You will also pass the ruined monastery of the **Panaghia,** founded in the 15th century. Though damaged by fires and earthquakes, the chapel and several red-tile-roofed buildings remain. Carriages here do not climb the hills above the harbor, where the old mansions and gardens are. The walk, however, is not that strenuous.

### LODGING

**$$$** ⊞ **Merit Halki Palas.** A member of the Merit chain, the Halki Palas was opened in 1994 after its predecessor, which had been built in the 1850s, burned down. But the character of the old hotel has been retained, with white-painted wood, ornate eaves, and large, airy rooms. It's one of the most restful hotels in Istanbul, and though the island has few sights of its own, the old city is only an hour away by ferry. ⊠ *Refah Şehitleri Cad. 88, 81340, Heybeliada,* ☎ *216/351–8890,* FAX *216/351–8483. 45 rooms with bath. Restaurant, pool. MC, V.* ⊛

## Princes Islands Essentials

### ARRIVING AND DEPARTING

**Ferries** (80¢–$1.70) make the trip from Sirkeci or Bostancı (Asian side) docks in half an hour to an hour, depending on where they depart. Go straight to Büyükada and catch a local ferry to Heybeli later. You must pay each way to and from Istanbul but can travel for free between the islands themselves. For the return journey you can buy a ticket on the islands, but you must hold on to it and hand it over on disembarkation in Istanbul. In summer the early evening ferries returning to the mainland are often very crowded on weekends. Much quicker, though less romantic, is the sea bus, departing from Kabataş near the Dolmabahçe Mosque and from Bostancı sea-bus terminals on the Asian side. Buy tokens for the sea bus at the terminals.

GETTING AROUND

Since no cars are allowed on the islands, you do most of your exploring on foot. Horse-drawn carriage tours cost $10 to $15. The other, perhaps more strenuous but definitely fun, option, is to rent a bicycle ($2 per hour) from one of the shops near the clock tower on Büyükada. To get from one of the Princes Islands to the other, hop aboard any of several daily ferries.

# Edirne

*235 km (146 mi) northwest of Istanbul.*

Unlike Istanbul, which every conqueror and pretender within marching distance hoped to have as his capital, Thrace was the sort of region that most warriors passed on through. The climate is harsh—sizzling in summer, bitter in winter—and the landscape unexceptional. But the area has some worthy sights, particularly Edirne, founded in the 2nd century AD as Hadrianopolis by the Roman emperor Hadrian. The city has been fought over by Bulgars, crusaders, Turks, Greeks, and Russians through the centuries, though once the Ottoman capital was moved to Istanbul, it became something of a picturesque backwater. The overhanging balconies of traditional Ottoman wooden houses shade Edirne's still-cobbled lanes, and its rich collection of mosques and monuments remains mostly unspoiled by the concrete towers so prevalent in Turkey's boomtowns.

**Hürriyet Meydanı,** Edirne's central square, makes a good starting point. Standing in the middle of it is a monument to the city's great passion, wrestling: Two enormous wrestlers steal the spotlight from the obligatory Atatürk statue.

Just off the north side of the Hürriyet Meydanı (Freedom Square) is the **Üç Şerefeli Cami** (Mosque with Three Galleries), built between 1437 and 1447. The galleries circle the tallest of the four minarets, which are notable for their fine brick inlay. On the mosque grounds is the 15th-century **Sokurlu Hamam,** built by Sinan, and one of the country's more elegant baths. It is open to the public from about 8 AM until 10 PM and costs $4 for a bath, $10 for a bath with massage.

Walking east from the square along Talat Paşa Caddesi brings you to the **Eski Cami** (Old Mosque). The mosque is appropriately named: Completed in 1414, it is the city's oldest. The huge-scale calligraphy illustrating quotes from the Koran and naming the prophets is exceptional in its grace and intricacy. Adjoining it is the **Rüstempaşa Kervansaray** (Rüstempaşa Caravansary), restored and reopened as a hotel, just as it was in the 16th century. Also alongside the mosque is the 14-domed **bedestan** (market), and one block away, the **Ali Paşa Bazaar.** Both are more authentic than Istanbul's Grand Bazaar, as the wares sold—coffeepots, kilims, soap shaped like fruits and vegetables, towels—are meant for locals rather than tourists. ⊠ *Talat Paşa Cad., east from Hürriyet Meyd.,* ☎ *no phone.* 🎟 *Free.* ⊙ *Daily 9–7.*

The **Selimiye Cami** (Selimiye Mosque), not Istanbul's Süleymaniye, is the mosque Sinan described as his masterpiece, and it is certainly one of the most beautiful buildings in Turkey. Today a statue of the architect stands in front, but it is hardly necessary; the mosque remains his greatest monument. The architect was 85 years old when it was completed. The central dome, more than 100 ft in diameter and 148 ft high, rests on eight pillars, set into the walls so as not to disturb the interior space. External buttresses help support the weight of 999 windows; legend has it that Sultan Selim thought 1,000 might be a bit greedy. The marble mimber is exquisitely carved, and the mihrab is set back in an apse adorned with exceptional İznik tiles. The *medrese* (mosque compound) houses Edirne's **Türk-Islâm Eserleri Müzesi** (Museum of Turkish and Islamic Art), which displays Islamic calligraphy and photos of local wrestlers, as well as collections of weapons and jewelry from ancient Thrace, folk costumes, kilims, and fine embroidery. ⊠ *Hürriyet Meyd.* 🖾 *Free.* ☉ *Daily sunrise–sunset; usually closed to tourists at prayer times, particularly Fri. noon prayers.*

The other great mosque in Edirne is the striking **Beyazıt Cami** (Beyazıt Mosque), on the outskirts of the city across the Tunca River. The immense complex is about a 20-minute walk northwest from Hürriyet Meydanı via the fine-hewn, six-arched **Beyazıt Bridge,** which dates from the 1480s, as does the mosque. You can also take a *dolmuş* (shared taxi) from the square. The mosque was built by the Sultan Beyazıt, hence its name, at the end of the 15th century. The complex includes both the mosque itself—with a remarkable indented dome and a beautifully fretted mihrab—and two schools, a hospital, a kitchen, and storage depots. Apart from visiting tourists or a handful of young boys from the neighboring village playing soccer in the shadow of its walls, the complex is usually deserted by all but the custodian and fluttering pigeons, making it not only one of the most peaceful spots in Edirne but also a poignant reminder of the city's imperial past. ⊠ *Head northwest from Hürriyet Meydanı, across Beyazıt Bridge,* 🕾 *no phone.* 🖾 *Free.* ☉ *Daily sunrise–sunset during summer; mosque is often locked during winter, but custodian will sometimes open it up.*

**Sarayiçi,** a field with an arena on one side, is the site of Edirne's famous wrestling tournament. Usually held in June, it is the best known of those held in villages throughout the country: Its burly, olive-oil-coated men have been facing off annually here for more than 600 years. Thousands of spectators turn out. Sarayiçi is a 20-minute walk up the Tunca River from Benazıt Cami.

## Dining and Lodging

$ ✕ **Emirgan.** On the outskirts of town amid plane trees on the western bank of the Meriç River, this popular local haunt serves a passable range of Turkish meatballs, *köfte* and *şiş kebab.* In summer you can sit outside and watch the river flow. ⊠ *Karaağaç Yolu,* 🕾 *284/212–2906. No credit cards.*

$ ✕ **Bulvar Kebap.** Just north of the main square on the way to the Selimiye Mosque, the Bulvar offers not only kebabs but a tasty range of *pide,* filled with ground beef, cheese, and grilled lamb served in clean, if unprepossessing, surroundings. ⊠ *Emekli Öğretmenler Derneği Altı.,* 🕾 *284/225–6624. No credit cards.*

$$ 🏨 **Hotel Rüstem Paşa Kervansaray.** Built in the 1500s, reputedly by the celebrated architect Sinan, today this hotel is the most impressive in Edirne, at least from the outside. The inside is more functional: Rooms have high ceilings and decorative fireplaces, plain furniture, and low, single beds; avoid rooms near the nightclub, which are noisy. The building sprawls around a pleasant courtyard full of flowers and

shaded by a huge plane tree. ⊠ *İki Kapılı Han Cad. 57, Sabuni Mah.,
22800,* ☎ *284/225–2195 or 284/225–6119,* FAX *284/212–0462. 79
rooms with bath. Restaurant, nightclub, bar. MC, V.*

$  🖫 **Şaban Açıgöz Oteli.** Modest and nondescript, the Açıgöz Oteli is
efficient, clean, and well located, just off the main square and opposite the Kervansaray. The hotel does not have the charm of its neighbor, but its rooms are functional, with all the basic amenities. A small
restaurant serves breakfast but no midday or evening meals. ⊠ *Tah-
mis Meyd., Çilingirler Cad. 9, 22800,* ☎ *284/213–1404 or 284/213–
0313,* FAX *284/213–4516. 34 rooms with shower. Restaurant. MC, V.*

### Edirne Essentials

ARRIVING AND DEPARTING

**Buses** headed for Edirne depart frequently from Istanbul's Esenler Terminal. The trip takes four hours and costs $4. If you're going by **car,**
take the toll road—the E80 TEM (the toll from Istanbul to Edirne costs
$3.50), which is faster and much easier than Route 100. The trip takes
about 2½ hours. Three **trains** leave Istanbul's Sirkeci Station daily for
the painfully slow 6- to 10-hour trip; the cost is about $5, so you are
better off taking the bus or driving.

GETTING AROUND

The bus and train stations are on the outskirts of town, too far to walk.
Take a taxi into the center, asking for Hürriyet Meydanı. Sights in town
can all be reached on foot.

CONTACTS AND RESOURCES

Edirne's **tourist information office** (⊠ Talat Paşa Cad., near Hürriyet
Meyd., ☎ 284/213–9208) is open every day in summer and is generally closed off-season.

# ISTANBUL A TO Z

## Arriving and Departing

### By Bus

Buses arrive at the **Esenler Otogar** (Esenler Station; ☎ 212/658–0036),
outside the city near Bayrampaşa. This terminal is accessible by the Hızlı
Tren (rapid train) system, which leaves from Aksaray. However, the train
is often very crowded, particularly at rush hour, and you might be better
off taking a taxi. A few buses from Anatolia arrive at the **Harem Terminal** (☎ 216/333–3763), on the Asian side of the Bosporus. Most bus companies have minibus services from the bus terminals to the area around
Taksim Square and Aksaray, which is close to many hotels. Private taxis
cost about $12 from Esenler Terminal to Taksim or Sultanahmet and about
$10 from the Harem Terminal. Note that you'll have to pay the Bosporus
Bridge toll when crossing from Asia to Europe, or vice versa.

### By Car

E80 runs between Istanbul and central Anatolia to the east; this toll
road is the best of several alternatives. You can also enter or leave the
city on one of the numerous car ferries that ply the Sea of Marmara
from the Kabataş docks. There's an overnight ferry to İzmir from the
Eminönü docks. To get out of the city by car, your best bet is to buy
a map, as the signs aren't always so clear.

### By Plane

All international and domestic flights arrive at Istanbul's **Atatürk Airport** (☎ 212/663–6400). The main airlines flying into the airport include **Air France, British Airways, Delta, Lufthansa,** and **Turkish Airlines**
(☞ Air Travel *in* the Gold Guide for phone numbers).

BETWEEN THE AIRPORT AND THE CITY CENTER

**Shuttle buses** (☎ 212/252–1106) make the 30- to 40-minute trip from the airport's international and domestic terminals—which are some distance apart—to the Turkish Airlines office in Taksim Square; buses to the airport depart from Taksim Square every hour from 6 AM until 11 PM and as demand warrants after that. Allow at least 45 minutes for the bus ride in this direction and plan to be at the airport two hours before international flights to allow for the time-consuming security and check-in procedures. **Taxis,** which are metered, charge about $15 to Taksim Square and $11 to Sultanahmet Square.

## By Train

Trains from Europe and the west (and service is limited) arrive at **Sirkeci Station** (☎ 212/527–0051), in Old Stamboul, near the Galata Bridge. Trains from Anatolia and the east come into **Haydarpaşa Station** (☎ 216/336–0475), on the Asian side.

# Getting Around

The best way to explore the magnificent monuments in Old Stamboul is to walk. The setting shifts frequently, from narrow, cobbled streets to wide, tree-lined boulevards. To get to other areas, you can take a bus or one of the many ferries that steam between the Asian and European continents. Dolmuşes and private taxis are plentiful, inexpensive, and more comfortable than city buses.

## By Boat

You would expect a sprawling city surrounded by water to be well served by ferries, and Istanbul does not disappoint. The main docks are at Eminönü, on the Old Stamboul side of the Galata Bridge; Karaköy, on the other side of the bridge; Kabataş, near Dolmabahçe Palace; and across the Bosporus on the Asian shore, at Üsküdar and Kadiköy.

**Commuter ferries** of various sizes crisscross between these points day and night and provide great views of the city at a most reasonable price (usually $3 or less round-trip). Information on all city ferries is available between 9 and 5 from the Istanbul **Ferry Lines office** (☎ 212/244–4233). One of the most practical and speedy innovations on Istanbul's waterways has been the *deniz otobüsü* (sea buses), which are large, powerful catamarans painted blue, red, and white, operating to and from Karaköy, Kadıköy, Kabataş, Bostancı, the Princes Islands, Yalova, and Bakırköy. The interiors are air-conditioned and reminiscent of a large aircraft. Schedules are available at docks marked DENIZ OTOBÜSÜ TERMI-NALI and are also available on a 24-hour Turkish-language telephone service (☎ 216/362–0444).

Best for sightseeing is the **Anadolu Kavağı** boat (☎ 212/522–0045), which makes all the stops on the European and Asian sides of the Bosporus. It leaves year-round from the Eminönü Docks, Pier 5, next to the Galata Bridge on the Old Stamboul side, at 10:35 and 1:35, with two extra trips on weekdays and four extra trips on Sunday from April through August. Unless you speak Turkish, have your hotel call for boat schedules, as English is rarely spoken at the docks. The round-trip fare is $6; the ride each way lasts one hour and 45 minutes. You can disembark at any of the stops and pick up a later boat, or return by taxi, dolmuş, or bus.

## By Bus or Tram

The city's buses (mostly vermilion and blue, although an increasing number are now completely covered in brightly colored advertising) and trams are crowded and slow, but they are useful for getting around and—at about 50¢ per ride—inexpensive. The route name and number are posted on the front of each vehicle; curbside signboards list routes and itineraries. Buy tickets before boarding; they're available individually and in books of 10 from ticket stands near each stop or from news-stands around the city, and for a few cents above face value, they can also be purchased from shoeshine boys and men sitting on wooden crates at most bus stops. London-style double-deckers operate between Sul-tanahmet and Emirgan on the Bosporus and between Taksim and Bostancı on the Asian side. Unlike the older city buses, these are clean and offer a panoramic ride. A bus attendant collects fares of three in-dividual tickets (totaling $1.50).

### By Taxi or Dolmuş

Taxis are metered and inexpensive. Most drivers do not speak English and may not know every street, so write down the name of the one you want and those nearby and the name of the neighborhood you're visiting. Although tipping is not automatic, it is customary to round off the fare to the nearest 25,000 TL. Fares are 50% more expensive between midnight and 6 AM. Avoid taxi drivers who choose roundabout routes, which cost more money, by having your hotel's attendant or a Turkish speaker talk to the driver before you get in. The vast major-ity of Istanbul taxi drivers are scrupulously honest—but in one com-monly reported scam a driver will tell a foreigner customer unfamiliar with the local currency that he or she has handed over the wrong amount of Turkish lira, so be mindful when paying. It is always advisable to check that the taxi has a working meter that is switched on, but it is inadvisable to agree on a fare with a driver unless you know for cer-tain it is cheaper than the metered fare.

Dolmuşes (shared taxis), many of which are bright yellow minibuses, run along various routes. You can sometimes hail a dolmuş on the street, and as with taxis, dolmuş stands are marked by signs. The destination is shown on either a roof sign or a card in the front window. Dolmuş stands are placed at regular intervals, and the vehicles wait for cus-tomers to climb in. Though the savings over a private taxi are signif-icant, you may find the quarters a little too close for comfort, particularly in summer.

## Contacts and Resources

### Consulates

**U.S. Consulate.** (✉ Meşrutiyet Cad. 104, Tepebaşı, Beyoğlu, ☎ 212/251–3602). **Canadian Consulate** (✉ Büyükdere Cad. 107/3, Bengün Han, Gayrettepe, ☎ 212/272–5174). **U.K. Consulate.** (✉ Meşrutiyet Cad. 34, Tepebaşı, Beyoğlu, ☎ 212/293–7540).

### Emergencies

**Ambulance** (☎ 112); **International Hospital Ambulance** (☎ 212/663–3000).

**Tourism police** (☎ 212/527–4503).

Good sources for English-speaking doctors are: **American Hospital** (✉ Güzelbahçe Sok. 20, Nişantaşı, ☎ 212/231–4050); **German Hospital** (✉ Siraselviler Cad. 119, Taksim, ☎ 212/293–2150); and **International Hospital** (✉ Istanbul Cad. 82, Yeşilköy, ☎ 212/663–3000).

Information is available about **24-hour pharmacies** (☎ 111); note that operators generally don't speak English. There's a pharmacy in every neighborhood, and all Istanbul pharmacies post the name and address of the nearest one open around the clock. The names of 24-hour pharmacies are also available through the directory inquiries ser-vice (☎ 118), although it is advisable to ask a Turkish speaker to make

the call. **Taksim** (⌧ İstiklal Cad. 17, ☎ 212/244–3195), one good pharmacy, is centrally located in the Taksim district.

## Guided Tours

Arrangements for guided tours can be made through travel agencies
and also often can be made through hotels; the offerings are all pretty
similar, though names may change. Classical Tours takes in Aya Sofya,
the Museum of Turkish and Islamic Arts, the Hippodrome, Yerebatan
Sarayı, and the Blue Mosque in its half-day version ($25); the Topkapı
Palace, Süleymaniye Cami, the Grand or perhaps the Egyptian Bazaar,
and lunch in addition to the above sights in its full-day version ($50;
$60–$80 by private car). Bosporus tours often include lunch at Sarıyer
and visits to the Dolmabahçe and Beylerbeyi palaces. The Night Tour
($50) includes dinner, drinks, and a show at either the Kervansaray or
the Galata Tower nightclub.

## Travel Agencies

Most travel agencies are along Cumhuriyet Caddesi, off Taksim Square,
in the hotel area: **American Express** (⌧ Istanbul Hilton, Cumhuriyet
Cad., Harbiye, ☎ 212/241–0248 or 212/241–0249); **Ekin Tourism** (⌧
Cumhuriyet Cad. 295, Harbiye, ☎ 212/234–4300); **Intra** (⌧
Halâskârgazi Cad. 111–2, Harbiye, ☎ 212/234–1200); **Setur** (⌧
Cumhuriyet Cad. 107, Harbiye, ☎ 212/230–0336); and **Vip Turizm** (⌧
Cumhuriyet Cad. 269/2, Harbiye, ☎ 212/241–6514).

## Visitor Information

**Turkish Ministry of Tourism** (⌧ Atatürk Airport, ☎ 212/663–0793; ⌧
Istanbul Hilton, Cumhuriyet Cad., Harbiye, ☎ 212/233–0592; ⌧ International Maritime Passenger Terminal, Karaköy Meyd., ☎ 212/249–
5776; ⌧ In Sultanahmet district, Divan Yolu Cad. 3, ☎ 212/518–1802;
and ⌧ In Beyoğlu district, Meşrutiyet Cad. 57, ☎ 212/243–3731). Hours
are usually from 9 until 5, though some close for an hour around noon.

# 2 THE SOUTHERN MARMARA REGION

Whether you are heading out from Istanbul for the Aegean or for Ankara and Central Anatolia, you would do well to take two or three days to explore this region near the southern shore of the Sea of Marmara. Termal remains a singularly Turkish spa, and both Bursa and İznik have rich histories.

Revised and
Updated by
Gareth Jenkins

TERMAL IS NOTABLE FOR ONE and only one reason—its natural hot springs. A popular spa since Roman times, the springs were used by the Ottomans, refurbished in 1900 by Sultan Abdül Hamid II, and regularly visited by Atatürk during breaks from the frenzied business of running the country in the 1920s and '30s. Termal retains something of that 1930s air, and its restored baths, shady gardens, and piney woods are time-proven restoratives.

İznik was put on the map in 316 BC when one of Alexander the Great's generals claimed the city. Six years later it was conquered by another general, Lysimachus, who renamed it Nicaea after his wife. In AD 325 and again in 786, Nicaea hosted international ecumenical councils, which had profound effects on the practice of Christianity. The Seljuks made the city their capital for a brief period in the 11th century; Byzantine emperors in exile did the same in the 13th century while Constantinople was in the hands of Crusaders. Orhan Gazi (ruled 1326–61) captured it in 1331.

Following the Ottoman conquest of Istanbul, İznik became a center for the ceramics industry. To upgrade the quality of native work, Sultan Selim I (ruled 1512–15), known as "The Grim," imported 500 Persian potters from Tabriz after conquering it. The government-owned kilns were soon turning out exquisite tiles with intricate motifs of circles, stars, and floral and geometric patterns, executed in lush turquoise, green, blue, red, and white. Despite their costliness, their popularity spread through the Islamic world.

Bursa became the first capital of the nascent Ottoman Empire after the city was captured in 1326 by Orhan Gazi, the empire's first sultan. It was here that Ottoman architecture blossomed, laying the foundation for the more elaborate works to be found in the later capitals, Edirne and Istanbul. More than 125 mosques here are on the list kept by the Turkish Historical Monuments Commission, and their minarets make for a grand skyline. Present-day Bursa is one of Turkey's more prosperous cities, a pleasing mix of bustling modernity, old stone buildings, and wealthy suburbs with vintage wood-frame Ottoman villas. Residents proudly call their city Yeşil Bursa (Green Bursa)—for the green İznik tiles decorating some of its most famous monuments and also for its parks and gardens and the national forest surrounding nearby Mt. Uludağ, a popular ski resort. While the earthquake of 1999 took a severe toll in this region, recovery has been rapid and you will probably encounter very little evidence of the tragedy.

## Pleasures and Pastimes

### Bird-Watching
Western Turkey lies on one of the main bird migration routes between Africa and Europe. Millions of birds pass through the region each spring and fall. One of the best places to bird-watch is the Kuşcenneti (Bird Paradise) National Park, on the shore of Lake Kuş west of Bursa. More than 239 different species of migrants and year-round residents have been recorded in its marshland and forests.

### Dining and Lodging
Restaurants in the area near the Sea of Marmara's southern shore are not generally up to Istanbul standards, but there are some good choices, the fanciest being those at the Çelik and Dilmen hotels, in Bursa. Many establishments in Uludağ, except for those in hotels, are open only in winter during ski season. Bursa is the best place to use as a center for exploring the southern Marmara region. There are also hotels in

Yalova, Termal, and İznik, if you are in need of a one-night stopover. For charts that explain meal and room rates at the establishments in this chapter, *see* Dining and Lodging Price Categories in Smart Travel Tips A to Z at the back of this book.

### Skiing

The mountain of Uludağ, which towers above Bursa, is usually covered with 6 to 10 ft of snow from December into May. Skiing and lodging facilities are good, although less elaborate than those in Europe or North America. The resort gets very crowded on winter weekends and during holidays. The latest details of snow cover and facilities can be obtained from the visitor center in Bursa (☞ Visitor Information *in* The Southern Marmara Region A to Z, *below*).

### Spas

Turkish baths can be found throughout the country, but south of the Marmara at spas such as Termal you can do your soaking in thermal water piping hot from the depths of the earth. Rich in minerals, the waters are said to cure a variety of ills from rheumatism to nervous complaints.

## Exploring the Southern Marmara Region

### Great Itineraries

IF YOU HAVE 3 DAYS

*Numbers in the text correspond to numbers in the margin and on the Sea of Marmara map.*

Leave Istanbul early enough to be in Yalova by midday. From Yalova either catch a minibus or drive to 🏛 **Termal** ①. Spend the afternoon wandering in the gardens and soaking in the thermal water, then stay overnight at one of the spa's hotels. On the morning of the second day, return to Yalova and head toward 🏛 **İznik** ②. If you leave Termal soon after breakfast, you should be in İznik by midmorning. In İznik, head west along Kılıçaslan Caddesi and have lunch at a lakefront restaurant. Afterward, retrace your steps to the center of town and explore the sights there. If you are traveling by private car, return by Route 150 as far as Orhangazi and head south along Route 575 to 🏛 **Bursa** ③. If traveling by public transportaion, take either a minibus to Bursa or one of the much more frequent minibuses returning to Yalova and then catch a bus from there to Bursa. Spend the night in Bursa and the next day sightseeing.

### When to Tour the Southern Marmara Region

The southern Marmara region is considerably cooler than the Aegean and Mediterranean coasts. The best time to visit, unless you love winter sports, is from May through October; the national park at Uludağ remains refreshingly cool, even in midsummer. But the region is still accessible during the cooler seasons, and soaking in one of the thermal baths at Termal or elsewhere is a fine antidote to the winter blues.

# TERMAL, İZNIK, AND BURSA

If you're coming from Istanbul by car, you may have planned to head straight for Bursa. But if time permits, visit Termal or İznik beforehand. It is possible to see Termal or İznik in one day from Istanbul, but attempting to see both will make for a hurried and less than satisfying trip. By the same token, it is unwise to attempt to travel to and explore Bursa in a single day.

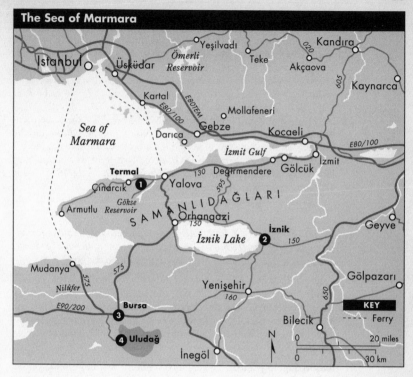

## The Sea of Marmara

## Termal

**❶** *12 km (8 mi) southwest of Yalova. Head west from Yalova, following signs to Çınarcık. Termal is signposted about 3 km (2 mi) outside Yalova.*

Termal is a self-contained resort with two hotels, exotic gardens, and three public thermal baths with rich mineral waters. The public baths have lockers where you can store your clothes while you have a soak. Both hotels have baths open to guests only, so if you plan an overnight stay, you can bathe at your hotel.

The grand **Sultan Baths** are an Ottoman institution, with baroque decor and hot mineral waters. You can rent your own cabin and soak to your heart's content in a deep gray-marble tub. 🎫 *$3.50 per person, $5 for 2 people.*

★ The less imposing **Valide Baths** (the *valide* was the mother of the reigning sultan in Ottoman times) also have ornate decor and individual cabins and tubs. 🎫 *$2 per person for 90 mins.*

★ The **Kurşunlu** (Lead-Roof Bath) has a large outdoor thermal pool, an indoor pool, and a sauna. 🎫 *$2.50 for outdoor pool, $2 for enclosed pool and sauna, $2.50 per person for private cubicle, $3.50 for 2 people.*

Atatürk liked Termal so much he had a house built for himself here. From the path from the Kurşunlu pool you can see **Atatürk's Cottage** and a white house with gingerbread trim that was used by his guests. When you're finished soaking, make a quick stop at the museum devoted to Atatürk; it has a delightful tea garden on one side. 🎫 *$1.* ⊙ *During daylight hrs.*

## Dining and Lodging

**$$** ✕🆇 **Turban Yalova Termal Çamlık Oteli.** Adjoining the baths, this
**★** pleasant hotel sits on a ridge overlooking the resort's grounds and dates
from Termal's modern heyday in the 1930s. It has a good Turkish restau-
rant and modern white-tile tubs filled with thermal waters. Guest
rooms in the back are less expensive (because the view is not as nice),
and in the off-season rates drop significantly. ☎ 226/675–7400, FAX 226/
675–7413. *83 rooms with bath. Restaurant. AE, DC, MC, V.*

**$$** ✕🆇 **Turban Yalova Termal Çınar Oteli.** This hotel has the same owners, managers, accommodations, and phone number as the nearby
Çamlık. The view isn't as nice, and it's a bit less atmospheric, but it's
still comfortable. Its thermal baths have old-fashioned gray-marble tubs
like those at the Sultan Baths. ☎ 226/675–7400, FAX 226/675–7413.
*18 rooms with bath. Restaurant. AE, DC, MC, V.*

# İznik

**➋** *60 km (37 mi) from Yalova. Take Rte. 575 south from Yalova for ap-*
*proximately 25 km (16 mi) to Orhangazi, head east at the sign for İznik,*
*and follow Rte. 150 around the north shore of Lake İznik.*

Lakeside İznik is rather run-down today, but it has a notable past: It
was here that the famed İznik tiles were made. The ceramic industry
went into decline in the 18th century, and İznik artisans are only now
making a comeback by reproducing the rich colors of the original tiles.
The revival is on a small scale and has met with only modest success
thus far.

**Sancta Sophia** (Church of the Holy Wisdom) was built in the center
of İznik in the 6th century, during the reign of Justinian. Its primitive
mosaic floor is believed to date from that time. The wall mosaics were
added as part of a reconstruction in the 11th century, after an earthquake toppled the original church. There are some fine fragments of
Byzantine fresco and mosaic works, including a mural of Jesus with
Mary and St. John the Baptist. It was here that the great ecumenical
councils of the 4th and 8th centuries were held. ✉ *Atatürk Cad. and*
*Kılıçaslan Cad.,* ☎ *no phone.* 💰 *$1.* 🕘 *Daily 9–noon and 2–5. If closed,*
*ask for key at İznik Museum, a few blocks away.*

The Ottoman style of the **Hacı Özbek Cami** is very primitive. This small-
scale mosque, which dates from 1332, lacks the ornamentation seen
in later buildings in Bursa and Istanbul. ✉ *Kılıçaslan Cad., east of the*
*Belediye Sarayı (town hall),* ☎ *no phone.* 💰 *Free.* 🕘 *Daily sunrise–*
*sunset.*

**★** The **Yeşil Cami,** a Seljuk-style mosque near İznik's east wall, is known
as the Green Mosque because of the color of much of its tile work.
The Seljuk style is simpler than the Ottoman: Seljuk mosques usually
have just one room under a single dome and borrow Persian and In-
dian architectural and decorative traditions; Ottoman mosques, as ex-
emplified by Bursa's Ulu Cami, draw on Byzantine structures such as
Istanbul's Aya Sofya. The Green Mosque's blue-and-green tiles are not
the original İznik work, which was damaged by various earthquakes
and replaced during the 19th century. ✉ *Teke Sok., off Kılıçaslan*
*Cad.,* ☎ *no phone.* 💰 *Free.* 🕘 *Daily sunrise–sunset.*

The building that houses the **İznik Müzesi** (İznik Museum) was built
in 1388 as a soup kitchen. Such kitchens, serving free food to the poor,
were often constructed by the wealthy as demonstrations of Muslim
charity. Today the museum contains artifacts such as Greek tombstones,
Ottoman perfume bottles, and İznik tiles. If you have time, ask at the
museum about a visit to the Byzantine Tomb, the **Yeraltı Mezar,** on

the outskirts of town. Discovered in the 1960s, this 5th-century burial place of an unknown family has well-preserved painted murals of peacocks, flowers, and abstract patterns in the Byzantine style. ⊠ *Kılıçaslan Cad., opposite Yeşil Cami,* ☎ *224/757–1027.* 🎫 *$1.* ☉ *Daily 9–noon and 1–5.*

The gray-stone **Lefke Kapısı** (Lefke Gate), the eastern gate to the ancient city, was built in honor of a visit by the Roman emperor Hadrian in AD 120. Its old inscriptions, marble reliefs, and friezes remain intact. You can scramble up onto the old city walls for a good view. Thick, sturdy fortifications like these were what saved many a town from ruin. Outside the gate are the city graveyard and Muslim tombs belonging to a nobleman named Hayrettin Paşa and to lesser luminaries. The oldest is 600 years old.

### Dining and Lodging

$–$$  ✕ **Balıkçı Restaurant.** The specialties at this lakeside eatery include fish dishes, grilled meatballs, and mezes. ⊠ *Göl Kenarı,* ☎ *224/757–1152. No credit cards.*

$–$$  ✕ **Kırık Çatal.** Open since 1964, this restaurant is run by the same people who manage the Motel Burcum. No one knows how it got its name, which means "broken fork." Fresh appetizers and hot main dishes, including local eel, are served on an open-air terrace. ⊠ *Göl Kenarı,* ☎ *224/757–2990. Reservations essential for large groups.* MC, V.

$  🏨 **Çamlık Motel.** In this quiet lakefront establishment, rooms are sparsely furnished and unadorned, but the garden on the lake is pleasant and doubles as a café. ⊠ *Göl Kenarı,* ☎ *224/757–1362,* ᖴᴬˣ *224/757–1631. 33 rooms with bath.* V.

$  🏨 **Motel Burcum.** This is another lakeside hotel with sparsely furnished rooms. The music from the adjacent café might bother you if you like quiet, but the staff is friendly, and the restaurant prepares fresh vegetable and meat dishes. ⊠ *Göl Kenarı,* ☎ *224/757–1011,* ᖴᴬˣ *224/757–1202. 25 rooms with bath.* MC, V.

## Bursa

**❸**  *247 km (153 mi) from Istanbul via Rte. 100 or E80 to İzmit, Rte. 130 to Yalova, and Rte. 575 south from Yalova to Bursa. As an alternative, take Rte. 100 from Istanbul to Darıca, the ferry across to Yalova ferry terminal, Rte. 130 for 10 km (6 mi) into Yalova, and finally Rte. 575 for 63 km (39 mi).*

Bursa, along the slopes of Uludağ, suffers a bit from the sprawls. It stretches along an east–west axis, and its main street winds and changes names many times between the city center and the neighborhood known as Çekirge, a couple of miles to the west. The town square, at the intersection of Atatürk Caddesi and İnönü Caddesi, is a logical starting point. The area, officially Cumhuriyet Alanı (Republic Square) is popularly called **Heykel** (Statue), after its imposing equestrian statue of Atatürk. Head east from here, turn left onto Yeşil Caddesi, and walk another few blocks.

An incredible juxtaposition of simple form, inspired stone carving, and spectacular İznik tile work, the **Yeşil Cami** (Green Mosque) is among the finest mosques in Turkey. Work on the mosque began in 1421, during the reign of Mehmet I Çelebi (ruled 1413–21). Its beauty starts in the marble entryway, where complex feathery patterns are carved in the stone. Inside is a sea of blue-and-green İznik tiles, many with floral designs. The central hall rests under two shallow domes; in the one near the entrance, an oculus sends down a beam of sunlight at midday, illuminating a fountain delicately carved from a single piece of marble. The *mihrab* (prayer niche) towers almost 50 ft, and there are intricate carvings near the top. On a level above the main doorway is the sultan's loge, lavishly decorated and tiled; a caretaker will sometimes take visitors up to see it. ⊠ *Yeşil Cad.*, ☎ *no phone.* ☎ *Free.* ⊙ *Daily sunrise–sunset.*

The **Yeşil Türbe** (Green Mausoleum) is Mehmet I Çelebi's tomb, built in 1424. The "green" tomb is actually covered in blue tiles, added after an earthquake damaged the originals in the 1800s. Inside, however, are incredible original İznik tiles, including those sheathing Mehmet's immense sarcophagus. The other tombs belong to his children. ⊠ *East end of Yeşil Cad., opposite Yeşil Cami*, ☎ *no phone.* ☎ *Free.* ⊙ *Daily 8:30–noon and 1–5:30.*

The **Bursa Etnoğrafya Müzesi** (Bursa Ethnographic Museum) is on the site of a former theological school that is part of the complex that includes Yeşil Cami and Yeşil Türbe (☞ *above*). It houses a fine collection of tile work, inlaid wood, jewelry, books and almanacs, pottery, and bits of Seljuk architectural decoration. ⊠ *Yeşil Cad., on west side of Yeşil Cami*, ☎ *no phone.* ☎ *$1.* ⊙ *Tues.–Sun. 8:30–noon and 1–5:30.*

NEED A BREAK? Several **tea gardens** on the west side of the Yeşil Mosque and Yeşil Tomb are pleasant places to have a sandwich or pastries and take in views of the city. The two mosques in the distance, the Emir Sultan (1431, to the right) and the Yıldırım Beyazıt (1391, to the left), are not worth visiting because earthquakes have damaged their interiors.

The **Orhan Gazi Cami** (Orhan Gazi Mosque) was built for Sultan Orhan Gazi in 1335. This is the first truly Ottoman mosque. Although small, it has a graceful porch and fountain. ⊠ *Set back from Atatürk Cad.* ☎ *Free.* ⊙ *Sunrise–sunset.*

★ The **bedestan** (covered bazaar) was built in the 1300s by Yıldırım Beyazıt I (ruled 1389–1402) but was flattened by a massive earthquake in 1855. It has been lovingly restored, and many of the old Ottoman *hans* (markets) inside still provide the flavor of the 16th century. Best buys include silver and gold jewelry, thick Turkish cotton towels (for which Bursa is famous), and silk goods (☞ Shopping, *below*, for additional details about the bazaar). ⊠ *Cumhuriyet Cad., near intersection with Maksem Cad.*

The striking **Ulu Cami** (Grand Mosque) dates from 1396. Sultan Beyazıt had it built after vowing to build 20 mosques if he was victorious in the battle of Nicopolis in Macedonia; this one mosque with 20 domes was something of a compromise. Its interior is decorated with an elegantly understated display of quotations from the Koran in fine Islamic calligraphy. ⊠ *Near intersection of Atatürk Cad. and Maksem Cad.*

The neighborhood known as **Hisar** (Fortress) is where Bursa started, like so many cities of old, within the walls of a fortress. Pınarbaşı Caddesi is the main street through this part of town; make a detour on Kale Caddesi, an atmospheric block lined with wood-frame houses from the 17th to 19th centuries. In a small park not far from the citadel walls, overlooking Cemal Nadir Caddesi, are the tombs of Osman and Orhan, considered founders of the Ottoman Empire. The word Ottoman derives from Osmanlı, the people led by Osman. The son of a warrior chieftain named Ertuğrul Gazi, who had taken control of an area near Bursa, Osman sought to expand the boundaries of his father's state and eventually laid siege to Bursa. But it wasn't until 1326, several years after he died, that the city fell and the Ottomans, under Orhan, claimed the victory. The tombs date from the 19th century; the originals were destroyed in an earthquake.

The **Sultan Murat II Cami** (Sultan Murat II Mosque) and surrounding complex, Bursa's Muradiye neighborhood, were built in 1425–26, during the reign of Mehmet the Conqueror, in honor of Murat, Mehmet's father. The mosque is unexceptional, perhaps because Mehmet's attentions were so firmly focused on Constantinople, which he would soon win. Outside, next to the mosque in what is surely the city's most serene resting place, there is a fountain ringed by 12 tombs. Among those buried here are Murat himself, Mehmet, and Mustafa, the eldest son of Süleyman the Magnificent, who was strangled in his father's tent. The sultan's ambitious wife, Roxelana, had persuaded her husband that Mustafa was a traitor. ⊠ *Kaplıca Cad.,* ☎ *no phone.* ⊡ *Free.* ☉ *Sunrise–sunset.*

The 17th-century **Osmanlı Evi** (Ottoman House), built on what is believed to have been the site of a pavilion belonging to Sultan Murat II, is one of the oldest and best preserved of Bursa's historic homes, complete with authentic period carpets and furniture. The main room on the upper floor has wooden cupboards covered with painted floral motifs and an intricately carved wooden ceiling. ⊠ *Kaplıca Cad., opposite Sultan Murat II Cami complex,* ☎ *224/222–0868.* ⊡ *$1.* ☉ *Tues.– Sun. 8:30–12:30 and 1:30–5.*

Dominating the view on Çekirge Caddesi is the refreshingly green **Kültür Parkı** (Culture Park). Many Turkish towns have such a park, with restaurants, tea gardens, a pond with paddleboats, a sports stadium, and a Ferris wheel. This park is quite large, stretching for about a dozen city blocks and containing Bursa's **Arkeoloji Müzesi** (Archaeology Museum). The museum is pleasant enough, with its Roman coins and other artifacts, but there are better ones in Istanbul, Ankara, and elsewhere. The same goes for the nearby **Atatürk Müzesi** (Atatürk Museum), with old-fashioned furniture and a few exhibits on the great leader's life. ⊠ *Kültür Parkı: Çekirge Cad. and Stadyum Cad.,* ☎ *224/ 234–4818 Archaeology Museum; 224/220–2029 for Atatürk Museum.* ⊡ *$2.* ☉ *Tues.–Sun. 8:30–12:30 and 1:30–5.*

The affluent suburb called **Çekirge** starts at Kültür Parkı and continues westward. Bursa has been a spa town since Roman times; the thermal springs run along these slopes, and mineral baths are an amenity at many hotels in this area.

## Dining and Lodging

**$$** ✕ **Cumurcul.** In the Çekirge section of town, this old house converted into a restaurant is a local favorite. Grilled meats and fish are attentively prepared. In addition to the usual cold mezes are hot starters, including the tasty *avcı böreği* (hunter's pie), a deep-fried or oven-baked pastry filled with meat or cheese. ⊠ *Çekirge Cad.,* ☎ *224/220–9695. Reservations essential on weekends. AE, MC, V.*

**$** ✕ **Hacı Bey.** Arguments never end over where to find the best Bursa kebab, but this downtown stop is always a contender. The setting is basic cafeteria style, but the food is what counts. ⊠ *Ünlü Cad., Yılmaz İş Han 4C,* ☎ *224/221–6440 or 224/222–0000. DC, MC, V.*

**$** ✕ **Kebapçı İskender.** Bursa is famous for the main dish served here: İskender kebab, skewer-grilled slivers of meat and pita bread immersed in a rich tomato sauce topped with butter and yogurt. ⊠ *Ünlü Cad. 7, Heykel,* ☎ *224/221–4615. No credit cards.*

**$** ✕ **Özömür Köftecisi.** *Köfte,* a rich, grilled patty of ground beef or
★ lamb, is a regional specialty, and that's the thing to order here. This restaurant benefits from its charming location, in the covered market by the Ulu Cami. ⊠ *Ulu Cami Cad. 7,* ☎ *no phone. No credit cards.*

**$** ✕ **Selçuk.** Another Kültür Park restaurant with the usual Turkish specialties, this one offers a shady terrace and slightly lower prices than its neighbors, as well as live music on Friday and Saturday evenings. ⊠ *Kültür Park,* ☎ *224/234–4951. No credit cards.*

**$$$$**  ⊞ **Çelik Palas.** At the poshest hotel in Bursa, the main attraction is the
★  domed, Roman-style pool fed by hot springs; you will find your fellow guests constantly traipsing through the hallways in their robes en route. The hotel has a lively 1930s design scheme, and some rooms have balconies. ⊠ *Çekirge Cad. 79,* ☎ *224/233–3800,* FAX *224/236– 1910. 173 rooms with bath. Restaurant, bar, dance club. AE, MC, V.*

**$$$**  ⊞ **Hotel Dilmen.** The lobby in this fancy, modern hotel in the Çekirge section is accented by gleaming brass and stained-glass windows. Rooms, however, are simply furnished. It has the requisite thermal baths, a pleasant garden terrace and bar, and views of the valley. ⊠ *1 Murat Cad. 20,* ☎ *224/233–9500,* FAX *224/235–2568. 91 rooms with bath. Restaurant, bar, exercise room. MC, V.*

**$$**  ⊞ **Ada Palas.** On every floor of this Çekirge hotel are thermal baths, and the price tag is lower than that at the nearby Çelik. Rooms are unexceptional but in good condition. ⊠ *1 Murat Cad. 21,* ☎ *224/233– 3990,* FAX *224/236–4656. 36 rooms with bath. V.*

**$$**  ⊞ **Hotel Dikmen.** Although less grand than Çekirge hotels, the Dikmen (not to be confused with the Dilmen (☞ *above*) is conveniently located downtown just opposite the Ulu Cami. It has large, plain guest rooms, a spacious lobby, and a sunny garden with a marble fountain. It is often filled by tour groups. ⊠ *Maksem Cad. 78,* ☎ *224/224–1840,* FAX *224/224–1844. 53 rooms with bath. Restaurant, bar. No credit cards.*

### Nightlife

The **Kervansaray Termal Hotel** (⊠ Çekirge Meyd., ☎ 224/233–9300) has a fine floor show, with noted local singers and belly dancers. The presentation is more traditional and less touristy than similar offerings in Istanbul, although there is no skimping on the glitz. The price is about $30 per person with dinner. The **Çelik Palas** (☞ Lodging, *above*) has a somewhat more refined lounge act.

### Shopping

In Bursa the **bedestan** (covered bazaar), behind the Ulu Cami, is where the action is from 8 to 5, Monday through Saturday. As is traditional, each section is dominated by a particular trade: jewelers, silk weavers, antiques dealers. The Koza Han section, in a historic courtyard by the east entrance, is the center of the silk trade. The Emir Han, in the southwest section, is another silk market and has a fountain and a courtyard tea garden. These *hans* (markets) are lively in June and September, the silk harvesting months, when buyers swarm in from around the country to place orders. Bursa has been a center of the silk industry since the coming of the Ottoman sultans and remains a good place to buy silk scarves, raw-silk fabric by the yard, and other silk products. Antiques can be found in the small Eski Aynalı Çarşı section of the bazaar. Of note is a shop called Karagöz, which has a fine collection of old copper and brass, kilims, jewelry, and the translucent, vividly colored shadow puppets from which the store takes its name.

OFF THE  **KUŞCENNETİ NATIONAL PARK –** If you're heading on from Bursa to
BEATEN PATH  Çanakkale and the Aegean Coast, consider stopping at Kuşcenneti (Bird Paradise) National Park, beside Lake Kuş. There are benches and tables for picnics, a viewing tower for bird-watching, and a small information center with exhibits describing the more than 200 species of birds that visit the park. ⊠ *Take Rte. 200 west about 100 km (62 mi) from Bursa; signs for the park appear before the city of Bandırma.*

# Uludağ

❹ *33 km (20 mi) southeast of Bursa; start from Çekirge Cad. heading west and follow the signs for Uludağ.*

Bursa is the jumping-off point for excursions to Uludağ, where you will find a lush national park, **Uludağ Ulusal Parkı** (Uludağ National Park) and Turkey's most popular ski resort. To appreciate fully why the town is called Green Bursa, take the 30-minute ride up the **teleferik** (cable car) from Namazgah Caddesi in Bursa to the mountain's summit for a panoramic view. You can also make the hour-long drive; heading west on Çekirge Caddesi, the turnoff to Uludağ is about 4 km (2½ mi) from the city center. The road is narrow and winding, and sometimes in winter it is only passable in all-terrain vehicles. All Uludağ resort hotels are in an area near the highest peak, called **Oteller**. From here you can reach undeveloped spots for blissfully cool hikes in summer. ☎ 224/221–3635. 🎟 *Teleferik: $8 round-trip; park: $2.50 per car.* ⊙ *Teleferik operates year-round every 30 or 40 mins during daylight.*

## Lodging

**$$–$$$** 🏨 **Grand Hotel Yazıcı.** This slanted-roof, seven-story hotel is the most luxurious and expansive of the resorts. Rooms are pleasant, and the lobby is huge and showy. Your lasting impressions may be of acres of marble and the boisterous live music on weekends. ⊠ *Oteller Mevkii,* ☎ *224/285–2050,* 🖷 *224/285–2048. 260 rooms with bath. Restaurant, bar, café, pool, sauna, exercise room, dance club. MC, V.*

**$$–$$$** 🏨 **Otel Beceren.** This Turkish version of an alpine ski lodge is notable for its service. The hotel does not have as many amenities as the Yazıcı, however. ⊠ *Oteller Mevkii,* ☎ *224/285–2111,* 🖷 *224/285–2119. 86 rooms with bath. Restaurant, bar. No credit cards.* ✍

**$$** 🏨 **Akfen Hotel.** One of the smaller hotels in Uludağ, the Akfen has a wonderful, warm atmosphere, literally as well as figuratively, along with cozy rooms. ⊠ *Oteller Mevkii,* ☎ *224/285–2021,* 🖷 *224/285–2027. 50 rooms with bath. Restaurant, dance club. MC, V.* ✍

## Nightlife

The **Akfen** and **Grand Hotel Yazıcı** (☞ Dining and Lodging, *above*) have lively discos. The settings are far from flashy, but there are usually plenty of people out to have fun.

## Outdoor Activities and Sports

Uludağ is Turkey's largest ski resort. It has 30 intermediate and beginner trails, with five chairlifts and six T-bars. There are ski-rental shops at the base of the mountain. Prime season is January–April, and the resort is packed on weekends.

# THE SOUTHERN MARMARA REGION A TO Z

## Arriving and Departing

### By Boat

Sea buses and express ferries operate daily between Istanbul's Kabataş docks and Yalova. A sea bus from Kabataş costs only about $4 and takes just under an hour; the express ferry costs about $2 and takes two hours. Sea buses also travel to Yalova from Kartal, and less frequently, from the Bostancı docks, on the Asian side, but Kartal is difficult to reach by public transportation. There is a car ferry from Darıca to Yalova that also accepts passengers, although the dock isn't served by public transportation.

### By Bus

Several buses daily make the trip from Istanbul's terminal at Esenler to Yalova and Bursa. The journey takes about four hours to Yalova and five to Bursa, including the ferry trip from Darıca to Yalova. The bus trip costs about $3.50. A better option is the sea bus to Yalova. Near the sea bus quay in Yalova are buses to Bursa and minibuses to İznik.

### By Car

From Istanbul take dreary Route 100, lined with factories and slowed by heavy truck traffic headed for Ankara. At İzmit take Route 130 to Yalova, a small transportation center east of Termal; Route 575 connects Yalova and Bursa. As an alternative, you can take the TEM toll road (E80), which is almost as dreary as Route 100 but much quicker, as far as İzmit before linking up with Route 130 to Yalova.

Better still, take Route 100 only as far as the car ferry from Darıca, 45 km (28 mi) east of Üsküdar, on the Asian side of Istanbul, to Yalova. The ferry trip costs about $10 one-way but lops 140 km (87 mi) off the journey. From Bursa, Route 200 runs west toward Çanakkale and the Aegean, east toward Ankara. There are often huge lines for ferries from Darıca at the beginning and end of local religious holidays, and there may be a wait of up to an hour on summer weekends as the ferries become crowded leaving Darıca on Friday evening and leaving Yalova on Sunday evening.

### By Plane

AIRPORTS AND AIRLINES
Although Bursa does have an airport, regular scheduled flights to and from Istanbul ceased in 1999. With the exception of occasional charter flights, only private planes currently use the airport.

## Getting Around

### By Bus and Dolmuş

The telephone number for the **Bursa bus station** is ☎ 224/254–6072 or 224/254–1260. Just off the sea-bus quay in Yalova you will find minibuses headed for İznik and Bursa, both 90 minutes and a $2 bus fare away. Make sure not to mistake the İznik bus for those headed for İzmit. *Dolmuşes* (shared taxis) also wait off the docks; they cost a bit more than the bus and offer comparable comfort and speed. Between Bursa and İznik, service is by bus (about $2) and dolmuş ($2–$5). The telephone number of the **İznik bus station** is ☎ 224/757–1418.

To get from Yalova to Termal, walk from the ferry dock straight ahead to the traffic circle with the big statue of Atatürk, turn right, and walk one block. Bus 4 (marked TAŞKÖPRÜ–TERMAL) departs from here; the fare is about 50¢ for the 20-minute ride. Minibuses run more frequently but cost slightly more.

### By Car

From Yalova, Termal is 12 km (7½ mi) west via the road marked ÇINARCIK; Bursa is 60 km (37 mi) south via Route 575; İznik is 62 km (38 mi) southeast (via Route 575 south and Route 150, which loops around İznik Lake).

## Contacts and Resources

### Emergencies

**Ambulance** (☎ 112). **Police** (☎ 155). Note: It is unlikely that an English speaker will answer either of these phones. In addition, ambulances are often slow in coming. Your best bet is to ask for help from people around you or at your hotel; they will invariably know about the nearest doctor or hospital.

## Guided Tours

**Yöntur Turizm** (✉ İnönü Cad., Hüzmen Plaza Çarsısı 29 B 15, Bursa, ☎ 224/220–9132) arranges tours of Bursa and İznik.

## Visitor Information

**Bursa** (✉ Valilik Binası, Atatürk Cad., Heykel, ☎ 224/233–2649; and an information kiosk on ✉ Orhangazi Alt Geçit 1, Heykel, ☎ 224/220–1848). **İznik** (✉ Belediye Ishanı, 2nd floor, Kılıçaslan Cad., ☎ 224/757–1933). **Termal** (☎ 226/675–7400).

# 3  THE AEGEAN COAST

Along the Aegean Coast are long stretches of sandy beaches and pine-clad hills punctuated by old port villages—Foça, Çeşme, Kuşadası, Bodrum—some reincarnated as modern resorts. You'll find Greek and Roman cities here, including the 3,000-year-old ruins of Troy, made famous by the poet Homer; Pergamum, on its windswept hilltop; and the magnificent temples, colonnaded streets, and theater in Ephesus.

| **N THE 2ND CENTURY AD,** the Greek travel writer Pausanias wrote glowingly of the Aegean Coast, lauding its climate and magnificent buildings. Not all the wonders Pausanias mentioned are visible today, but enough are left to give you a good idea of what life was like when this part of the world could fairly have been called the center of the universe.

Revised and
Updated by
Gareth Jenkins

## Pleasures and Pastimes

### Beaches

Alluring white-sand beaches (*plajlar* in Turkish) are among the Aegean Coast's big draws. The most notable are the ones are in Akçay (on the Gulf of Edremit); Sarmısaklı, outside Ayvalık; those along Akburun (the White Cape) and Ilıca, 5 km (3 mi) south and north of Çeşme, respectively; deserted Gümüşsu, down the hill from the ancient city of Colophon; and the long strand at Pamucak, 2 km (1 mi) west of Selçuk. The beach within Bodrum proper is not one of the reasons you'd come to the town. You'll find better in the outlying villages on the peninsula—Torba, with its big resort village; Türkbükü, quiet and family-oriented; Turgutreis, more of a scene; Akyarlar, which is rarely crowded; Ortakent, backed by old wooden town houses; Bitez, on a small bay; Gümbet, popular for windsurfing and diving; and Gümüşük, rimming a perfect bay with the half-submerged ruins of ancient Mindos. At all these the water is clear, and outdoor restaurants abound; all are easy to reach from Bodrum by minibus or *dolmuş* (shared taxi). Sedir Island, in the Gökova Gulf, is delightful when not overrun with day-trippers.

### Cruises

One of the most enjoyable ways to see the coast is from the water. You can take a one- or two-week "blue-voyage cruise"—as the locals call almost every boat trip in the area. Many of these are on *gulets,* converted wooden fishing craft with full crew, though yachts can be chartered with or without a crew. It's a good idea to try to arrange your trip before you leave home, although it's possible to arrange a cruise on the spot by doing your own negotiating at the docks. Note, however, that some trip operators at the docks try to fill their boats with as many passengers as possible, which means you won't necessarily know with whom you'll be traveling or under what conditions. Ask a travel agent or someone at your hotel to recommend a reputable company with a good boat and crew (☞ Guided Tours *in* The Aegean Coast A to Z, *below*; Outdoor Activities and Sports *in* Bodrum, *below*; and Tour Operators *in* Smart Travel Tips A to Z).

### Dining

Eating along the Aegean Coast is a pleasure, especially if you like seafood. The main course is often whatever was caught that day, though there are always beef and lamb kebabs. Regional specialties generally begin with the sea—mussels stuffed with rice, pine nuts, and currants (one of the many stuffed dishes that fall under the heading of dolma); *ahtapot salatası,* a cold octopus salad, sometimes with shrimps thrown in and tossed in olive oil, vinegar, and parsley; and grilled fish, including *palamut* (baby tuna), *lüfer* (bluefish), *levrek* (sea bass), and *kalkan* (turbot). Your standard eatery might have sturdy wooden tables and chairs, paper napkins on the tables, and maybe a fishnet draped on the wall, but, especially in the resort towns, you'll also find restaurants with crystal and linens. Because the Aegean is the most heavily visited region of the country, prices are higher than in the interior or on the Mediterranean but are still reasonable. For a chart that ex-

## The Aegean Coast

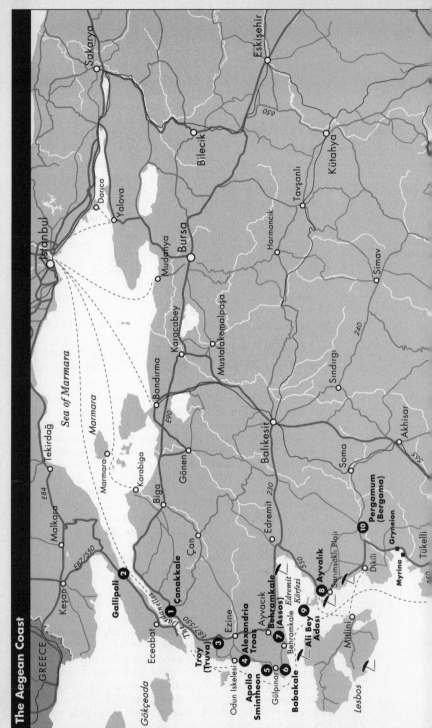

GREECE

Sea of Marmara

*Marmara*

*Marmara*

Istanbul

Darıca

Yalova

Sakarya

Eskişehir

Bilecik

Tavşanlı

Kütahya

Mudanya

Bursa

Karacabey

Mustafakemalpaşa

Harmancık

Simav

Bandırma

Balıkesir

Sındırgı

Gönen

Soma

Akhisar

Biga

Çan

Karabiga

Marmara

Tekirdağ

Malkara

Keşan

Eceabat

Gallipoli **2**

Çanakkale **1**

*The Dardanelles*

Ezine

Troy (Truva)

Alexandria Troas **3 4**

Apollo Smintheon **5**

Gülpınar **6**

Babakale

Ayvacık

Behramkale **7** (Assos)

Behramkale

Ali Bey Adası **9**

Edremit **230**

Edremit Körfezi

Ayvalık **8**

Sarımsaklı Plajı

Dikili

Pergamum (Bergama) **10**

Gryneion

Myrina

Tükelli

Odun İskelesi

Gökçeada

Mitilini

Lesbos

E84

E87/550

E87/550

E90

TEM/Dardanelles

650

240

550

565

230

450

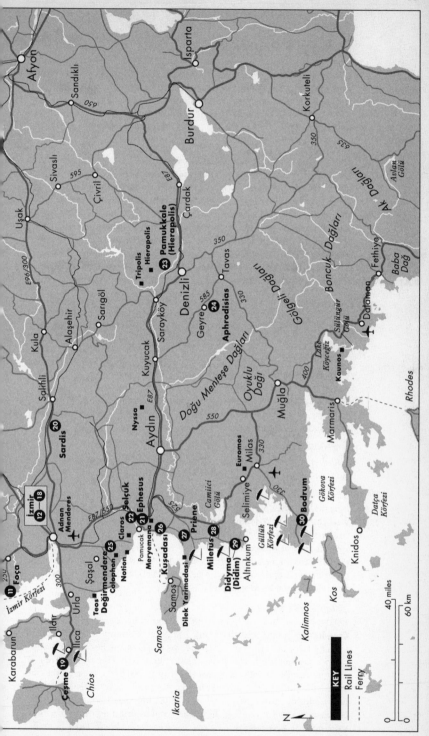

plains the cost of meals at restaurants in this chapter, *see* Dining and Lodging Price Categories at the front of this book.

## Diving and Snorkeling

The warm, placid bays along the coast are ideal for snorkeling, and many big beach resorts have gear. However, Turkish authorities frown on exploring near archaeological ruins without a permit. To obtain permits, contact the local tourist information office (☞ The Aegean Coast A to Z, *below*). Specialized boat trips are available for scuba divers and snorkelers.

## Lodging

If you want something fancy and upscale, you'll have to stay in İzmir or Bodrum. Elsewhere, accommodations are more modest. Expect clean, simply furnished rooms, with low wooden beds, industrial carpeting or Turkish rugs, and maybe a print on the wall. As many hotels are near the water, don't forget to ask for a room with a view—you'll pay little extra, sometimes nothing extra. For a chart that explains room rates for the accommodations listed in this chapter, *see* Dining and Lodging Price Categories in Smart Travel Tips A to Z at the back of this book.

# Exploring the Aegean Coast

The Aegean Coast can be divided into three main regions: the northern coast from Çanakkale to the northern outskirts of İzmir; the city of İzmir itself; and the southern coast down to Bodrum, including a detour inland to the ruins at Aphrodisias and the natural hot springs of Pamukkale.

## Great Itineraries

Given distances and the wealth of interesting sights, you should allow from 8 to 10 days to explore the region thoroughly. If you are pressed for time, it is best to head straight for İzmir and use it as a base from which to take in some of the main sights nearby.

IF YOU HAVE 4 DAYS

*Numbers in the text correspond to numbers in the margin and on the Aegean Coast, İzmir, and Ephesus and Selçuk maps.*

Take an early morning flight from Istanbul to **İzmir** ⑫–⑱. Head by bus or rental car to explore **Ephesus** ㉑ and 🏨 **Selçuk** ㉒. On the second day, visit the ruins of **Priene** ㉗, **Miletus** ㉘, and **Didyma** ㉙ before looping back to 🏨 **Kuşadası** ㉖. On the third day, move on to 🏨 **Pamukkale** ㉓, stopping off at **Aphrodisias** ㉔ on the way. Early the next day, soak in one of Pamukkale's hot springs and visit **Hierapolis** before returning to İzmir, where, if you have time, you can stroll the city's waterfront promenade, the **Kordonboyu** ⑰.

IF YOU HAVE 10 DAYS

Arrive by car, bus, or ferry from Istanbul, check into a hotel in 🏨 **Çanakkale** ①, and tour the Army and Navy Museum if time permits. On day two, take the ferry back across the Dardanelles to the battlefields of **Gallipoli** ②. Early on day three, stop briefly at the ruins of **Troy** ③ and the **Apollo Smintheon** ⑤ on the way to **Assos** ⑦, where you can spend the bulk of the day exploring the ruins. Stay overnight in 🏨 **Behramkale**, near Assos. The next morning, head south along the coast, stopping for lunch in **Ayvalık** ⑧ and taking a detour to the hilltop ruins of **Pergamum** ⑩ before continuing on to 🏨 **Foça** ⑪ or 🏨 **İzmir** ⑫–⑱. If you stay in İzmir, be sure to stroll the **Kordonboyu** ⑰, the city's waterfront promenade. On day five, visit **Ephesus** ㉑ and 🏨 **Selçuk** ㉒—the Ephesus Museum in Selçuk is definitely worth a stop. Swim and catch the sunset at deserted Gümüşsu, down the hill from the ancient city of Colophon on the way to 🏨 **Kuşadası** ㉖.

On the following morning, visit the ruins of **Priene** ㉗, **Miletus** ㉘, and **Didyma** ㉙. Return to Kuşadası. On day seven, head for ⊡ **Pamukkale** ㉓, stopping off at **Aphrodisias** ㉔ on the way. Early the next day, soak in one of Pamukkale's hot springs and visit **Hierapolis** before moving on to ⊡ **Çeşme** ⑲, where you can either tour the nearby Genoese castle or hang out on the beaches at **Akburun** or **Ilıca**. Spend day nine and as much of day 10 as you can along the beach. If you have a rental car, you can drop it off in İzmir and return to Istanbul by plane. Or you might consider taking the ferry from İzmir to Istanbul.

### When to Tour the Aegean

The best time to tour the Aegean is probably in May, when the countryside is still swathed in spring flowers and the more popular tourist destinations have not become too crowded (Bodrum in particular can become very hot and crowded during July and August). During high summer several of the towns along the coast host open-air concerts and plays, the most famous of which are held in the old Greek theater at Ephesus. Although the fall is also a good time to travel, most of the countryside is parched rather than carpeted with flowers.

# THE NORTHERN AEGEAN COAST

## From Gallipoli to İzmir

This region covers the area from the tip of the Çanakkale Peninsula to the battlefields of Gallipoli, taking in legendary Troy and ending in İzmir. A detour along one of Turkey's grandest back-country drives will bring you to the cliff-top ruins of ancient Pergamum. You will need at least two overnights to cover the ground comfortably, though you could easily spend a whole week.

## Çanakkale and Gallipoli

*320 km (200 mi) southwest of Istanbul, E80 to Tekirdağ, E84 to Keşan, and E87 to Eceabat, from where an hourly ferryboat crosses the Dardanelles to Çanakkale.*

❶ For centuries **Çanakkale** has been the guardian of the Dardanelles, the narrow straits that separate Europe from Asia and connect the Aegean Sea with the Sea of Marmara. This strategic point has been fought over since the days of the Trojan War. En route to Greece, the invading armies of the Persian conqueror Xerxes used a bridge made of boats to cross the straits in 480 BC; the Spartans crushed the Athenians here in 404 BC, effectively ending the Peloponnesian War. A century later the straits were crossed by Alexander the Great (356 BC–323 BC, ruled 336–323) on his march from Macedonia to conquer Asia and, in the 14th century, provided the nascent Ottoman Empire with its first access to Europe. During World War I, Britain (with soldiers from Australia and New Zealand, which were then still British colonies) and France tried to breach Çanakkale's defenses in the Gallipoli campaign, devised by the young Winston Churchill, then lord of the admiralty. The goal was to capture Istanbul and control the entire waterway from the Aegean to the Black Sea and open up a supply channel to Russia. After nine months and bloody fighting that left more than 50,000 Allied and an unknown number of Turks dead, the Allies admitted defeat and evacuated their forces, beaten by the superior strategy of Lieutenant-Colonel Mustafa Kemal—the man who would later be called Atatürk. Nowadays, Çanakkale is an agricultural center and garrison town, with drab, utilitarian architecture and few frills, but it serves as the gateway to historic Gallipoli.

The **Askeri Ve Deniz Müzesi** (Army and Navy Museum) occupies the imposing **Çanak Kale** (Fortress of Çanak), built in the 15th century under the aegis of Mehmet the Conqueror. Inside the high, sturdy, gray walls, all kinds of weaponry are on display, including dozens of cannons, ancient and modern. But the real reason to come here is for the sweeping view of the mouth of the Dardanelles and the Aegean. ⊠ *Waterfront, 3 blocks south of ferry dock.* 🎫 *Free.* ⊙ *Museum Tues.–Thurs. and weekends 9–noon and 1:30–5; fortress grounds daily 9 AM–10 PM.*

**②** **Gallipoli** lies to the north of the Dardanelles. Thirty-one beautifully tended military cemeteries of the Allied dead from World War I line the Gallipoli battlefields. The major battles were in two sections—along the coast between Kabatepe and Sulva Bay, and at Cape Helles.

If you don't have a car, either hire a taxi for the day (about $20) or sign up for the half-day excursion to Gallipoli run by **Troy-Anzac Tours** (⊠ İskele Meyd., south side near clock tower, Çanakkale, ☎ 286/217–5849 or 286/217–5847, FAX 286/217–0196; 🎫 about $15 per person, including breakfast). The ferry from Eceabat, which crosses to the military sites, leaves from the main square.

From where the ferry from Eceabat lands, it's a 20-minute drive east via the single road skirting the coast. A major forest fire in 1994 destroyed many of the region's trees, although a replanting program is now beginning to reforest the hillsides. Start with the small but poignant exhibit of photographs at Kabatepe. There are several cemeteries here,

★     all with long, mesmerizing rows of austere white crosses. The **Anzac Memorial at Lone Pine Cemetery** bears the names of the Australian and New Zealand troops killed during the battle. Farther along the same road is the French cemetery and the Turkish trenches into which Atatürk's men dug themselves. You can also look down on Sulva Bay as the Turkish defenders did and imagine the coming onslaught.

At **Cape Helles,** on the southernmost tip of the peninsula, there is a massive, four-pillared memorial to Turkey's war dead. No one knows how many there were; estimates vary from 60,000 to 250,000. When returning on the ferry to Çanakkale, look for the memorials to the campaign carved into the cliffs on the European side. The large one at Kilitbahır reads: "Stop, O passerby. This earth you tread unawares is where an age was lost. Bow and listen, for this quiet place is where the heart of a nation throbs."

## Dining and Lodging

**$–$$**  ✕ **Rıhtım Restaurant.** This waterside eatery, a couple of minutes' walk west of the ferry landing, specializes in fish, although it also serves grilled meats. Try the *kalamar* (squid fried in batter), followed by a grilled version of whatever looks freshest. If the weather is good, you can sit outside on the terrace, which has fine views across the Dardanelles. ⊠ *Eski Balıkhane Sk. 7,* ☎ *286/217–1770. No credit cards.*

**$**  ✕ **Trakya Restaurant.** Run by six brothers who prepare the food daily, this popular restaurant has three branches in the main square. The oldest branch has strictly functional decor, but it serves good quality kebabs, moussaka, and the ever-present *kuru fasulye* and *pilav* (beans and rice). The two other locations specialize in *doner* kebabs (meat roasted on a spit) and grilled meats. ⊠ *Cumhuriyet Meyd. 32,* ☎ *286/217–3152. No credit cards.*

**$**  ✕ **Yalova Liman.** The menu at this upstairs waterfront restaurant includes appetizers and grilled fish or meat. Ask the chef which fish is in season and order it grilled or fried. The best part of eating here is the evocative setting: the photographs of old Çanakkale on the walls, the views across the Dardanelles, and the hum of locals crooning folk songs or discussing the latest soccer match. ✉ *Gümrük Sok. 7,* ☎ *286/217–1045. MC, V.*

**$$** 🏨 **Akol.** In this modern hotel on the Çanakkale waterfront, the lobby is bright and full of cool white marble and brass fixtures. Rooms resemble better roadside motels in the United States, but if you've been staying in guest houses, you will appreciate the good water pressure in the showers. Ask for a room with a terrace overlooking the Dardanelles; you'll be able to see the memorials to World War I in the distance. ✉ *Kordonboyu, 17100,* ☎ *286/217–9456,* 🖷 *286/217–2897. 137 rooms with bath. Restaurant, bar, pool. MC, V.*

**$$** 🏨 **Grand Truva Oteli.** This establishment is a training school for aspiring young hotel professionals, and the students in charge are solicitous. The older section has views of the Dardanelles; the modern section in back lacks the views but is spiffier. The location near Çanakkale's center makes the hotel an excellent base for sightseeing. ✉ *Mehmet Akif Ersoy Cad. 2, Cevat Paşa Mahallesi, Kordonboyu, 17100,* ☎ *286/217–1024 or 286/217–1886,* 🖷 *286/217–0903. 69 rooms with bath. Restaurant, bar. AE, MC, V.*

**$** 🏨 **Hotel Bakır.** This small hotel near the clock tower in Çanakkale is acceptable if you're on a tight budget. The accommodations are unexceptional and the decor a little dowdy, but some rooms have views, and the prices are low. Request a room overlooking the water when making your reservation. ✉ *Rıhtım Cad. 12, 17100,* ☎ *286/217–2908,* 🖷 *286/217–4090. 35 rooms with bath. Restaurant, bar. MC, V.*

**$** 🏨 **Tusan Güzelyalı.** A pine forest on the beach at Intepe, 14 km (8½ mi) south of Çanakkale on the road to Troy, surrounds this popular hotel. The beautiful setting is the draw, since the two-story stucco-and-brick structure has the usual comfortable but nondescript rooms. Reserve well in advance. ✉ *Güzelyalı, 17001,* ☎ *286/232–8746 or 286/232–8747,* 🖷 *286/232–8226. 64 rooms with bath. 2 restaurants, bar, exercise room, beach, dance club. MC, V. Closed Nov.–Mar.* ✎

# Troy (Truva)

❸ *32 km (20 mi) south of Çanakkale on Rte. E87.*

Troy, known as Truva to the Turks and Ilion to the Greeks, is one of the most evocative names in literature. Long thought to be the figment of the Greek poet Homer's imagination, depicted in his epic *Iliad*, the site was excavated in the 1870s by Heinrich Schliemann, a German businessman who had struck it rich in California's gold rush. While scholars scoffed, he poured his wealth into the excavations and had the last laugh: He found the remains not only of the fabled Troy but of nine successive civilizations, one on top of the other, dating back 5,000 years (and now known among archaeologists as Troy I–IX). Archaeologists believe the Troy of the Trojan War represents the seventh layer (1300 BC–900 BC). Subsequent excavations during the 1930s revealed 38 additional layers of settlements. A more recent dig by a German team revealed the footings of a late Bronze Age wall; the find enlarges the supposed Troy fivefold.

Schliemann found a hoard of jewels that he believed were those of the Trojan War's King Priam, but they have more recently been dated to the much earlier Troy II (2600 BC–2300 BC). Adding to the controversy that surrounded his discoveries, Schliemann smuggled the jewels out of the country, and his wife was seen wearing them at fashionable social events. Schliemann later donated them to Berlin's Pergamon Museum, but they disappeared during the Red Army's sack of Berlin in World War II. They reappeared in 1993, when Moscow announced that their state Pushkin Museum of Fine Arts housed what they called the lost "treasure of Priam." Although Germany, Greece, and Turkey all have pressed claims to the treasure, recent custom dictates that archaeological finds belong to the country in which they were originally found.

As Homer's story was written 500 years after the war—traditionally believed to have taken place around 1184 BC—it is hard to say how much of it is history and how much is invention. Nonetheless, it makes for a romantic tale: Paris, the son of King Priam, abducted the beautiful Helen, wife of King Menelaus of Sparta, and fled with her to Troy. Menelaus enlisted the aid of his brother, King Agamemnon, and launched a thousand ships to get her back. His siege lasted 10 years and involved such ancient notables as Achilles, Hector, and the crafty Odysseus, king of Ithaca. It was Odysseus who ended the war, after ordering a huge wooden horse to be built and left outside Troy's gates. When it was completed, the Greeks retreated to their ships and pretended to sail away. The Trojans hauled the trophy into their walled city and celebrated their victory. Under cover of darkness, the Greek ships returned, and the attackers at last gained entry to Troy, after soldiers hidden inside the horse crept out and opened the city's gates. Hence the saying: "Beware of Greeks bearing gifts."

What you will see today depends on your imagination. You may find the site highly suggestive, with its remnants of massive, rough-hewn walls, a paved chariot ramp, and strategic views over the coastal plains to the sea. Or you may consider it an unimpressive row of trenches with piles of earth and stone. Considering Troy's fame (and the difficulties involved in conquering it), the city is surprisingly small. The best-preserved features are from the Roman city, with its *bouleuterion* (council chamber), the site's most complete structure, and small theater. There's little to see in the exhibit space (the impressive artworks are in Istanbul and Ankara); a site plan shows the general layout and marks the beginning of a signposted path leading to key features from several historic civilizations. Labeling is cursory, so to appreciate Troy's significance fully, it's best to come prepared with a detailed history such as scholar George Bean's *Aegean Turkey* or to take a guided tour. English-speaking guides may or may not be available at the site; if you don't want to take your chances, arrange a tour in advance with a travel agent. As for the oft-debated horse, a giant wooden replica sits out near the parking area, duly entertaining to children, who climb up inside for a look around. ✉ *Follow signs from Rte. E87,* ☎ *no phone.* ⌨ *$2.50.* ☉ *Daily 8–5.*

## Alexandria Troas

❹ *32 km (20 mi) from Troy off Rte. E87.*

Alexandria Troas was built at the behest of Alexander the Great in approximately 330 BC. It became a wealthy commercial center and the region's main port. The city, called at one point Antigonia, surpassed Troy in its control over the traffic between the Aegean and the Sea of Marmara and was even considered a capital under the Roman and Byzantine empires. The seaside location that won it prosperity also invited plundering by raiders, which led to its demise. St. Paul visited twice on missionary journeys in the middle of the 1st century AD, proceeding by land to Assos at the end of the second trip. In the 16th and 17th centuries, when the city was called Eski Stamboul (Old Istanbul), Ottoman architects had stones hauled from here to Istanbul for use in the building of imperial mosques, the Blue Mosque in particular. Visit today not so much for seeing the scanty remnants of the city's monumental baths and its aqueduct as for the setting, tucked away in a deserted stretch of wilderness you can often have all to yourself.

## The Apollo Smintheon

**❺** *20 km (12 mi) south of Alexandria Troas via the coast road.*

The Apollo Smintheon is, as the name suggests, a temple dedicated to the god Apollo. It dates from the 2nd century BC. Smintheus—one of the sun god's many names, meaning "killer of mice"—alludes to a problem that Teucer, the town's founder, had with mice eating his soldiers' bowstrings. The temple is just a trifle, but it has some interesting carved pillars and is surrounded by wild pomegranate trees.

## Babakale

**❻** *10 km (6 mi) from the Apollo Smintheon on the coast road, south from Gülpınar.*

Babakale is a minuscule, sleepy fishing village at the southern tip of the Çanakkale Peninsula. No one is sure who built the 16th-century castle above the harbor, only that it was a haven for pirates until a Turkish naval officer named Mustafa Paşa routed them in the late 18th century. Mustafa Paşa went on to build a small mosque and *hamam* (Turkish bath). Particularly in the spring when the castle grounds are carpeted in flowers, Babakale conveys a sense of peace and spaciousness that contrasts dramatically with its turbulent, often violent past.

## Behramkale (Assos)

★ **❼** *20 km (12 mi) southeast of Gülpınar on coast road.*

The lofty ruins of Behramkale, known in ancient times as Assos, provide a panoramic view over the Aegean. As you approach, the road forks, one route leading to the ancient village atop the hill and the other twisting precariously down to the tiny modern port (it's harrowing at night, so arrive before dark). The port is a marvel, pressed against the sheer cliff walls. There are a few small hotels, built of volcanic rock, that seem much older than they are, a fleet of fishing boats, and a small, rocky beach. The crowd at this low-key resort is an interesting mix of Turkish elite, artists, and intellectuals.

The **ruins** of Assos, on a site measuring about five square city blocks, lie at the top of a hill. Founded about 1000 BC by Aeolian Greeks, the city was successively ruled by Lydians, Persians, Pergamenes, Romans, and Byzantines, until Sultan Orhan Gazi (1288–1360) took it over for the Ottomans in 1330. Aristotle is said to have spent time here in the 4th century BC, and St. Paul stopped en route to Miletus, where he visited church elders in about AD 55. The old stone village just under the ruins is little changed in the last century, though the carpet and trinket sellers have grown more aggressive of late. Abandon your car on one of the wider streets and make your way up the steep, cobbled lanes to the top of the acropolis, where you will be rewarded with a sensational view of the coastline and, in the distance, the Greek island of Lesbos, whose citizens were Assos's original settlers.

In Assos are a gymnasium, theater, *agora* (marketplace), and, carved into the hillside below the summit of the acropolis, the site of the **Temple of Athena** (circa 530 BC), which has splendid sea views and is being reconstructed. A more modern addition is the **Murad Hüdavendigâr Cami,** a mosque built in the late 14th century. The mosque is very simple, a dome atop a square, with little decoration. The Greek crosses carved into the lintel over the door indicate the Ottomans used building material from an earlier church, possibly one on the same site. Back down the slope, on the road toward the port, are a parking area for the **necropolis** and city walls stretching 3 km (2 mi). Assos was known for its sarcophagi, made of local limestone, which were shipped throughout the Greek world. Unfortunately, most tombs here are in pieces.

## Dining and Lodging

**$$**  ✕🏨 **Assos Kervansaray.** The best situated of the trio of Assos hotels,
**★**  at the farthest edge of the harbor, the Kervansaray has an aura of antiquity, probably because of the gray lava stone of which it was built just a few years ago. Rooms are small and functional, but most have terrific views of the Aegean. The restaurant serves dressed-up versions of traditional Turkish dishes. There is a swimming pier, though the beach itself is rocky. ✉ *Behramkale, Ayvacık, 17860,* ☏ *286/721–7093 or 286/721–7199,* 𝔽𝔸𝕏 *286/721–7200. 42 rooms with bath, 2 suites. Restaurant, pool, windsurfing. MC, V.* 🐾

**$$**  ✕🏨 **Hotel Assos.** This blocky hotel between the Kervansaray and the Behram draws a decidedly international crowd. Built in Mediterranean-style gray lava stone, it has burnished wood paneling inside and a refined Turkish restaurant that opens up to the bay in good weather. Rooms are done in the same minimalist style as those of its neighbors. ✉ *Behramkale, Ayvacık, 17860,* ☏ *286/721–7017 or 286/721–7034,* 𝔽𝔸𝕏 *286/721–7249. 36 rooms with bath. Restaurant, bar. MC, V.*

**$$**  ✕🏨 **Hotel Behram.** The third in the line of hotels in Assos, this is the first one you reach when driving into town. Rooms are tidy and simple, with whitewashed walls and Scandinavian-style furniture; not all have a view, however, so ask for one when you book. The restaurant has a cozy fireplace and stone walls and turns out standard Turkish fare. ✉ *Behramkale, Ayvacık, 17860,* ☏ *286/721–7016,* 𝔽𝔸𝕏 *286/721–7044. 17 rooms with bath. Restaurant. MC, V.*

# Ayvalık

**★ ⑧**  *131 km (81 mi) from Assos, east on coast road to Rte. E87 south.*

Ayvalık first appears in Ottoman records at the late date of 1770, when an Ottoman naval hero, Gazi Hasan Paşa, was aided by the local Greek community after his ship sank nearby. Soon after, the town was granted autonomy, perhaps as a gesture of gratitude, and the Muslim population was moved to outlying villages, leaving the Greeks to prosper in the olive oil trade. In 1803 an academy was founded following Plato's instructions, with courses in Attic Greek, physics, logic, philosophy, rhetoric, and mathematics. Nothing remains of the school today. At the close of World War I, the Greeks invaded Turkey and claimed the Aegean Coast. The Turks ousted the Greek army in 1922, and the entire Greek community of Ayvalık was deported.

This rapidly growing town has some of the finest 19th-century Greek-style architecture in Turkey. Unlike the typical Ottoman house (tall, narrow, and built of wood, with an overhanging bay window), Greek buildings are stone, with classic triangular pediments above a square box. The best way to explore is to turn your back to the Aegean and wander the tiny side streets leading up the hill into the heart of the old residential quarter (try Talat Paşa Caddesi and Gümrük Caddesi). Several historic churches in town have been converted into mosques. St. John's is now the **Saatlı Cami** (Clock Mosque). St. George's is now the **Çınarlı Cami** (Plane Tree Mosque). The **Taxiarchis Church,** a museum, displays a remarkable series of paintings done on fish skin depicting the life of Christ. The church is currently closed for renovations, and no reopening date has been set.

After wandering through town, take the main street, Atatürk Caddesi, west along the coast to reach the fine 10-km (6-mi) stretch of beach called **Sarmısaklı Plajı.** The resorts a few miles down provide a good place to stay overnight before tackling the ruins at Pergamum, southeast from Ayvalık.

## Dining and Lodging

**$$** ✕ **Canlı Balık.** This fish restaurant at the end of Ayvalık Pier delivers
★ excellent food in a romantic setting. With its starched white tablecloths and weathered decor, the interior has an air of faded grandeur. In fine weather you can sit on the terrace at the very tip of the pier, with local fishing boats swaying in the water a few feet away and the Aegean stretching to the horizon. Start with mezes, such as fried squid or mussel salad in local olive oil, then move on to fresh, grilled local fish, perhaps *barbunya* (red mullet). ✉ *2nd bldg. north of Inönü Cad., on harbor,* ☎ *no phone. No credit cards.*

**$$** 🏨 **Büyük Berk.** This modern hotel is on Ayvalık's best beach, about 3½ km (2 mi) from the center of town. Rooms are functional, with low wooden beds and whitewashed walls, but all have balconies, most looking out over the Aegean. ✉ *Sarmısaklı Plaj, 10425,* ☎ *266/324–1045 or 266/324–1046,* FAX *266/324–1194. 250 rooms with bath. Restaurant, pool, tennis court, exercise room, dance club. MC, V.*

**$$** 🏨 **Grand Hotel Temizel.** Away from the other hotels on Sarmısaklı Beach, this fairly luxurious lodging has a private beach, a casino, a diminutive Turkish spa, and an elegant lobby, all cool marble and gleaming brass. Guest rooms are also a cut above the usual, with bigger beds, wooden dressers, and minibars. Most have Aegean views. ✉ *Sarmısaklı Plaj, 10425,* ☎ *266/324–2000,* FAX *266/324–1274. 164 rooms with bath. Restaurant, bar, pool, sauna, Turkish bath, tennis court, exercise room, soccer, windsurfing, casino, dance club. MC, V.*

**$$** 🏨 **Ayvalık Beach Hotel.** This hotel, which is reached by driving across a causeway, comprises a cluster of two-story chalets nestled among pine trees on a wooded slope overlooking a sheltered inlet. Wonderful sea views more than compensate for the lack of frills in the clean and comfortable but sparsely furnished rooms. ✉ *Şeytan Sofrası Yolu, Altınkum Mev., Ayvalık, 10425,* ☎ *266/324–5301,* FAX *266/324–5304. 68 rooms with bath. Restaurant, bar, pool, beach. MC, V.*

**$** 🏨 **Ankara Oteli.** This is the least expensive of the hotels on Sarmısaklı Beach, just a few feet from the surf. Although rooms are nondescript, they do have balconies; book ahead to get one facing the beach. ✉ *Sarmısaklı Plaj, 10425,* ☎ *266/324–1195 or 266/324–1048,* FAX *266/ 324–0022. 108 rooms with bath. Bar, café, recreation room. No credit cards. Closed Nov.–Mar.*

# Ali Bey Adası

**❾** *Just off coast at Ayvalık (connected by a causeway to mainland).*

Like Ayvalık, Ali Bey Adası (also known as Cunda Island) was once predominantly Greek, and some Greek is still spoken here. The fishing town has good seafood restaurants lining its atmospheric quay; they're noted for their grilled *çipura* (a local fish) and for dishes made with octopus, served grilled, fried, or in a cold seafood salad. The island's Greek houses are well preserved and varied, and the 19th-century **St. Nicholas Church,** in the middle of town, is a must-see. Though the frescoes have been defaced—the eyes of the apostles have been gouged out—there is an amusing depiction of Jonah with a whale that looks a lot like the grouper you could order for lunch. With its large cracks, caused by an earthquake in 1924, and the birds flying around its airy domes, the whole place has a ghostly air. If the church is closed, wait by the front door, and someone will eventually come by to let you in.

# Pergamum (Bergama)

★ 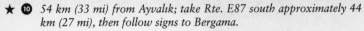 *54 km (33 mi) from Ayvalık; take Rte. E87 south approximately 44 km (27 mi), then follow signs to Bergama.*

The windswept ruins of Pergamum, about 8 km (5 mi) from the modern city of Bergama, are among the most spectacular in Turkey. The attractions here are spread out over several square miles, so if you don't have a car, negotiate with a taxi driver in Bergama (you have to pass through the town anyway) to shuttle you from site to site—this shouldn't cost more than $10 or $20, depending on how long you take. All told, you will probably want to spend half a day.

Pergamum was one of the ancient world's major powers, though it had a relatively brief moment of glory. Led by a dynasty of maverick rulers, it rose to prominence during the 3rd and 2nd centuries BC. Because he was impressed by the city's impregnable fortress, Lysimachus, one of Alexander the Great's generals, decided this was the place to stow the booty he had accumulated while marching through Asia Minor. When Lysimachus was killed in 281 BC, Philetaerus (circa 343 BC–263 BC), the commander of Pergamum, claimed the fortune and holed himself up in the city. After defeating the horde of invading Gauls who had been sacking cities up and down the coast in 240 BC, the Pergamenes were celebrated throughout the Hellenic world as saviors. The dynasty established by Philetaerus, known as the Attalids, ruled from then until 133 BC, when the mad Attalus III (circa 170 BC–133 BC) died and bequeathed the entire kingdom to Rome. By a liberal interpretation of his ambiguous bequest, his domain became the Roman province of Asia and transformed Rome's economy with its wealth.

The city was a magnificent architectural and artistic center in its heyday—especially under the rule of Eumenes II (197 BC–159 BC), who lavished his great wealth on it. He built Pergamum's famous library, which contained 200,000 books. When it rivaled the great library in Alexandria, Egypt, the Egyptians banned the sale of papyrus to Pergamum, which responded by developing a new paper—parchment, made from animal skins instead of reeds. This *charta pergamena* was more expensive but could be used on both sides; because it was difficult to roll, it was cut into pieces and sewn together, much like today's books. The library of Pergamum was transported to Alexandria by Cleopatra, where it survived until the 7th century AD, when it was destroyed by the fanatical Caliph Omar, who considered the books un-Islamic.

The most dramatic of the remains of Pergamum are at the **acropolis.** Signs point the way to the 6-km (4-mi) road to the top, where you can park your car and buy a ticket and perhaps one of the reasonably good picture books containing site maps; then begin to explore. Broken but still mighty triple ramparts enclose the **upper town,** with its temples, palaces, private houses, and gymnasia (schools). In later Roman times, the town spread out and down to the plain, where the Byzantines subsequently settled for good.

After entering the acropolis through the Royal Gate, you can follow a couple of different paths. To start at the top, pick the path to the far right, which takes you past the partially restored **Temple of Trajan,** at the summit. This is the very picture of an ancient ruin, with burnished white-marble pillars high above the valley of the Oç Kemer Çayi (Selinos River). On the terraces just below, you can see the scant remains of the **Temple of Athena** and the **Altar of Zeus.** Once among the grandest monuments in the Greek world, the Altar of Zeus was excavated by German archaeologists who sent Berlin's Pergamon Museum every stone they found, including the frieze, 400 ft long, that vividly depicted the battle of the gods against the giants. Now all that's left is the altar's flat stone foundation. The **Great Theater,** carved into the steep slope west of the terrace that holds the Temple of Athena, is another matter; it can seat some 10,000 spectators and retains its astounding acoustics. You can test them by sitting near the top and having a companion do a reading in the stage area. ☎ 232/632–6663. 🎫 $2. ☉ Apr.– Oct., daily 8:30–5:30; Nov.–Mar., daily 8:30–5.

The **Kızıl Avlu** (Red Courtyard) in Bergama is named for the red bricks from which it is constructed. You will pass it on the road to and from the acropolis—it's right at the bottom of the hill. This was the last pagan temple constructed in Pergamum before Christianity was declared the state religion in the 4th century. At that time it was converted into a basilica dedicated to St. John. The walls remain, but not the roof. Most interesting are the underground passages, where it is easy to imagine how concealed pagan priests supplied the voices of "spirits" in mystic ceremonies. ☎ 232/633–1096 at Archaeology Museum for information. 🎫 $1. ☉ Apr.–Oct., daily 9–noon and 1–7; Nov.–Mar., daily 9–noon and 1–5.

Bergama's **Arkeoloji Müzesi** (Archaeology Museum) is one of Turkey's better provincial museums. It houses a substantial collection of well-presented statues, coins, and other artifacts excavated from the ancient city. ⊠ Hükümet Cad., ☎ 232/633–1096. 🎫 $2.50. ☉ Apr.–Oct., daily 8:30–5:30; Nov.–Mar., Tues.–Sun. 9–noon and 1–5:30.

The **Asklepion** is believed to have been the world's first full-service health clinic. The name is a reference to Asklepios, god of medicine and recovery, whose snake and staff are now the symbol of modern medicine. In the heyday of the Pergamene Asklepion in the 2nd century AD, patients were prescribed such treatments as fasting, colonic irrigation, and running barefoot in cold weather. The nature of the treatment was generally determined by interpretation of the patient's dreams. You enter the complex at the column-lined **Holy Road,** once the main street connecting the Asklepion to Pergamum's acropolis. Follow it for about a city block into a small square and through the *propyleum,* the main gate to the temple precinct. Immediately to the right are the **Shrine of Artemis,** devoted to the Greek goddess of chastity, the moon, and hunting, and the **library,** a branch of the one at Pergamum. Patients also received therapy accompanied by music during rites held in the intimate theater, which is now used each May for performances of the Bergama Arts Festival. Nearby are pools that were used for mud and sacred water baths. A subterranean passageway leads down to the sacred cellar of the **Temple of Telesphorus,** where the devout would pray themselves into a trance and record their dreams upon waking; later, the dreams would be interpreted by a resident priest. ⊠ Follow Hükümet Cad. west to Rte. E87; near tourist information office, follow sign pointing off to right 1½ km (1 mi), ☎ 232/633–1096. 🎫 $2.50. ☉ Daily 8:30–5:30.

## Dining and Lodging

**$** ✕ **Bergama Restaurant.** This inexpensive eatery, on the main street not far from the Archaeology Museum, offers an excellent range of kebabs and starters, including a few local specialties such as the tasty spicy meatballs *bergama köftesi.* The tables are set around a small pond filled with plump goldfish; the walls are covered in stripped pine and local stone. ⊠ Bankalar Cad. 5, ☎ 232/632–3492. No credit cards.

**$$** 🏨 **Hotel Iskender.** Rooms at this plain-looking hotel in the center of town are comfortable and air-conditioned. An outdoor restaurant serves typical Turkish food. ⊠ İzmir Cad., Ilıca Önü Mev. P. K. 35, 35700, ☎ 232/632–9711 or 232/632–9710, FAX 232/632–9710. 60 rooms with bath. 2 restaurants, bar, air-conditioning. MC, V.

**$$** ⊡ **Asude Hotel.** Some of the rooms at the front of this distinctive brick-red five-story hotel on the outskirts of town have distant views of the ancient ruins of Pergamum. The rooms are plainly decorated, with whitewashed walls and wooden furnishings, but they are clean and well maintained, and the restaurant serves a passable selection of grilled meats. ⊠ *İzmir Asfaltı 93, Fatih Mah. 35700,* ☎ *232/631–3903,* FAX *232/631–3904. 52 rooms with bath. Restaurant, bar. MC, V.*

## Foça

⑪ *70 km (43 mi) from Bergama, south on Rte. E87 and west on Rte. 250.*

Foça is a typical Aegean fishing village with good restaurants, a few cozy *pansiyons* (guest houses), and a big Club Med nearby. Odysseus is said to have lost six men in the straits between Scylla and Charybdis, but these islands, rather more tame today, have the best beaches in the area; you can hire a boat in the village for $10 or $20 for the ride out. If it's late in the day, or you just prefer staying in a small town instead of big-city İzmir, Foça is a good spot to stay overnight.

### Dining and Lodging

**$** ✕ **Restaurant Foça.** The restaurants along Foça's little harbor usually prepare an appropriately dizzying array of fresh fish. In this one, the best of a good bunch, you can have your *palamut* (bonito), *lüfer* (bluefish), or *levrek* (sea bass) grilled to perfection. ⊠ *Sahil Cad., Eski Foça,* ☎ *232/812–1307. AE, MC, V.*

**$$$$** ⊡ **Club Méditerranée.** The fishing village of Foça seems an unlikely spot for one of these all-inclusive vacation resorts, but the French vacation operation does a creditable job here. Red-tile-roof bungalows are grouped into two small hamlets, one atop a hill overlooking the Aegean, the other in an olive grove. ⊠ *In Eski Foça, 12 km (7 mi) north of Foça,* ☎ *232/812–1607, 232/812–2176; 212/750–1687 in U.S;* FAX *232/812–2175. 376 rooms with bath. Restaurant, bar, pool, tennis court, dive shop, windsurfing, waterskiing. AE, DC, MC, V.* ✆

**$$** ⊡ **Hanedan.** This unassuming four-story hotel in what looks like a town house is right on the harbor. Public areas are scattered with Turkish rugs and kilims; guest rooms are small and simple. ⊠ *Büyükdeniz Sahil Cad. 1,* ☎ *232/812–3650,* FAX *232/812–2451. 30 rooms with bath. Restaurant. No credit cards.*

## İzmir

*70 km (43 mi) from Foça, east on Rte. 250 and south on Rte. E87.*

Turkey's third-largest city, with a population of 2 million, İzmir was called Smyrna until 1923. A vital trading port, though one often ravaged by wars and earthquakes, it also had its share of glory. Many believe that Homer was born in Old Smyrna sometime around 850 BC. Alexander the Great favored the city with a citadel atop its highest hill.

The city fell into assorted hands after the Romans, starting with the Byzantines and Arabs. From 1097 on, Smyrna became a battlefield in the Crusades, passing back and forth between the forces of Islam and Christendom. Destroyed and restored successively by Byzantines and Seljuks, Smyrna was held by the Knights of Rhodes in 1402 when the Mongol raider Tamerlane came along, sacked it yet again, and slaughtered its inhabitants. Thirteen years later Sultan Mehmet I Çelebi incorporated it into the Ottoman Empire.

Toward the end of the 15th century, Jews driven from Spain settled in Smyrna, forming a lasting Sephardic community. By the 18th and 19th centuries Smyrna had become a successful, sophisticated commercial port with an international flavor. Its business community included sizable Italian, Greek, Armenian, British, French, and Jewish contingents. This era came to an end with World War I, when Ottoman Turkey allied itself with Germany. In 1918 the Greek army, encouraged by the British and French, landed at the harbor and claimed the city. The occupation lasted until 1922, when Turkish troops under Atatürk defeated the Greek forces and forced them to evacuate. On September 9, 1922, Atatürk made a triumphant entry into the port. The joy of the local Turks was short-lived; a fire shortly thereafter blazed through the city. Fanned by the wind, it burned wooden houses like matches while hidden stores of munitions exploded.

The city was quickly rebuilt—and given the Turkish name İzmir. Like the name, much of the city dates from the '20s, from its wide boulevards to the office buildings and apartment houses painted in bright white or soft pastels. This important industrial center is not particularly pretty, though it has a harbor-front promenade and peaceful green Kültür Parkı at its center.

The sweeping view of the city and its harbor from the windy restored
⑫ ramparts of the **Kadifekale** (Velvet Fortress), built by Alexander the Great, make it a good spot to orient yourself to İzmir. The name, according to romantics if not to scholars, alludes to the resemblance of the present-day citadel's walls to rubbed velvet. Rebuilt after various mishaps and enlarged and strengthened by successive conquerors, the structure looks like a childhood fantasy of a medieval castle, with solid stone blocks (some dating from Alexander's day), Byzantine cisterns, and Ottoman buttresses jutting out to support the walls.

⑬ The **agora** at the foot of Kadifekale Hill, just off 816 Sokak (816 Street), was the Roman city's market. The present site is a large, dusty, open space surrounded by ancient columns and foundations. There are well-preserved Roman statues of Poseidon, Artemis, and Demeter in the northwest corner. To get there from Kadifekale, exit from the fortress's main gate and take the road that descends to the left; when you see steps built into the sidewalk, turn right and go down. ⊠ *Namazgah, Anafartalar Cad.* ⌐ *$1.* ⊙ *Daily 8:30–5:30.*

⑭ **Konak Meydanı** (Konak Square), at the water's edge, is one of the two main squares in the city (the other, Cumhuriyet Meydanı, or Republic Square, is to the north along Atatürk Caddesi). Konak marks the start of the modern-day marketplace, a maze of tiny streets filled with shops and covered stalls. Unlike Istanbul's Grand Bazaar, İzmir's is not covered. **Anafartalar Caddesi** is the bazaar's principal thoroughfare, but try the smaller side streets, too, where you'll find minimarkets dedicated to musical instruments, songbirds, clothing, blankets, and many other treats. ⊙ *Mon.–Sat. 8–8.*

⑮ The **Arkeoloji Müzesi** (Archaeology Museum) contains the 2nd-century statues of Demeter and Poseidon found when the agora was excavated, as well as an impressive collection of tombs and friezes and the memorable, colossal statue of the Roman emperor Domitian (AD 51–96, ruled 81–96). ⊠ *Cumhuriyet Bul., Bahribaba Parkı,* ☎ *232/489–0796.* ⌐ *$2.50.* ⊙ *Tues.–Sun. 8:30–5:30.*

⑯ The **İzmir Etnoğrafya Müzesi** (İzmir Ethnographic Museum) focuses on folk arts and daily life, housing everything from period bedrooms to a reconstruction of İzmir's first pharmacy. ⊠ *Cumhuriyet Bul., Bahribaba Parkı,* ☎ *232/489–0796.* ⌐ *$1.50.* ⊙ *Tues.–Sun. 8:30–5:30.*

⑰ The **Kordonboyu** (Cordon), the waterfront promenade, is the most fashionable section of town. It starts at the museum complex in **Bahrib-**

# İzmir

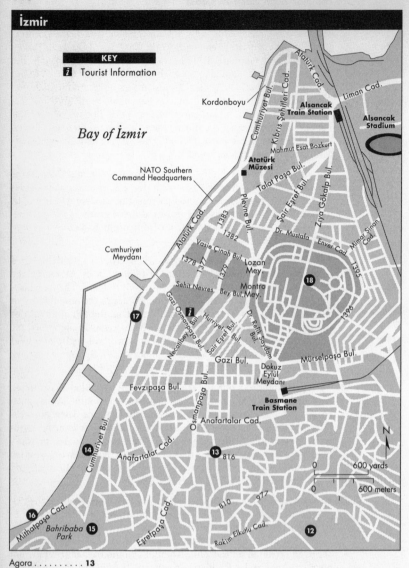

**KEY**

*i* Tourist Information

Bay of İzmir

Kordonboyu

**Alsancak Train Station**

Liman Cad.

Atatürk Cad.

Cumhuriyet Bul.

Kıbrıs Şehitleri Cad.

**Alsancak Stadium**

Mahmut Esat Bozkurt

**Atatürk Müzesi**

Talat Paşa Bul.

NATO Southern Command Headquarters

Plevne Bul.

Atatürk Cad.

Şair Eşref Bul.

Ziya Gökalp Bul.

Dr. Mustafa

Enver Cad.

Mimar Sinan Cad.

1383

1382

Vasıf Çınah Bul.

Cumhuriyet Meydanı

1378   1377   1379

**Lozan Mey.**

1395

**18**

Şehit Nevres

**Montro Mey.**

**Bey Bul.**

**17**

Gazi Osmanpaşa Bul.

*i*

Hürriyet Bul.

Şair Eşref Bul.

Dr. Refik Saydam Bul.

Necatibey Bul.

1396

Gazi Bul.

Mürselpaşa Bul.

**Dokuz Eylül Meydanı**

Osmanpaşa Bul.

Fevzipaşa Bul.

**Basmane Train Station**

Anafartalar Cad.

Cumhuriyet Bul.

**14**

Anafartalar Cad.

**13**   816

N

0          600 yards

0          600 meters

**16**

Mithatpaşa Cad.

*Bahribaba Park*

**15**

Eşrefpaşa Cad.

810      977

Rakin Elkuflu Cad.

**12**

aba Parkı and stretches north along the busy harbor, past the 19th-century Ottoman **Saat Kulesi** (Clock Tower), **NATO's Southern Command headquarters,** and the small **Atatürk Müzesi** (Atatürk Museum; ⊠ Atatürk Cad., Alsancak 248, ☎ 232/421–7026). The museum, housed in a pale yellow Levantine building, is open Tuesday–Sunday 8:30–noon and 1–5. Along the strip are several good seafood restaurants, all with a few tables outside overlooking the water.

(18) **Kültür Parkı** (Culture Park), İzmir's central park, has gardens, a zoo, amusement rides, and nightclubs. It is the site of a major industrial fair from late August to late September. ⊠ *East of Lozan and Montrö Meyds.*

### Dining and Lodging

$$ ✕ **Altınkapı.** Probably the best of the many kebab houses on 1444 Sokak, this is the only one to have received the Turkish Standards Institute seal of approval. Its specialties include excellent *İnegöl köfte* (grilled lamb patties)and a fine selection of *pide* (Turkish pizza). ⊠ *1444 Sok. 9, Alsancak,* ☎ *232/422–5687. MC, V.*

$$ ✕ **Deniz.** Befitting its bayside location, the main event in this attractive spot on the ground floor of the İzmir Palas Hotel is the seafood. Options range from sole to sea bass, mussels to mullet. *Kılıç şiş* (grilled swordfish kebab) is a house specialty. ⊠ *Atatürk Cad. 188, Alsancak,* ☎ *232/422–0601. DC, MC, V.*

$$ ✕ **Ömür Balık Lokantası.** Open only at lunchtime, this pleasant restaurant in a restored Ottoman building serves all sorts of seafood, including fresh fish, octopus, and shrimp. ⊠ *902 Sok. 44, Hisarönü,* ☎ *232/425–6839. No credit cards.*

$ ✕ **Elif İskender.** Everybody in İzmir has a favorite kebab place, and this one is on a lot of lists. It's a lively sidewalk café in the center of the city, a block in from the water, with tasty doner kebabs and budget-wise prices. ⊠ *Cumhuriyet Bul. 194,* ☎ *no phone. No credit cards.*

$$$$ ☷ **İzmir Hilton.** At 34 stories, the Hilton is one of the tallest buildings on the Aegean Coast. Striking and modern, it looms over the city center. From the 10-story atrium to the elegant rooftop restaurant, the public spaces are suitably grand. Guest rooms are plush, with thick floral comforters and matching drapes. About the only complaint you could make is that there's nothing particularly Turkish about the place. ⊠ *Gazi Osman Paşa Bul. 7, 35210,* ☎ *232/441–6060,* ℻ *232/441–2277. 381 rooms with bath. 2 restaurants, 2 bars, air-conditioning, pool, 2 tennis courts, health club, squash, shops, casino, business services. AE, DC, MC, V.* ☜

$$$ ☷ **Mercure Konak Hotel.** This hotel right on the water has lots of cool marble and greenery. Guest rooms have full-size beds, plush carpeting, and big windows with views. The city's museums are within easy walking distance. ⊠ *Mithatpasa Cad. 128, 35210,* ☎ *232/489–1500,* ℻ *232/489–1709. 82 rooms with bath. Restaurant, bar, meeting room. AE, MC, V.*

$$ ☷ **Hotel Kilim.** Rooms here are comfortable, and some have bay views. Those close to the street can be noisy, so ask for one higher up. The hotel's nondescript restaurant serves seafood and traditional Turkish lamb dishes—in good weather you can eat at sidewalk tables overlooking the harbor. ⊠ *Kazim Dirik Cad. 1, 35210,* ☎ *232/484–5340,* ℻ *232/489–5070. 75 rooms with bath. Restaurant, bar. MC, V.*

$$ ☷ **Karaca Otel.** This mid-rise hotel is on a little side street; some rooms have a view of the gardens, and some have terraces. The decor is contemporary, with wall-to-wall carpeting and some Turkish touches. The location is convenient, and the rates are lower than at larger, neighboring properties. ⊠ *1379 Sok. 55, at Necatibey and Gazi Osmanpaşa Buls., 35210,* ☎ *232/489–1940,* ℻ *232/483–1498. 74 rooms with bath. Restaurant, bar, meeting room. AE, MC, V.*

**$–$$** 🏨 **Kısmet.** The public spaces and guest rooms at this comfortable hotel are tastefully decorated, but since it doesn't have a great view and is an older property, you'll pay less. The side-street location makes it quieter than places on the main drag, and the staff is friendly. ⊠ *1377 Sok. 9, 35210,* ☎ *232/463–3850,* ℻ *232/421–4856. 62 rooms with bath. Restaurant. AE, MC, V.*

**$** 🏨 **Hotel Baylan.** This four-story property with a shiny marble facade is a good value. Its bright and pleasant rooms, on the small side, have unprepossessing Scandinavian-style furniture. ⊠ *Anafartalar Cad., Basmane, 1299 Sok. 8, 35240,* ☎ *232/483–1426,* ℻ *232/483–3844. 30 rooms with bath. Restaurant, bar. AE, MC, V.*

### Nightlife

There is an open-air restaurant/nightclub, the **Kubana** (☎ 232/425–4773), in Kültür Parkı. **Charlie's Cocktail Bar** (⊠ 1386 Sok. 8/B, Alsancak, ☎ 232/421–4981) is popular with an expatriate crowd. The **Mexican Bar** (⊠ Atatürk Cad. 192, Alsancak, ☎ 232/464–3347) offers live Latin jazz most nights. If you're into barhopping, 1469 Sokak is known as the bar strip, and the favorite place to be seen is the **Punta Bar** (☎ 232/463–1504). The two-story **British Bar** (⊠ Atatürk Cad. 174/A, ☎ 232/463–1020) offers good live music and is famous for its cocktails. The metal-and-wood interior of the **Diva Bar** (⊠ Cengiz Topel Cad. 30/1, Bostanlı, Karşıyaka, ☎ 232/330–7171) provides a rugged backdrop to the musical menu of blues and jazz and to the house drink, the Diva Cocktail.

# THE SOUTHERN AEGEAN COAST

## Ephesus, Pamukkale, Priene, and Bodrum

Between the beaches of Çeşme and the resort town of Bodrum, the southern Aegean Coast encompasses some of Turkey's most famous archaeological sites—Aphrodisias, Priene, Didyma, and the stunning ruins of the ancient city of Ephesus. You should allow at least three overnights in the region, although you could easily spend two weeks, mixing visits to the sites with lounging on some of the areas's beautiful beaches.

## Çeşme

⑲ *81 km (50 mi) west of İzmir on Rte. 300.*

Çeşme's honey-colored Genoese castle and clean beaches have made it a popular resort town. But life was not always peaceful here. A historic sea battle fought off Çeşme's coast in 190 BC ended with the defeat of Hannibal, the famed general of Carthage, at the hands of the Romans. Nearly 2,000 years later, in 1770, the Russian fleet utterly destroyed the Ottoman navy, a blow from which the empire never recovered. Things are quieter now, and the only boats you will see today are yachts and pleasure craft tied up along the quay that curves around Çeşme Bay.

The 14th-century **Genoese castle** is picturesque, its stone walls given over to basking lizards and its keep often deep in wildflowers. The castle's museum displays weaponry from the glory days of the Ottoman Empire. 🎫 *$2.* ☉ *Daily 8:30–11:45 and 1–5:15.*

**Beaches** are the main highlight of Çeşme. About 5 km (3 mi) south of town, out along Akburun (White Cape), are several nice stretches, including **Pirlanta** and numerous unnamed coves. The same distance north of town is the popular **Ilıca Beach**.

## Dining and Lodging

**$$** ✕ **Körfez.** With its chic terrace, lively piazza section, and indoor disco, this popular waterfront restaurant fills with vacationers in summer. At white-linen-covered tables on the terrace you can sample appetizers and order grilled or stewed fish—or allow the chef to send you his specialty, *sütlü balık* (baked fish in a special sauce topped with mushrooms and cheese). ✉ *Yalı Cad. 12,* ☎ *232/712–6718 or 232/712–0191. Reservations essential in summer. V.*

**$** ✕ **Sahil.** A waterfront eatery across from the Ertan Hotel, Sahil serves fresh, tasty appetizers like eggplant salad and typical Turkish dishes such as lamb kebabs and grilled fish. You may sit indoors or outdoors on a terrace. For scenery you have the pretty but unremarkable Bay of Çeşme as well as promenading vacationers. ✉ *Cumhuriyet Meyd. 12,* ☎ *232/712–8294. Reservations essential in summer. No credit cards.*

**$** ✕ **Sevim Café.** Despite its location on an awkward corner at the edge of the main square by the sea, this establishment is charming and serves its dishes in a style that you won't find elsewhere. The owner, Ms. Zehra, hand-prepares the main dish for which the café is famous: *mantı* (meat-filled ravioli topped with garlicky yogurt and served with a sprinkle of hot pepper and saffron). The chef, whose expertise is enhanced by international experience, also juggles meats on the grill and arranges beautiful salads on the side. Come early for a good seat. ✉ *Hal Binası 5, opposite Kervansaray,* ☎ *no phone. No credit cards.*

**$$$** ✕🏨 **Kervansaray.** Built in 1528 during the reign of Süleyman the
★ Magnificent, this old property in the town center, next to Çeşme's medieval castle, is largely decorated in traditional Turkish style, with kilims, low wooden furniture, and brass fittings. The bathrooms are tiled, motel-modern affairs. Good choices for lunch or dinner in the excellent restaurant include lamb kebabs with yogurt, cold eggplant salad, and *börek* (deep-fried pastry shells, here filled with goat cheese). In pleasant weather you can dine outdoors in a courtyard surrounded by the ancient stone walls of the Kervansaray. ✉ *Kale Yanı,* ☎ *232/712–7177 or 232/712–6491,* FAX *232/712–2906. 34 rooms with bath. Restaurant, bar. AE, DC, MC, V. Closed Nov.–Mar.*

**$$$** 🏨 **Altın Yunus Tatilköyü.** The low, bright white cuboid buildings of this
★ big resort—whose name translates as "golden dolphin"—curve along an attractive white-sand beach edging a cove dotted with sailboats. Rooms are done in Mediterranean style, with lots of white and pale ocean blue. You'll find thicker carpets, bigger beds, and a more plush feel than is usual for Turkey. With almost every imaginable recreational facility, the resort is a destination unto itself. ✉ *Kalemburnu Boyalık Mev., Ilıca,* ☎ *232/723–1250,* FAX *232/723–2252. 517 rooms with bath. 6 restaurants, 2 bars, 2 indoor pools, 2 outdoor pools, beauty salon, Turkish bath, 5 tennis courts, exercise room, windsurfing, boating, dance club, nightclub, playground. AE, MC, V.* ✺

**$$$** 🏨 **Şifne Hotel.** As much a thermal resort as a hotel, the Şifne is named for the nearby seaside hamlet, 11 km (6 mi) from Çeşme. Rooms are functional rather than luxurious, although most have fine sea views. The water in the two large open-air thermal pools is reputed to cure numerous diseases. The hotel also has its own beach. ✉ *Şifne,* ☎ *232/717–1099. 36 rooms with bath. Restaurant, bar. MC, V.*

**$$** 🏨 **Ertan Oteli.** This five-story white-stucco hotel, on the water on the north side of Çeşme's main square, is modern and efficient. Many rooms have views of the Aegean, as does the terrace restaurant. ✉ *Cumhuriyet Meyd. 12,* ☎ *232/712–6795,* FAX *232/712–7852. 67 rooms with bath. Restaurant, bar. MC, V.*

**$** 🏨 **Tani Pansiyon.** A friendly retired couple runs this very modest pansiyon. The simple rooms have low wooden beds and views of the bay through handmade crocheted lace curtains. Be sure to ask for one facing the bay. Bathrooms and showers are shared, as is a lace-decked kitchen upstairs on the terrace, where breakfast is served. ⊠ *Çarşı Sok. 5, Musalla Mah.,* ☎ *232/712–6238. 8 rooms without bath. No credit cards.*

## Sardis

**⑳** *171 km (106 mi) east of Çeşme on Rte. 300 (also called E96 east of İzmir).*

The ancient city of Sardis was the capital of Lydia under King Croesus (ruled 560 BC–546 BC), who put a lot of money into building temples, the most famous of which is the Temple of Artemis. The Lydians' main claim to fame comes from their invention of minted coinage at the end of the 7th century BC. Today it is possible to see the remains of the equipment that was used to melt and shape the gold they were so skillful in extracting. In 546 BC the city came under Persian rule, when Cyrus captured Sardis but spared Croesus's life. In Byzantine times it was the site of a diocese, and in the 14th century AD it was taken by the Turks. The older city was almost completely destroyed by a major earthquake in AD 17. Most remains date from the Roman Empire, which held sway in the area until the 3rd century AD.

The **Temple of Artemis,** slightly bigger than Athens's Parthenon, is unfortunately not as well preserved, but reerected columns with fine Ionic capitals and the one wall still standing hint at the temple's former grandeur. The acropolis behind it offers splendid views, but the hike up and down can take two hours. ⊠ *South of the village of Sartmustafa; a sign points the way down an unpaved but passable road.* ☎ *no phone.* 🎟 *$1.* ⊙ *Daily 8:30–dusk.*

Other **Sardis ruins** are across the highway from the Temple of Artemis. At the **gymnasium complex,** bathers would enter through the colonnaded *palaestra* (exercise hall), continue through the row of changing rooms, and end up in the enormous *caldarium* (hot pool). The ornate **Marble Court,** where you can see the remains of Byzantine-era shops, has been reconstructed, revealing a multistory facade with carved reliefs. The **restored synagogue** dates from the 4th century AD and has some intact mosaic pavements. ⊠ *On dirt road heading north, across highway from road to Temple of Artemis (10 mins on foot, less by car),* ☎ *no phone.* 🎟 *$1 for each site.* ⊙ *Daily 8:30–dusk.*

## Ephesus and Selçuk

*79 km (49 mi) south of İzmir on Rte. E87.*

★ **㉑** **Ephesus** (Efes in Turkish) is the best-preserved and probably the most evocative ancient city in the eastern Mediterranean. The Delphi oracle led the Ionian Greeks here from their original home in central Greece in the 11th century BC by giving this advice to Androkles, the Ionian leader: "The site of the new town will be shown . . . by a fish; follow the wild boar." According to the legend, as Androkles and his men were traveling in the vicinity of what became Ephesus, they came across some people cooking. A fish, about to be cooked over an open fire, jumped and knocked embers into nearby brush. The fire spread, and a boar fleeing the flames was followed to Mt. Koressos, later called Bülbül Dağ, or Mount of the Nightingale, by the Turks. And that is where the Ionians settled.

Ephesus, on the sea at the time, quickly became a powerful trading port and sacred center for the cult of Artemis. Its fame drew the attention of a series of conquerors, among them Croesus of Lydia and 6th-century BC Cyrus of Persia. After a Greek uprising against the Persians failed,

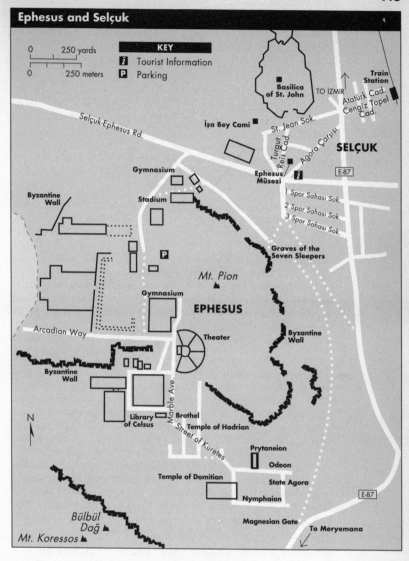

## Ephesus and Selçuk

**KEY**
- **ℹ** Tourist Information
- **P** Parking

0 — 250 yards
0 — 250 meters

Basilica of St. John

TO İZMIR

Train Station

Atatürk Cad.
Cengiz Topel Cad.

İşa Bey Cami

St. Jean Sok.

Turgut Reis Cad.

Agora Çarşısı

**SELÇUK**

Gymnasium

Ephesus Müsezi

ℹ

E-87

Byzantine Wall

Stadium

1 Spor Sahası Sok.
2 Spor Sahası Sok.
3 Spor Sahası Sok.

Graves of the Seven Sleepers

P

Mt. Pion ▲

Gymnasium

**EPHESUS**

Arcadian Way

Theater

Byzantine Wall

Byzantine Wall

Marble Ave.

Library of Celsus

Brothel

Street of Kuretes

Temple of Hadrian

Prytaneion

Odeon

N

Temple of Domitian

State Agora

Nymphaion

E-87

Bülbül Dağ ▲
Mt. Koressos ▲

Magnesian Gate

To Meryemana

Ephesus managed to stay out of trouble, often by playing up to both sides of any conflict. Perhaps because the Temple of Artemis was consumed by fire on the day Alexander the Great was born, Alexander himself aided the city in its efforts to rebuild after his rise to power.

Like most Ionian cities in Asia Minor, Ephesus became a Roman city, and eventually a Christian one, though not without a struggle. In the Acts of the Apostles, St. Luke writes at length about the popularity of the cult of Artemis, referring to the goddess by her Latin name, Diana. The city's silversmiths drove St. Paul out of Ephesus for fear that his preaching would lessen the sale of the "silver shrines for Diana," claiming, "By this craft we have our wealth." When St. Paul addressed the town in its amphitheater, saying that "there are no gods made with hands," the local silversmiths rioted; they were "full of wrath, and cried out, saying, 'Great is Diana of the Ephesians'" (Acts 19:24–40). Paul is believed to have written some of his Epistles here. St. John visited between 37 and 48 AD, perhaps with the mother of Jesus, and again in 95, when he is supposed to have written his Gospel here and died. In 431 Ephesus was the scene of the Third Ecumenical Council, during which Mary was proclaimed the Mother of God.

Ephesus was doomed by the silting in its harbor. By the 6th century the port had become useless, and the population had shifted to what is now Selçuk; today Ephesus is 5 km (about 3 mi) from the sea. The new city was surrounded by ramparts, and a citadel was built. In the year 1000, crusaders came from the West, Turks from the East. Ephesus became known as Hagios Theologos (Holy Word of God) and then by the Turkish version of that name, Ayasoluk. The first Seljuk invaders were fought off in 1090, and the Byzantines held out until 1304. The town was incorporated into the Ottoman Empire at the beginning of the 15th century.

Ephesus is the showpiece of Aegean archaeology and one of the grandest reconstructed ancient sites in the world. The remarkably preserved ruins were rediscovered in the late 1800s, and excavations have been going on for nearly a century. The site is a pleasure to explore: Marble-paved streets with grooves made by chariot wheels lead past partially reconstructed buildings and monuments. The remains are especially appealing out of season, when the place can seem deserted. In summer it's packed with tourists, many of whom come off the Greek ships that cruise the Aegean and call at Kuşadası, 20 km (12 mi) to the south. Go early or late in the day, if possible. Site guides are available at the trinket stands ringing the parking lot.

The road leading to the site parking lot passes a 1st-century AD **stadium,** where chariot and horse races were held on a track 712 ft long and where gladiators and wild beasts met in combat before 70,000 spectators. On your left after you enter the site is the 25,000-seat **theater,** backed by the western slope of Mt. Pion. A huge semicircle, with row upon row of curved benches, it was begun by Alexander's general Lysimachus and completed by emperors Claudius and Trajan in the 2nd century AD. There is a fine view from the top of the steps; higher still, near the top of Mt. Pion, are vestiges of the city's Byzantine walls. The theater is used for music and dance performances each May during the Selçuk Ephesus Festival of Culture and Art. Leading away from the theater toward the ancient port, now a marsh, is the **Arcadian Way.** This 1,710-ft-long street was once lined with shops and covered archways. Only a long line of slender marble columns remains.

In front of the theater is Marble Avenue. Follow it to the beautiful, two-story **Library of Celsus.** The courtyard of this much-photographed building is backed by wide steps that climb to the reading room, where you can still see rolls of papyrus. The library is near Marble Avenue's intersection with the **Street of Kuretes,** a still-impressive thoroughfare named for the college of priests once located there. Strategically positioned at this corner is a large house believed to have been a **brothel.** Look for the floor mosaics of three women. To the right along the street are the multistoried houses of the nobility, with terraces and courtyards. To the left are public buildings. A block down from the brothel is the fine facade of the **Temple of Hadrian,** with four Corinthian columns and a serpent-headed hydra above the door to keep out evil spirits; beyond is a partially restored fountain dedicated to the emperor Trajan. The street then forks and opens into a central square that once held the **Prytaneion,** or town hall; the **Nymphaion,** a small temple decked with fountains; and the **Temple of Domitian,** on the south side of the square, which was once a vast sanctuary with a colossal statue of the emperor for whom it was named. All are now a jumble of collapsed walls and columns.

Returning to the Street of Kuretes, turn right to reach the **odeon,** an intimate semicircle with just a few rows of seats, where spectators would listen to poetry readings and music. Columns mark the northern edge of the state **agora** (market). Beyond, the **Magnesian Gate** (also known as the Manisa Gate), at the end of the street, was the starting point for a caravan trail and a colonnaded road to the Temple of Artemis. ⊠ *Site entry 4 km (2½ mi) west of Selçuk on Selçuk–Ephesus road,* ☎ *232/892–6402 or 232/892–6940.* 🎫 *$5.* ⊙ *Daily 8–5:30.*

According to the legend attached to the **Graves of the Seven Sleepers,** seven young Christian men hid in a cave to avoid persecution by the Romans in the 3rd century AD. They fell into a sleep that lasted 200 years, waking only after the Byzantine Empire had made Christianity the official state religion. When they died, they were buried here, and the church that you see was built over them. The tombs in the large cemetery are largely from the Byzantine era. ⊠ *South of Sor Sahasi Sok. 3.* 🎫 *Free.*

㉒ Huddled under its crenellated, honey-colored-stone Byzantine fortress that, when floodlighted at night, seems to float above the town, **Selçuk** has retained a special charm. The fortress itself holds nothing of interest.

★ The small **Ephesus Müzesi** (Ephesus Museum), in Selçuk, has one of the best collections of Roman and Greek artifacts found anywhere in Turkey. Along with some fine frescoes and mosaics are two white statues of Artemis. In each she is portrayed with several rows of what are alternatively described as breasts or a belt of eggs; in either case, they symbolize fertility. ⊠ *Agora Çarsısı, opposite visitor center,* ☎ *232/ 892–6010.* 🎫 *$2.50.* ⊙ *Daily 8:30–noon and 1–5:30.*

**İsa Bey Cami** (İsa Bey Mosque) is one of the oldest mosques in Turkey, dating from 1375. Its jumble of architectural styles suggests a transition between Seljuk and Ottoman design: Like later Ottoman mosques, this one has a courtyard, something not found in Seljuk mosques. The structure is built out of "borrowed" stone: marble blocks with Latin inscriptions, Corinthian columns, black-granite columns from the baths at Ephesus, and pieces from the altar of the Temple of Artemis. ⊠ *St. Jean Sok.* ⊙ *Daily 9–6.*

The fragments of the **Temple of Artemis** on display at the İsa Bey Mosque (☞ *above*) are about all you will see of the holy site that drew pilgrims from around the ancient world and was one of its Seven Wonders. Begun in the 7th century BC, greatly expanded by the wealthy Lydian king Croesus, and redone in marble in the 6th century BC, the temple was burned down by a disgruntled worshiper in 356 BC. Alexander the Great had it rebuilt, but it was sacked by Goths in AD 263 and later stripped for materials to build Istanbul's Aya Sofya and Selçuk's St. John Basilica. Today a lone column towering over a scattering of fallen stones in a green field on the Selçuk–Ephesus road is all that remains of a temple that was once four times larger than the Parthenon in Athens.

The emperor Justinian built the **St. John Basilica** over a 2nd-century tomb on Ayasoluk Hill, believed by many to have once held the body of St. John the Evangelist. Eleven domes formerly topped the basilica, which rivaled Istanbul's Aya Sofya in scale. The barrel-vaulted roof collapsed after a long-ago earthquake, but the church is still an incredible sight, with its labyrinth of halls and marble courtyards. It provides beautiful views both of Selçuk's castle and the Plain of Ephesus. ⊠ *Entrance off St. Jean Sok., just east of İsa Bey Cami,* ☎ *no phone.* 🎫 *$2.* ⊙ *Daily 8–5.*

NEED A
BREAK? Tea and a wide selection of excellent *lokum* (Turkish delight candies) are
sold at tiny **Tadim** (⊠ In Emlak Bankası arcade, ☎ 232/892–3999).
Hikmet Çeliker's family has been making the confection for the last 250
years and shipping it the world over.

**Meryemana,** the House of the Virgin Mary, is becoming an increasingly
popular pilgrimage for Catholics. A small church was built above a leafy
gully on what had been the site of an ancient house believed by many
to have been the place where St. John took the mother of Jesus after
the crucifixion and from which she ascended to heaven. ⊠ *Off Rte. E87,
5 km (3 mi) south of Ephesus.* 🖼 *$1.50.* ☉ *Daily 7:30–sunset.*

## Dining and Lodging

**$$** ✕ **Artemis.** Artemis's superb setting overlooking a verdant valley and
its excellent range of appetizers and meat dishes, particularly its baked
lamb, make it well worth the 9 km (5 mi) ride by taxi or dolmuş from
Selçuk to the picturesque village of Şirince. Try the local wine, which
is produced by the villagers in their homes—an unusual practice in
Turkey. ⊠ *In Şirince (9 km [5 mi] southwest of Selçuk),* ☎ *232/898–
3201 or 232/898–3202,* 𝔽𝔸𝕏 *232/898–3204. MC, V.*

**$** ✕ **Günhan Restaurant.** One of the few places to eat at the Ephesus ruins,
this restaurant prepares a variety of foods, from sandwiches to tradi-
tional stewed Turkish dishes, kebabs, and grilled lamb chops and
steaks. The spot, shaded by awnings, is perfect for a rest and cool drink
before or after a trip to the ruins. ⊠ *Ephesus Ruins,* ☎ *232/892–2291.
MC, V. No dinner.*

**$$** 🏨 **Hotel Pınar.** This four-story concrete hotel is the only one in town
with a government three-star rating, but don't expect more than a mod-
ern motel, with small beds and industrial carpeting. On the plus side,
the management is efficient, the location central, and there is always
plenty of hot water and good pressure in the showers. ⊠ *Sehabettin
Dede Cad., 35920, Selçuk,* ☎ *232/892–2561,* 𝔽𝔸𝕏 *232/892–3033. 40
rooms with bath. Restaurant, bar. MC, V.*

**$$** 🏨 **Kale Han.** A friendly family runs this hotel built around a walled
garden. It is designed to resemble an old stone inn and decorated with
antiques and old photographs. Rooms are simple, with bare whitewashed
walls and dark timber beams. Ask for one facing the castle behind the
hotel. One of the buildings in the garden has a four-bed suite with its
own bathroom. In the airy dining room, with large windows and a big
fireplace, simple grilled meats and fish are served. ⊠ *Atatürk Cad. 49,
Selçuk,* ☎ *232/892–6154,* 𝔽𝔸𝕏 *232/892–2169. 54 rooms with bath, 1
suite. Restaurant, pool. V.* ☕

**$** 🏨 **Esra Pansiyon.** This is one of several pansiyons in Şirince, 9 km (5
mi) outside Selçuk and one of the most beautiful villages in the Aegean
region. The whitewashed walls, the cleanliness and simplicity of its rooms,
and the early morning quietness of its terrace shaded by creeping vines
make the Esra charming and romantic. ⊠ *Şirince, 35927, Selçuk,* ☎
*232/898–3140 or 232/898–3140. 5 rooms, 3 with bath. MC, V.*

**$** 🏨 **Hotel Akay.** This relatively new hotel, set in a quiet residential
neighborhood by the İsa Bey Mosque, has old-Ottoman flourishes—
whitewashed walls inside and out, latticed balconies, arched windows
and doors, kilims on the floor, and copper and brass pots here and there.
⊠ *İsa Bey Cami Kar., Serin Sok. 3, Selçuk,* ☎ *232/892–3172,* 𝔽𝔸𝕏 *232/
892–3009. 16 rooms with bath. Restaurant. MC, V.*

**$** 🏨 **Tusan Efes Motel.** This white-stucco compound next to the Ephesus
archaeological site feels removed from the action since it's surrounded
by eucalyptus trees and next to a campground. Though the rooms are
bare and unimpressive, the location is great: You can get to the site
well ahead of the bus tours. The restaurant prepares delicious Turk-

ish foods. ⊠ *Ephesus*, ☎ *232/892–6060*, 𝖥𝖠𝖷 *232/892–2665. 10 rooms with bath. Restaurant, pool. MC, V.*

**$**
**ᴟ Victoria Hotel.** The name of this four-story hostelry in the heart of Selçuk recalls the owners' time in England. It's a tidy, cheerful little place, with marble floors in the lobby and whitewashed walls set off by honey-colored wood trim throughout. Rooms have delightful views of storks nesting on the ancient columns of an aqueduct. The restaurant is a good bet for traditional Turkish fare. ⊠ *Cengiz Topel Cad. 4, Selçuk*, ☎ *232/892–3203*, 𝖥𝖠𝖷 *232/892–3204. 24 rooms with bath. Restaurant. MC, V.*

# Pamukkale (Hierapolis)

**㉓** *170 km (105 mi) from Selçuk on Rte. E87 (follow road signs after Sarayköy).*

Pamukkale (pronounced pam-*uck*-al-lay) first appears as an enormous, chalky white cliff rising 330 ft from the plains. Mineral-rich volcanic spring water cascades over basins and natural terraces, crystallizing into white curtains of solidified water seemingly suspended in air. It is believed these hot springs can cure rheumatism and other problems. In the mid-1990s, the diversion of water from the springs to fill **thermal pools** in nearby luxury hotels reduced the volume of water reaching the site to a trickle; that, combined with a huge increase in the number of visitors, discolored the water's once-pristine whiteness. Large sections of the site are now cordoned off, and water is pumped across others as the authorities strive to conserve and restore a still-striking natural wonder to its former magnificence. In spite of these efforts, the springs are not as beautiful as they once were, and the area around them is very commercialized.

**Hierapolis** demonstrates how long the magical springs of Pamukkale have cast their spell. The ruins that can be seen today date from the time of the Roman Empire, but there are references to a settlement here as far back as the 5th century BC. Because the sights are spread over about ½ km (¼ mi), prepare for some walking. Between the theater and the Pamukkale Motel are the ruins of a **Temple of Apollo** and a bulky **Byzantine church.** The monumental fountain known as the **Nymphaion,** just north of the Apollo Temple, dates from the 4th century AD. Near the northern city gates, a short drive or long walk, is another indication of the town's former popularity, a vast **necropolis** (cemetery) with more than 1,000 cut-stone sarcophagi spilling all the way down to the base of the hill.

The stone building that enclosed Hierapolis's baths is now the **Pamukkale Müzesi,** a museum with a fine display of marble statues found at the site. ☎ *258/272–2077 for visitor center (for information); 258/272–2034 for museum.* ▨ *$1.* ⊙ *Tues.–Sun. 8–noon and 12:30–6.*

## Lodging

Although Pamukkale village has numerous pansiyons, the best are those clustered in one short strip at the top of the slope, overlooking the hot pools. They cost more than places down below, but they give you a better opportunity to take advantage of Turkey's famous spa waters and offer views over the calcified cliffs. It's unfortunate that most hotels around the pool are grouped in an unsightly mass.

**$$$**
**ᴟ Polat Thermal Hotel.** Clean and spacious, with a full range of facilities, the Polat Thermal is almost a thermal resort in itself, consisting of one- and two-story buildings around a large outdoor pool. The rooms are comfortable, although plain, with functional furnishings and whitewashed walls. ⊠ *Karahayıt, Denizli 20227*, ☎ *258/271–4110*, 𝖥𝖠𝖷 *258/271–4092. 296 rooms. 2 restaurants, 2 pools, sauna, dance club. MC.*

$$$   🏨 **Colossae Hotel Thermal.** More of a health resort than a hotel, the Colossae offers thermal and mud baths and even its own masseurs, beauticians, and health consultants. The low-rise complex is set among well-tended gardens around an Olympic-size pool. The rooms are plush and tastefully decorated in pastel tones, and many have shaded terraces overlooking the gardens. ⊠ *Karahayıt, Denizli 20227,* ☎ *258/271–4156,* FAX *258/271–4250. 230 rooms with bath. 4 restaurants, 2 pools, beauty salon, massage, sauna, Turkish bath, 2 tennis courts, exercise room, dance club. MC, V.* 🐾

$$    🏨 **Koray Hotel.** This hotel is in the village, at the foot of the falls, which are a five-minute walk, but it has its own thermal pool. Rooms are attractive, with simple pine furnishings and whitewashed walls. ⊠ *Karahayıt, Denizli,* ☎ *258/272–2300; 258/272–2222 for reservations,* FAX *258/272–2095. 35 rooms with bath. Restaurant, pool. MC, V.*

# Aphrodisias

★ ㉔   *80 km (50 mi) from Pamukkale, west on E87 and south on Rte. 585 at town of Kuyucak.*

The city of Aphrodite, goddess of love, is one of the largest and best-preserved archaeological sites in Turkey. Though most of what you see today dates from the 1st and 2nd centuries AD, archaeological evidence indicates the local dedication to Aphrodite follows a long history of veneration of pre-Hellenic goddesses, such as the Anatolian mother goddess and the Babylonian god Ishtar. Only about half the site has been excavated to date.

Aphrodisias, which was granted autonomy by the Roman Empire in the late 1st century BC, prospered as a significant center for religion, arts, and literature in the early 1st century AD. Imposing Christianity on its citizens proved far more difficult than granting autonomy to the pagan city, however, because of the cult of Aphrodite. One method used to wipe out remnants of paganism was renaming the city, first Stavropolis (City of the Cross), then simply Caria, which archaeologists believe is the origin of the name of the present-day village of Geyre.

The excavations here have led archaeologists to believe Aphrodisias was a thriving sculpture center, with patrons beyond the borders of the city. The signatures of Aphrodisian artists on statues, fragments, and bases as far away as Greece and Italy attest to this. The towering Babadağ range of mountains, east of the city, offered ancient sculptors a copious supply of white and delicately veined blue-gray marble, which has been used to stunning effect in the statues in the site museum, in the spiral, fluted, and other columns that sprout throughout, and in the delicate reliefs of gods and men, vines, and acanthus leaves on decorative friezes.

The beauty of Aphrodisias is in its details, and a good place to start taking them in is the **site museum**, just past the ticket booth. The museum's collection includes several impressive statues from the site, among them one of Aphrodite herself. Pick up a guide and a map—you'll need them, as the signage is poor.

From the museum, follow the footpath to the right, which makes a circuit around the site and ends up back at the museum. The **Tetrapylon** is a monumental gateway with four rows of columns and some of the better remaining friezes. The **Temple of Aphrodite** was built in the 1st century BC on the model of the great temples at Ephesus. Its gate and many of its columns are still standing; some bear inscriptions naming the donor of the column. Next to the temple is the fine **Odeon**, an intimate, semicircular concert hall and public meeting room. Farther on is the **stadium**, which once was the scene of footraces, boxing and wrestling matches, and other competitions. One of the best preserved of its kind anywhere, the stadium could seat up to 30,000 spectators. The **theater,** built into the side of a small hill, is still being excavated. Its 5,000 white-marble seats are simply dazzling on a bright day. The adjacent **School of Philosophy** has a colonnaded courtyard with chambers lining both sides where teachers would work with small groups of students. ☎ *256/448–8084 for museum.* ⌦ *Site $2.50, museum $2.50 additional.* ⊙ *Site and museum daily 8:30–5.*

## Değirmendere (Colophon)

❷❺ *35 km (22 mi) from Selçuk, west to Pamucak, north on coastal road, and then north on marked road to Ahmetbeyli and Değirmendere.*

Less than 2 km (1 mi) west of the present-day village of Değirmendere is the ancient site of **Colophon,** the farthest inland of the Ionian cities. Colophon prospered in the 8th and 7th centuries BC, and the fine horses and fierce cavalry for which it was known were often enlisted as allies by foreign armies to finish off unending wars. The popularity of the nearby oracle at Claros, the fertility of their land, and their skill as mariners made the citizens of this city very wealthy—so wealthy, it was said, it was possible to spot more than a 1,000 musk-scented men dressed in purple strolling through the agora (musk and the dye to make the color purple were very expensive). In Colophon's heyday women musicians were paid an official salary by the government to play from dawn to dusk, and puppies were sacrificed to the Wayside Goddess of the underworld. The combination of extreme wealth and apparent decadence, along with the founding of nearby Ephesus, brought about Colophon's decline. In the 3rd century, the population was moved by Lysimachus to his new, walled city of Ephesus, and according to Pausanias, those who resisted were "buried left of the road to Claros." Today there is not much to see at Colophon except the remains of a wall, though excavations have uncovered streets, a *stoa* (colonnaded porch), and a temple dedicated to Demeter.

**Claros,** 7 km (4 mi) south of Colophon, was the site of a highly regarded oracle and a **Temple of Apollo,** now standing alongside the road. Claros is mentioned in Homer's verses as the site of an important cult as far back as the 7th and 6th centuries BC. Because the location, in a low-lying valley that was probably the site of a sacred spring and wood, is subject to flooding, the temple is often buried in mud, but ongoing excavations should be clearing up that problem. Excavations have also revealed much information about how the oracles were performed in the temple. A mazelike corridor leads you to the sacred oracle chamber, where annually appointed male prophets would drink holy water and make predictions through a priest and a *thespios,* a composer of poetry, who would versify the prophet's utterings. Fragments of colossal statues of Apollo, Artemis, and Leto are scattered about; it's estimated that the statue of Apollo was 24 or 25 ft high. Inscriptions of oracles from the temple have been found as far away as southern Russia, Algeria, Sardinia, and even Great Britain. According to one source, an oracle at this temple predicted the destruction of Europe and Asia in a war over the beautiful Helen.

The crumbling remains of **Notion,** Colophon's port, are scattered along a cliff top 2 km (1 mi) to the south of Claros along the same road. After Lysimachus depopulated Colophon to furnish Ephesus, Notion had a brief period of prosperity, when it was known as New Colophon, but as Ephesus grew, Notion's population and wealth dwindled. You can make out the foundations of a temple, an agora, and a theater. Down below is a beach.

# Kuşadası

**㉖** *20 km (12 mi) southwest of Selçuk on Rte. 515.*

One of the most popular resort towns in the southern Aegean, Kuşadası is an ideal base from which to explore the surrounding area. It was a small fishing village as late as the 1970s, but now is a sprawling, hyperactive town packed with curio shops and a year-round population of around 60,000, which swells several times over in summer with the influx of tourists (particularly Brits) and Turks with vacation homes. Good hotels and restaurants are more plentiful here than elsewhere along the coast, and there's even a bit of nightlife. Kuşadası is the jumping-off point for the 2½-hour boat trip to the Greek island of Samos. Tickets, which should be obtained a day in advance, can be purchased at any travel agency in town (☞ Guided Tours *in* The Aegean Coast A to Z, *below*); the cost is about $35 each way, and departures are at 8 and 5 daily.

A causeway off Kadınlar Denizi, just south of the harbor, connects Kuşadası to an old **Genoese castle** on Güvercin Adası (Pigeon Island). Today the site of a popular disco and several teahouses with gardens and sea views, the fortress was home to three Turkish brothers in the 16th century. These infamous pirates—Barbarossa, Oruc, and Hayrettin—pillaged the coasts of Spain and Italy and sold passengers and crews from captured ships into slavery in Algiers and Constantinople. Rather than fight them, Süleyman the Magnificent (ruled 1520–66) hired Hayrettin as his grand admiral and set him loose on enemies in the Mediterranean. The strategy worked: Hayrettin won victory after victory and was heaped with honors and riches.

Kuşadası's 300-year-old **caravansary** (✉ Atatürk Bul. 1), now the Club Kervansaray (☞ Dining and Lodging, *below*), is loaded with Ottoman atmosphere. Its public areas are worth a look even if you're not staying here.

If you're looking for beaches, either head north from Kuşadası to Pamucak or travel 33 km (20 mi) south to lovely, wooded **Samsundağ Milli Parkı** (Samsundağ National Park, also known as Dilek Peninsula National Park), which has good hiking trails and several quiet stretches of sandy beach. To get there, take the coast road, marked Güzelçanlı or Devutlar, from about 10 km (6 mi) south of Kuşadası. It's open April–December. ☞ *Park $2.* ☉ *Apr.–Dec.*

## Dining and Lodging

**$$$**  ✕ **Sultan Han.** This excellent restaurant is in the heart of town, just off Barbaros Hayrettin Caddesi, the main shopping street, in an old house built around a courtyard with a stately, gigantic palm tree. You can dine in the open-air courtyard or upstairs in small rooms piled with kilims, where you sit on cushions at low brass tables. Much of the seafood is grilled. Fish baked in salt is a local specialty. ✉ *Bahar Sok. 8,* ☎ *256/614–6380. Reservations essential. No credit cards.*

**$$**  ✕ **Ada Restaurant.** At this spacious Pigeon Island restaurant, choose from local fish, appetizers, and kebabs—all displayed at the entrance along with their prices. The food is good, but most people come here for the location, not the cuisine. ✉ *Güvercin Adası,* ☎ *256/614–1725. AE, MC, V.*

**$$**  ✕ **Ali Baba Restaurant.** An appetizing and colorful display of the day's catch meets you at the entrance to this waterside fish restaurant. The decor is simple, the view over the bay is soothing, and the food is fabulous. For starters, try the cold black-eyed pea salad, the marinated octopus salad, or the fried calamari. Follow it with a grilled meat dish or whatever fish is in season. It's worth reserving in advance since this place usually fills up by 8 PM. ⊠ *Belediye Turistik Çarşısı 5,* ☎ *256/614–1551. Reservations essential. MC, V.*

**$$** ✕ **Alize.** Five minutes' walk from the waterfront, this excellent bistro more than makes up for its lack of a sea view with a superb range of meat, fish, and pasta dishes. It's a favorite hangout for locals, particularly the young trendy set for whom it doubles as a café and bar. There is live acoustic music in the evenings. ⊠ *Karagöz Sok. 7, Sağlık Cad.,* ☎ *256/612–0360. MC, V.*

**$$** ✕ **Tarihi Çınar Et.** This popular eatery on the outskirts of town takes its name from the 800-year-old Oriental plane tree (*çınar* in Turkish) whose spreading branches shade its tables. House specialties are lamb and chicken cooked on a spit. There is also a wide range of *mezes* and superb ice cream. ⊠ *Davutlar Yolu, Saraydamlı,* ☎ *256/681–1177. MC, V.*

**$** ✕ **Özurfa.** The focus at this Turkish fast-food spot is kebabs. The Urfa kebab—spicy, grilled slices of lamb on pita bread—is the house specialty, and the fish kebabs are tasty. The location just off Barbaros Hayrettin Caddesi is convenient to the market. ⊠ *Cephane Sok. 7,* ☎ *256/612–6070. No credit cards.*

**$$$** ⊞ **Club Kervansaray.** A refurbished 300-year-old inn that was once a way station for camel caravans, this hotel in the center of town has massive armor-plated doors at its main entrance and is decorated in Ottoman style. The central courtyard—where the camels once were kept—is paved with marble and planted with palm trees. Rooms are decorated with kilims and Turkish folk art. In the dressy Turkish restaurant, there's live entertainment: singers, perhaps a belly dancer, and, later, a pop band. ⊠ *Atatürk Bul. 2, 09400,* ☎ *256/614–4115,* FAX *256/614–2423. 26 rooms with bath. Restaurant, bar, nightclub. AE, DC, MC, V.* ✾

**$$$** ⊞ **Kismet.** Surrounded by beautifully maintained gardens, the Kismet
★ is set on a promontory overlooking the marina on one side and the Aegean on the other and feels almost like a private Mediterranean villa. Each room has a private balcony, most with sea views. Kismet's popularity makes reservations a must. ⊠ *Akyar Mev., Türkmen Mah., 09400,* ☎ *256/618–1290,* FAX *256/618–1295. 107 rooms with bath. Restaurant, tennis court, beach. MC, V. Closed Nov.–Mar.* ✾

**$$** ⊞ **Atınç Otel.** The Atınç, a mid-rise hotel, is in a good location: It's just a 5- to 10-minute walk from the center of town, but not so close you're bothered by the noise. Other pluses include the Aegean views from the front rooms and the rooftop pool that looks out on the whole town. Guest rooms have balconies but not much style. ⊠ *Atatürk Bul. 42, 09400,* ☎ *256/614–7608,* FAX *256/614–4967. 75 rooms with bath. 2 restaurants, 2 bars, pool. MC, V.*

**$$** ⊞ **Efe Otel.** This midprice hotel sits on the waterfront a little beyond the path to Pigeon Island. A four-story whitewashed box with dark-wood trim, it's small but has a personable staff. Rooms are nondescript— the carpeting drab, the walls bare, and the beds low, with wooden frames—but many have balconies and views of Pigeon Island. ⊠ *Güvercin Ada Cad. 37, 09400,* ☎ *256/614–3661,* FAX *256/614–3662. 84 rooms with bath. 2 restaurants, bar. AE, MC, V.*

**$** ⊞ **Bahar Pansiyon.** A block from Hayrettin Barbaros Caddesi is this cozy hotel. Front rooms have balconies, and all are quiet, affordable, and simply furnished. ⊠ *Cephane Sok. 12, 09400,* ☎ *256/614–1191,* FAX *256/614–9359. 16 rooms with bath. Restaurant, bar. No credit cards.*

**$** ⊞ **Liman Hotel.** Very close to the port in a whitewashed, narrow building with black cast-iron balconies, the Liman has basic but clean rooms with comfortable furniture. Be sure to ask for one in the front of the building, facing the sea. The staff is attentive and sincere. ⊠ *Buyral Sok. 4, Kıbrıs Cad., 09400,* ☎ *256/612–3149. 16 rooms with bath. Indoor café, outdoor café, air-conditioning. No credit cards.*

### Nightlife

The **Kapı Bar** (⊠ Cephane Sok. 20, ☏ 256/614–7070), in the market area, is a club with a dance floor. The **Club Kervansaray** (⊠ Atatürk Bul. 2, ☏ 256/614–4115) has dining, dancing, and a show on most nights. A younger crowd heads to the vast **Ecstasy Bar** (⊠ Sakarya Sok. 22, ☏ 256/613–1391), which plays the latest chart-topping sounds and has an official capacity of 1,000 spread over two floors. On Barlar Sokak, Kuşadası's bar strip, the spacious and popular **Queen Victoria** (☏ no phone) has live music in summer. There are several Irish and British-style pubs farther along **Barlar Sokak.** For a lively night of dancing, young Turks and energetic tourists walk across the causeway to **Pigeon Island** to the "Disco"—there's no other name on the sign, but you can hear its music almost everywhere on this minuscule landfall.

## Priene

★  ㉗  *37 km (23 mi) from Kuşadası, southeast on Rte. 515, south on Rte. 525, west on Rte. 09–55 (follow signs).*

Priene sits spectacularly atop a steep hill above the flat valley of the Büyük Menderes (Maeander River). Dating from about 350 BC, the city you see today was still under construction in 334, when Alexander the Great liberated the Ionian settlements from Persian rule. At that time it was a thriving port. But as in Ephesus, the harbor silted over, commerce moved to neighboring Miletus, and the city's prosperity waned. As a result, the Romans never rebuilt Priene, and the simpler Greek style predominates as in few other ancient cities in Turkey. Excavated by British archaeologists in 1868–69, it's smaller than Ephesus and far less grandiose.

From the parking area, the walk up to the Priene ruins is fairly steep; because the routes through it are well marked, you won't need a map. After passing through the old city walls, you follow the city's original main thoroughfare; note the drainage gutters and the grooves worn into the marble paving stones by the wheels of 4th-century BC chariots. Continuing west, you come to the well-preserved *bouleterion* (council chamber) on the left. Its 10 rows of seats flank an orchestra pit with a little altar, decorated with bulls' heads and laurel leaves, at the center. Passing through the doors on the opposite side of the council chamber takes you to the **Sacred Stoa,** a colonnaded civic center, and the edge of the **agora,** the marketplace. Farther west along the broad promenade are the remains of a row of **private houses,** each of which typically has two or three rooms on two floors; of the upper stories, only traces of a few stairwells remain. In the largest house a statue of Alexander was found.

A block or so farther along the main street is the **Temple of Athena.** Its design—the work of Pytheos, architect of the Mausoleum of Halicarnassus (one of the Seven Wonders of the Ancient World)—was repeatedly copied at other sites in the Greek empire. Alexander apparently chipped in on construction costs. The temple was not a place for worshipers to gather but a dwelling for the goddess Athena; only priests could enter. Earthquakes have toppled the columns; the five that have been reerected evoke the former appearance of the temple, which once had a stunning view over the Menderes Valley. A walk north and then east along the track leads to the well-preserved little **theater,** sheltered on all sides by pine trees. Enter through the stage door into the orchestra section; note the five front-row VIP seats, carved thrones with lions' feet. If you scramble up a huge rock known as Samsun Dağı (behind the theater and to your left as you face the seats), you will find the scanty remains of the **Sanctuary of Demeter,** goddess of the harvest; a few bits of columns and walls remain, as well as a big hole through which blood of sacrificial victims was poured as a gift to the deities of the underworld. Since few people make it up here, it is an incredibly peaceful spot, with a terrific view over Priene and the plains. Above this, should you care to go farther, are the remnants of a Hellenistic fortress. ☏ *no phone.* ⌨ *$1.50.* ◷ *Daily 8:30–6.*

## Miletus

**28** *16 km (10 mi) south of Priene on Rte. 09–55.*

Miletus was one of the greatest commercial centers of the Greek world before its harbor silted over. The first settlers were Minoan Greeks from Crete, who arrived between 1400 BC and 1200 BC. The Ionians, who arrived 200 years later, slaughtered the male population and married the widows. The philosopher Thales was born here in the early 6th century BC; he calculated the height of the pyramids at Giza, suggested that the universe was actually a rational place despite its apparent disorder, and coined the phrase "Know thyself." An intellectual center, the city was also home to the mathematicians Anaximenes, who held that air was the single element behind the diversity of nature, and Anaximander, whose ideas anticipated the theory of evolution and the concept of the indestructibility of matter. Like the other Ionian cities, Miletus was passed from one ruling empire to another and was successively governed by Alexander's generals Antigonus and Lysimachus and Pergamum's Attalids, among others. Under the Romans the town finally regained some control over its own affairs and shared in the prosperity of the region. St. Paul preached here before the harbor became impassable and the city had to be abandoned once and for all.

The archaeological site is sprawled out along a desolate plain. Well-marked trails make a guide or map unnecessary. The parking lot is right outside the city's most magnificent building—the **Great Theater,** a remarkably intact 25,000-seat amphitheater built by the Ionians and kept up by the Romans. Along the third to sixth rows some inscriptions reserving seats for notables are still visible, and the vaulted passages leading to the seats have the feel of a modern sporting arena. Climb to the top of the theater for a look at the defensive walls built by the Byzantines and a view across the ancient city.

To see the rest of the ruins, follow the dirt track to the right of the theater. A stand of buildings marks what was once a broad processional avenue. The series begins with the **Delphinion,** a sanctuary of Apollo; a **Seljuk hamam** added to the site in the 15th century, with pipes for hot and cold water still visible; a **stoa** (colonnaded porch) with several reerected Ionic columns; the foundations of a **Roman bath** and **gymnasium;** and the first story of the **Nymphaion,** all that remains of the once highly ornate three-story structure, resembling the Library of Celsus at Ephesus, that once distributed water to the rest of the city.

To the south, the dirt track becomes a tree-lined lane that leads to the **İlyas Bey Cami,** a mosque built in 1404 in celebration of its builder and namesake's escape from Tamerlane, the Mongol terror. The mosque is now a romantic ruin: The ceiling is cracked, dust covers the tiles, and birds roost inside. The path from the mosque back to the parking lot passes a small museum, the **Miletus Müzesi,** containing some finds from the site and the surrounding area. ☏ *no phone.* ⌨ *Ruins $1.50, museum $2.* ◷ *Tues.–Sun. 8:30–6.*

# Didyma (Didim)

**㉙** *20 km (12 mi) south of Miletus on Rte. 09–55.*

Didyma (Didim in Turkish) is famous for its magnificent **Temple of Apollo.** As grand in scale as the Parthenon—measuring 623 ft by 167 ft—the temple has 124 well-preserved columns, some still supporting their architraves. Started in 300 BC and under construction for five centuries, it was never completed, and some of the columns remain unfluted. The temple's oracles rivaled those of Delphi. Beneath the courtyard is a network of underground corridors where the temple priests would consult the oracle. The corridor walls would throw the oracle's voice into deep and ghostly echoes, which the priests would interpret. The tradition of seeking advice from sacred oracles probably started long before the arrival of the Greeks; in all likelihood, the Greeks converted an older Anatolian cult based at the site into their own religion. The Greek oracle had a good track record, and at the birth of Alexander the Great (356 BC), predicted that he would be victorious over the Persians, that his general Seleucus would later become king, and that Trajan would become an emperor.

The popularity of the oracle dwindled with the rise of Christianity, around AD 385. The temple was later excavated by French and German archaeologists; its statues are long gone, hauled back to England by Sir Charles Newton in 1858. Fragments of bas-reliefs on display by the entrance to the site include a gigantic head of Medusa and a small statue of Poseidon and his wife, Amphitrite. ☎ *No phone.* 🎟 *$1.50.* ☉ *Daily 8:30–6.*

For a rest after all this history, continue another 5 km (3 mi) south to **Altınkum.** The white-sand beach, which stretches for a bit less than 1 km (½ mi), is bordered by a row of decent seafood restaurants, all facing the water, and some small hotels.

*En Route*   Shortly before you reach Milas, along the road to Bodrum, Route 525 skirts the south shore of **Çamiçi Gölü** (Bafa Gölü, or Lake Bafa). The lake is relatively small and largely undeveloped, especially away from the main road. For a real change of pace, rent a boat to go across the lake, or drive the rough 10-km (6-mi) road along the eastern shore, to the village of Kapıkiri and the ancient ruins of Heracleia. Though a minor town in antiquity, Heracleia has a wonderful setting, surrounded by high mountains. The villagers are Türkilometersen, descended from the Turkish tribes that settled Anatolia in the 13th and 14th centuries. The ruins, a Temple of Athena and some city walls, are also unusual: They were left by Carians, a native Asian people who adopted Greek language and culture. On an islet facing the village are the remains of a Byzantine monastery, and huge volcanic boulders are scattered about. The combination of elements is incredibly atmospheric.

# Bodrum

**㉚** *161 km (100 mi) from Kuşadası, southeast on Rte. 515 to Rte. 525 south to Rte. 330 heading southwest; 125 km (78 mi) from Didyma, northeast on town road to Rte. 525 south to Rte. 330 southwest.*

Bodrum, known as Halicarnassus in antiquity, has a good claim to being Turkey's leading resort. The modern town stretches along the shore of two crescent-shape bays and has for years been the favorite haunt of the Turkish upper classes. Today thousands of foreign visitors have joined the elite, and the area is bursting at the seams with villas, hotels, guest houses, cafés, restaurants, and discos. But it is still beautiful, with its gleaming whitewashed buildings covered with bougainvillea and its un-fettered vistas of the sparkling bays.

Founded around 1000 BC, Halicarnassus was one of the first Greek colonies in Asia. The northern cities of the Aegean formed the Ionian League, but those farther south—Halicarnassus, Kos, Rhodes, Knidos, Lalysos, Lindos, Camiros—joined the Dorian Federation. Halicarnassus reached its height under Mausolus, who ruled from 377 BC to 353 BC as a *satrap* (governor) of what was then a distant outpost of the far-flung Persian Empire. After his death, his wife (who was also his sister), Artemisia, succeeded him. On learning that a woman ruled Halicarnassus, Rhodes sent its fleet to seize the city, only to be promptly—and soundly—defeated.

Artemisia ordered the construction of the great white-marble tomb for Mausolus at Halicarnassus that made the Seven Wonders list and gave us the word *mausoleum*. The **mausoleum** consisted of a solid rectangular base topped by 36 Ionic columns, surmounted by a pyramid, and crowned with a massive statue of Mausolus and Artemisia riding a chariot. The mausoleum has been dismantled, and the site—two blocks north of the bay and indicated by signs on Neyzen Tevfik Caddesi, the shore road ringing the west bay—is not worth the price of admission. ☎ 252/316–1095. 🎟 $4. ☉ Tues.–Sun. 8:30–noon and 1–5.

The ancient **theater** is one of the few surviving pre-Hellenic theaters in Asia Minor and thus one of the oldest; it's a popular place to take in a sunset. ⊠ North of mausoleum. 🎟 Free.

The **Petronion** (Castle of St. Peter) is the most outstanding historic site in modern Bodrum and one of the great showpieces of late-medieval military architecture. The European crusaders known as the Knights of St. John seized Bodrum in 1402 and dismantled the mausoleum, using many of the stones to build the Petronion. The castle and its beautiful gardens, visible from every part of town, look as if they belong in a fairy tale. On the ramparts, you may recognize prominent coats of arms—those of the Plantagenets, d'Aubussons, and others. The five turrets are named after the homelands of the knights, who came from England, France, Germany, Italy, and Spain. Inside is an unusual and interesting **Museum of Underwater Archaeology**, with treasures recovered from historic wrecks discovered off the Aegean Coast. ⊠ Kale Cad., ☎ 252/316–2516. 🎟 $4. ☉ Tues.–Sun. 8:30–noon and 1–5.

## Dining and Lodging

$$$ ✕ **Restaurant Han.** This restaurant benefits from a fine location, in an 18th-century caravansary with a tree-shaded courtyard a block from the harbor. The decor is minimal—you eat at trestle tables in the open air. But the kebabs, köfte, and grilled fresh prawns are crowd pleasers. So is the belly dancer who performs most nights. ⊠ Kale Cad. 29, ☎ 252/316–7951. Reservations essential in summer. No credit cards.

$$ ✕ **Amphora.** The options are dazzling: 20 or so mezes (including eggplant pureed, sautéed with garlic, or in tomato sauce) and two dozen kinds of kebabs. Another plus is the setting, opposite the marina at the edge of town in an old stone building decorated with kilims and boating and fishing gear. ⊠ Neyzen Tevfik Cad. 172, ☎ 252/316–2368. Reservations essential in summer. MC, V.

$$ ✕ **Club Pirinç.** This restaurant is notable for its Turkish-French cuisine and pleasant bar. ⊠ Yeni Çarşi 8, ☎ 252/316–2902. MC, V.

$$ ✕ **Kortan Restaurant.** This seaside fish house has outdoor seating with
★ views of Bodrum's castle and of Chios, off the coast. The better dishes include fish kebabs, octopus salad, and whatever the catch of the day

happens to be, usually served grilled. ✉ *Cumhuriyet Cad. 32,* ☎ *252/ 316–1241. Reservations essential in summer. AE, MC, V.*

**$$$** 🏨 **Çömça-Manzara Hotel.** On a hill facing Bodrum's castle across the bay, this hotel complex looks like a little Mediterranean village. But don't expect high-style furnishings—the interiors recall American motels of the 1950s. Each of the 30 small whitewashed buildings has apartments—each with a living room, kitchen, and terrace—as well as ordinary guest rooms. In peak season half board may be required. ✉ *Kumbahçe Mah., Meteoroloji Yanı, 48400,* ☎ *252/316–2012 or 252/ 316–1719,* 𝔽𝔸𝕏 *252/316–1720. 30 apartment units and 60 rooms with bath. Restaurant, pool. AE, DC, MC, V.*

**$$$** 🏨 **Lavanta Hotel.** Surrounded by well maintained grounds on a hill-
★ side overlooking the Bodrum peninsula just outside the village of Ya-likavak, the Lavanta is a tranquil, distinguished retreat in an area where many hotels are bland and geared to package tourism. All of the attractive rooms overlook the sea from private terraces and are furnished with tasteful traditional pieces and antiques the owners, Tosun and Maria Merey, have collected from around the world. Dinner, served to hotel guests only, features traditional Turkish home cooking. ✉ *Yalikavak-Bodrum, 48430,* ☎ *252/385–2167,* 𝔽𝔸𝕏 *252/385–2290. 11 apartment units and 8 rooms with bath. Pool. MC, V.* 🐌

**$$** 🏨 **Ayaz Hotel.** This hotel is on a small bay just east of the Bodrum harbor, away from the noise and bustle of town, yet less than a five-minute drive from the center. It has its own gardens and a beach with a bar where you can listen to the waves and while away the hours. The guest rooms are done in contemporary style and have balconies and sea views. ✉ *On Gümbet Bay, 48400,* ☎ *252/316–1174 or 252/316–2956,* 𝔽𝔸𝕏 *252/316–4751. 96 rooms with bath. Restaurant, bar, pool, waterski-ing, playground. V.*

**$$** 🏨 **Manastir Hotel Bodrum.** The bar in this comfortable whitewashed-stucco Mediterranean-style hotel was once the site of a monastery. Front rooms have balconies and look out on the Petronion; all are cool and spacious, with whitewashed walls and tasteful, modern furnishings. ✉ *Barış Sitesi Mev., Kumbahçe, 48400,* ☎ *252/316–2854,* 𝔽𝔸𝕏 *252/316– 2112. 59 rooms with bath. 2 restaurants, bar, 2 pools, sauna, tennis court. AE, DC, V.*

**$$** 🏨 **Maya Hotel and Pansiyon.** Though it's in the center of town, this hotel feels secluded, with its private garden and swimming pool bordered by bright flowers. Rooms, in low white-stucco buildings, are utilitarian and nondescript, with Scandinavian-style furniture. In the associated pansiyon, on a tiny side street behind the marina, rooms are smaller, and you have to walk over to the hotel for a dip in the pool, but the prices are lower. ✉ *Gerence Sok. 32, Gümbet, 48400,* ☎ *252/ 316–4741,* 𝔽𝔸𝕏 *252/316–4745. 72 rooms with bath. Restaurant, bar, pool, sauna, exercise room. MC, V.*

**$** 🏨 **Mylasa Pansiyon.** An Australian archaeologist who found it hard to leave Bodrum runs this pansiyon in an attractive white-stucco building in the center of town. It has a comfortable lounge and a roof deck with a view of the Aegean. Rooms are just what you find in most pansiyons—the beds are low, with simple wooden frames, and there's no decor to speak of. ✉ *Cumhuriyet Cad. 34, 48400,* ☎ *252/316–1846,* 𝔽𝔸𝕏 *252/316–1254. 16 rooms with bath. Bar, breakfast room. MC, V.*

## Nightlife

The scene in Bodrum is more sophisticated than anywhere else along the Aegean. The **Halikarnas Disco** (✉ Cumhuriyet Cad. 178, ☎ 252/ 316–8000) bills itself as "probably the most amazing nightclub in the world." It is, in fact, rather like discos more commonly found in western Mediterranean resorts, complete with fog machines and laser lights.

## ONE LAST TRAVEL TIP:

# Pack an easy way to reach the world.

**123 456 7891 2345**
J.D. SMITH

Wherever you travel, the MCI WorldCom Card℠ is the easiest way to stay in touch. You can use it to call to and from more than 125 countries worldwide. And you can earn bonus miles every time you use your card. So go ahead, travel the world. MCI WorldCom℠ makes it even more rewarding. For additional access codes, visit **www.wcom.com/worldphone**.

## MCI WORLDCOM.

## EASY TO CALL WORLDWIDE

1. Just dial the WorldPhone® access number of the country you're calling from.

2. Dial or give the operator your MCI WorldCom Card number.

3. Dial or give the number you're calling.

| | |
|---|---|
| Argentina | 0800-222-6249 |
| Belize (A) | 557 or 815 |
| Brazil | 000-8012 |
| Chile | 800-207-300 |
| Colombia ◆ | 980-9-16-0001 |

| | |
|---|---|
| Costa Rica (A) ◆ | 0800-012-2222 |
| Ecuador ⁛ | 999-170 |
| Egypt ◆ | 7955770 |
| El Salvador (A) | 800-1567 |
| Guatemala ◆ | 99-99-189 |
| Honduras (A) ⁛ | 8000-122 |
| Israel | 1-800-920-2727 |
| Mexico | 01-800-021-8000 |
| Nicaragua | 166 |
| Panama (A) | 00800-001-0108 |
| Turkey ◆ | 00-8001-1177 |
| Venezuela ◆ ⁛ | 800-11140 |

**(A)** Calls back to U.S. only. ◆ Public phones may require deposit of coin or phone card for dial tone. ⁛ Limited availability.

## EARN FREQUENT FLIER MILES

**Bureau de change**

**Cambio**

**外国為替**

# In this city, you can find money on almost any street.

## NO-FEE FOREIGN EXCHANGE

The Chase Manhattan Bank has over 80 convenient locations near New York City destinations such as:

Times Square
Rockefeller Center
Empire State Building
2 World Trade Center
United Nations Plaza

**Exchange any of 75 foreign currencies**

 CHASE

**THE RIGHT RELATIONSHIP IS EVERYTHING.®**

**Hadigari** (✉ Dr. Alım Bey Cad. 37, ☎ 252/313–1960) and the **Mavi Bar** (✉ Cumhuriyet Cad. 175, ☎ 252/316–3932) are venerable meccas in Bodrum drinking circles, attracting Turkish artists, writers, and their numerous hangers-on. **MM Dancing** (✉ Dr. Alım Bey Cad., 1025 Sok. 44, ☎ 252/316–2725), a bar and nightclub near the marina, is a pleasant place to while away the night. MM also has a floating disco on a huge boat tied up at the quay, which sails out to sea after 1 am, when other nightclubs are required by law to turn the volume down or close up altogether.

## Outdoor Activities and Sports

### CRUISES

The primary place to go on a cruise in Bodrum is in the mountain-rimmed **Gökova Körfezi** (Gökova Gulf), the body of water between the Bodrum Peninsula and the Datça Peninsula, 30 km (18 mi) or so to the south. The densely pine-forested region along the coast is punctuated by tiny farming and fishing settlements. Travel agencies in Bodrum can provide information and make arrangements in advance, or you can make arrangements before you leave home (☞ Tour Operators *in* the Gold Guide). The cost of a cruise is about $600 a day for a boat with six double berths and crew.

Although there are many classical and Byzantine remains along the Datça Peninsula, **Knidos**, at its tip, is the only major site (☞ Chapter 5). **Sedir Island** (and the ancient city called Cedreae), due north of Marmaris, is delightful when not overrun with day-trippers attracted by the golden sands of the lovely Cleopatra Beach. Mark Antony is said to have sent for the sand from the Sahara to please his love.

For information about cruises, contact: **Era Tourism** (☎ 252/316–2310, 🖷 252/316–5338); **Neyzen Tours** (☎ 252/316–7204); **Borda Yachting** (☎ 252/316–6252 or 216/313–7764, 🖷 252/316–6198); and **Motif Travel** (☎ 252/316–1536, 🖷 252/316–3522). Also *see* Tour Operators *in* the Gold Guide.

### DIVING

The sea around Bodrum provides some of the best diving in the Aegean. For further details contact **Motif Diving** (✉ Neyzen Tevfik Cad. 80, ☎ 252/316–6198) or **Bodrum Spor** (✉ Yeni Çarşi 4, ☎ 252/313–2074).

# THE AEGEAN COAST A TO Z

## Arriving and Departing

### By Boat

#### FROM ECEABAT

You can reach Çanakkale by car and passenger ferry across the Dardanelles, the straits dividing Europe and Asia. Boats depart on the hour from Eceabat, near the battlefields, about 330 km (205 mi) and a three- or four-hour drive from Istanbul. The crossing takes about 30 minutes, and the cost is $6 for a car and driver and 50¢ per additional passenger and per passenger on foot.

#### FROM ISTANBUL

**Turkish Maritime Lines** (✉ Rıhtım Cad. 1, ☎ 212/244–0207 for information; 212/249–9222 for reservations) operates passenger and car ferry services to İzmir. Boats leave in the afternoon and arrive the next morning. Fares range from $25 for a single seat to $110 for a suite accommodating from two to four. In summer there is also service between İzmir and Marseille, Genoa, Venice, and Piraeus, the port for Athens.

## By Bus

Buses, typically modern and air-conditioned, operate between the larger and smaller towns and from there depart for the major archaeological sites. Typical travel times are: Istanbul to Çanakkale, six hours; Çanakkale to İzmir (via Bergama, Ayvalık, and Ayvacık), six hours; İzmir to Bodrum, 3½ hours.

## By Car

A car is a plus for exploring this region since it allows you to stop at will at picturesque towns and to track down lesser-known ruins and less crowded beaches. However, it's a long haul from Istanbul to İzmir—565 km (350 mi), an exhausting seven- or eight-hour drive. To make this trip, pick up Route 200 heading west toward Çanakkale. From there the E87 follows the coast south all the way to Kuşadası, where it turns inland toward Antalya. Route 525 continues along the coast, past Priene and Miletus; Route 330 branches off in Bodrum and connects with the main Mediterranean highways.

## By Plane

The major airport serving the region is **Adnan Menderes Airport,** 2 km (16 mi) south of İzmir. **Turkish Airlines** (THY; ☎ 212/252–1106 for information in Istanbul; 212/663–6363 for reservations in Istanbul; 232/274–2424 in İzmir; 232/445–5363, extension 232 for reservations in İzmir) and **Istanbul Airlines** (☎ 212/231–7526 or 212/231–7527) make the hour-long flight direct from Istanbul. In summer you have two other options on THY: Flying nonstop from London or Frankfurt into İzmir. Or you can connect through Istanbul to **Dalaman Airport,** on the Mediterranean coast, near Marmaris, and drive north. Dalaman is 395 km (245 mi) from İzmir.

## By Train

Trains to İzmir from Istanbul take a good 10 to 12 hours. You start out by taking a boat across the Sea of Marmara, and about four hours later you connect with a train at Bandırma. Take the morning departure rather than the night one if you want to enjoy the scenery of the cruise and the northern Aegean. Contact **Turkish Maritime Lines** (☞ *above*) in Istanbul for schedules and fares.

# Getting Around

## By Boat

The Aegean Coast is one of the more popular routes for yachting. In most towns the harbor is in the city center, and the main archaeological sites are a cheap, easy cab ride away. Kuşadası and Bodrum are charter centers.

## By Bus

Though it's slower and more restrictive than traveling by car, bus travel is a viable option if you don't want to drive. It's exceptionally inexpensive, as fares are rarely more than a few dollars, and all the towns and attractions are well served by bus. When you arrive at the main bus station for one town, simply ask about connecting service to the next town along the line.

## By Car

Except around İzmir, where heavy and hectic traffic requires serious concentration to keep you from getting lost, the highways are generally in good condition, the traffic fairly light, and the main attractions relatively close together. As you head south, distances are: Çanakkale to Bergama, 245 km (152 mi); Bergama to İzmir, 98 km (61 mi); İzmir to Ephesus, 79 km (49 mi); Ephesus to Bodrum, 172 km (107 mi).

CAR RENTALS

All the following agencies are in İzmir: **Airtour Türkiye** (☎ 232/441–6252). **Avis** (☎ 232/441–4417 or 232/441–4418). **Budget** (☎ 232/482–0505; 232/274–2203 at the airport). **Hertz** (☎ 232/274–2193).

# Contacts and Resources

## Emergencies

**Ambulance** (☎ 112). **Gendarme** (☎ 156), only in rural areas. **Police** (☎ 155). Unfortunately, the person who answers the telephone is unlikely to speak English. Your best bet is to ask a Turkish speaker to place the call for you.

## Guided Tours

Travel agencies in all the major towns organize tours of the historical sites. At the harbor in Ayvalık, dozens of small tour boats operate two-hour outings along the coast and to nearby islands (around $5, $10 including a meal). *See* Tour Operators *in* the Gold Guide for companies operating longer boat trips.

In İzmir, go to **Setur Travel** (✉ Atatürk Cad. 194/A, ☎ 232/463–6100). In Kuşadası, try **Last Minute Tours** (✉ Central Station 11, ☎ 256/614–6332 or 256/612–3365) and **Akdeniz Turizm** (✉ Atatürk Bul. 26, ☎ 256/614–1140), as well as travel agencies along Teyyare Caddesi in Kuşadası, in order to arrange escorted tours to Ephesus; to Priene, Miletus, and Didyma; and to Aphrodisias and Pamukkale.

## Visitor Information

**Ayvalık** (✉ Yat Limanı Karşısı, ☎ 266/312–2122). **Bergama** (✉ İzmir Cad. 54, Zafer Mah., ☎ 232/633–1862). **Bodrum** (✉ Eylül Meyd. 12, ☎ 252/316–1091 or 252/316–7694). **Çanakkale** (✉ İskele Meyd. 67, ☎ 286/217–1187; ✉ Hükümet Konağı Kat 1, ☎ 286/217–3791 or 286/217–5012). **Çeşme** (✉ İskele Meyd. 8, ☎ 232/712–6653). **İzmir** (✉ Adnan Menderes Airport, ☎ 232/274–2214; ✉ Gaziosmanpasa Bul. 1/C, ☎ 232/489–9278). **Kuşadası** (✉ İskele Meyd., ☎ 256/614–1103). **Selçuk** (✉ Agora Çarsısı 35, Atatürk Mah., ☎ 232/892–6328 or 232/892–6945).

# 4 THE MEDITERRANEAN COAST

St. Paul was born ⟍ ⟍rkey's Mediterranean Coast and preaches ⟍ ⟍ shores; Mark Antony gave a piece of it ⟍ ⟍ ⟍patra; Hittites, Lycians, Lydians, Romans, ⟍ ⟍eeks, Byzantines, Seljuks, Ottomans, and many other peoples have come and gone from this region. Even today this coast offers something for everyone: upscale resorts with all the modern conveniences; tiny hamlets where virgin forest is separated from the sea by strips of unspoiled beach; and, above all, the knowledge that to walk the Mediterranean shore is to walk hand in hand with history.

By Michael
Severn

Revised and
Updated by
Eli Newell

THE MODERN TURKISH MEDITERRANEAN is its ancient counterpart. Unspoiled fishing villages, among them Üçağiz on Kekova Sound, share the shoreline with busy resort towns such as Marmaris and Antalya. The coast's bustling bazaars are stocked with bright, baggy trousers; piles of *halvah* (a tasty candy made from sesame seeds); and jams made of eggplant, rose, and other exotic ingredients. Though tourism has developed considerably here in recent years and big tour buses are an everyday sight now, it has not yet gotten to the point where restaurants are serving mainly fish-and-chips or where the locals think of you only in terms of the trinkets you might buy (though you will find some who do). Here if you ask a young man directions to the main highway, he is still apt to jump onto his motorcycle and lead you the 5 km (3 mi) or so to find it.

The Turkish Riviera, as it is billed, isn't just about beaches and fishing villages. The region also has ancient cities of Greek, Roman, Arab, Seljuk, Armenian, Crusader, and Byzantine origin. According to legend, Termessos, known as the Eagle's Nest and one of the region's most important sites, defied Alexander the Great (although many historians believe he wasn't really interested in conquering the town anyway). The Roman theater in Aspendos rivals the Colosseum. St. Paul came here spreading the Gospel to the Seven Churches of Asia, a fact the Turkish government is using to promote "faith tourism." Later, the might of Islam overcame the Byzantines, setting the foundation for a great Muslim empire.

Whether you come to Turkey in search of history or to lie on the beach along a perfect turquoise-colored sea, you can do both along its Mediterranean coast.

# Pleasures and Pastimes

### Beaches

İstuzu Beach, near Dalyan, and Patara, a bit farther east, are two of the most exceptional beaches in all of Turkey. Phaselis is the nicest place to swim west of Antalya; east of the city are the splendid beaches of Side and, even better, Alanya. Near Marmaris, head for İçmeler, Turunç, or Kumlubük. All are blissfully clean, and many have fine white sand, though the azure lagoon of Ölüdeniz and the beach by the ruins of Olympos are pebbled, as are others.

### Cruises

Perhaps the most romantic way to tour the coast is to cruise for several days in a *gület,* the traditional wooden sailboat that looks so graceful on the turquoise water. In this dreamy, private world, timbers creak, brass fittings glint in the sun, hidden bays beckon off the bow, and beaches and ancient cities not on landlubbers' maps become your personal hideaways. Make arrangements before you leave home or ask at any of the seaside towns—even during the height of the season, boats are available (just make sure you are going with a reputable company and that you find out who else will be on the boat), especially from Marmaris. Most of these tours follow a regular itinerary, and a few will put together a trip to suit you. Many tour companies now specialize in yacht tourism, with tours sometimes called "blue voyages" (☞ The Mediterranean A to Z, *below,* and Tour Operators *in* The Gold Guide).

### Dining

Regional specialties along the coast include mussels stuffed with rice, pine nuts, and currants (one of the many stuffed dishes that fall under the general heading *dolma*); *ahtopot salatası,* a cold octopus salad, tossed in olive oil, vinegar, and parsley; and grilled fish—*palamut* (baby tuna), *lüfer* (bluefish), *levrek* (sea bass), *kalkan* (turbot), and more. As in other parts of Turkey, the main difference between good inexpensive restaurants and good expensive restaurants is the setting: Higher tabs get you linen or cotton tablecloths and napkins rather than paper mats, crystal rather than glass. Restaurants of all grades are required by law to display prices, a rule often flouted in the case of fish for the good reason that market prices can fluctuate wildly within a short period. Always ask before you eat—certain varieties of fish can be very expensive at certain times of year. Unless otherwise noted, dress is casual at all restaurants described below, and reservations are not required. For a chart that explains the cost of meals at restaurants in this chapter, *see* Dining and Lodging Price Categories at the back of this book.

## Lodging

Most of the region's upscale lodgings are in Marmaris, Kemer, Belek, Alanya, and Antalya. Accommodations elsewhere are more modest. As a rule, expect clean, simply furnished rooms with low wooden beds, industrial carpeting or Turkish rugs, and maybe a print on the wall. Since many establishments are near the water, be sure to ask for a room with a view. The rare surcharges are insignificant. For a chart that explains room rates at the accommodations in this chapter, *see* Dining and Lodging Price Categories at the back of this book.

## Nightlife

Nightlife in the Mediterranean Coast's small towns and villages can be limited and largely depends on the tourist population. However, you will find a wide variety of discos and bars in the main resort areas, usually in hotels. In Kemer, for example, it's hard to find a place without a disco. Elsewhere, do as the locals do and let dinner in a waterfront setting be the evening's entertainment. Sometimes your meal will be accompanied by music and always by raki—Turkey's distinctive anise and grape-seed schnapps. It shouldn't be hard to strike up a conversation with residents and vacationing Turks. If you are headed for a disco, the action usually starts around 10 PM and ends around 2 AM.

## Outdoor Activities and Sports

The warm, placid bays along the coast are ideal, and many big beach resorts have snorkeling and diving gear. Sunken archaeological sites, where the ocean floor is littered with ancient columns and bits of stairways and tombs, put Turkey's Mediterranean Coast among the world's top diving experiences, as indicated by the number of diving schools springing up (but note that it is prohibited to go snorkeling or diving around certain sites).

One way to enjoy the wonderful landscape of the Mediterranean hinterland is to go rafting and trekking in three main areas—around Fethiye and Ölüdeniz, in the Köprülü National Park near Antalya, and along Alanya's Dimçay River.

## Shopping

Increasingly large tourist-oriented shopping centers are opening in the area, particularly around Antalya, Marmaris, and Kemer. These sell a full range of items, from leather goods to gold jewelry, carpets, and textiles. On the other hand, smaller shops are more intimate, more fun, and if you enjoy bargaining, often a lot less expensive. In addition to bigger items, herbs, spices, nuts, jams, and cologne all make good presents. So does Kütahya porcelain, which comes in all varieties and prices. Also, be sure to get to the markets, where locals shop. Antalya has a fruit-and-vegetable market every day in a different part of town. Smaller towns usually have weekly markets.

# Exploring the Mediterranean Coast

Until the mid-1970s, Turkey's southwest coast was inaccessible to all but the most determined travelers—those intrepid souls in four-wheel-drive vehicles or on the backs of donkeys. Today, well-maintained highways wind through the area. The countryside along the Turquoise Coast, east of Marmaris, is less crowded, although these days, resorts are even developing east of Alanya at such spots as Gazipaşı and Silifke. If you're more adventurous, you can continue all the way to Antakya, near the Syrian border. The attractions below are listed roughly from east to west from Marmaris, with a loop to Loryma and the Datça Peninsula, west of Marmaris.

## Great Itineraries

If you have seven full days, you will have time to travel from Marmaris to Antalya, stopping at all the highlights in between. You'll have to stick to the beaten path to cover all this ground in a week, but fortunately in Turkey the beaten path isn't all that beaten. Even three days gives you time to comb the beaches, explore local villages, and visit ancient ruins. With a car you will be able to pack more into each day, though bus travel is a viable option since local service is so good. Another option, outlined in the five-day itinerary below, is to fly into Antalya and work your way west by car or bus. Or you could do it the other way—fly into Dalaman Airport, just under 100 km (62 mi) from Marmaris, and work from east to west.

*Numbers in the text correspond to numbers in the margin and on the Western and Eastern Mediterranean Coast and Antalya maps.*

IF YOU HAVE 3 DAYS

On your first morning, proceed north and then east from **Marmaris** ① on Route 400. Relax for an hour or so in the sulfurous hot springs along the eastern shore of **Lake Köyceğiz** ⑤. In the afternoon, head to the intimate village of 🏛 **Dalyan** ⑥, where you can catch a boat to Kaunos. Explore the ruins in Kaunos before continuing on to İstuzu Beach. Return to Dalyan for a quiet riverside dinner. The next morning, head to 🏛 **Fethiye** ⑧ to view the town's famous rock tombs, then board a boat for a visit to Gemiler Island, where there are ruins of several civilizations. Spend your third day on the beach in **Ölüdeniz** ⑩.

IF YOU HAVE 5 DAYS

Fly to 🏛 **Antalya** ㉔–㉛ on day one. The next morning, head west on Route 400, stopping for a picnic or a swim at **Phaselis** ㉒ before exploring the unexcavated remains of nearby **Mt. Olympos** ㉑. Arrive in 🏛 **Kaş** ⑰ in time for dinner. On day three, take a boat trip to Kekova Sound. Stay another night in Kaş. The next morning, head to 🏛 **Fethiye** ⑧ and **Ölüdeniz** ⑩. Dine in Fethiye and stay overnight there. On your final day, visit **Marmaris** ①.

IF YOU HAVE 7 DAYS

Begin your first day in **Marmaris** ① and then drive north and east on Route 400, stopping at **Lake Köyceğiz** ⑤ on the way to 🏛 **Dalyan** ⑥. Have dinner along the waterfront in Dalyan. The next day, take a boat to Kaunos and İstuzu Beach before returning to Dalyan. On day three, stop in 🏛 **Fethiye** ⑧. Take a swim and have a late lunch or an early dinner at nearby **Ölüdeniz** ⑩. The following day, continue east on Route 400 to 🏛 **Kaş** ⑰, stopping en route at the Lycian cities of **Tlos** ⑪, **Pınara** ⑫, and **Xanthos** ⑭. In the evening, stroll along the harbor in Kaş. On day five, take a boat trip from Kaş to Kekova Sound. After spending a second night in Kaş, continue east on day six to **Mt. Olympos** ㉑ and **Phaselis** ㉒. Have dinner overlooking the harbor and stay

# The Western Mediterranean Coast

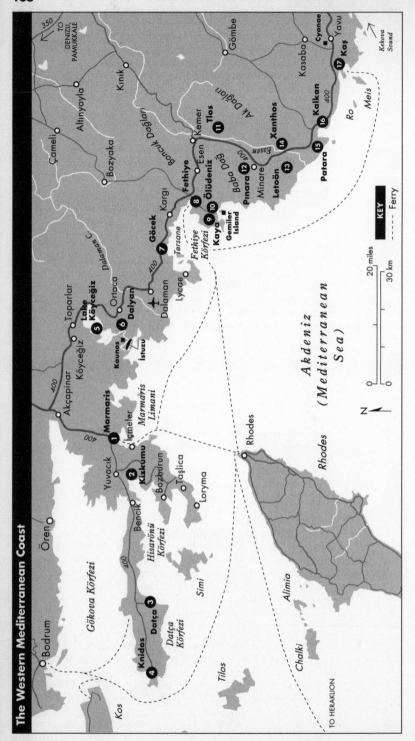

TO
DENIZLI,
PAMUKKALE

*Kekova
Sound*

Yavu

Cyanae ⑰ Kaş

Gömbe

Kasaba

Kınık

Altınyayla

Ak Dağları

Kalkan ⑯

Çameli

Bozyaka

*Boncuk Dağları*

Kemer
Tlos ⑪

Xanthos
⑭

Ro

Meis

Esen

Fethiye

Kargı

Ölüdeniz ⑧
⑩

Pınara ⑫

Minare

Letoön ⑬

Patara

⑮

Göcek ⑦ ⑨ Kaya
Gemiler
Island

*Baba Dağ*

Toparlar

Lake
Köyceğiz ⑤ ⑥ Dalyan

Ortaca

Dalaman Ç

*Fethiye
Körfezi*

Tersane

Köyceğiz

Akçapınar

Kaunos

*istuzu*

Dalaman

Lycae

Lydae

*Marmaris
Limanı*

Marmaris ①

İçmeler

Yuvacık

Kızkumu ②

Akdeniz
*(Mediterranean
Sea)*

Bencik

Bozburun

Taşlıca

Loryma

*Hisarönü
Körfezi*

Rhodes

Ören

Datça ③

*Gökova Körfezi*

Knidos ④

*Datça
Körfezi*

Simi

Rhodes

Bodrum

Kos

Tilos

Alimia

Chalki

KEY

---- Ferry

20 miles

30 km

N

TO HERAKLION

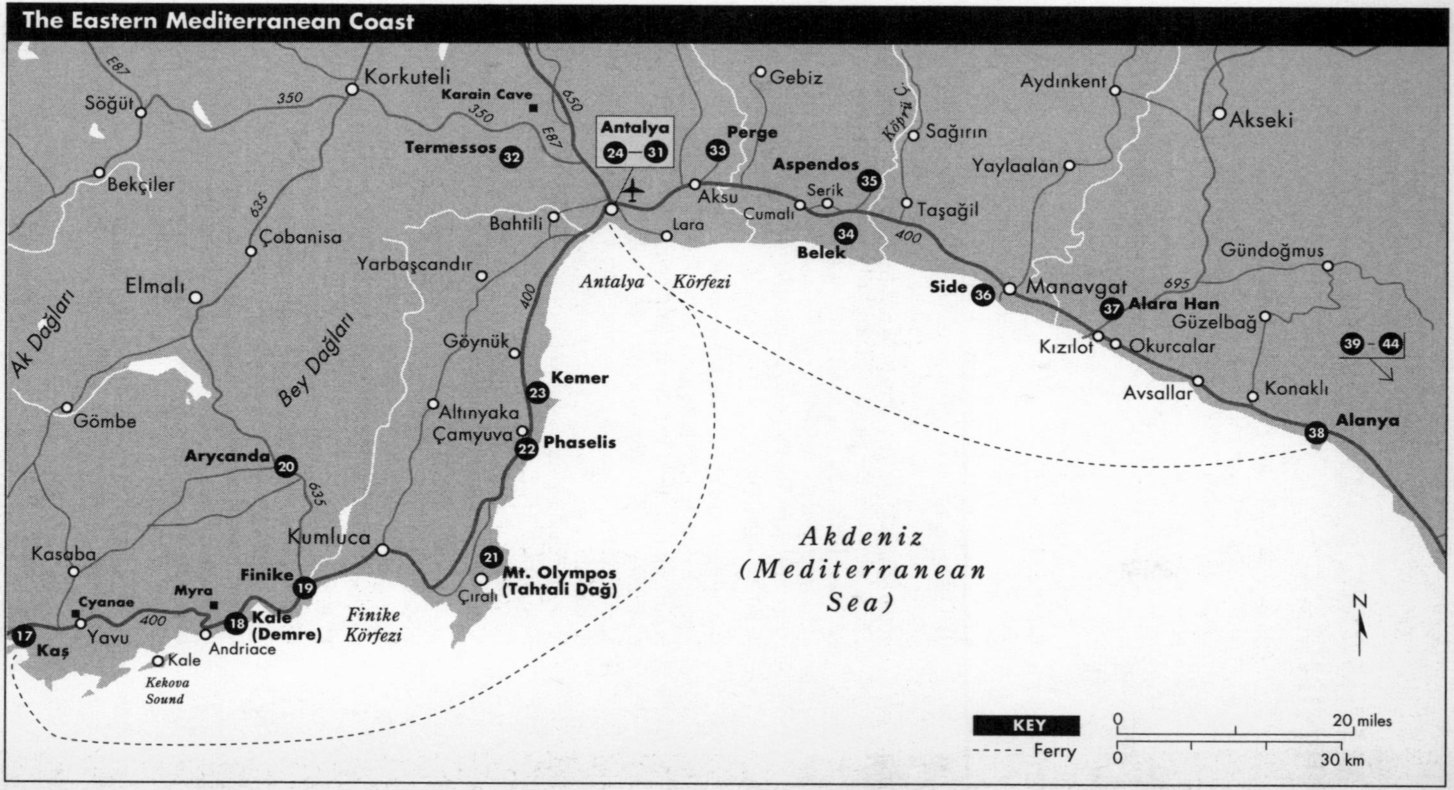
The Eastern Mediterranean Coast
Korkuteli
Karain Cave
Söğüt
Bekçiler
Termessos 32
Antalya 24—31
Perge 33
Gebiz
Aspendos 35
Serik
Cumalı
Aksu
Lara
Bahtili
Köprü Ç.
Sağırın
Taşağil
Aydınkent
Akseki
Yaylaalan
Belek 34
Gündoğmus
Side 36
Manavgat
Alara Han 37
Güzelbağ
Kızılot
Okurcalar
Avsallar
Konaklı
Alanya 38
39 - 44
Çobanisa
Elmalı
Yarbaşcandır
Antalya Körfezi
Ak Dağları
Bey Dağları
Göynük
Kemer 23
Altınyaka
Çamyuva
Phaselis 22
Gömbe
Arycanda 20
Kumluca
Kasaba
Finike 19
Mt. Olympos (Tahtali Dağ) 21
Çıralı
Myra
Cyanae
Kale (Demre) 18
Yavu
Kaş 17
Andriace
Kale
Kekova Sound
Finike Körfezi
Akdeniz (Mediterranean Sea)
E87
350
650
635
400
695
N
KEY
Ferry
0 20 miles
0 30 km

overnight in ⊞ **Antalya** ㉔–㉛. On day seven, hit as many of Antalya's highlights as your schedule permits.

# MARMARIS AND THE DATÇA PENINSULA

Modernity confronts antiquity in the westernmost portion of the Mediterranean Coast. An international party crowd headquarters itself in Marmaris. Heading west from the town are several ancient ruins of note.

## Marmaris

❶ *178 km (110 mi) from Bodrum northeast on Rte. 330 to Milas and east and south, bypassing Muğla, on Rte. 550 to link up with the Great East Rd., Rte. 400.*

A broad boulevard lined with eucalyptus trees leads into Marmaris, a fashionable but often overcrowded resort town between two bays, backed by an old castle. The jumping-off point for some of the best sailing on the Mediterranean, it has sprouted the boutiques, restaurants, and nightlife that seem to be a requirement for the yachting set. The result is a scene that's a far cry from anything in rural Turkey. Because of this, you may feel it's not authentically Turkish and push quickly on into the hinterland; or you may be mesmerized by the interface between Turkish culture and international tourism and settle in for a longer stay.

Until the growth of tourism, Marmaris was a sleepy little fishing village, but its origins go back more than 2,500 years. The modern town is built on the site of the ancient Greek city of Phryscus, the remains of which can still be seen on Asar Tepe, a hill 1½ km (1 mi) to the north of the modern town. Its fine natural harbor once attracted warships rather than today's yachts and pleasure boats. Süleyman the Magnificent launched his successful seaborne assault on the island of Rhodes from here in 1522, and the fleet of the British admiral Horatio Nelson sheltered in Marmaris before setting forth to defeat the ships of Napoléon Bonaparte at the Battle of Aboukir, in Egypt in 1798.

Modern Marmaris has a palm-lined waterfront promenade and a well-stocked bazaar where you can pick up local honey and rose jam, frankincense, and other items. Urban sprawl—literally every block has a construction site—is making the city less attractive than in days gone by.

### Dining and Lodging

$$–$$$ ✕ **La Campagna.** This upscale restaurant, opened by an Italian chef and her Turkish husband, is a real treat. Although the original chef recently returned to her native Italy, the kitchen is now in the able hands of a student of hers since boyhood. Enjoy authentic homemade Italian pasta and tiramisu while watching boats head out to sea. There is also fresh fish, a full bar, an excellent wine list, and outdoor seating overlooking the Mediterranean during the summer. ✉ *Netsel Marina*, ☎ 252/412–5557. *MC, V.*

$–$$ ✕ **Birtat.** Opened in 1964 by the same brothers that run it today, Birtat is one of the oldest and best restaurants along the waterfront promenade at the yacht harbor. Fish dishes are the specialty, and there is also a good selection of starters. Depending on the weather, you can opt for either indoor or outdoor seating. ✉ *Yat Limani*, ☎ 252/412–1076. *MC, V.*

**$–$$**
**★** ✕ **Pineapple.** The menu is eclectic at this international restaurant in the Marmaris marina. The house specialty is roast lamb, but the chef also prepares Thai chicken, French onion soup, steak Diane, and fish-and-chips. Above Pineapple is its sister restaurant, My Marina English Pub. ☒ *Netsel Marina,* ☎ *252/412–0976. DC, MC, V.*

**$$$$** ▥ **Hotel Grand Azur.** This international resort is without question the nicest place to stay in Marmaris. With a sleek modern design and lush tropical gardens, the Grand Azur has so many activities and amenities you may not find a need to leave during your entire stay. ☒ *Kenan Evren Bulv. 13,* ☎ *252/417–4050,* 🖷 *252/417–4060. 254 rooms with bath, 30 suites. 3 restaurants, 3 bars, minibars, no-smoking rooms, room service, 2 pools, massage, sauna, 2 tennis courts, exercise room, private beach, water sports, boating, shops, dry cleaning, laundry service, baby-sitting. AE, DC, MC, V.* ⊗

**$$–$$$** ▥ **Hotel Elegance.** Rooms at this beach resort 3 km (2 mi) from the center of town are done in pastels, with floral-print curtains and bedspreads. All have terraces, and some have sea views. The grounds are dotted with palm trees, and the beach is a long strip of white sand. There are more amenities here than in most Turkish hotels. ☒ *Uzunyali Cad. 130,* ☎ *252/412–8101,* 🖷 *252/412–2005. 190 rooms with bath. 2 restaurants, 4 bars, minibars, room service, 2 pools, Turkish bath, windsurfing, boating, waterskiing, shops, dance club, baby-sitting. AE, DC, MC, V.*

**$$** ▥ **Hotel Lidya.** It's in no way intimate, but the Lidya has pretty gardens filled with jasmine and bougainvillea, as well as a full range of amenities. It's also one of the few hotels in town with a private beach. The property is a long walk (or a fairly short drive) from the center of town, but its disco still manages to draw a crowd. ☒ *Siteler Mah. 130, Uzunyalı,* ☎ *252/412–2940,* 🖷 *252/412–1478. 343 rooms with bath. 2 restaurants, 5 bars, indoor pool, beach, windsurfing, boating, dance club. AE, DC, MC, V.*

**$** ▥ **Özcan Hotel.** This is a modern but attractive hotel in an even better setting in the center of Turunç village, 23 km (14 mi) south of Marmaris, on the other side of the bay. With its own private beach, it's ideal if you want to spend time away from the somewhat overdeveloped town. ☒ *Turunç Köyü,* ☎ *252/476–7140,* 🖷 *252/476–7036. 78 rooms with bath and 9 suites. Restaurant, snack bar, shops, beach, water sports. No credit cards. Closed Nov.–Apr.*

## Nightlife

Marmaris comes alive at night with an incredible selection of bars and dance clubs. If you're looking to imbibe seriously, make your way to **Bar Street** in the old town and its four solid blocks of drinking establishments, visiting as few or as many as you want. **İçmeler Beach** offers dance clubs and karaoke bars with raucous crowds partying into the night.

### BOATS AND CHARTERS

You don't have to go far to escape the crowds that gather in Marmaris in high season (May–September). The Marmaris and Datça peninsulas, which together form a sort of lobster claw at the far southwestern edge of the country, are blissfully untrammeled. The best way to see them is by boat; inquire at the Marmaris harbor about charters, both with crew and without, or make arrangements before you leave home (☞ Tour Operators *in* the Gold Guide). Rates are about $500 a day for a craft with six double berths and crew, but the exact fare is a direct reflection of your ability to bargain (note that it's harder to make arrangements on the spot in high season). **Alkor Yachting** (☎ 252/412–4385, 🖷 252/412–4384) and **Yeşil Marmaris** (☎ 252/412–6486, 🖷 252/412–4470) are good sources.

# Kizkumu

**②** *30 km (19 mi) from Marmaris, west on Rte. 400 and south on road to Bozburun.*

Pine-covered mountains surround this tiny village (known as Keci Buku on navigational maps) around an idyllic bay. You can get here by boat from Marmaris or by car. In the middle of the bay is a stretch of red sand just under the surface of the water, for which there is a local legend as to its origin: Long ago a young girl was fleeing from marauding pirates. While running, she gathered red dirt in her dress and cast it in front of her to form a path across the bay. She ran out of dirt, but her efforts were said to have created a coastal spit, which makes it possible to walk into the middle of the bay. Just south of the spit are signs for Şekule Waterfall. You've probably seen more spectacular falls, but the 15-minute walk to them through a forest complete with babbling brook is like a visit to Arcadia.

OFF THE BEATEN PATH
**LORYMA** – A vast citadel stands guard over lonely Bozuk Bay in Loryma, one of the most beautiful spots on the coast. The citadel dates from Hellenistic times—the late 3rd through 1st centuries BC. Also along the coast are Amos, with its heavily fortified towers and gates, and Gerbekse, with the romantic ruins of several Byzantine churches. Approaching each of these cities from the sea (by boat from Marmaris or Kizkumu) is all the more dramatic. ⊠ *20 km (12 mi) west of Marmaris, turn south on local road signposted* BOZBURUN *and continue to follow signposts to Loryma.*

# Datça Peninsula

*76 km (47 mi) west of Marmaris (to town of Datça) on Rte. 400.*

**③** Getting to **Datça** is easiest and quickest by sea: By land the trip from Marmaris has startlingly beautiful views but takes as much as two hours on a winding road. The peninsula is heavily forested and lightly populated. Datça is more than the fishing village it once was, though it's not yet a real resort. The town's residents are refreshingly less obsessed with tourism than their counterparts elsewhere along the coast, though here, too, things are changing as shops, pansiyons, and bars spring up.

**④** Windswept **Knidos** sits on a headland at the very end of the Datça Peninsula, 38 km (24 mi) west of Datça, where the Aegean meets the Mediterranean. A very primitive site, its ruins are strewn amid olive groves and few hints of modern civilization. The city was founded in the 7th century BC by Dorian Greeks; because of its prime location on shipping routes between Egypt, Rhodes, Ephesus, the Greek mainland, and other major ports, it later served as the meeting place for a federation of Dorian cities—including Rhodes, Kos, and Halicarnassus. Its main claim to fame was a temple to Aphrodite that housed a 4th-century BC statue of the goddess by Praxiteles, a realistic nude that the historian Pliny called the finest statue in the world. The statue became a tourist attraction, drawing travelers from afar, among them Cicero and Julius Caesar; eventually it vanished.

Though Knidos is pretty much a do-it-yourself site, with few descriptive markers, the site custodian may be willing to show you around if the day is not too hot. As you approach, you will see the original stairway that led to the upper portion of the city to your right. Climb up, and you will find the excavations of a **sanctuary to the goddess Demeter.** The British archaeologist Sir Charles Newton found a statue of her here in the 1850s and duly had it shipped to the British Museum.

To see the foundations of the unusual **circular temple** that housed the statue of Aphrodite, make your way to the restaurants by the harbor and follow the path leading uphill to the right. In 1970, a fragment of what may have been the original statue, inscribed PRAX(iteles) and APH(rodite), was found at the top of the hill. Back by the harbor, there is a small *odeon,* or concert hall. On the promontory with the lighthouse is the rectangular, stone **Lion Tomb**—the lion, however, has been removed and now resides in the British Museum.

### Dining and Lodging

$$ ✕⊞ **Club Datça Altın Yunus Hotel.** If you want to stay in an upscale, modern resort with full amenities, this place near the center of Datça is typical of that type, though it's a lot less garish than some. Rooms, which are functionally but cheerfully furnished, are in villas throughout the extensive, well-manicured grounds. The clientele tends to be made up of European package-tour groups, though there are some independent travelers as well. ⊠ *İskele Mah.,* ☎ *252/712–8820 or 252/ 712–8821,* FAX *252/712–8819. 108 rooms with shower. 2 restaurants, 2 bars, pool, Turkish bath, sauna, beach, water sports, children's activities, shops. MC, V. Closed Nov.–Apr.*

$ ✕⊞ **Hotel Mare.** Though the bright white building looks like a suburban corporate headquarters, the grounds are cool and pleasant. This is the quintessential spot for getting away from it all while remaining close to the center of Datça. Rooms have balconies but are otherwise clean and simple. Modest suites make good choices for large families. ⊠ *Şükrü Efendi Cd.,* ☎ *252/712–3397 or 252/712–3211,* FAX *252/712– 3396. 50 rooms with shower. Restaurant, bar, pool, beach, water sports, shops. MC, V.*

$–$$ ✕⊞ **Olimpos Hotel.** Airy and clean, the Olimpos is decorated with old kilims and wooden furniture. The staff is very accommodating, and the restaurant is good. ⊠ *Koru Mah.,* ☎ *252/712–2001,* FAX *252/712– 2653. 30 rooms with bath. Restaurant, bar, outdoor café. V. Closed Oct.–Apr.*

# THE TURQUOISE COAST
## From Köyceğiz to Kemer

Lycia, a compact, mountainous, and isolated area extending all the way to Antalya, begins just east of Köyceğiz. The first mention of the Lycians appears in Hittite records dating from the 14th century BC. Egyptian documents written a century later tell of a troublesome sea people called the Lukki, whom some historians believe to be the Lycians. The historian Herodotus, writing in the 5th century BC, said that the Lycians were descended from Sarpedon, who was exiled by his brother, King Minos of Crete, sometime around 1400 BC. To confuse the issue further, some Turkish archaeologists now claim them as indigenous Anatolians. Homer places them on the side of Troy in the Trojan War. The Lycians were considered an extraordinarily independent people, with their own language (even now not completely deciphered) and a fierce determination not to be conquered.

Like the rest of Anatolia, Lycia was ruled by a succession of overlords, starting with the Persians in the 6th century BC. It was the last region on the Mediterranean Coast to be incorporated into the Roman Empire (at the end of the 2nd century BC). The six major cities in the Lycian Union—Xanthos, Patara, Pinara, Tlos, Myra, and Olympos—grew wealthy from sea trade. Its citizens made an art of building monumental tombs. There were regal rock tombs carved directly into cliff walls, resembling everything from Ionic temples to rustic houses; pillar tombs, such as the one at Xanthos, with a massive rectangular grave chamber 26 ft high; and giant sarcophagi with arched lids.

## Lake Köyceğiz

**❺**  *63 km (39 mi) east of Marmaris on Rte. 400.*

The entire Lake Köyceğiz area is a wildlife preserve, inhabited by kingfishers, kestrels, egrets, and cranes. The peaceful market town of **Köyceğiz** has a lakeside promenade and broad, shady trees. The lion statues displayed in the town square, dredged out of nearby marshes, hint at the buried riches yet to be found in the region. Dotting the lake's eastern shore are the Sultaniye sulfurous hot springs, said to have medicinal value. Although their smell can be off-putting, the hot, muddy pools make for a bathing experience many pay good money for at posh spas. But there are no facilities, so bring your own towels.

### Dining and Lodging

**$–$$**  ✕🏨 **Panorama Plaza.** One of the plusher hotels along the lakeside promenade, the Panorama has a lobby filled with antiques and kilims. Rooms of varying sizes are furnished in simple modern style with a few antique touches. All have terraces and a view of the lake. The hotel can plan day trips for you, but since most of the guests are German, there's no guarantee your guide will speak English. Note that the hotel offers special reduced rates for families staying more than five days. ✉ *Cengiz Topel Cad. 69, Ulucamii Mah.,* ☎ *252/262–3773 or 252/ 262–2642,* 📠 *252/262–3633. 28 rooms with shower. Restaurant, snack bar, 2 bars, minibars, pool. MC, V.* 🍽

**$**  ✕🏨 **Hotel Özay.** On the shore of Lake Köyceğiz with views across to the mountains beyond is this quiet, efficiently run, family-managed hotel. Its outdoor café is in a garden draped with vines, bougainvillea, and jasmine, and its restaurant is above average. Daily boat trips to nearby sites can be arranged through the hotel. ✉ *Kordon Boyu 11,* ☎ *252/ 262–4300,* 📠 *252/262–2000. 32 rooms with shower. Restaurant, bar, outdoor café, pool. MC, V.*

## Dalyan

**★ ❻**  *12 km (7 mi) south of Köyceğiz on Rte. 400 to local road (follow signs).*

Carian tombs are carved into the cliff that rises from behind the reed-backed Dalyan River in the quiet fishing town of Dalyan. When the cliff is lighted up at night, it's a grand sight. Dalyan has tried to resist development as a tourist destination, but it has only partially succeeded. The several restaurants and hotels, however, make it a good base for exploring the ancient city of Kaunos, 10 km (7 mi) west. To reach Kaunos and İstuzu Beach, just downstream from Dalyan at Ekincik, board a boat at the harbor in Dalyan (they'll be lined up waiting for you).

**★**  **İstuzu Beach** stretches for 5 unspoiled miles, with the Mediterranean on one side and a freshwater lagoon on the other. In June and July *Caretta caretta* sea turtles lay their eggs here; signs along the beach mark possible nesting places and warn you not to stick umbrellas in the sand or behave in other ways that could disturb the turtles. Although this is supposed to be a conservation area—the city has agreed to prohibit high-rise development to protect the turtles—some tourism development has started.

In his *Metamorphosis,* Ovid immortalized **Kaunos,** who fled from the amorous advances of his sister Byblis and founded the city that now bears his name; nymphs turned Byblis, who wept inconsolably at the loss, into a fountain. The remains at Kaunos (which is about 15–30 minutes by boat from Dalyan, depending on weather conditions) include a crumbling Byzantine basilica, a massive Roman bath restored as a site museum, and a well-preserved semicircular 4th-century BC theater cut into the hillside in the Greek style. The rock tombs here, although evocative and beautiful, are not strictly Lycian, as they appear to be. Instead it was the Carians, whose kingdom bordered Lycia, who carved these tombs in the 4th century BC in the Lycian style.

### Dining and Lodging

$$–$$$   ✗ **Denizatı.** At probably the best restaurant in Dalyan, the putter of *caïques* out on the water and the chirp of crickets in the evening set the tone. The waitstaff is thoroughly pleasant, and the gray mullet are caught locally and usually grilled to perfection. ✉ *South of main square and statue of Atatürk,* ☎ *252/284–2129. MC, V. Closed Nov.–Apr..*

$$–$$$   ✗ **Deniz Yıldızı.** This fish restaurant lacks the view of its nearby sibling, Denizatı. Still, with its white tablecloths, excellent service, and good selection of Turkish wine, it's a classy establishment that isn't so fancy you can't bring the kids. ✉ *Çarşı İçi,* ☎ *252/284–4183. MC, V.*

$$–$$$   ✗🏨 **Dalyan Hotel.** Rooms at this hotel are comfortable and clean and have views across the Dalyan River of ancient tombs. The attentive staff organizes bird-watching and moonlight excursions on Lake Köyceğiz and hiking, bicycling, and motorcycling trips on nearby mountain paths, so you can work up an appetite to eat at the hotel's excellent restaurants. ✉ *Yali Sok., Maraş Mah.,* ☎ *252/284–2239,* 🅵🅰🆇 *252/ 284–2240. 20 rooms with shower. 2 restaurants, 2 bars, pool, snorkeling, windsurfing, playground. MC, V. Closed Nov.–Mar.* ✍

$   ✗🏨 **Binlik Hotel.** Rooms at this family-run hotel are not luxurious, but
★   they do have more amenities—such as hair dryers and full-size beds— than do most places this size. If you like meeting fellow travelers, this is the place to stay; guests generally gather in the comfortable common area after meals. Take the half-board option, as dinners here are satisfying. ✉ *Sulungur Sok. 16,* ☎ *252/284–2148 or 252/284–2280,* 🅵🅰🆇 *252/284–2149. 82 rooms with shower. Restaurant, bar, cafeteria, snack bar, minibars, 2 pools. MC, V.* ✍

$$–$$$   🏨 **Hotel Assyrian.** With modern bathrooms, 24-hour room service, and a large pool overlooking the Dalyan River, this relatively new property is a pleasant place to escape civilization (it's 1 km [½ mi] from the center of town) without having to suffer for lack of amenities. The hotel encourages long stays by offering reduced rates for extended visits. ☎ *252/284–3232,* 🅵🅰🆇 *252/284–3244. 34 rooms with bath. Restaurant, bar, outdoor café, snack bar, air-conditioning, minibars, room service, pool. AE, DC, MC, V. Closed mid-Nov.–mid-Mar.*

## Göcek

❼   *40 km (25 mi) east of Dalyan on Rte. 400.*

From Göcek, just east of Dalaman Airport, a water taxi can take you to any of the **Twelve Islands,** or you can rent a yacht or a *gulet,* a converted wooden fishing craft. These tiny islands don't have exceptional ruins, but they do have coves with beaches. The most popular anchorages include Tersane, Kapi Creek, Cleopatra's Bay, and Tomb Bay.

You can also take a water taxi to **Kızılkuyruk Köyü,** a village on a small, remote bay near ancient Lydae. Little is known about the history of this scenic but often-deserted site that has bits of ruined walls, foundations of ancient buildings, and fragments of decorative carved marble. **Katrancı,** in a rocky headland about halfway between Göcek and Fethiye, is a secluded cove and one of the prettiest spots in the area for a swim.

# Fethiye

**8** *52 km (32 mi) east of Göcek on Rte. 400.*

Fethiye was rebuilt after the original town was destroyed in an earthquake in 1957. Although it looks modern as a result, it's still an old-fashioned agricultural community where goats and sheep are herded along the main roads on their way to market. At night residents promenade along the lighted harbor or relax, sipping tea, in their gardens. During the day the town lacks charm, except for the spirited produce market, where herbs, dried fruits, frankincense, and saffron are displayed and bartered. Saffron goes for a fraction of its price abroad, but beware of so-called Turkish saffron, which usually turns out to be turmeric. Fethiye was known in antiquity as Telmessus (not to be confused with Termessos, near Antalya), and was the principal port of Lycia from the Roman period onward. In front of the town hall is the finest of several scattered tombs, representing a two-story Lycian house, with reliefs of warriors on both sides of its lid.

Fethiye's museum, the **Fethiye Müzesi,** has some fine statues and jewelry from the glory days of Telmessus, and the English-language label interpretation is lively, even provocative, as in the following: "If you consider history as a period of time that has no significance for you, then it is only natural that you are indifferent to the destruction of cultural values." ⊠ *Off Atatürk Cad. (look for signs).* ⌨ *$1.50.* ⊙ *Tues.–Sun. 8:30–5.*

Impressive **rock tombs** were carved into the cliff that looms above town. The largest is the **Tomb of Amyntas,** presumably the burial place of a 4th-century BC ruler or nobleman. The portico imitates an Ionic temple; the door to the main grave chamber even has faux iron studs. Inside are the slabs where corpses were laid out. To reach the tombs, you'll have to climb many steps—the stairway starts at Kaya Caddesi, near the bus station—but your effort will be well rewarded, particularly at dusk, when the cliffs take on a reddish glow. West via Kaya Caddesi is the requisite crusader **castle,** probably dating from the 12th century and attributed to the Knights of St. John.

You can take one of the boats or water taxis in Fethiye's harbors on a variety of **boat tours,** some including meals, to Göcek, the Twelve Islands, Gemiler Island, and Ölüdeniz (☞ Göcek, *above*). Itineraries are posted, and there are people are on hand to answer questions. Be sure to shop around, as packages vary widely. The cost ranges from around $12 to $20 per person. Ask to inspect the boat before booking. And if a meal is involved, check whether a choice of entrées is available—this can be particularly important if you're a vegetarian. Companies operating boat tours are all basically the same, though **Carole & Tayfun's** (☎ 252/612–4715 or 532/263–3159) is slightly better than the rest: Carole, who is English, goes on all the trips herself, and the company prides itself on taking special care of older passengers.

**Gemiler Island** is a scenic must, surrounded by an amphitheater of mountains and scattered with Byzantine remains dating from the 7th to the 9th centuries. There are also some Lycian tombs from the 2nd century BC, as well as a 19th-century Greek church with some intact mosaics dedicated to St. Nicholas.

*En Route* If you're traveling from Fethiye to Antalya, you may want to follow the coast road. If you are in a hurry or have already seen the coastal sites, take the well-signposted inland route. This involves branching northeastward off Route 400 22 km (14 mi) east of Fethiye toward

Korkuteli. The road has been improved recently and is relatively traffic-free compared to the coastal route. If you're traveling by bus, note that some buses travel to Antalya via Elmalı, and the journey typically takes four hours. Around the coast, it is more likely to take seven hours and can be even longer in summer traffic. If you're driving, the inland route presents an opportunity to take in the ancient city of Termessos (☞ *below*) along the way.

## Dining and Lodging

$$ ✕ **Meğri Restaurant.** Stone walls, high-wood ceilings, and decorative kilims give this upscale fish restaurant in the middle of the bazaar the feel of a Swiss chalet as imagined by Turks. It's often crowded, so reservations are a good idea. ⊠ *Eski Cami Geçidi Likya Sok. 8–9,* ☎ *252/ 614–4046,* 𝖥𝖠𝖷 *252/612–0446. MC, V.*

$–$$ ✕ **Yacht.** As its name suggests, this waterfront restaurant opposite the marina attracts the international yachting crowd. Fish (usually grilled), lamb (in stew and kebabs), and *bonfilé* (steaks) are the specialties. You can eat indoors or out in the garden. Some nights musicians and a belly dancer perform. ⊠ *Yat Limanı Karşısı (yacht harbor),* ☎ *252/614– 7014. MC, V.*

$$ ▥ **ATA Park Hotel** This new hotel on the outskirts of town enjoys a pleasant view of the harbor and hills beyond. There's a homey feel to the traditionally furnished rooms, the staff and management are eager to meet the needs of their guests, and there are many more amenities than you would expect to find in a hotel in this price range. ⊠ *Karagözler 2,* ☎ *252/612–4081,* 𝖥𝖠𝖷 *252/612–4082. 50 rooms with shower. 2 restaurants, 2 bars, air-conditioning, minibars, Turkish bath, pool. MC, V.* ✍

$ ▥ **Otel Dedeoğlu.** This reliable old hotel is in a convenient spot near the yacht harbor and the tourist information office. Rooms are basic and have views of the bay. ⊠ *İskele Meyd.,* ☎ *252/614–4010,* 𝖥𝖠𝖷 *252/ 614–1707. 44 rooms with shower. Restaurant, bar, air-conditioning. MC, V.*

# Kaya

**⑨** *From Fethiye take the local road toward Ölü Deniz; as you head east, about 5 km (3 mi) before turnoff to Ölü Deniz, look for signs to Kaya on right side.*

Highly atmospheric Kaya is a ruin of an entirely different order from all others along the Mediterranean Coast. It was a thriving Greek community until 1923, when all the village's residents were repatriated to Greece following a population-exchange agreement between the two countries in the 1920s. Nowadays it's a much smaller Turkish agricultural village. Spread across three hills, Kaya is eerily quiet and slowly crumbling. You can wander through small cuboid houses reminiscent of those in the Greek Islands, some with a touch of bright Mediterranean blue or red on the walls. In the two basilicas the murals have all been defaced, although Christ and the apostles are visible in one. A few Turkish families living near the ruins sell soda and trinkets to the occasional tourist. They may invite you inside their homes and serve you tea, after which you'll probably (they hope) feel obligated to buy something from them.

# Ölüdeniz

★ **⑩** *15 km (9 mi) south of Fethiye; follow signposts on local road.*

Ölüdeniz is one of Turkey's great natural wonders, an azure lagoon rimmed by white-sand-and-pebble beaches. The area, a national park, can be reached by ferry, car, or *dolmuş* (shared taxi). The water is warm and the setting entirely delightful, even with the crowds.

Ölüdeniz means "dead sea," and there are two local explanations for the name. One is prosaic—the waters of the lagoon are always flat calm. But then there is the legend of a sea captain who in the 2nd century AD fell in love with a beautiful local girl. On his last voyage he was caught in a storm at sea and aimed his boat for the safety of the lagoon. His father, who was traveling with him, could see no inlet, just waves crashing against the rocks. Thinking that death was imminent, he accused his son of placing them in a trap and threw him overboard. Moments later the boat was hurled through the hidden entrance into the calm lagoon, where the father realized his tragic mistake. Distraught at the loss of her lover, the girl committed suicide and her name, Belcekız, was given to another nearby inlet and village. Ölüdeniz was so called because it was the place of the sea captain's death.

### Dining and Lodging

$$ ✕ **Beyaz Yunus.** Wicker chairs and wooden floors are set beneath a domed ceiling at this, probably the nicest restaurant in the Ölüdeniz area, whose name is White Dolphin in English. It's on the adjacent Bay of Belcekız on a promontory near Padiralı, a spot with fine views of the placid turquoise waters. Continental and Turkish dishes are imaginatively prepared and presented. ⊠ *Beyaz Yunuz, Belcekız,* ☎ *252/ 616–6036. MC, V.*

$ ✕ **Asmali Restaurant.** On the road to the Meri Oteli (☞ *below*), this simple family-run restaurant serves homemade dishes, which vary from day to day, and cold mezes, grilled meats, and fish. It has a beautiful garden terrace with overhanging vines. ⊠ *On road to Meri Otel,* ☎ *no phone. No credit cards.*

$$$–$$$$ ▦ **Meri Oteli.** This hotel's setting on a steep incline above the lagoon, alongside terraced gardens and overlooking one of Turkey's most beautiful bays, is a delight. Rooms are another story: Although perfectly clean, they're a bit down-at-the-heels and overpriced. But the area is short on accommodations, other than a few small guest houses. To get here, look for signs for Meri. ⊠ *Ölüdeniz,* ☎ *252/617– 0001,* FAX *252/617–0010. 75 rooms with bath. Restaurant, bar, beach. MC, V.* ✎

$$$–$$$$ ▦ **Montana Pine Resort.** Though it's a long way from Montana, this hotel is also in a stunning setting, 3 km (2 mi) above Ölüdeniz, which means the views are sensational. Rooms are large and airy and have balconies, and there's daily shuttle service to the Ölüdeniz Beach. ⊠ *Ölüdeniz,* ☎ *252/616–7108 or 252/616–6366,* FAX *252/616–6451. 154 rooms with bath and 5 suites. 2 restaurants, 2 bars, 3 pools, airconditioning, minibars, sauna, hot tub, health club, shops, airport shuttle. MC, V. Closed Nov.–Mar.* ✎

## Tlos

⓫ *About 22 km (14 mi) east of Fethiye; exit to Rte. 400 and follow the local road north to Kemer, where a yellow sign marks the right turn that leads southwest for 15 km (9 mi) to Tlos.*

Tlos, an ancient Lycian city high above the valley of the Xanthos River, was called Tlawa in Lycian. Archaeologists believe it to be the Dalawa mentioned in 14th-century BC Hittite records. Park, pay your admission to the site custodian, and climb up to the **acropolis** for a stunning view of the Xanthos Valley, to the west, and mountains—holding a Roman theater—to the east. The fortress at the summit is Turkish from the 18th century and was a popular haunt of the pirate Kanlı ("Bloody") Ali Ağa. Below the fortress, off a narrow path, is a cluster of rock tombs. Note the relief here of Bellerophon, son of King Glaucus of Corinth, mounted on Pegasus, the winged horse. The monster he faces is the dreaded Chimera—a fire-breathing creature with a lion's head, goat's body, and serpent's tail. (According to legend, Bellerophon won.) If you have time, hike over to the theater you saw from the fortress; among the ruins are carved blocks depicting actors' masks. Nearby, the old baths provide a magnificent view of the Xanthos Valley. This is a do-it-yourself site, and though there are no descriptive signs or maps, you should have little trouble finding the main sights. 🎫 *$1.* ☉ *Daily 8:30–sunset.*

| | |
|---|---|
| OFF THE BEATEN PATH | **SAKLIKENT GORGE –** Tlos is very close to this gorge, a popular spot for picnicking. There are also several places to eat: In the nearby village of Yaka Köyü (signposted), for instance, is the vast but peaceful **Yaka Park Restaurant** (☎ 252/638–2011). On the site of a now-demolished windmill, it has its own trout farm, guaranteeing the fish will always be fresh. |

# Pınara

**⓬** *40 km (24 mi) southeast of Fethiye, look for sign on Rte. 400, 20 km (12 mi) south of Tlos.*

Pınara is an exceptionally romantic ruin atop a steep dirt road and backed by high cliffs. It was probably founded as early as the 5th century BC, and it eventually became one of Lycia's most important cities. You need time and determination to explore, as it is widely scattered, largely unexcavated, and overgrown with plane, fig, and olive trees. Park down in the village of **Minare** and make the half-hour hike up the clearly marked trail. At the top, the site steward will collect your admission and point you in the right direction—there are no descriptive signs or good site maps.

The spectacular **Greek theater,** which has overlooked these peaceful hills and fields for thousands of years, is one of the finest in Turkey. It is perfectly proportioned, and unlike that of most other theaters in Turkey, its stage building is still standing, so you can get a clear picture of what it looked like in use. The site also contains groups of rock **tombs** with unusual reliefs, one showing a cityscape, and a cliff wall honeycombed with hundreds of crude rectangular "pigeonhole" tombs. Nearby villagers volunteer to show tourists this site; it's not a bad idea to accept the offer as they know the highlights. A tip is customary. 🎫 *$1.* ☉ *Daily 8:30–sunset.*

# Letoön

**⓭** *22 km (13 mi) south of Pınara off Rte. 400; follow the signpost on the local road to the east of Rte. 400.*

Excavations have revealed three temples in Letoön. The first, closest to the parking area, was dedicated to Leto, the mother of Apollo and Artemis. It dates from the 2nd century BC. The middle temple, the oldest, is dedicated to Artemis and dates from the 5th or 4th century BC. The last, dating from the 1st century BC, belongs to Apollo and contains a rare Lycian mosaic depicting a bow and arrow (a symbol of Artemis) and a sun and lyre (Apollo's emblems). Compare the first and last temples: The former is Ionic, topped by a simple, triangular pediment and columns with scroll-shape capitals. The latter is Doric, with an ornate pediment with scenic friezes and detailing, and its columns have undecorated capitals. 🎫 *$1.* ☉ *Daily 8:30–sunset.*

# Xanthos

 *25 km (16 mi) south of Pınara on Rte. 400.*

Xanthos, perhaps the greatest city of ancient Lycia, earned the region its reputation for fierceness in battle. Determined not to be subjugated by superior forces, the men of Xanthos twice set fire to their own city, with their women and children inside, and fought to the death. The first occasion was against the Persians in 542 BC, the second against Brutus and the Romans in the 1st century BC. Though the site was excavated and stripped by the British in 1838 and most finds are now in London's British Museum, the remains are worth inspecting. Largely undeveloped, with no snack shop, no detailed signage, and no paved walk, Xanthos is nonetheless easily explored on the dusty paths around the ruins. Allow at least three hours and expect some company: Unlike the other Lycian cities, Xanthos is on the main tour-bus route.

Start across from the parking area at the 2nd-century BC **theater,** built by Lycians in the Roman style. Inscriptions indicate it was a gift from a wealthy Lycian named Opromoas of Rhodiapolis. Alongside it are two much-photographed pillar **tombs.** The more famous of the pair is called the Harpy Tomb after the half-bird, half-woman figures carved onto the north and south sides. Other reliefs show a seated figure receiving various gifts, including a bird, a pomegranate, and a helmet. The tomb has been dated to 470 BC, although the reliefs are plaster casts of originals in the British Museum. The other tomb consists of a sarcophagus atop a pillar, an unusual arrangement; the pillar section is probably as old as the Harpy Tomb, the sarcophagus added later. On the side of the theater, opposite the Harpy Tomb and past the agora, is the Inscribed Pillar of Xanthos, a tomb dating from about 400 BC and etched with a 250-line inscription that recounts the heroic deeds of a champion wrestler and celebrated soldier named Kerei.

Cross the road and walk past the parking area to see the large Byzantine **basilica** and its abstract mosaics. Along a path up the hill, you will find several sarcophagi and a good collection of rock-cut house tombs, as well as a spot of shade. Xanthos's center was up on the acropolis behind the theater, accessible by a trail. 🖼 *$1.* ☉ *Daily 8:30–sunset.*

# Patara

 *18 km (11 mi) south of Xanthos, off Rte. 400.*

Patara was once Lycia's principal port. Cosmopolitan in its heyday—Hannibal, St. Paul, and the emperor Hadrian all visited, and St. Nicholas, the man who would be Santa Claus, is said to have been born here—the port eventually silted up. The **ruins** you'll find today are scattered among marshes and sand dunes. The city was famous for a time for its oracle and its temple of Apollo, still lost beneath the sands. Herodotus wrote that the oracle worked only part-time, as Apollo spent summers away in Delos (probably to escape the heat). Although the sight of the 2,000-year-old theater half-buried in sand is unique, the real reason to come here is the **beach,** a superb 11-km (7-mi) sweep of sand dunes popular with Turkish families yet never so crowded you need to walk far to find solitude. Please regard warning signs concerning the nesting of *Caretta caretta* turtles. In terms of accommodations, there are pansiyons, but since this is an official conservation area, most have been constructed illegally. Some are actually on top of parts of the ancient city, and any further development seriously endangers the turtles. For this reason it is not recommended that you stay here.

# Kalkan

**⑯**   *16 km (10 mi) southeast of Xanthos on Rte. 400.*

You may find that Kalkan is the perfect Mediterranean hideaway, with century-old houses topped by red-tile roofs and with blue waters lapping at the harbor. Or you may bemoan its rapid development and the lack of a beach, though this has not proven to be a problem for the rich Turks, who have made Kalkan into "their" resort. One of the most popular nearby spots is **Kapıtaş,** a small strand of white sand set dramatically at the foot of a sheer cliff wall; take a water taxi there.

## Dining and Lodging

**$-$$**   ✕ **Palanın Yeri.** As in most small seaside towns, most of Kalkan's restaurants are down by the harbor, as is this one, "Pala's Place" in English. It has a vine-covered terrace and a good selection of fresh fish and meat dishes with salads and starters. Eating outdoors has only one downside: the presence of town cats that crowd around you waiting for leftovers. ⊠ *Yat Limanı,* ☎ *242/844–3047. MC, V.*

**$**   ✕ **Özgür Cafe** This open air café serves up a variety of traditional Turkish pancakes and snacks, but the real attractions are the atmosphere—you can nap in one of the hammocks—and the welcome provided by the owners, Oz and Anna. ☎ *242/844–2569. No credit cards.*

**$$**   🏨 **Hotel Pirat.** Some complain that this large property, the first really modern addition to this resort town full of old Greek houses, doesn't suit Kalkan. But the location is good, right on the harbor and a short walk from the swimming platform, and the rooms have terraces and are bigger than those in local pansiyons. Ask for accommodations that overlook the water rather than the town. ⊠ *Kalkan Marina,* ☎ *242/ 844–3178,* 𝔽𝔸𝕏 *242/844–3183. 136 rooms with bath. 2 restaurants, 2 bars, 3 pools. MC, V.*

**$-$$**   🏨 **Kalkan Han.** Near the back part of the village, this restored Ottoman caravansary has a roof terrace with sweeping bay views; it's splendid at breakfast and perfect after dark, when the rooftop becomes the Star Bar. An old kilim decorates the small lobby, and dark-wood accents add character inside and out. ⊠ *Köyiçi Mevkii,* ☎ *242/844–3461,* 𝔽𝔸𝕏 *242/844–2048. 16 rooms with bath. Restaurant, bar. MC, V. Closed Nov.–Apr.*

**$**   🏨 **Balıkçı Han.** This delightful pansiyon, on a small street edging the waterfront, is in a converted 19th-century inn. In the lobby is a faded Ottoman Victorian–style café-bar that is open to the sea. Some rooms have old brass beds, a nice change from the usual wooden platforms. This place is extremely popular, so book ahead, and in summer be sure to ask for an air-conditioned room: the price difference is insignificant and the comfort so much greater. ⊠ *Yalı Boyu Mah.,* ☎ *242/844–3075,* 𝔽𝔸𝕏 *242/844–3641. 10 rooms with bath. MC, V. Balıkçı Han has a flexible policy on winter closure: if there's business, it stays open, but don't rely on it Nov.–Apr.*

# Kaş

**⑰**   *30 km (18 mi) east of Kalkan on Rte. 400.*

Luxury hotels have replaced some of the tiny, traditional houses on the hills above the water in lively Kaş, yet there are still plenty of inexpensive, old-fashioned pansiyons in town. Kaş has a few ruins, including a monumental **sarcophagus** under a massive plane tree, up the sloping street to the left of the tourist office. The tomb has four regal lion's heads carved onto the lid. In 1842 a British naval officer counted more than 100 sarcophagi in Kaş—then called Antiphellus—but most have been destroyed over the years as locals nabbed the solid, flat side pieces to use in construction of new buildings. This practice appears to have been halted. A few hundred yards west of the main square, along Hastane Caddesi, is a small, well-preserved **theater** with a lovely view of the Greek island of Kastellorizon (called Meis in Turkish).

Kaş makes a good base for boat excursions. The hour-long boat ride to **Kastellorizon** gives you a taste of Greece. Although immigration regulations limit your stay to a day, it's a good trip: The island is completely undeveloped and has an impressive 12th- to 16th-century crusader castle with crenellated gray-stone walls. Other excursion options include Kekova Sound, the 5th- to 14th-century Byzantine fortress at Kale, or Demre, site of St. Nicholas Basilica. Or head back toward Patara and Kapıtaş Beach. To hire a boat, stop at the quay, survey the vessels and their posted itineraries, and strike a deal. Trips start at about $10 per person ($7 if you haggle a bit); boats with crew can be chartered for less than $100. Lunch—delicious grilled chicken, salad, and rice—is usually extra (around $4–$10 per person, but be sure to ask the price in advance), or you can pack your own.

<table><tr><td>OFF THE<br>BEATEN PATH</td><td>**KEKOVA SOUND –** Venturing to Kekova Sound may be one of the high points of your visit to Turkey. Most local transportation is by water, but a new road to Üçağiz off Route 400 has made the overland journey, which has magnificent views, easier. Kekova Island is close by the notched shore, whose many inlets create a series of lagoons. Anchoring each is a little fishing community. The apse of a Byzantine church backs Tersane, whose bay is a favorite swimming spot. Üçağiz has small pansiyons and waterside restaurants. Kale, the jewel of the sound, is a pleasing jumble of boxy houses built up a steep rocky crag alongside layers of history: Lycian tombs, a tiny Greek amphitheater, and atop the rocky hill, the medieval ruins of Simena Castle. As you cruise the waters between the villages, you can look overboard to see ancient Roman and Greek columns, buildings, stairways, and ubiquitous Lycian tombs, the last up to their lids in water—the sunken remains of a succession of ancient cities. To go diving, you must obtain a permit in advance (☞ Turkish Diving Federation *in* The Mediterranean Coast A to Z, *below*), but you don't need official papers to swim in the crystal-clear water of perfect, private little bays while your boatman naps. Accommodations on Kekova Sound are clean but basic, with plumbing, hot water, and some of the most incredible views $20 or so a night can buy.</td></tr></table>

## Dining and Lodging

$$–$$$  ✕ **Chez Evy.** This French-run place is a bit of everything—café, bar, and restaurant. Its garden dining area has attracted many celebrities. The food is fine, hearty French country cooking, and it's so popular that booking in advance is strongly recommended. ☒ *Terzi Sok. 2,* ☏ *242/836–1253. MC, V.*

$$  ✕ **Eriş.** Fifty yards north of Kaş's main square in a restored Ottoman house, this long-established, popular restaurant serves the usual Turkish grilled meats and appetizers. But its specialty is fresh seafood—the squid, lobster, octopus (in a stew or on a kebab), and prawns are especially excellent. ☒ *Cumhuriyet Meyd., Orta Sok. 13,* ☏ *242/836–2134. MC, V.*

$$–$$$  ✕ **Sun Cafe.** This restaurant just east of the harbor serves enormous plates of traditional Ottoman cuisine. Outdoor seating is in a stone garden setting accentuated by an authentic Lycian house tomb dating back to the 4th century BC. ☒ *Hükümet Cad.,* ☏ *242/836–1053. MC, V.*

$–$$  ✕ **Bahçe.** This courtyard restaurant serves delightful Turkish dishes in a quiet garden setting. The waitstaff here operates like one large family—each one taking part in the preparation and serving of food. ✉ *Anit Mezar Karşisi 31,* ☎ *242/836–2370. No credit cards.*

**$–$$** 🏨 **Club Hotel Phellos.** If you're looking for a break from simple pansiyons and are willing to pay just a bit more, this hotel with a most gracious staff could be the answer. The building is modern, but old-fashioned wooden balconies in each room add a nice touch, as do marble floors and Turkish carpets in the public spaces. Rooms are decent in size, though most have the usual pair of single beds. ✉ *Küçk Çakıl Mevkii,* ☎ *242/836–1953,* 𝖥𝖠𝖷 *242/836–1890. 81 rooms with bath. Restaurant, 2 bars, pool. MC, V.*

**$–$$** 🏨 **Hotel Linda.** At the end of a long line of hotels and pansiyons on the outskirts of town, the Hotel Linda has simple, clean rooms, most of which have balconies with sea views. The staff is friendly and helpful and happy to arrange excursions along the coast. ✉ *Küçk Çakıl Mevkii,* ☎ *242/836–1328,* 𝖥𝖠𝖷 *242/836–1788. 39 rooms with shower. Restaurant, bar, pool. MC, V.*

*En Route*   Yellow signs on Route 400 mark the turnoff for Yavu, a short drive beyond the road to Kekova, where you can park and hike up to uncrowded ancient **Cyaneae** and perhaps the greatest concentration of tombs on the coast. The 45-minute trek to reach them—along a rough trail about 2 km (1 mi) long—takes in a theater, a bath, and a library, all from the Roman era, all heavily overgrown. The tombs vary in age, a few dating as far back as the 3rd or 2nd century BC, with most from the 2nd or 3rd century AD.

# Kale (Demre)

**⑱**  *37 km (23 mi) east of Kaş on Rte. 400.*

The legend of jolly old St. Nick started here, in Kale (not to be confused with the same-named town on Kekova Sound), also known as Demre. Made bishop of Myra in the first half of the 4th century, St. Nicholas was said to have carried out nocturnal visits to the houses of local children to leave gifts, including gold coins as dowries for poor village girls; if a window were closed, said the storytellers, he would drop the gifts down the chimney.

A church was built around the tomb of St. Nicholas in the 6th century but was later destroyed in an Arab raid. In 1043 the **St. Nicholas Basilica** was rebuilt with the aid of the Byzantine emperor Constantine IX and the empress Zoë near the center of town, a couple of blocks from the square. St. Nicholas's remains, however, were stolen and taken to Bari, Italy, in 1087, where the church of San Nicola di Bari was built to house them. A few bones remained, so the story goes, and these can be seen in the Antalya Museum. The church in Kale today is mainly the result of restoration work financed by 19th-century Russian noblemen. It is very difficult to distinguish between the original church, parts of which may date back to the 5th century, and the restorations, although the bell tower and upper story are clearly late additions. A service is held in the church every year on December 6, the feast day of St. Nicholas, as part of the annual symposium and festival organized by the Father Christmas and Call to World Peace Foundation. 🎟 *$1.* ☉ *Daily 8:30–5:30.*

The monuments of ancient **Myra**—a striking Roman theater and a cliff face full of Lycian rock tombs—are about 2 km (1 mi) north of Kale, well marked by signs. The theater dates from the 2nd century BC and for a time was used for gladiator spectacles involving wild animals. There are some fine reliefs on the tombs (a stairway leads to a raised viewing platform so you can see them up close) and on the bits of pediments and statuary scattered about the grounds of the site. ☒ *$2.* ☉ *Daily 8:30–5 or 5:30.*

### Lodging

$ ☷ **Topçu Hotel.** On Route 400 at the turn to Kale is a typical, clean whitewash-and-wood provincial hotel. The staff is very keen to be of assistance, and an excellent breakfast of fresh bread, eggs, and cheese is served. ☒ *Şehir Merkez Girişi,* ☎ *242/871–2200,* ℻ *242/871–2201. 42 rooms with shower. No credit cards.*

## Finike

⑲ *28 km (15 mi) west of Kale along Rte. 400*

Though it's the jumping off point for Arycanda and its yacht marina was recently developed, Finike remains relatively untouched by tourism, possibly because most local landowners are already doing very well from growing citrus fruits. Finike has few sights of note, but it is a pleasant, sleepy little town with some of the friendliest and most helpful people around and some fine beaches both east and west.

### Dining and Lodging

$$ ✕ **Petek Restaurant.** At the harbor entrance, this establishment is renowned locally for its fish, though the usual grilled dishes are served here, too. Inside, the decor is plain and a little run-down, but outside you get to enjoy a terrific view. ☒ *Liman Girişi,* ☎ *242/855–1782. No credit cards.*

$ ✕ **Birlik Restaurant.** Birlik (the name means "unity") is away from the marina and a place few tourists find. A very local, almost entirely Turkish crowd comes here to dine on plain and simple but fine Turkish cookery. Be sure to try the *hibeş,* a local specialty made from tahini and hot-pepper paste. ☒ *Akın Sok.,* ☎ *242/855–3184. No credit cards.*

$ ☷ **Motel Urallı.** This motel is longer established and more reliable than most. Three kilometers (2 miles) out of town, it's made up of simply but tastefully furnished chalets and bungalows, surrounded by orange groves and across the road from the beach. The friendly German/Turkish owners can help you arrange day trips. ☒ *Sahil Yolu,* ☎ *242/855–1060,* ℻ *242/855–3744. 16 rooms or bungalows with shower. Restaurant, bar. No credit cards. Closed Oct.–Mar.*

## Arycanda

⑳ *7 km (5 mi) east of Kale, turn north at Finike on the Korkuteli road (Rte. 635), also signposted for Arycanda, which is around 40 km (25 mi) farther on, to the east of the main road.*

By virtue of its location, Arycanda remains one of Mediterranean Turkey's best undiscovered archaeological sites. The city first appeared in historical records in the 5th century BC, although it is probably considerably older. It passed through Persian hands, fell to Alexander, joined the Lycian League, and became a Roman province under the emperor Claudius in AD 43. Arycanda's setting is in an alluring valley punctuated by gorges, pine forests, and waterfalls, the first of which is right by the yellow sign, about 1 km (½ mi) from the site. There is a parking area and an easy-to-follow but unsigned trail up to the acropolis and across the little stream, which is dry in summer. It leads first to the monumental **Roman baths,** perhaps Turkey's best-preserved bathhouse, with its intact mosaic floors, standing walls, and windows framing the valley. The tombs, farther east along the trail, are Roman rather than Lycian. North of the baths, toward the cliff face, you will come to a sunken agora, a market with arcades on three sides; the middle gate leads into an intimate odeon, a small concert hall topped by a Greek-style theater with a breathtaking view of the valley and the snow-covered mountains. Paved streets, mosaics, and an old church are scattered among these structures.

## Mt. Olympos (Tahtali Dağ)

**㉑** *36 km (22 mi) from Kale on Rte. 400.*

Past the town of Kumluca, Route 400 ascends to dizzying heights, where, just past the summit, a sign points to Mt. Olympos, 9 km (5½ mi) south of the coast road. One of the 20 mountains to bear the name Olympos in antiquity, this one, known as Tahtali Dağ in Turkish, is the one where the hero Bellerophon is said to have defeated the legendary fire-breathing Chimera.

This is wild, undeveloped country—the first spot of civilization you reach is **Çavuş Village,** where a fragment of wall here and there among the pink oleander and a crumbling temple to Marcus Aurelius mark the unexcavated remains of the ancient city of Olympos. The beach where the river reaches the sea is quite busy. Not only is it a popular swimming and sunbathing spot for people arriving by road, but it's also a popular stop on many yacht-tour itineraries.

You have to hike for about an hour from Çavuş (ask for directions) up a dusty, rock-strewn mountain trail to discover the secret of the Chimera. From a gash in the rock, at a site known as the **Sanctuary of Hephaistos,** a natural gas produces a flickering flame, barely visible during the day but seen clearly by sailors far out at sea after dark since ancient times.

A winding 7-km (4-mi) road off Route 400 leads to the coastal village of Çıralı. The Lycian ruins and sandy beach are striking, and from here it's only an hour's walk to the Sanctuary of Hephaistos, on Mt. Olympos. Though Çıralı is small and out of the way, there are a dozen or so pansiyons, most with restaurants. As the best time to visit the sanctuary, on what is locally called Yanardağ, or Burning Mountain, is at dusk, it's not a bad idea to stay the night in Çıralı—or in the nearby town of Andrasan, which also has several pansiyons.

## Phaselis

★ **㉒** *56 km (35 mi) northeast of Finike on Rte. 400 to local road (look for yellow sign) through pine forest.*

For romantic ruins it would be hard to beat Phaselis. Still existing are substantial remains of this town, which was founded in the 7th century BC by settlers from Rhodes and was a successful trading post through the Roman era. A broad, grassy lane cuts through the half-walls of the Roman **agora;** a small **theater** sits just behind that; and fine **sarcophagi** are scattered throughout a necropolis in the pine woods that surround the three bays. Overgrown streets descend to the translucent water, which is ideal for swimming. This is not so much an important place as a poetic one, ideal for a picnic or a day at the beach. 🎫 *$2.* ☉ *Fall–spring, daily 8–5; summer, daily 8–6.*

## Kemer

**㉓** *15 km (9 mi) north of Phaselis on Rte. 400.*

Kemer is a center of intensive and unappealing package-tourism development, with hotels and restaurants, a well-equipped marina, and all-inclusive resort villages that make you forget you're in Turkey.

## Lodging

Kemer and the surrounding resort towns of Çamyuva and Tekirova, to the south, and Göynük and Beldibi, to the north, have so many accommodations only a representative selection is listed below.

**$$$–$$$$**    🏨 **Türkiz Hotel.** If you want to stay in the center of Kemer itself, near the marina, this hotel is the best choice. The hotel is a friendlier place than the space-age decor suggests, and it has a full range of services, including its own large beachside water-sports and entertainment complex, with the very popular Moonlight disco. ✉ *Yalı Cad. 3, 07980,* ☎ *242/814–4100,* FAX *242/814–2833. 139 rooms and 6 suites, all with bath. 2 restaurants, 7 bars, patisserie, 2 pools, sauna, Turkish bath, exercise room, beach, shops, dance club, nightclub. AE, DC, MC, V.* 🕭

**$$–$$$**    🏨 **IFA Beach Hotel International.** In Tekirova, just south of Kemer, this environment-friendly establishment is in a magnificent spot between the Taurus Mountains and the sea. The hotel's manager insists on recycling all hotel waste, to the extent of having a large compost heap in the garden. As a result, the garden is flourishing with shade trees and riotous blooms. Rooms are modern and comfortable, if a little impersonal. ✉ *P. K. 137, Kemer 07137,* ☎ *242/821–4032,* FAX *242/821– 4044. 373 rooms, 7 suites, all with bath. 2 restaurants, 6 bars, pool, sauna, Turkish bath, beach, shops. AE, DC, MC, V. Closed mid-Oct.– Mar.*

## Nightlife

Daytime in Kemer is about going to the beach, and nighttime is about going out. Many of the hotels and resorts have bars and discos open to nonguests. But Kemer's most fashionable bar (and one of its most crowded and noisiest) is **Prima** (✉ Liman Cad.). Another hot spot with live music is the **Sherlock Holmes,** on the beach.

## Outdoor Activities and Sports

The **Erendiz Ranch** (✉ 2 km [1 mi] west of Kemer, in Aslanbucak, 4 Yekickeköy Sok., ☎ 242/814–2504) organizes tours of various lengths, from an hour to a day, for about $3–$4 per hour, guide included. Erendiz can also provide overnight accommodations on premises. Accommodations are fairly rudimentary, but the cooking and the welcome more than make up for it. The **Berke Ranch** (✉ 10 km [6 mi] west of Kemer on D400 in nearby Çamyuva, ☎ 242/814–5218 or 242/814– 2748) and **Tukan Ranch** (✉ Part of Tukan shopping and entertainment complex opposite Marco Polo Hotel, ☎ 242/824–6868) also arrange horseback-riding tours.

*En Route*    Eastward along the Mediterranean Coast toward Antalya, the wild, mountainous terrain of Lycia gives way to the broad plains of Pamphylia (Greek for "land of all tribes," or according to some translations, "land of all languages"). As you approach Antalya, hotels, motels, and pansiyons start to appear alongside the pebbly Konyaaltı Beach. The section of this beach closest to the city is currently being developed to provide more facilities for tourists.

# ANTALYA TO ALANYA

Alexander snapped up Pamphylia without much of a fight, although by simply passing around it, he avoided Termessos and its fortress stronghold high atop a mountain rather than wage a lengthy siege. Under the Romans, the major cities of Pamphylia—Attaleia (Antalya), Perge, Aspendos, Sillyon, and Side—were considered backwaters and left relatively free to run their own affairs. In about 67 BC, after Rome launched a naval campaign against pirates who had been raiding the coast, the cities prospered under the *Pax Romana*.

# Antalya

*35 km (22 mi) north of Kemer on Rte. 400.*

A latecomer among Pamphylian cities, Attaleia, now Antalya, was founded in about 160 BC by Attalus II, king of Pergamum, as his port on the southern coast (though there had been various settlements on the site before). It has been the coast's major port ever since. Christian armies used it en route to the Holy Land during the Crusades, the Seljuk Turks held it for most of the 13th century, and the Ottomans kept a fleet here from the 1390s to the fall of their empire in the 20th century. Today the city is a boomtown and a good base for excursions to the region's major archaeological sites: Perge, Aspendos, Side, and Termessos.

A big city, downright ugly on its outskirts, Antalya has a beautifully restored harbor area whose narrow streets are lined with small houses, restaurants, and pansiyons. On the hilltop above the harbor are tea gardens where the brew comes from old-fashioned samovars. The view extends beyond the bay to the Taurus Mountains, which parallel the coast.

You may notice that many signs are in Hebrew, German, and Russian—a response to the influx of tour groups from these countries. Most locals are friendly and glad to help tourists find their way around town, but women of any nationality traveling alone should beware of overzealous men eager to "practice their English."

**㉔ ㉕** The **old harbor,** filled with yachts, fishing vessels, and tourist-excursion boats, is the place to begin. **İskele Cami** (Jetty Mosque), a mosque on pillars, overlooks the harbor.

Head up any of the lanes leading north and east out of the harbor to get to the heart of the **Kaleiçi** (Inner Bailey), the area that was within the fortified city wall. It's a fine example of a traditional Ottoman neighborhood. A restoration project launched in the 1980s saved hundreds of houses, dating mostly from the 19th century, and these were converted into pansiyons, rug shops, restaurants, and art galleries. However, much of the restoration was out of keeping with the original: Note the use of timber, brick, and stone, and the ornate bay windows, but also note that no Ottoman house had a swimming pool in its courtyard.

**㉖** Several of the old town's cobbled lanes lead north from Antalya's harbor to the old stone **Saat Kulesi** (Clock Tower), at the junction known to Antalyans as Kalekapısı, one of the interfaces between the old town and the new. Behind the clock tower, the **Tekeli Mehmet Paşa Cami,** a mosque believed to have been built around the end of the 16th century, is one of the finest surviving Ottoman mosques in the region.

**㉗** Dark blue and turquoise tiles decorate the **Yivli Minare** (Fluted Minaret), a graceful 13th-century cylinder commissioned by the Seljuk sultan Alaaddin Keykubat I. The adjoining mosque, named for the sultan, was originally a Byzantine church. Within the complex are two attractive *türbes* (tombs) and an 18th-century *tekke* (monastery), which once housed a community of whirling dervishes. Of late, the monastery has been used as an art gallery. The Nigar Hatun Türbe (Tomb of Lady Nigar), next to the monastery, though built in Seljuk style, is a 15th-century copy. The *medrese* (theological school) adjacent to the Fluted Minaret has now been glassed in under a bus-station-style roof and is a tourist-oriented shopping center. ✉ *Cumhuriyet Cad., south side of Kalekapısı Sq.*

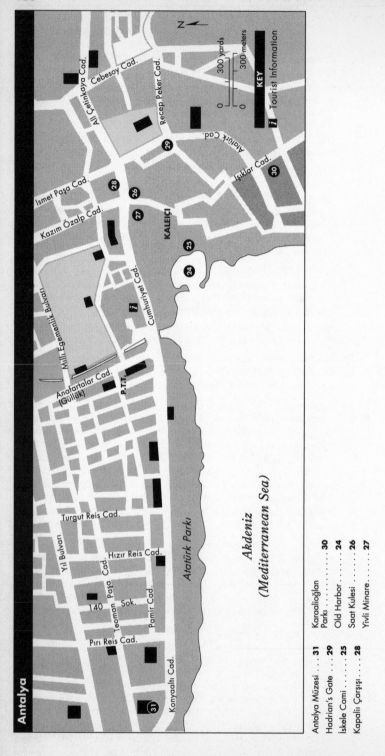

# Antalya

## KEY

ℹ️ Tourist Information

300 yards

300 meters

Ali Çetinkaya Cad.

Cebesoy Cad.

Recep Peker Cad.

Atatürk Cad.

Işıklar Cad.

İsmet Paşa Cad.

Kazım Özalp Cad.

KALEİÇİ

Cumhuriyet Cad.

Milli Egemenlik Bulvarı

Anafartalar Cad.
(Güllük)

P.T.T.

Turgut Reis Cad.

Yıl Bulvarı

Hızır Reis Cad.

Teoman Paşa Cad.

Pamir Cad.

140

Pırı Reis Cad.

Konyaaltı Cad.

Atatürk Parkı

Akdeniz
(Mediterranean Sea)

Antalya Müzesi . . . . **31**

Hadrian's Gate . . . **29**

İskele Cami . . . . . . . **25**

Kapalı Çarşısı . . . . **28**

Karaalioğlan
Parkı . . . . . . . . . . . . **30**

Old Harbor . . . . . **24**

Saat Kulesi . . . . . . **26**

Yivli Minare . . . . . . **27**

㉘ Antalya's **Kapalı Çarşısı** (Covered Bazaar) was once the real thing but is now for the most part sells a collection of tourist trinkets and cheap shoes and textiles. Of the old craftsmen, only one saddle maker remains, and a row of men work old sewing machines by an ancient wall. ✉ *Cumhuriyet Cad., north side of Kalekapısı Sq.*

Close to the covered bazaar is the **İki Kapılı Han,** an old Ottoman caravansary, restored using authentic materials as far as possible, though now it has been given over to jewelry and carpet shops. Back across the street is a row of shops purveying local honey, Turkish delight candy, and pistachio and rose jam. If you are really interested in true Turkish craftsmen, check out the **Demirciler Çarşısı** (Ironsmiths' Market), which survives on two narrow alleys behind the main Tekel (government alcohol and tobacco monopoly) store on the corner of Ali Çetinkaya Caddesi and İmetpaşa Caddesi. Unfortunately, this is prime property, and it's inevitable that the iron smiths will be driven out before long. While you're there, stop in for a drink or a quick lunch at Teneke, a restaurant at the entrance to the market, with an eccentric mix of fishermen, blacksmiths, and Russian tourists.

㉙ **Hadrian's Gate** (✉ Atatürk Cad., west of Cumhuriyet Cad.), constructed in honor of a visit by the Roman emperor in AD 130, has three arches, each with coffered ceilings decorated with rosettes. Because of its triple-arched construction, it is known locally as Uckapılar, or the Three Gates.

㉚ Shady **Karaalioğlan Parkı** (✉ Agustos Cad. at Atatürk Cad.) has a view of the Mediterranean and, at the northwest end, a stone tower 49 ft tall, called Hıdırlık Külesi. It dates from the 2nd century AD, and though no one knows for sure what it is, the best guess is that it was a combined lighthouse and fort.

★ ㉛ The first-rate collection at the **Antalya Müzesi** (Antalya Museum) encompasses Turkish crafts and costumes and artifacts from the classical and Roman eras (including the notable statues of the gods, from Aphrodite to Zeus, in the Gods Gallery), with bits of Byzantine iconography and some prehistoric fossils thrown in. Also, don't miss the remains of prehistoric man and the Seljuks, the children's and ethnographic sections, and the fabulous open-air sculpture gallery. There is also a cafeteria and a gift shop. If you have the time, walk to the museum from the center of town along the coastline promenade. ✉ *Konyaaltı Cad., heading west out of town,* ☎ *242/241–4528.* ☞ *$3.* ☉ *Tues.–Sun. 9–6.*

## Dining and Lodging
The fanciest places in town are the restaurants at the Talya, Sheraton Voyager, Dedeman, Falez, and Marina hotels. At the intersection of Cumhuriyet Caddesi and Atatürk Caddesi is the **Dönerciler Çarşısı,** the Döner Kebab sellers' market, now in a bland, utilitarian concrete building that replaced the old market. Though the food here is still good, the place doesn't have the feel it once did. Nonetheless, look for Bursa Kebapçısı (for carryout) and try the *kokoreç* (grilled sheep's intestines)—then you'll be a local.

$$–$$$ ✕ **Hemmingway.** Tucked into a hill in Kaleiçi, this steak house is not exactly a traditional Turkish restaurant, but for a guaranteed good meal, this is the place. Dine outside in the wonderfully ambient courtyard or just come for a drink at the well-stocked bar. ✉ *Tophane Yokuşu Iskele Cad. 64,* ☎ *252/244–5815. MC, V.*

$–$$ ✕ **Gaziantep Restaurant.** Serving food similar to that at Güneyliler's (☞ *below*), as well as seafood, this is a well-established favorite. In a lovely setting overlooking the bay inside the Atatürk Park, it has a roof terrace, which is a sublime place to eat on a warm summer evening. There are two other of these restaurants—one near the Covered Bazaar and one in the Lara district—but this one is the best. ⊠ *Konyaaltı Cad., inside Atatürk Parkı,* ☎ *252/241–7150. No credit cards.*

**$–$$**   ✕ **Kırk Merdiven Restaurant.** Once the barn of an Ottoman house, this restaurant is in the heart of Kaleiçi, where the winding streets can make it difficult to find. The easiest way is to start from the marina and climb the 40 stairs from which the restaurant takes its name; they're just behind the İskele Mosque. High-quality meats, fish, and a large selection of mezes and salads are served either inside or outside in the garden. ⊠ *Musalla Sok. 2, Selçuk Mah.,* ☎ *242/242–9686. MC, V.*

**$–$$**   ✕ **Sini.** This restaurant is an experiment in bringing Turkish *sulu yemekleri* (literally, "dishes with water")—a style of home cooking in which meats and vegetables are simmered slowly in various sauces—to fine dining. The excellent food is served in the beautiful wood-filled interior. Just point to what you want. Note that no alcohol is served and that although Sini is supposed to be open 24 hours, it's not. ⊠ *Hükümet Cad. 34,* ☎ *242/241–1912 or 242/241–1163. MC, V.*

**$**   ✕ **Güneyliler.** The family that runs Güneyliler (the name means "southerners") hail from Adana, and they mostly cook food from their native region. Up a side street near the Hotel Kişlahan's main entrance (☞ *below*), the restaurant is plainly furnished but is embellished with flowers and potted plants. Try the Adana kebab, spicy skewer-grilled meat, or its milder relative, the Urfa kebab, along with fresh pita bread. No alcohol is available, though you can opt for *ayran,* a refreshing yogurt drink, or another Adana specialty, turnip juice (*şalgam suyu*). ⊠ *4. Sok. 12/A Elmalı Mah.,* ☎ *242/241–1117. MC, V.*

**$**   ✕ **Tophane.** This tea garden overlooks Antalya's harbor and serves inexpensive drinks and snacks along with its priceless views. Adjacent to Cumhuriyet Square, with its statue of Atatürk, it's an Antalya institution. Sooner or later everybody meets everybody here. But, in line with what is happening to the rest of Kaleiçi, nowadays burgers and toasted sandwiches are served rather than traditional Turkish fare. There are several other tea gardens around Tophane, and if you need to send e-mail, the attractive park next to it contains the Bilişim Internet Café. ⊠ *Cumhuriyet Alanı,* ☎ *no phone. No credit cards.*

**$$$–$$$$**   ✕🏨 **Sheraton Voyager Antalya.** West of town near the museum, this bright and shiny resort resembles a sleek cruise ship. Rooms are plush, with thick carpeting, minibars, and terraces (most with sea views). The restaurants—where Turks go to impress business associates and dates—serve Turkish and international cuisine; the Maritime Restaurant is one of the best places for fish in town, but it's also one of the priciest. ⊠ *100 Yil Bul.,* ☎ *242/243–2432,* ⅁ *242/243–2462. 409 rooms with bath. 2 restaurants, 4 bars, outdoor café, air-conditioning, 2 pools, sauna, Turkish bath, 4 tennis courts, health club, windsurfing, boating, waterskiing, casino, dance club. AE, DC, MC, V.* ✎

**$$$–$$$$**   ✕🏨 **Talya Hotel.** This luxurious resort curves around its own beach, ★   which is accessible via an elevator that runs up and down the side of the cliff. Rooms are spacious, with big beds, private terraces, and a view of the sea from every window. The restaurants have the same views and high standards as the rest of the hotel. One serves international cuisine, the others traditional Turkish fare. Reserve early in high season, as this hotel is often completely full. ⊠ *Fevzi Cakmak Cad. 30,* ☎ *242/248–6800,* ⅁ *242/241–5400. 204 rooms with bath. 3 restaurants, 3 bars, minibars, pool, Turkish bath, tennis court, health club, casino. AE, DC, MC, V.*

**$$$**   ✕🏨 **Marina Hotel.** Three vintage Ottoman houses of white stucco ★   with bay windows and dark-wood trim were restored and connected

# When it Comes to Getting Local Currency at an ATM, Same Thing.

Whether you're in Yosemite or Yemen, using your Visa® card or ATM card with the PLUS symbol is the easiest and most convenient way to get local currency.

For example, let's say you're in France. When you make a withdrawal, using your secured PIN, it's dispensed in francs, but is debited from your account in U.S. dollars.

This makes it easy to take advantage of favorable exchange rates. And if you need help finding one of Visa's 627,000 ATMs in 127 countries worldwide, visit **visa.com/pd/atm**. We'll make finding an ATM as easy as finding the Eiffel Tower, the Pyramids or even the Grand Canyon.

It's Everywhere You Want To Be.

# SEE THE WORLD IN FULL COLOR

**Fodor's** Exploring Guides bring all the great sights vividly to life with hundreds of photographs, fascinating historical background, and colorful anecdotes. Detailed maps and practical information keep you headed in the right direction.

Pair a **Fodor's** Exploring Guide with your trusted Gold Guide for a complete planning package.

## Termessos

★  *37 km (23 mi) northwest of Antalya; take E87 north toward Burdur, bear left at fork onto Rte. 350 toward Korkuteli and follow signs to Termessos.*

Writers in antiquity referred to Termessos as the Eagle's Nest, and it is not hard to see why. The city is impregnable, high in the mountains behind Antalya amid the beautiful scenery of the Termessos National Park. The warlike people who made their home here launched frequent raids on their coastal neighbors. They were not Greek but a native Asian people who called themselves the Solymians, after ancient Mt. Solymus, which rises above the city. Termessos remained independent for much of its history and was quite wealthy by the 2nd century AD. Most of its remains date from this period. A massive earthquake in 567 leveled the city, and it never recovered.

The attractions in Termessos start right by the parking area, with a monumental **gate** dedicated to Hadrian. The steepness of the path that leads up to the craggy remains of the city walls soon makes it clear just why Alexander declined to attack. It's from here that the Termessans dumped boulders onto Alexander's soldiers. Next come a **gymnasium** and **bath** complex built of dark gray stone blocks, and the 5,000-seat **theater**, whose perch at the edge of a sheer cliff garners many votes as the most spectacular setting in Turkey. From this staggering height you can view the Pamphylian plain, Mt. Solymus, and the occasional mountain goat or ibex. Termessos has one more wonder: a vast **necropolis,** with nearly 1,000 tombs scattered willy-nilly on a rocky hill. To get there, head back to the main trail and make a left. There is no restaurant at the site, so pack a picnic lunch. And wear sturdy shoes! ⌨ *$1.* ☉ *Daily 8–7.*

One kilometer (½ mile) north of the Termessos turnoff from E87 is the **Karain Cave** (follow yellow signs for Karain). This is where it all began 50,000 years ago. Digs still continue in the Karain Cave, first discovered in 1919, but it has already been proved that it was inhabited as far back as the Paleolithic Age, making it the oldest known settlement site in Turkey. Later it seems to have become a religious center for primitive man. Many of the Karain finds—stone implements, bones of people and animals, and fossilized remains including those of hippopotamuses—are on display in Antalya Museum, but there is also a small museum on the edge of the high meadow where the cave is. Part of the cave itself is also electrically lighted and open to the public. ⌨ *$2.* ☉ *Tues.–Sun. 8–5.*

## Perge

 *22 km (14 mi) from Antalya, east on Rte. 400 to turnoff at Aksu and then north (follow yellow signs).*

Perge suffers from comparison with more dramatic Termessos, and its 14,000-seat theater, though in good shape (at press time it was closed for renovation but is due to reopen), is no match for its counterpart in nearby Aspendos. But a climb to the top of the theater rewards you with a panoramic view of the **Perge ruins,** including a stadium that is one of the best preserved in the ancient world, just to the north, and beyond it the city's sturdy 3rd-century BC garrison towers. The vaulted chambers under the stadium bleachers held shops; marble inscriptions record the proprietors' names and businesses.

The rest of the site is about 1 km (½ mi) north. You enter through the old gates, after parking just outside the old city walls. Directly ahead is a fine colonnaded avenue. The slender, sun-bleached columns lining the street once supported a covered porch filled with shops. You can still see floor mosaics in places, and delicate reliefs of gods and famous citizens decorate the entablatures between some columns. The long grooves in the paving are ruts worn by chariot wheels; the channel running down the center carried water from a fountain at the far end. St. Paul, who sailed here from Cyprus, preached at the basilica near the end of the street, on the left. 🏛 *$1.* ☉ *Daily 8–7.*

# Belek

**③④** *30 km (19 mi) east of Antalya; 8 km (5 mi) east of Perge turnoff at Aksu on Rte. 400, then turn south on local road (follow signs).*

Belek is a relatively new resort town with a good deal going for it. It has fine sandy beaches and woodlands that are a paradise for naturalists and ornithologists. But Belek's chief claim to fame is as the Mediterranean's new golf center, with four 18-hole courses. You can't find inexpensive accommodations in Belek—development has been deliberately restricted to top hotels and resort complexes. Don't look for restaurants, either. If you're staying in Belek and want to eat out, you have a choice between visiting another hotel or making a trip to the nearby village of Kadriye. For nongolfers, Belek makes a good center for exploring the local sites, but a car is necessary; although there is bus service to and from Antalya, it is infrequent and unreliable.

## Lodging

**$$$** 🏨 **Gloria Golf Resort.** One of the newest hotel complexes in Belek (opened in 1997), the Gloria is also one of the best. Its par-72 golf course has been widely praised. Rooms are large and modern, with touches of Turkish crafts and antiques; many have excellent views. ⊠ *Acısu Mevkii,* ☎ *242/715–1525,* 📠 *242/715–1525. 289 rooms, 59 suites, all with bath. 2 restaurants, 3 bars, snack bar, air-conditioning, 2 pools, sauna, Turkish bath, tennis, squash, beach, shops. AE, DC, MC, V.*

**$$$** 🏨 **Tatbeach Golf Hotel.** This hotel is older than Gloria, but the golf course only opened in 1998. From the unusually light and airy lobby and rooms to the colorful and well-manicured gardens, this is a splendid hotel. Service is excellent, and a variety of water sports are available. ⊠ *Belek, Box 1,* ☎ *242/725–4080,* 📠 *242/725–4099 or 242/725–4100. 269 rooms, 33 suites, 3 bungalows, all with bath. 2 restaurants, 6 bars, snack bar, 3 pools, sauna, tennis, health club, beach, shops. AE, DC, MC, V.* 🍴

# Aspendos

**★ ③⑤** *31 km (19 mi) from Perge, east on Rte. 400 to turnoff past Belkis and north (follow yellow signs).*

Most experts agree that the **theater** in Aspendos is the best preserved in Turkey. Its quality rivals that of the Colosseum in Rome. A splendid Roman **aqueduct** that traverses the valley north of the **acropolis,** another superior example of Roman engineering, utilized the pressure of the water flowing from the mountains to supply the summit of the acropolis. The water tower here dates from the 2nd century AD; its stairway is still intact.

Pay your admission to the main site at what was once the actors' entrance to the theater. Built during the reign of Emperor Marcus Aurelius (ruled AD 161–180) by a local architect called Xenon, it is striking for the broad curve of seats, perfectly proportioned porticoes, and rich decoration. The Greeks liked open vistas behind their stages, but the

Romans preferred enclosed spaces; the stage building you see today was once covered in marble tiles, and its niches were filled with statues, some now on view in the Antalya Museum (☞ Antalya, *above*). The only extant relief depicts Dionysus (Bacchus) watching over the theater. The acoustics are fine, and the theater is still in use—for concerts and for the Antalya International Opera and Ballet Festival, held every June, rather than for the wild-animal and gladiator spectacles as in Roman times. Aspendos is not just a Roman site—the Seljuks used it as an imperial palace in the 13th century, and one of the two towers they added to the structure remains standing. There are traces of the distinctive Seljuk red-and-yellow paintwork here and there, too.

Seeing the remainder of the site requires a hike up the zigzagging trail behind the theater, a trek of perhaps an hour or more. The rewards are a tall **Nymphaion**—a sanctuary to the nymphs built around a fountain decorated with a marble dolphin—and the remains of a Byzantine **basilica** and **market hall.** ☐ *$1.* ⊙ *Daily 8–7.*

# Side

⌾ *22 km (14 mi) east of Aspendos on Rte. 400.*

The peninsular city of Side has an excellent museum, two long and beautiful beaches, and ancient ruins (some right by the water's edge). The downside is too much development and garish souvenir shops. Thousands *love* its jumbled mix of old and new, its energy and spirit, and its fun-in-the-sun hedonism. A vocal minority finds it honky-tonk and less deserving of their time than other Turkish destinations.

The name means "pomegranate" in some mysterious pre-Greek language. The town's known history starts with Greeks fleeing Troy after its fall. Following Alexander's reign, the city was dominated by the Seleucids of Syria and the Ptolemies of Egypt; after the demise of the Seleucids in 129 BC, pirates overran the coast, and Side became a major slave-trading center. A naval expedition in 67 BC cleaned things up, and for the next couple of centuries Side was a thriving Roman provincial town. By the 10th century it had been abandoned, most likely as a result of earthquakes and Christian and Arab raids. It was not finally resettled until a group of ethnic Turkish fishermen migrated from Crete in the early 20th century.

Its **beaches** need little explanation: The one on the west side of the peninsula runs for miles; the one on the east is smaller but usually emptier. **Ruins** are all around: a lovely theater in the dead center of town, with city and sea views from the top row, and 2nd-century AD temples to Apollo and Athena, a few blocks south, on the tip of the peninsula. The theater is unique in the area: At other theaters the sloping terrain was used to rake the terraces upward, but the Side theater is built on flat land, and the tiers of seating were supported by a purpose-built vaulted structure 65 ft high.

The **Side Müzesi** (Side Museum), in the center of town, has a small but rich collection of Roman statues: the Three Graces, various cherubs, a brilliant satyr, and a bust of Emperor Hadrian. The sculpture garden behind the museum is larger than the museum itself and overlooks the Mediterranean. ⊠ *Selimiye Köyü,* ☎ *242/753–1006.* ☐ *$2.50.* ⊙ *Tues.–Sun. 8–noon and 1–5.*

## Dining and Lodging

$$ ✕ **Aphrodite Restaurant.** If you go to this restaurant, on the square next to Side's waterfront in summer, order the *kuzu baligi* (mutton fish), a local specialty that tastes something like swordfish. The kitchen also

prepares a good range of other fish and meat dishes. ⊠ *İskele Cad.,* ☎ *242/753–1171. MC, V.*

**$–$$**  ✕ **Nergis Restaurant and Bar.** On the waterfront just east of the square is this justifiably popular restaurant, which is particularly notable for its seafood. Sit upstairs to enjoy the excellent service coupled with the best views of the waterfront and square. ⊠ *İskele Meyd.,* ☎ *242/753–1467. MC, V.*

**$–$$**  ✕ **Paşaköy Bar and Restaurant.** Paşaköy's food is no better or worse than other places, but what differentiates this pleasant restaurant is its weird and wonderfully kitschy garden, decked out with bizarre mock-classical statuary and stuffed animals. The grilled meat dishes are good, the waitstaff is friendly and attentive, and the bartender makes mean cocktails. ⊠ *Liman Cad. 98,* ☎ *242/753–3622,* ℻ *242/753–4170. AE, MC, V.*

**$–$$**  ✕ **Sur Restaurant.** Close to the waterfront, this place has a first-floor terrace overlooking the square and a panoramic view. Fish dominates the menu and varies according to what is in season. Kebabs and good salads are also served. ⊠ *İskele Cad.,* ☎ *242/753–1087.*

**$$$**  🏨 **Sunrise Queen Hotel.** Three and a half kilometers (2 miles) from the town center is this ritzy resort that's fairly typical but also better designed and more attractive than others. It's often filled with tour groups, though many Turks also stay here. The hotel has its own private beach and water slides for kids. Suites have whirlpool baths. Ask about short-stay special offers off-season. ⊠ *Side,* ☎ *242/753–4783,* ℻ *242/753–4760. 339 rooms, 35 suites, all with bath. 2 restaurants, 9 bars, air-conditioning, 8 swimming pools, beauty salon, health club, 7 tennis courts, nightclub. MC, V.*

**$$–$$$**  🏨 **Hotel Acanthus.** This modest four-story hotel is done in Mediterranean style, with whitewashed walls, dark-wood trim and terraces, and a red-tile roof. Rooms are comfortable if unimpressive. The same family that runs the Acanthus owns three other establishments in the area—the Arum, the Cennet, and the Hemera—all worth looking into. The owners sponsor the Aspendos Opera and Ballet Festival in June, so you may find the hotels full of musicians at that time. ⊠ *Side Köyü, Box 55,* ☎ *242/753–3050,* ℻ *242/753–1913. Cennet:* ☎ *242/753–1017,* ℻ *242/753–1438; Arum:* ☎ *242/753–4560,* ℻ *242/753–4140; Hemera:* ☎ *242/753–2450,* ℻ *242/753–2458. 104 rooms with bath. 2 restaurants, 2 bars, air-conditioning, minibars, 2 pools, tennis court, beach, windsurfing. MC, V.*

**$**  🏨 **Hanimeli Pansiyon.** This charming, traditional Side-style stone house, with simple rooms overlooking the Mediterranean or the lush garden, is right downtown, but it's quiet and feels private. Breakfast is served in the extraordinary garden where the owner can often be found tending to his beautiful flowers. Since this delightful retreat is often booked months in advance, you're well advised to reserve. ⊠ *Turgutreis,* ☎ *242/753–1100,* ℻ *242/753–1100. 12 rooms with shower. MC, V.*

**$**  🏨 **Özlem Motel.** Side has hundreds of smaller hotels, motels, and pansiyons to pick from, but this one, 1 km (½ mi) from the town center, is in an orange grove and has beach access. The small, single-story bungalows sleep three or four and are particularly popular with families. ⊠ *Deniz Bükü Mevkii,* ☎ *242/753–3517 or 242/753–1408,* ℻ *242/753–3518. 55 bungalows with shower. Restaurant, bar, beach. No credit cards.*

## Nightlife

Most big hotels have discos; otherwise, nightlife centers on the bars (note that bars open up and shut down with some frequency, so one listed here may not be open the next season). **Barracuda Café and Bar** (⊠ Barbaros Cad., ☎ 242/753–2724), on the street along the seafront, is one of the more popular places in town. The **Blues Bar** (✉ Camii Sokağı, ☎ 242/753–1197) has great live music and a staff that goes out of its way to ensure that women are not bothered. One other place to see live music is the **Temple Bar** (☎ 242/753–1181), which, as the name suggests, is near the Temple of Apollo.

## Outdoor Activities and Sports

**Boat trips** along the Manavgat River can be arranged in the town of Manavgat (on Route 400 1 km [½ mi] east of the turnoff for Side); in addition, several Side companies organize trips from the harbor there. In Manavgat you can find someone to take you on a boat tour (though that someone will probably find you first) at the bridge in the town center. Prices vary widely according to the length of the trip and whether food is provided; you should definitely bargain. Boats stop to let you swim, and some arrange for activities such as jet skiing, waterskiing, or water parachuting; be warned, however, that not all the operators are properly licensed or insured, and serious accidents have occurred.

**Centaurus Riding School** (✉ Club Robinson Kavşağı, ☎ 242/756–9047), just outside Side, arranges trips through the surrounding countryside; someone can pick you up in town or from your hotel.

# Alara Han

**37** *27 km (17 mi) east of Manavgat, turn north off Rte. 400 onto local road signposted* ALARA HAN; *the site is 8 km (5 mi) inland.*

The empire of the Rum Seljuks was the first Muslim empire to extend into Anatolia, long before the Ottomans arrived. It reached its height in the 13th century, when the Seljuks established full control of Turkey's Mediterranean and Black Sea coasts. Their capital was at Konya (Iconium), in central Anatolia, where winters were bitterly cold. As a consequence, the Seljuks established Alanya (☞ *below*) as a secondary winter capital, and there are many Seljuk remains in the area, including the Alara Han.

The Alara Han was built by Sultan Alaaddin Keykubat I in 1231. Though *han* is usually translated as "inn" or "caravansary," for the Seljuks, hans were more than just way stations for travelers. In Seljuk times the word *han* was applied to a wide variety of public buildings serving many functions—as depots for goods or as centers for tax collection, for instance. Alara Han, with its carved lamps, lions' heads, fountain, prayer room, and majestic vaulted interior, is different in design from other surviving Seljuk hans, and it is believed to have been a treasury or imperial archive.

A steep climb above the Alara Han is the Alara Kalesi (Alara Castle). Some remains of Seljuk frescoes survive in the old palace and bathhouse.

# Alanya

**38** *75 km (47 mi) east of Side on Rte. 400.*

Like Side, Alanya arouses strong reactions. Many people love its harbor area and beaches; others are concerned the town is rapidly turning into a hideous concrete jungle with far too many boxy hotels. But Alanya is worth a stop for its Seljuk remains, among the finest surviving remnants of the Seljuk empire.

Ancient sources had a hard time deciding exactly where on their maps to place the town, known to the Greeks as Korakesion and to the Romans as Coracesium. The rocky peninsula on which it is set forms a natural boundary between Pamphylia, to the west, and Cilicia, to the east, which Mark Antony gave to Cleopatra as a gift. Though the lovers are said to have enjoyed the fine beaches, it was Cilicia's forests that Cleopatra was after; lumber was one of Egypt's major imports, and the queen had a mind to build a navy. The city of Alanya, which Mark Antony included in the package, was fairly insignificant until the arrival of the Seljuk Turks in 1220. Several amusing stories explain the Seljuk sultan Alaaddin Keykubat's conquest: One says he married the commander's daughter, another that he tied torches to the horns of thousands of goats and drove them up the hill in the dark of night, suggesting a great army was attacking. Most likely, he simply cut a deal; once settled, he renamed the place and built defensive walls to ensure he would never be dislodged.

The road into Alanya passes through an area of modern resorts and affords splendid views of Keykubat's **kale** (citadel). The outer wall is 8 km (5 mi) long and took 12 years to build; through the battlement crenellations and its 150 towers, arrows could be sent down on attackers. Up the hill, past another wall, is the **İç Kale** (Inner Fortress), where you can park and strike out on foot along tree-shaded lanes into the old city's residential area. Many a crumbling building here dates from Seljuk times. At its center are the remains of the original *bedestan* (bazaar) and caravansary. A path leading west from these buildings takes you to the attractive tomb of Sultan Akşabe, the **Akşabe Sultan Tekke**. The exterior is stone; the interior, the dome, and truncated minaret are redbrick. Continue up the path to the top of the promontory, where you will find a third wall, around the **İç Kale** (İç Keep). Inside are the foundations of Keykubat's palace and the ruins of a Byzantine church, with some 6th-century frescoes of the evangelists. Steps ascend to the battlement on the summit. From there the panorama takes in the Mediterranean's Technicolor blue-green, the two beaches, and a seemingly unending succession of cliffs jutting into the sea from the foothills of the Taurus Mountains. This apparently was the spot where condemned prisoners and unfaithful wives were tossed to their deaths. ☎ 242/512–3304. ▨ $3 for İç Kale and Byzantine church; admission free to other sites. ⊙ Tues.–Sun. 8–7.

The **Kızıl Kule** (Red Tower), built in 1225 by an architect known as Abu Ali, was patterned on other Mediterranean Coast crusader castles. Bricks are used inside. Archers manned the many loopholes, and a series of troughs conveyed boiling tar and melted lead, which was dumped onto attackers. Nowadays the Red Tower houses a small but interesting ethnographic museum. A short walk south along the water or along the castle walls, if you prefer, is a second defensive tower rising above the *tersane*, a 13th-century Seljuk shipyard, the only one still in existence. A guardroom is to the left of the entrance, a mosque to the right. ⊠ *Eastern harbor at south end of İskele Cad.*

The **Alanya Müzesi** (Alanya Museum) has some Greek and Roman pieces, including a bronze statue of Hercules and a big collection of Seljuk and Ottoman artifacts—beautiful old kilims, illustrated Korans and other religious books, and silver and gold jewelry. ⊠ *Azaklar Sok., south of Atatürk Cad., Sekerhane Mah.,* ☎ 242/513–1228. ▨ *$1.* ⊙ *Tues.–Sun. 8–noon and 1:30–5:30.*

The **Damlataş Magarasi** (Weeping Cave) is named for the dazzling multihued stalactites and stalagmites inside. Many Turks while away the hours here in the belief that the high humidity and cool temperature alleviate asthma, bronchitis, and other respiratory illnesses. Sick people are encouraged to visit in the four hours prior to the official opening time every morning. ⊠ *At south end of West Beach, 2 blocks south of Alanya Museum.* 🖼 *$1.25.* ⏲ *Daily 10–8.*

## Dining and Lodging

$–$$ ✕ **İskele Restaurant.** An agreeable view, outdoor seating, and a fully stocked bar are among the draws at this restaurant close to the harbor. Fish and a range of mezes are served, as well as European dishes such as chicken Kiev, Wiener schnitzel, filet mignon, and lasagna. ⊠ *İskele Cad.,* 🕾 *242/511–0304. MC, V.*

$–$$ ✕ **Janus Restaurant.** This restaurant close to the harbor is famous for its fish dishes. The menu varies depending on what is available, but ask for levrek or *barbunya* (red mullet). After dinner, dancing usually continues into the wee hours. ⊠ *Rıhtım Meyd.,* 🕾 *242/513–2694. MC, V. Closed Oct.–Apr.*

$ ✕ **Dimçayı Mangal Tesisleri.** This tree-shaded open-air restaurant near the water makes a pleasant lunch stop on your way east from Alanya. You choose your meat (chops, shish kebab, or *köfte*) and then grill it yourself over a barbecue while the waiters bring salads and drinks. ⊠ *Mersin Yolu, Dimçayı, 3 km (2 mi) east of Alanya on Rte. 400,* 🕾 *242/514–0141. No credit cards.*

$$$–$$$$ 🏨 **Club Hotel Alantur.** Like most of the other big seaside resorts in Alanya, this one is a bright, white midrise complex with many facilities. The beach is exceptional, and the garden is cool and well tended. The comfortable rooms recall Holiday Inns; you can choose to stay in the main hotel or in one of the many bungalows. ⊠ *20 Dimçayı Mev., Çamyolu Köyü,* 🕾 *242/518–1740,* 🖷 *242/518–1756. 100 rooms, 252 bungalows, all with bath. Restaurant, 4 bars, 4 pools, miniature golf, 4 tennis courts, beach, windsurfing, jet skiing, dance club. MC, V.*

$$$ 🏨 **Grand Kaptan Hotel.** For luxury, comfort, and friendly service, this beachside hotel, 3 km (2 mi) east of town, is hard to beat. You can be assured of special care because the owner, Müfit Kaptanoğlu, takes a personal interest in his guests. The hotel is very popular with international tour groups as well as Turks. The restaurant serves many French-influenced dishes. ⊠ *Oba Göl Mevkii,* 🕾 *242/514–0101,* 🖷 *242/514–0092. 268 rooms, 2 suites, most with bath. 2 restaurants, 4 bars, snack bar, pool, sauna, tennis, beach, dance club. MC, V.*

$–$$ 🏨 **Alaiye Hotel.** You can expect modern rooms with balconies (some with sea views) and a bright, clean lobby at this hotel. The restaurant has a magnificent view of the water, and the pool has a bar. The beach is just a short walk away. ⊠ *Atatürk Cad. 228,* 🕾 *242/513–4018,* 🖷 *242/512–1508. 98 rooms with shower. Restaurant, 4 bars, pool, parasailing, waterskiing. MC, V.* ⊜

$–$$ 🏨 **Kaptan Hotel.** Overlooking the harbor and near the Red Tower, this hotel is small and modern in a minimalist vein. It has a lively poolside café and rooftop restaurant with a delightful view and good traditional Turkish fare. ⊠ *İskele Cad. 70,* 🕾 *242/513–4900,* 🖷 *242/513–2000. 43 rooms with shower. Restaurant, 3 bars, air-conditioning, 2 pools. MC, V.*

$–$$ 🏨 **Kleopatra Inn Hotel.** The hotel's location next to the town bus terminal makes it ideal for a short stay if you're traveling by bus. Though it's one of those ubiquitous concrete boxes, it's clean and well-kept and has a pleasant small garden around a pool. The nearest public beach is in walking distance, and it's 1 km (½ mi) from the center of town (there's good bus and dolmuş service). ⊠ *Kızlarpınarı Mah. Otogar Mevkii,* 🕾 *242/519–3140 or 242/519–3126,* 🖷 *242/519–3091. 60 rooms with shower. 2 restaurants, 3 bars, pool, tennis. V.*

## Nightlife

Alanya's nightlife centers around its harbor and on İskele Caddesi, although there are a few large dance clubs outside town in Dimçay. Bars often have extensive menus, and restaurants frequently have live music or turn into impromptu discos after dinner. The **James Dean Bar** (✉ İskele Cad., ☎ 242/512–3195) is popular and less expensive than some of the others. **Zapf Hahn** (✉ İskele Cad., ☎ 242/513–8285) is the spot to go if you like techno.

### Outdoor Activities and Sports

Alanya's main **beach** remains relatively uncrowded except in the height of summer. It's also easy to reach other nearby beaches, coves, and caves by boat. Legend has it that buccaneers kept their most fetching maidens at **Korsanlar Mağarası** (Pirates' Cave) and **Aşıklar Mağarası** (Lovers' Cave), two favorite destinations. Tour boats charge from $5 to $10 per person; hiring a private boat, which you can do at the dock near the Red Tower, should cost less than $20—don't be afraid to bargain.

**Alraft Rafting and Riding Club** (✉ In Bıçakçı village, ☎ 242/513–9155) organizes rafting tours on the Dimçay River, as well as horseback-riding trips. The Azak Hotel (✉ Atatürk Cad.) acts as Alraft's agent in Alanya; here you can get information or make reservations. From mid-April through October, **bungee jumping** at the harbor in the afternoon and evening is the big event; fear not, safety standards are high.

The major sporting event of the year is the **Alanya International Triathlon,** in October. But Alanya's sporting season begins in May with the **Alanya International Rafting Triathlon** on the Dimçay River. Between the two triathlons, you'll find beach volleyball, basketball, handball, and other sporting events, especially in summer. Ask at your hotel or at the tourist information office (☞ The Mediterranean Coast A to Z, *below*).

# EAST OF ALANYA

East of Alanya, the road winds tortuously along the coast. Road improvements have made it easier to travel here, and resorts are starting to bloom between Alanya and Mersin. As you travel the 55 km (34 mi) from Alanya to Gazipaşa on Route 400, the coastal plain narrows, and you come to a long stretch reminiscent of the Amalfi Coast or the French Riviera.

## Gazipaşa

**39**  *47 km (29 mi) southeast of Alanya on Rte. 400.*

On your way along the coast you may want to stop in Gazipaşa. It's being touted as the Mediterranean's next big resort, with its own airport and hotels and restaurants springing up. The question is whether Gazipaşa will become another Side or Alanya or will retain the charm and tranquillity that led one of Turkey's leading writers and painters, Fikret Otyam, to make it his home for the last 20 years.

## Anamur

**40**  *83 km (51 mi) southeast of Gazipaşa on Rte. 400.*

Anamur is one of the fastest developing resorts east of Alanya. In the small **Anamur Müzesi** (Anamur Museum), local finds, including earthenware phalluses buried in the fields by farmers as part of a fertility ritual, are on display. This ritual predated the arrival of Christianity but continued well into Christian times; today phalluses still occasionally turn up when farmers are plowing. ☒ *$1.* ☉ *8–5.*

South of town on the shore is the **Mamure Kalesi** (Mamure Castle, also known as Mamuriye). Its precise date of construction is uncertain, but it was built in Roman times to protect the city, then known as Anemurium, from seaborne raiders. The castle was renovated and partially rebuilt by the Seljuks, who captured it in the 13th century, and again by the Karamanoğulları, who controlled this part of Anatolia after the Seljuk empire collapsed. Note the inscription to the Karamanoğulları prince, İbrahim Bey II, dating from 1450.

## Lodging

**$–$$** ☎ **Hermes Hotel.** From Anamur to Mersin you won't find luxury hotels or gourmet restaurants, though there are plenty of perfectly adequate, modern, plainer places to sleep and eat. This hotel in the center of Anamur is a case in point: What differentiates it is air-conditioning in all rooms. ✉ *İskele Cıvarı Mevkii,* ☎ *324/814–3950,* 𝖥𝖠𝖷 *324/814–3995. 70 rooms with shower. 2 restaurants, 3 bars, cafeteria, air-conditioning, pool, sauna, dance club. MC, V.*

*En Route*   Eleven kilometers (7 miles) before Silifke is the town of **Taşucu.** If you want to make an excursion to the Turkish republic of Northern Cyprus, this is the place to get a hovercraft to Girne (Kyrenia). Another alternative is to take the ferry from Mersin.

# Silifke

④⑴   *Silifke is 120 km (74 mi) east of Anamur on Rte. 400, Kız Kaleiçi 21 km (13 mi) farther.*

The small town of Silifke is dominated by its Byzantine castle; the exact date of construction is unknown. In the vicinity of the castle, remains have been found indicating there was a settlement here as far back as the Bronze Age, though most of what can be seen today is from the Roman city known as **Seleuceia Trachea,** or Calycadnos Seleuceia. The ruins include a theater, a stadium, and the Corinthian columns of the 2nd-century AD Temple of Zeus. Also left are a basilica and tomb dedicated to St. Thecla, St. Paul's first convert and the first female Christian martyr. Local finds are displayed in the small **Silifke Müzesi** (Silifke Museum). ☉ *Daily 8–5.*

★   On an island just off the coast is the **Kız Kalesi** (Maiden's Castle). The island is known to have been a settlement as early as the 4th century BC, though the castle is nowhere near that old. As might be expected from the setting and name, Kız Kalesi comes with a legend: Locals will tell you it was built by a king to protect his only daughter. The beautiful daughter, the apple of her father's eye, had her fortune read by a wandering soothsayer who declared she would die of a snakebite. The king therefore sent her to the island, where there were no snakes, and the castle takes its name from the maiden's exile. But she did die from a snakebite in the end: the offending serpent was delivered to the castle by accident in a basket of grapes sent as a gift from her father's palace.

Across the main highway from the castle are the remains of **Korykos** (Corycos), the ancient city the castle protected. Part of Cilicia, Korykos, which Mark Anthony presented to Cleopatra in about 36 BC and which was taken back into the Roman Empire by Antiochus III in 197 AD, was ruled for many years by the monarchs of Egypt. It enjoyed its finest flowering as a major port city in the Roman and Byzantine periods and, unlike some of its neighbors along this coast, regained much of this importance under the Ottomans. It wasn't until the 19th century that it was abandoned. Excavations are not complete, but finds include parts of a Byzantine rampart, a Roman gate, buildings believed to be temples, column bases, and a necropolis.

Two kilometers (1 mile) inland from Korykos are two **caves.** More than 400 ft deep and close to Korykos's Temple of Zeus, **Cennet** (Heaven) can be entered via a path that has stone steps dating from Roman times. At the westernmost point of the cave is a small Byzantine church. Cehennem (Hell) is not accessible. It's believed that the Romans used the cave as a prison and that the monster Typhon was walled up inside Cehennem—curious because most versions of Roman mythology have it that Zeus slew Typhon on the slopes of Mt. Etna, in Sicily.

### Dining and Lodging

**$–$$** ✕🏨 **Club Barbarossa Hotel.** To explore this area thoroughly, an overnight stop is recommended. This modern hotel, 27 km (17 mi) east of the Kız Kalesi, has great views of the castle, its own beach, and air-conditioning. Furnishings are simple, and the staff is very friendly. The Barbarossa restaurant serves good, simple Turkish fare. Also nearby, along the coastal highway, are a number of inexpensive fish restaurants. ⊠ *Kız Kalesi, Erdemli,* ☎ *324/523–2364,* FAX *324/523–2090. 103 rooms with shower. 2 restaurants, 5 bars, cafeteria, snack bar, air-conditioning, 2 pools, sauna, Turkish bath, beach. AE, MC, V.*

## Mersin

**㊷** *68 km (42 mi) east of Silifke on Rte. 400.*

A commercial center, Mersin is not very attractive, but it has a good selection of hotels and therefore makes a fine base for exploring this part of the coast. Note that from June through September, the combination of extreme heat and humidity makes Mersin one of the most inhospitable places in this region. Do what the locals do: get out, either to the waterfront bars and restaurants or to the resort areas along the coast.

One of the highlights is on the outskirts of town—**Viranşehir,** a colony settled by Rhodes that later became a pirate stronghold. Here you'll find a long row of Corinthian columns and, in winter, the goatskin tents of Turkoman nomads known as the Yörük.

### Lodging

**$$$** 🏨 **Mersin Hilton.** This Hilton is thoroughly modern, efficient, more luxurious than the competition, and filled with amenities. At 12 stories it's one of the tallest buildings on the coast. Rooms are good-sized, and all have views of the Mediterranean. ⊠ *Adnan Menderes Bul. 3310,* ☎ *324/326–5000,* FAX *324/326–5050. 188 rooms with bath. Restaurant, bar, minibars, pool, sauna, 2 tennis courts, health club, shops. AE, DC, MC, V.* ♨

**$$** 🏨 **Mersin Oteli.** The Mersin aspires to be like the nearby Hilton but doesn't quite succeed. Though it, too, is a big, white, modern box of a hotel, it's older and its public and private spaces are less grand. Of course, it costs less, too. ⊠ *Gümrük Meyd. 112,* ☎ *324/238–1040,* FAX *324/231–2625. 105 rooms with shower. Restaurant, bar, sauna, exercise room, casino, nightclub. AE, DC, MC, V.*

*En Route*  St. Paul was born some 2,000 years ago in Tarsus, 28 km (17 mi) east of Mersin on Route E90, though little sign of the saint remains nowadays in what has become a dusty, sleepy provincial town of no great interest.

## Adana

**㊸** *69 km (43 mi) east of Mersin on Rte. E90.*

Adana is Turkey's fourth-largest city after Istanbul, Ankara, and İzmir, but it's the least known to tourists because it's a commercial and industrial center with few sights. The city is the center of the enormously fertile Çukurova Plain, where cotton and rice are staple crops. It's a bustling, clamorous city with many *gecekondu* suburbs. *Gecekondu* means "erected overnight," and the houses in these areas are just that—built without permission, usually on publicly owned land. Because of the large migrant population here, you may hear Kurdish and even Arabic in the streets.

The region is the home of one of Turkey's leading contemporary novelists, Yaşar Kemal. Kemal began his career as a public letter writer in the town of Kozan, 65 km (40 mi) northeast of Adana, and much of his work is set in this region of Turkey, including *İnce Memed* (translated into English and filmed as *Mehmet My Hawk*), published in 1955.

Adana's earliest migrants were the Hittites in the 19th century BC, believed to be the first people to establish a settlement on the site of the present city. Their empire grew and extended far beyond Anatolia. But in the early 7th century BC, they were pushed out of Anatolia through the combined pressure of the Assyrians, the Egyptians, and the area's indigenous peoples. For a good introduction to Hittite culture, head to the **Adana Arkeoloji Müzesi** (Adana Archaeological Museum). Also here are finds from other, later civilizations. ☎ *322/454–3855.* ✉ *$1.* ⊙ *Daily 9–5.*

Adana also has an **Ethnographic Museum.** ☎ *322/363–3717.* ✉ *$1.* ⊙ *Daily 9–5.*

In addition, the city has a good many reminders of the Ottoman period, of which the **Ulu Cami** (Great Mosque), completed in 1541, and its *medrese* (theological school) are among the finest. The mosque's *mihrab* (the prayer niche indicating the direction of Mecca) is a splendid example of İnik tile work.

More tile work is found at the nearby **Ramazanoğlu Türbe** (Ramazanoğlu Tomb). Also finished in 1541, it's a memorial to Ramazanoğlu Halil Bey, one of the most powerful leaders of the Ramazanoğlu principalities, which ruled this part of Turkey for more than 250 years. Although they accepted Ottoman sovereignty in 1517, they continued their rule until 1608, when the province started being governed directly from Istanbul. It was Halil Bey who began the building of the Ulu Mosque in 1513, but he did not live to see it completed.

OFF THE
BEATEN PATH

**KARATEPE –** About 130 km (81 mi) northeast of Adana, this important late Hittite site makes for a long day trip but a worthwhile one. And if you're traveling between İskenderun and Antakya, definitely make the detour. To reach Karatepe from Adana, take Route E90 east as far as Osmaniye, then go northwest on the local road, signposted to Karatepe and Kadirli. The road forks 8 km (5 mi) farther on: left for Kadirli and right for Karatepe, which is 19 km (12 mi) from the fork. Close to the modern village is the ancient city of Karatepe, whose most important building is the summer palace of Asitavanda, monarch of the late Hittite kingdom of Kue in the 8th century BC. Although some of the more fragile finds have been removed to museums elsewhere, a number of objects are exhibited in the open-air museum. A treasure trove of artifacts, the museum has fine examples of Hittite and Phoenician statuary and some remarkable pictorial friezes that bring Asitavanda's court to life. The area around the site is a beautiful national park. Also here, 4 km (2½ mi) north of Karatepe, is Kum Castle, which has survived remarkably intact since Crusader times. Some travel agencies in Adana organize day trips to these sites, which also take in Anavarza, a ruined Byzantine city near the village of Dilekkaya, around 50 km (31 mi) west. ▨ *$1, including guided tour.* ☉ *Daily 8–5.*

## Lodging

**$$$$**    ⚇ **Seyhan Hotel.** In the heart of the city, this high-rise hotel with a mirrored-glass exterior is a modern Adana landmark. Inside, it lives up to the five-star rating the eccentric Turkish system gives it. It even has its own farm and a small zoo. ⊠ *Turhan Cemal Beriker Bul. 18,* ☎ *322/457–5810,* ℻ *322/454–2834. 140 rooms, 20 suites, and 20 apartments, all with bath. Restaurant, 5 bars, snack bar, pool, sauna, Turkish bath. AE, DC, MC, V.*

**$–$$**    ⚇ **Çetinel Tesisleri.** An alternative to staying in the center of town is this small but well-run hotel, 3 km (2 mi) west of Adana in Yüreğirn. It has lovely gardens and camping facilities. ⊠ *Girne Bul. 138, Yüreğir,* ☎ *322/321–2758, 322/321–2759, or 322/321–2766,* ℻ *322/321–2775. 30 rooms with shower. Restaurant, bar, pool. MC, V.*

*En Route*    Traveling east, then south from Adana, you come to a part of Turkey little frequented by tourists. You'll cross the plain of Issos, where Alexander the Great defeated Darius III of Persia in 333 BC and founded a city that still bears his name, though it is now translated into Turkish: **İskenderun.** This pleasant, modern seaside town 50 km (31 mi) north of Antakya is a good place to take a break, even if little trace now remains of its ancient history.

# Antakya (Antioch)

🌢 *191 km (118 mi) from Adana, east on Rte. E90, south on Rte. E91.*

Antakya is better known by its old name, Antioch. Founded in about 300 BC by Seleucus Nikator, one of Alexander's generals, the city grew quickly, thanks to its strategic location on the trade routes between Asia, the Middle East, and the Mediterranean. After the Roman occupation began in AD 64, Antioch became the empire's third most important city, after Rome and Alexandria. Famed for its luxury and notorious for its depravity, it was chosen by St. Paul as the objective of his first mission to the gentiles. After enduring earthquakes and Byzantine and Arab raids, it fell to the crusaders in 1098; Egyptian raiders nearly leveled it in 1268. A late addition to the Turkish Republic, it was occupied by France after 1920 as part of its mandate over Syria, which still has an outstanding territorial claim on it. Though the city reverted to Turkey just before World War II, it still maintains a distinctive character. The people of Antakya are mostly bilingual, speaking both Turkish and a local dialect of Arabic. In the cobbled streets of the old quarter, on the east bank of the River Orontes, you can also hear Syriac (Aramaic), the language spoken by many of Turkey's Christians (although the Syriac Christian community is rapidly declining). This part of town has many attractive and interesting old houses.

On the northern edge of town is **Senpiyer Kilisesi** (church of St. Peter), a tiny cave high up on a cliff, blackened by centuries of candle smoke and dripping with water seeping out of the rock. It is here that the apostle preached to his converts and where they first came to be called Christians. The present facade to the cave dates from the 11th and 12th centuries. Mass is celebrated here on the first Sunday of every month. ⊠ *Off Kurtuluş Cad.*

The River Orontes (Asi in Turkish) divides Antakya in two. In the old town you will find the 17th-century **Habib Neccar Cami,** a mosque on Kurtuluş Caddesi, due south of St. Peter's. Just north is the bazaar quarter, a real change of pace: The feel here is more Syrian and Arab than

Turkish. On Hürriyet Caddesi, several winding blocks southwest of the mosque opposite the Atahan Hotel, is the fine loggia of a derelict **Latin monastery**; enter its cloister from the side street.

Experts consider the exceptional Roman mosaics of **Hatay Müzesi** (Hatay Museum)—portraying scenes from mythology and figures such as Dionysus, Orpheus, Oceanus, and Thetis—among the highest achievements of Roman art. ⊠ *Gündüz Cad. 1, in central square on right bank of Orontes,* ☎ *326/214–6167.* 🎫 *$1.* ☉ *Tues.–Sun. 8:30– 12:30 and 1:30–5:30.*

Most mosaics at the Hatay Museum come from villas in **Harbiye,** originally called Daphne, a beautiful gorge of laurel trees and tumbling waterfalls that was said to have been chosen by the gods for the Judgment of Paris and that contained one of the ancient world's most important shrines to the god Apollo (⊠ 7 km [4 mi] south of Antakya on Rte. E91). Mark Antony chose it as the venue for his ill-fated marriage to Cleopatra in 40 BC. Daphne was also a favorite resort for wealthy Antiochenes and developed such a reputation for licentiousness, it was put off-limits to the Roman army.

OFF THE BEATEN PATH

**SAMANDAG AND SELEUCEIA AD PIERIA** – You'll find a beach at Samandag (also known as Çevlik Beach), as well as tasty but inexpensive fish, 28 km (17 mi) south of Antakya. You'll also find the remains of Antioch's old port, Seleuceia ad Pieria, including an underground water channel, 1,400 meters (1,526 yards) long, which was built entirely by hand. Nearby rock tombs are still used by the local villagers to stable their donkeys.

## Lodging

$$–$$$ 🏨 **Büyük Antakya.** If you've made it this far, almost to the Syrian border, you deserve the best hotel available, and this is it: a giant, white pyramid of a building with cool marble in the lobby and bright rooms with big windows and nonstop sun. ⊠ *Atatürk Cad. 8,* ☎ *326/213– 5860,* 🗚 *326/213–5869. 72 rooms with shower. Restaurant, bar, air-conditioning, dance club. MC, V.*

$$ 🏨 **Arsuz Hotel.** On its own private beach in Arsuz (also called Uluçınar) is this clean, bright, airy hotel with a lush garden leading down to a private beach. ⊠ *Arsuz (Uluçınar),* ☎ *326/643–2444, 326/643–2445, or 326/643–2447,* 🗚 *326/643–2448. 104 rooms and 3 suites, all with bath or shower. Restaurant, 2 bars, beach. MC, V.*

$ 🏨 **Orontes Hotel.** This hotel has basic but air-conditioned rooms in the city center. ⊠ *İstiklal Cad. 58,* ☎ *326/214–5931,* 🗚 *326/214–5933. 35 rooms with shower. Restaurant, air-conditioning. No credit cards.*

# THE MEDITERRANEAN COAST A TO Z

## Arriving and Departing

### By Bus

Buses run frequently to this area. Routes are between Bodrum or İzmir and Marmaris; between Pamukkale's station in Denizli and Antalya; and between Ankara and Antalya or Mersin. The trip from Ankara to Antalya takes about eight hours (longer in winter) and costs about $15. The trip from Marmaris to Istanbul takes a grueling 13–14 hours and costs about $25.

### By Car

The main coast road from the Aegean becomes Route 330 at Milas and continues through Mugla toward Marmaris. From Marmaris the coast road going east is Route 400, which continues all the way to

Mersin, at which a branch of Route E90 goes on to Adana and E91 branches off for İkenderun and Antakya. If you're approaching the Mediterranean from the east end, take Route E90. The drive to Marmaris is 287 km (178 mi) from İzmir, 178 km (110 mi) from Bodrum. To Antalya, the inland route along E87 from Pamukkale is 296 km (184 mi). From Istanbul go via Antalya or Ankara; from Ankara just follow E90 south to Adana.

## By Plane

The main airports for flights between the coast and Istanbul, İzmir, or Ankara are in **Dalaman** (☎ 252/692–5899) and **Antalya. Adana** has a smaller airport with some domestic service; flights to far-eastern Turkey go from Adana. Charter flights, some direct from Europe, predominate in Dalaman. **Turkish Airlines** (☎ 212/663–6363 in Istanbul, 242/243–4381 in Antalya) also travels from Istanbul and Ankara to Dalaman in summer. Turkish Airlines and **Istanbul Airlines** (☎ 212/231–7526 in Istanbul, 242/243–3893 in Antalya) have several daily flights from Istanbul to Antalya and less frequent service from Ankara and İzmir. **Sun Express** (☎ 242/323–4047), a charter company that is a joint venture between Turkish Airlines and Lufthansa, will sell spare seats on its charter flights to and from the Dalaman and Antalya airports.

BETWEEN THE AIRPORTS AND CENTER CITY

Buses run frequently between Antalya's airport and the city center, 10 km (6 mi) away; the cost is $2. Taking a taxi to the city **bus station** (✉ Kazım Özalp Cad., ☎ 242/241–6231) should cost about $7.

From Dalaman Airport, buses travel frequently between Fethiye and Marmaris, 50 km (31 mi) east and 60 km (37 mi) west, respectively; the trip costs about $5. In Marmaris, the city **bus station** (☎ 252/412–3037) is two blocks north of İskele Meydanı, the main square. In Fethiye, the **bus station** (☎ 252/614–3531) is just off Atatürk Caddesi, about 1 km (½ mi) east of the town center.

## By Train

There is no service along the Mediterranean Coast.

# Getting Around

## By Boat

Traveling by boat is the best way to see the many otherwise-inaccessible coves and beaches. Local fishermen will transport you for a small fee, or you can hop on one of the many water taxis. You will see both types of transport lined up along the harbor in every seaside town. Many people charter boats and join the small flotillas that leave the Bodrum and Marmaris marinas daily for sightseeing tours in summer.

## By Bus

Every city has an intercity bus terminal. Routes connect **Antalya** (☎ 242/331–1250) with **Marmaris** (☎ 252/412–3037), **Mersin** (☎ 324/238–1648), and **Adana** (☎ 322/428–2047), with stops in between. Note that when the bus terminal is outside the city center (as it is in Antalya), it is customary for bus companies to provide minibus service from their city center locations to the station. Ask for *servis* (transfer service from the city center to the bus station) when you book your ticket, and you'll be given a pickup time. Otherwise, finding your own way to the terminal can be difficult and time consuming. The **Varan Bus Company** (☎ 212/551–7474 in Istanbul, 242/331–1111 in Antalya) is more expensive than others, but it has better service, no-smoking buses, and its own privately owned and spotlessly clean rest stops.

### By Car

Although the highways between towns are well maintained, the smaller roads are usually unpaved and very rough, and the twisty coastal roads require intense concentration. Some sample distances: Marmaris to Fethiye, 168 km (104 mi); Fethiye to Antalya, 318 km (197 mi); Antalya to Alanya, 115 km (71 mi). To estimate driving times, figure on about 70 km (43 mi) per hour.

## Contacts and Resources

### Car Rentals

On the Mediterranean you'll find international car-rental offices at the major tourist centers and in airports. Or you can make reservations when you first arrive at Atatürk Airport, in Istanbul: **Avis** (☎ 212/662–0852), **Budget** (☎ 212/574–1635), and **Hertz** (☎ 212/663–6400). For more information about car rentals, *see* Car Rental *in* the Gold Guide.

### Diving

The **Turkish Diving Federation** (✉ Ulus İşhane, A. Blok. 303–304, Ulus, Ankara, ☎ 312/310–4136, FAX 312/310–8288) can provide information on the permits you need for diving independently. If you are going to take a diving course, make sure the school is recognized by one or both international diving organizations, CMAS and PADI, and has instructors who speak English. Some of the best diving schools are the **Active Diving Center** (☎ 242/511–3662) in Alanya, the **Eurasia Diving Center** (☎ 242/814–3250), in Kemer; the **European Diving Center** (☎ 252/814–3250), in Fethiye; and the **İlter Diving Center** (☎ 242/311–8677), in Antalya.

### Emergencies

**Ambulance** (☎ 112). **Police** (☎ 155).

### Rafting and Trekking

In Alanya, contact **Alraft Rafting and Riding Club** (☎ 242/513–9155), which, as the name suggests, also organizes horseback-riding trips. In Fethiye, **Aventura** (☎ 252/616–6427) specializes in all kinds of activities, includes paragliding from Mt. Babadağ. In Side, **Get Wet** (☎ 242/753–4071) can arrange all kinds of outdoor activities such as rafting, trekking, and mountaineering. Yet another outdoor-sports specialist is Antalya-based **TransNature** (☎ 242/247–8688).

### Travel Agencies

**Kahramanlar Turizm** (✉ Cumhuriyet Meyd. 9, Kaş, ☎ 242/836–1062 or 242/836–2400, FAX 242/836–2422). **Pamphylia Travel** (✉ İstiklal Cad., Antalya, ☎ 242/243–1500, FAX 242/242–1400). **Sardes Tourism** (✉ Kordon Cad. 26, Dalyan, ☎ 252/284–2050, FAX 252/284–2189). **Tantur** (✉ Emre Oteli, K Evren Bul., Marmaris, ☎ 252/412–4616, FAX 252/412–6921).

### Visitor Information

Tourist offices: **Adana** (✉ Atatürk Cad. 13, ☎ 322/363–1448, FAX 322/363–1346). **Alanya** (✉ Damlataş Cad. 1, ☎ 242/513–1240, FAX 242/513–5436). **Antakya** (✉ Vali Ürgen Alanı 147, ☎ 326/216–0610, FAX 326/213–5740). **Antalya** (✉ Cumhuriyet Cad., Özel İdare Altı 2, ☎ 242/241–1747. **Dalaman** (✉ At airport, ☎ 252/692–5220). **Datça** (✉ Hükümet Binası, İskele Mah., ☎ 252/712–3163, FAX 252/712–3546). **Fethiye** (✉ İskele Karşısı 1, ☎ FAX 252/614–1527). **Kaş** (✉ Cumhuriyet Meyd. 5, ☎ FAX 242/836–1238). **Marmaris** (✉ İskele Meyd. 2, by marina, ☎ 252/412–1035, FAX 252/412–7277). **Mersin** (✉ /1, Liman Girişi, near docks, ☎ 324/238–3271, FAX 324/238–3272). **Side** (✉ Side Yolu Üzeri, Manavgat, ☎ 242/753–1265, FAX 242/753–2657). **Silifke** (✉ Veli Gürten Bozbey Cad. 6, Gazi Mah., ☎ 324/714–1151, FAX 324/714–5328).

# 5 ANKARA AND CENTRAL ANATOLIA

The civilizations that have inhabited Central Anatolia have bequeathed a richly textured region. Where else can you tread the same ground as the ancient Hattis, Hittites, Luwians, Phrygians, Cimmerians, Lydians, Persians, Macedonians, Bithynians, Galatians, Romans, Byzantines, Seljuks, and Ottomans? Many sights here are unique: churches carved into volcanic rock, underground cities, and the dance of the whirling dervishes. Here also is the political and cultural center of Ankara, which has attained Atatürk's ideal of a modern Turkish city.

Revised and
Updated by
Margaret Lynch

ISTORY HAS A WAY OF COMING FULL CIRCLE. In the 2nd millennium BC, Central Anatolia was the center of one of the earliest empires—the Hittites. In the 13th century AD, long after
the Hittites had disappeared, the Seljuks built a new empire in the center of Asia Minor. By the 19th century the region had become a backwater province in a failing Ottoman Empire, but after founding the
modern Turkish Republic in 1923, Kemal Atatürk chose Ankara to be
the seat of his government. Tens of thousands of Turks streamed into
the town, mostly on foot, to undertake the building of the new capital. Today the population has swelled to more than 3 million, and Central Anatolia is once again a political center.

Ankara is the natural starting point for exploring the ancient Hittite
cities of Hattuşaş, Alacahöyük, and Yazılıkaya; the wild lunar land-
scapes of Cappadocia (Kapadokya); and the old Seljuk capital at
Konya, home of the whirling dervishes. Although Ankara may be
physically close to these regions, its spirit is elsewhere. Atatürk was
determined to westernize Turkey; nowhere has that objective been
more fully realized than in Ankara. In the 1930s the neo-Ottoman architectural style popular in Turkey was scrapped in favor of a symbolic,
stark modernism influenced by the Vienna cubist and German Bauhaus
schools. A master plan for the city was devised by Hermann Jansen, a
Berlin city architect. Today's Ankara is thoroughly modern; it is the
haunt of politicians and civil servants, and its social calendar is studded with cocktail parties and diplomatic receptions.

The mood changes in the ancient towns of Central Anatolia. This region has been the homeland of numerous tribes and nations and has
served as a historical battleground as well as a melting pot of East and
West. Frontiers remained fluid, as even the Taurus mountain chain, to
the south, and higher chains to the southeast proved ineffective as natural boundaries of the interminable Anatolian plateau. As a result, the
landscape contains fascinating evidence of a long and complex human
occupation.

## Pleasures and Pastimes

### Dining
Central Anatolia's restaurants serve food similar to what you find
throughout Turkey: kebabs, kebabs, and more kebabs. Other common
dishes include mezes (appetizers), grilled fish and meat (especially
lamb), and vegetarian dishes. Many restaurants serve wine, beer, and
*rakı*, the ouzolike Turkish liqueur. Dress is casual, and unless otherwise noted, reservations are not necessary—in fact, you will seldom
need them except in Ankara, where dining is more sophisticated. For
a chart that explains the cost of meals at the restaurants in this chapter, *see* Dining and Lodging Price Categories at the back of this book.

### Lodging
Because Ankara is the nation's capital and host to many foreign embassies, hotels here tend to be grander, more Western, and more expensive than those in the rest of the country. Hotels in the surrounding
region have fewer amenities but much more charm—especially the hotels around Cappadocia. For a chart that explains room rates at the
accommodations in this chapter, *see* Dining and Lodging Price Categories at the back of this book.

### Nightlife
In much of Central Anatolia there is little nightlife, and the few bars and
discos to be found are local watering holes. Ankara, on the other hand,

has nightclubs with live bands at the Grand Hotel Ankara and the Hilton SA and Sheraton hotels. You can also head for the Luna Park Aile Gazinosu (Family Nightclub), in Gençlik Parkı, where Turkey's top pop singers perform nightly in summer. Though the good seats go early, the best acts come on late—about 11 PM. Tickets are available at the door.

## Shopping

The best bazaars can be found in Ankara, Kayseri, and Konya. Rugs and kilims are everywhere. In Ankara look for products made from angora, a local specialty; but check to see the origin of the material, as much of the angora now on sale in the city has been imported. Government-run stores called *dösim* are smart places to shop for handicrafts without the pressure of bargaining. There is one in the Göreme Open-Air Museum; in Ankara the Gesav Sanat Evi offers a similar collection of handicrafts, also with set prices.

# Exploring Ankara and Central Anatolia

If you are coming from the temperate Aegean or Mediterranean coasts, Central Anatolia provides a change. The climate is harsh, and temperatures can be extreme, especially in the north. Much of the plateau is an arid plain, slashed by ravines, centered on a huge salt lake, and scattered with mountains (often extinct volcanoes) and rivers dammed up into artificial lakes. In Cappadocia volcanic eruptions long ago covered the ground with tufa, a thick layer of mud and ash, over which lava spread. Erosion by rain, snow, and wind created "fairy chimneys"— surrealistic cones, needles, pillars, and pyramids. To the infinite variety of forms, oxidation added an improbable range of colors.

## Great Itineraries

You can cover the whole of Ankara in a day or two. From here, the Hittite cities to the east can easily be done as a day trip. Ankara, Cappadocia, and Konya form a rough triangle. Konya is en route to Antalya and the Mediterranean Coast or, if you stay inland, to Pamukkale and then to İzmir on the Aegean Coast. Cappadocia, to the southeast, is on the way to Diyarbakır and the far east of the country. You'll need at least two days to explore the wonders of Cappadocia, but Konya requires only a day.

IF YOU HAVE 3 DAYS
*Numbers in the text correspond to numbers in the margin and on the Central Anatolia and Ankara maps.*

You can easily cover Ankara and the Hittite cities in three days. Spend your first day exploring ⌖ **Ankara** ①–⑮. On day two, wake up early and head to the Hittite city of **Hattuşaş** ⑯. Continue 2 km (1 mi) northeast of Hattuşaş to view the rock carvings of **Yazılıkaya** ⑱. Return to Ankara in time for dinner. On your last day in Ankara, visit the rest of the city's sites.

IF YOU HAVE 7 DAYS
Spend days one and two in ⌖ **Ankara** ①–⑮. On day three, head to **Hattuşaş** ⑯ and **Yazılıkaya** ⑱. In the afternoon, drive south on the road to **Yozgat**. Take Route E88 west, then Route 785 heading south to Route 260, which eventually meets up with Route 765. Continue south on Route 765 to ⌖ **Nevşehir** ㉒. The morning of day four, drive 21 km (13 mi) south of Nevşehir on the road to Niğde, stopping at either **Kaymaklı** ㉓ or, farther south toward Niğde, at **Derinkuyu** ㉔, both underground cities. Break for lunch in **Ürgüp** ㉕, then head northwest to the vineyard-filled valley of ⌖ **Göreme** ㉖ and its open-air museum. On day five, visit **Zelve** ㉗ and stop by **Avanos** ㉘ to shop for onyx jewelry and pottery before breaking for lunch. Take a scenic drive south on

Route 300 until you reach the **Ihlara Valley** ㉝, where the Melendiz River has carved a rift into the sheer tuff cliffs. Spend another night in Göreme. Early on day six, continue on Route 300 to Konya, stopping along the way at Anatolia's largest and best-preserved caravansary, **Sultan Hanı.** Have lunch when you arrive in ⛽ **Konya** ㉞. Then head to Mevlâna Türbesi, the tomb of Mevlâna Celaleddin Rumi, the 13th-century poet and philosopher who founded the mystic order of the Mevlevi dervishes. From here, you can easily walk to the rest of the sights in Konya. On your last day in Central Anatolia, make your way to the ancient acropolis and enjoy the hilltop park, where you can have lunch at the café providing a scenic view. In the afternoon, walk around the bazaar.

### When to Tour Ankara and Central Anatolia

Ankara is always bustling, so there's no off-season when restaurants or hotels close. Elsewhere in Central Anatolia, though, museum hours are often shortened, and some sites close. It is especially difficult to explore the Hittite cities, even as late as April, because ice blocks some roads. Regardless of the season, try to visit the temple at Yazılıkaya around noon since that is when the stone reliefs are the most visible.

# ANKARA AND THE HITTITE CITIES

This city on the eastern edge of the high Anatolian Plateau may be physically close to the rest of the region, but in every other way Ankara feels a world apart from the surrounding steppe land. Turkey's capital provides a logical base for exploring the great sites of the Hittite Empire, which are contained within a triangle in northeastern Central Anatolia bounded by Hattuşaş, Yazılıkaya, and Alacahöyük. All the Hittite cities can be seen in a day trip if you have a car.

## Ankara

*454 km (281 mi) southeast of Istanbul, Rte. E80 to Rte. E89.*

Although Ankara is a young city, it has an ancient heart. It was here, at the dawn of the 15th century, that the Ottoman sultan Beyazıt I came face to face with the dreaded warrior Tamerlane, a descendant of Genghis Khan. Tamerlane came to Anatolia with an impressive record. He had subjugated Asia east of the Caspian Sea, invaded Persia, laid waste the Kirghiz plain, marched on Russia, turned south and attacked India, driven the Egyptians from Syria, and destroyed Baghdad, all in the course of 30 years. Beyazıt, called Yıldırım (Thunderbolt), had not done badly himself. He had wrested Bulgaria, Macedonia, and Thessaly from their Christian rulers and had slaughtered an army of crusaders at the Battle of Nicopolis.

The clash between Beyazıt and Tamerlane took place in July 1402, in the plain below the small town that was then called Ancyra. Beyazıt lost, decisively, providing much useful material for future poets. He was taken prisoner, and some say the ruthless Tamerlane took pleasure in humiliating and torturing him, scenes depicted with relish by the 16th-century playwright Christopher Marlowe in *Tamburlaine the Great.* Most authorities, however, agree the prisoner was treated with the regard due his rank. Beyazıt died after eight months of captivity, probably of a stroke, and Tamerlane, instead of continuing his march into Europe, turned his horse around and led his men back to the Mongol plains. He died the following year.

Before that epic battle, Ankara suffered a succession of conquerors. Legend attributes the city's foundation to the redoubtable Amazons,

# Central Anatolia

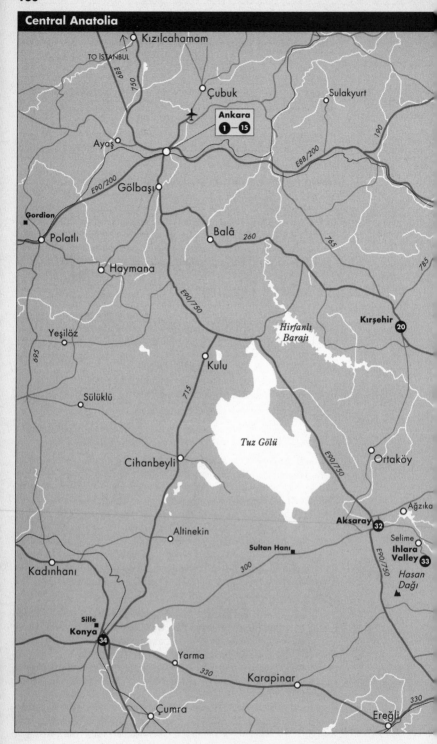

Kızılcahamam

TO İSTANBUL

Çubuk

Sulakyurt

Ankara
**1**—**15**

Ayaş

E88/200

Gölbaşı

E90/200

Gordion

Polatlı

Balâ  260

Haymana

Kırşehir
**20**

Yeşilöz

*Hirfanlı Barajı*

E90/750

Kulu

Sülüklü

715

*Tuz Gölü*

Cihanbeyli

Ortaköy

E90/750

Altinekin

Ağzıka

**Aksaray** **32**

Selime

Sultan Hanı

**Ihlara Valley** **33**

300

*Hasan Dağı*

E90/750

Kadınhanı

Sille
**Konya** **34**

Yarma

Karapinar

330

Çumra

Ereğli

330

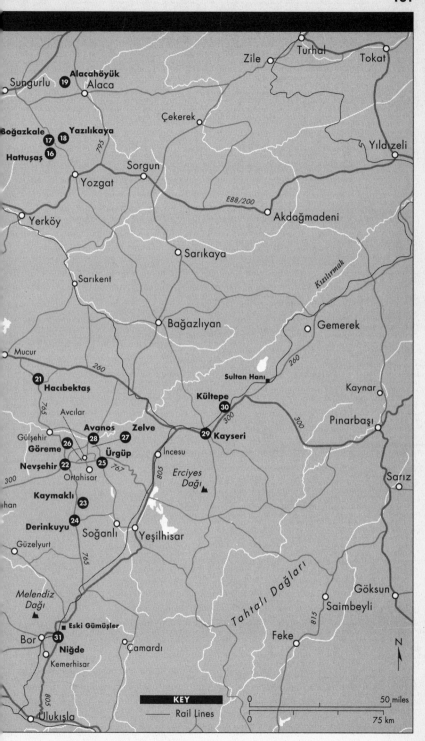

Sungurlu

Alacahöyük **19**
Alaca

**Boğazkale** **17** **18** **Yazılıkaya**
**Hattuşaş** **16**

Yozgat

Sorgun

Çekerek

Zile    Turhal    Tokat

Yıldızeli

795

E88/200

Yerköy

Akdağmadeni

Sarıkaya

Sarıkent

Bağazlıyan

Kızılırmak

Gemerek

Mucur

260

Hacıbektaş **21**

Sultan Hanı

Kültepe

260

Kaynar

765

Avcılar

Avanos **28** **27** **Zelve**
Göreme **26** **Ürgüp**
Nevşehir **22** **25**
Ortahisar

300

Kaymaklı **23**

Derinkuyu **24**
Soğanlı

Güzelyurt

300

**30**
**29** Kayseri

300

Pınarbaşı

İncesu

Erciyes
Dağı ▲

Sarız

805

767

765

Yeşilhisar

Melendiz
Dağı ▲

Eski Gümüşler

Bor **31**
**Niğde**
Kemerhisar

Çamardı

han

Tahtalı Dağları

Feke

Göksun
Saimbeyli

815

**N**
↑

805

Uluķışla

**KEY**
— Rail Lines

0 _____ 50 miles
0 _____ 75 km

but many archaeologists have identified it with the Hittite city of Ankuwash, which is thought to have been founded in around 1200 BC and taken over by the Phrygians in around 700 BC. It was later taken by Alexander the Great, the Seleucids, and the Galatians before being annexed to Rome by Augustus in 25 BC. Ankara retained its strategic significance through the Byzantine period, during which Persian, Arab, Seljuk, and Mongol invaders came and went through Ankara; but under the Ottomans its importance gradually declined. By the early 20th century it was little more than a dusty provincial town with an illustrious past, the perfect site for Atatürk to build an entirely new capital, just outside the old city.

To understand Ankara's layout, keep in mind that Atatürk Boulevard serves as the city's backbone. Ankara's modern development conveniently unfolds along this central north–south axis, with older settlements to the north and progressively newer districts stretching south. Much of what you will want to see is clustered in the old Ulus district, where narrow lanes surround some untidy Roman remains, several mosques, and the citadel. The first buildings of the modern Turkish Republic also are scattered here, around Ulus Meydanı. Here, as throughout the city, reminders of the country's revered founder are everywhere, from statues to streets bearing the names bestowed by his countrymen: Atatürk, the Father of the Turks; and Gazi, the Conqueror.

Begin exploring the city from some of its earliest material remains, at
❶ the **Hisar** (Citadel). Fortified by the Galatians, strengthened by the Romans, rebuilt by the Byzantines, and maintained by the Seljuks and Ottomans, the Hisar and its double walls are now crumbling away. Of the 20 towers that once guarded the structure, 15 are still standing at various heights. The citadel gates are fairly well intact; the best-preserved sections of the fortifications are near Parmak Kapısı (the inner gate). Hisar Kapısı (the outer gate) is topped by an inscription. Within the walls are ramshackle houses in the warren of narrow, cobbled lanes that gain a touch of elegance from incorporated bits of broken marble columns and slabs taken from Roman ruins. Some of the citadel's Ottoman houses now are being restored, and one contains the Gesav Sanat Evi (⊠ Kireçli Sok. 6), open Tuesday–Sunday 10–6:30 and a good place to buy fine handicrafts. The city's oldest *cami* (mosque), the small **Alaaddin Cami,** is also here. Originally built in 1178, much of what you see today was added later. To the south and west rise the skyscrapers of modern Ankara; the plains on which Tamerlane defeated Beyazıt stretch to the northeast; and crowded neighborhoods full of migrants to the capital from the countryside sprawl to the east.

★ ❷ The superb **Ankara Anadolu Medeniyetleri Müzesi** (Museum of Anatolian Civilizations) is housed in a restored 15th-century *bedestan* (covered bazaar and inn). Though the museum itself is relatively small, the collection is world class. Masterpieces from the Neolithic and Bronze ages and the Assyrian, Phrygian, Urartu, Hellenistic, and Roman eras are carefully displayed, all with explanations in English. (Note that the freelance "guides" who offer their services tend to overcharge and add little to your visit.) The heart of the museum is its comprehensive collection of Hatti and Hittite artifacts, dating from the dawn of the 2nd millennium BC. Here you will find the graceful, stylized deer standards that grace postcards throughout Turkey, as well as a bronze statuette of a bull (circa 2400 BC), a limestone Cappadocian idol with two heads (3rd millennium BC), a ram's-head vase (19th century BC), and a large bull's-head cauldron. Another huge cauldron, with clean, precise lines, is held up by four figures; it was found in Gordion, where a prophecy predicted Alexander the Great's rise to glory. There are small

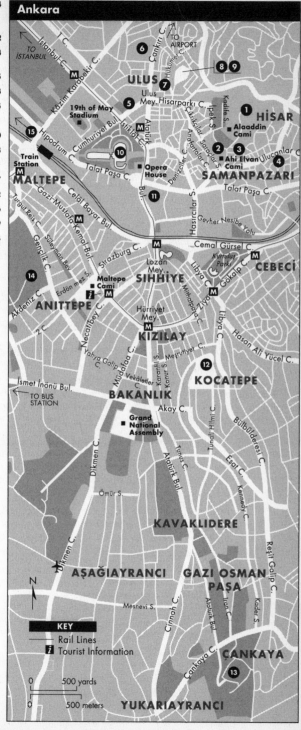

Ankara

statues, jewels worked in gold and iron, combs, and needles as well as wonderful bas-relief carvings in stone. The addition in 1998 of several frescoes from the site of Çatal Höyük (first occupied in the 7th millennium BC) offers an opportunity to view art that adorned the walls of homes in the oldest settled community in the world. Also displayed is a reconstruction of a ceremonial room from the site, decorated with clay bull's heads, along with several ceramic female figurines. ⊠ *Gözcü Sok. 2,* ☎ *312/324–3160.* ⊛ ⊠ *$4.* ☉ *Sun.–Tues. 8:30–5.*

South of the outer citadel walls is the neighborhood known as **Samanpazarı,** where you will find numerous mosques and small shops spilling out onto narrow lanes. This is prime hunting ground for rugs, crafts, antiques, and copperware. Three mosques, all open during daylight hours and with no admission charge, are in this bazaar area. The smallest of them, **Ahi Elvan Cami,** (⊠ Koyunpazarı Sok. 73) dates from the early
❸ 1400s and has Roman columns and a fine *mimber* (pulpit). **Aslanhane Cami** (Lionhouse Mosque; ⊠ Can Sok. 30), south of the citadel hill, took its name from the lion relief on a wall in front. It was built in
❹ 1289 by Emir Şeref Eddin. The 16th-century **Yeni Cami** (New Mosque; ⊠ Off Ulucanlar Cad.) was built by Süleyman's grand vizier, Çenabi Ahmet Paşa, supposedly using plans by the master architect Sinan, and executed by one of the great architect's pupils. The dark red porphyry of its walls is enhanced by the white-marble mimber and *mihrab* (prayer niche).

❺ The **Cumhuriyet Müzesi** (Republic Museum) originally housed the Büyük Millet Meclisi (Grand National Assembly). Here, between 1925 and 1960, the national parliament debated the decisions that would shape the extraordinary transformation of Turkey into a modern, secular nation. The early history of the parliament is shown through photographs, documents, and wax figures of the leaders of the first assembly. Most labels are in Turkish only. ⊠ *Cumhuriyet Bul. 22, off Ulus Meyd. (Nation Sq.),* ☎ *312/310–5361.* ⊠ *$1.75.* ☉ *Tues.–Sun. 9–noon and 1:30–5.*

❻ A 10-minute walk north of Ulus Meydanı, at the 3rd-century **Roma Hamamları** (Roman Baths), you can still see the oval soaking pool as well as the *frigidarium* and *caldarium* (cold and hot rooms). The steam rooms have raised floors; hot air once circulated below them from the furnace. Except for June–August, hours are reduced, so call ahead. ⊠ *Çankırı Cad. 43,* ☎ *312/310–7280.* ⊠ *$1.75.* ☉ *Daily 8:30–12:30 and 1:30–5:30.*

❼ The **Jülyanüs Sütunu** (Column of Julian) was erected in honor of the Roman emperor Julian the Apostate (ruled AD 361–63), so-called because he attempted to reverse his father's decision to make Christianity the empire's official religion. The column has 15 fluted drums topped by a Corinthian capital and commemorates a visit by the emperor in 362, when he was headed for battle with the Persians. Unfortunately, Julian didn't get to enjoy it; he died a year later. Storks arrive each spring to hatch their young in the huge nest atop the column. ⊠ *Hükümet Meyd., just northeast of Ulus Meyd.*

At the end of a lane lined with religious bookstores and stalls selling
❽ prayer beads is the **Hacı Bayram Cami,** built in the early 15th century of yellow stone and brick, with lavish touches of marble from the nearby Roman ruins and an unusual tiled roof. The glazed Kütahya tiles on the interior walls were added 300 years later. Hacı Bayram was a founder of an order of dervishes, and his tomb is near the entrance to the mosque. ⊠ *Bayram Cad., north of Hisarparkı Cad.,* ☎ *312/310–8297.* ⊠ *Free.* ☉ *Immediately after prayer times.*

**9**   **Temple of Augustus** was built 29–25 BC, probably on the site of a 2nd century BC shrine to Cybele, a nature goddess of Asia Minor, and dedicated to Augustus after a Roman law deified dead emperors. Augustus, who was opposed to this concept, nonetheless requested that a summary of the achievements of his rule (known today by its Latin title *Res Gestae,* or "Things Done") be carved into the walls of all his temples. The inscription discovered here in 1555 by a Flemish diplomat named Ghislain de Busbecq is the longest Latin inscription ever found and the only complete version of Augustus's text in the world. Fortunately Busbecq copied it down, as time has crumbled the stone and worn away most of the writing. ⊠ *Behind Hacı Bayram Cami.*

**10** The welcome green expanse of **Gençlik Parkı** (Youth Park) is in Ankara's new town. It has shady walks, tea gardens, a small amusement park with a Ferris wheel and rides for children, and a small lake where you can rent rowboats. ⊠ *Entrance on Atatürk Blvd.* ▨ *Free.* ◷ *Daily sunrise–sunset.*

**11** The **Etnoğrafya Müzesi** (Ethnographic Museum), up the hill across from the opera house, houses a rich collection of Turkish carpets, folk costumes, Anatolian handcrafts, weapons, and stunning Ottoman wooden mimbers. The building is done in Ottoman Revival style and includes a big dome and marble decoration. Atatürk lay in state here from 1938 to 1953, when his mausoleum was finished. The museum has been closed for restoration since 1999, and its reopening date has not yet been announced. Call ahead. ⊠ *Talat Paşa Cad., Opera,* ☎ *312/311–3007.* ▨ *$1.75.* ◷ *Tues.–Sun. 8:30–12:30 and 1:30–5.*

The **Resim ve Heykel Müzesi** (Painting and Sculpture Museum) displays works by contemporary Turkish artists. The building, completed in 1930, was used as a *Halk Evi* (People's House) by the ruling Republican People's Party to disseminate the ideals of secularism and republicanism. It was converted into a museum in the mid-1970s. ⊠ *Talat Paşa Cad., Opera,* ☎ *312/310–2094.* ▨ *Free.* ◷ *Tues.–Sun. 9–noon and 1–5.*

Atatürk Bulvarı runs south from Ulus through the **Sıhhiye district** and then into the **Kızılay district,** so named because of the Red Crescent (the Islamic world's version of the Red Cross) building that used to dominate Atatürk Bulvarı at Hürriyet Meydanı. Kızılay is the commercial center of the new city, its wide avenues and modern architecture built to contrast with the cramped old districts centered around the Hisar. Streets running parallel to Atatürk Bulvarı on the east side form a lively, colorful pedestrian area, with flower and fish markets, innumerable cafés, music shops, street vendors, and bookstores. Turhan Kitabevi, at the corner of Konur Sokak and Yüksel Caddesi, has an extensive offering of illustrated books on Turkish rugs, architecture, and archaeological sites. The main station for Ankara's new **metro,** opened in 1996, is at Hürriyet Meydanı.

**12** The vast **Kocatepe Cami** (Kocatepe Mosque), one of the largest mosques in the world, opened officially in 1987. You have to wonder what Atatürk would have thought of such a prominent religious structure in the capital of his secular state. Housed in the basement of the mosque is Beğendik, a Turkish department store. ⊠ *On Mithat Paşa Cad.*

Bakanlıklar, the government district, fills the west side of Atatürk Bulvarı from Hürriyet Meydanı to the **Türkiye Büyük Millet Meclisi** (Grand National Assembly), the parliament building, at the intersection with Ismet Inönü Bulvarı. Within walking distance, in the Kavaklıdere neighborhood, is Embassy Row, with gardens, fine restaurants, and world-class hotels.

⑬  The **Çankaya Köşkü** (Çankaya Pavilion) was occupied by Atatürk
    after he moved the capital to Ankara. The little house is on the grounds
    of the **Cumhurbaşkanlığı Köşkü** (Presidential Mansion), which has for-
    mal flower gardens and a fine view, though you can't visit the man-
    sion itself. You must have your passport for entry. ⊠ *Atatürk Bul., south
    of Çankaya Cad., Çankaya.* 🎫 *Free.* ⊙ *Sun. 1:30–4:30.*

★ ⑭  The most physically imposing of all of Ankara's attractions is the **Anıt
    Kabir** (Monumental Tomb), the mausoleum of Atatürk. Perched on a
    hilltop, it is reached by a marble-paved promenade lined with Hittite-
    style lions. To each side are pavilions with remarkable bas-relief carv-
    ings. At the entrance to the mausoleum are carved the words, WITHOUT
    CONDITION OR RESTRICTION, SOVEREIGNTY BELONGS TO THE PEOPLE. The
    mausoleum itself is a vast, soaring hall lined with brilliant gold mo-
    saics and marble, pierced by seven tall windows looking out over the
    city Atatürk built. The immensely impressive solitary marble sar-
    cophagus is only symbolic, however, as Atatürk's actual remains rest
    in the vault below. The **Atatürk Museum,** with personal belongings,
    objects associated with his life, and mementos from the War of Liber-
    ation (1919–22), is in an arcaded wing, along with a gift shop. ⊠ *Anıt
    Cad., south end,* ☎ *312/231–7975.* 🎫 *Free.* ⊙ *Daily 9–5.*

    When Turks want to get away from the heat of the city, many head
⑮  for **Atatürk Orman Çiftliği,** a model farm Atatürk had built in the city's
    western outskirts. In 1981, for the centenary of Atatürk's birth, a
    replica of his family home, the comfortable pink house of a merchant
    from Thessaloniki, was opened to visitors in the large park at the site.
    Pack a picnic lunch or try the excellent on-site restaurant ($–$$),
    which uses vegetables and dairy products produced on the farm.
    ⊠ *Hipodrom Cad., west from Talat Paşa Cad.,* ☎ *312/211–0170.*
    ⊙ *Daily 8–6.*

OFF THE          **GORDION –** The city made famous by King Midas, he of the golden
BEATEN PATH      touch, is only about 100 km (62 mi) southwest of Ankara. This was the
                 capital of Phrygia, whose population most likely emigrated from Mace-
                 donia and Thrace about 3,000 years ago. After a crushing defeat in
                 695 BC, Midas apparently committed suicide. There are a few remains
                 of the royal palace, but more interesting is the Great Tumulus, on the
                 edge of town, including what was once believed to be the tomb of King
                 Midas. It's a well-lighted tunnel, 230 ft long, that has been cut through
                 the mound to the burial chamber, which is framed with cedar and ju-
                 niper beams. When the tomb was opened, the skeleton of a short man,
                 about age 60, lay on a large table. It is believed that this was the body
                 of another king from the same dynasty; but who it was, nobody is sure.
                 The funerary artifacts were taken to the Museum of Anatolian Civiliza-
                 tions in Ankara; however, the small museum at Gordion, redesigned
                 and expanded in 1999, now provides a good overview of the site. *Take
                 Rte. E90 to Polatlı; then look for the road to Gordion, branching off to
                 the right, approximately 12 km (8 mi) west of Polatlı.*

## Dining and Lodging

$$$–$$$$   ✕ **Marco Polo.** This fine-dining restaurant specializes in classic inter-
           national cuisine such as steak and seafood. The menu is dynamic, fea-
           turing a nightly chef's recommended prix-fixe menu, the freshest fish,
           and seasonal food festivals. Excellent service, elegant decor, and live
           piano music make this Ankara's premier international dining option.
           ⊠ *Hilton Hotel, Tahran Cad. 12 Kavaklıdere,* ☎ *312/468–2800,* 🖷
           *312/468–0909. Reservations essential. AE, DC, MC, V. No lunch.*

$$$ ✕ **Amisos.** In a restored old villa, this inviting restaurant serves Turk-
★ ish, Black Sea, and international fare, ranging from fish and caviar to
soy chicken. One of Ankara's few fine-dining options that is open for
both lunch and dinner, Amisos is a favorite with business people for
lunch and with an elite crowd for dinner. Ask for a table in the green-
house. ⊠ *Filistin Sk. 28, Gazi Osman Paşa,* ☎ *312/446–6098,* FAX *312/
446–8345. Reservations essential. AE, DC, MC, V.*

$$ ✕ **Yakamoz.** Although the interior is a kitschy cross between a British
tearoom and a New England chowder house, Yakamoz serves out-
standing food. Be sure to have the grilled fish and seafood; they are
the high points of the menu. End your meal with the candied *ayva*
(quince) dessert. ⊠ *Tunalı Hilmi Cad. 114/J, off Kuğulu Parkı,* ☎ *312/
426–3752,* FAX *312/468–3697. Reservations essential for dinner. AE,
DC, MC, V.*

$–$$ ✕ **Göksu.** Black Sea cuisine is the specialty of Göksu (which means that
★ primarily seafood is served). The restaurant imports all its fish and cheese
from the region, making it a popular hangout for people from that area.
Rather incongruously, the walls are decorated with Hittite reliefs, but
the food is excellent. ⊠ *Bayındır Sok. 22/A, Kızılay,* ☎ *312/431–
2219. Reservations essential. AE, MC, V.*

$–$$ ✕ **Zenger Paşa Konağı.** The Mansion of Zenger Paşa, a traditional old
house within the citadel, has been restored and is now a fine restaurant. The food is traditional, too, from the *mantı* (Turkish ravioli) served
at lunchtime to the *saç kavurma* (sautéed lamb) at dinner. The city view
is an added attraction. ⊠ *Doyran Sok. 13, Ankara Kalesi,* ☎ *312/311–
7070. Reservations essential. AE, MC, V.*

$ ✕ **Akman Boza ve Pasta Salonu.** This spot has been serving tasty
breakfasts, sandwiches, desserts, and snacks since the 1930s. Tables
are set out in a courtyard with a small fountain. ⊠ *Ulus Çarşısı G Blok
1, off Atatürk Bulvarı, Ulus,* ☎ *312/311–8755. MC, V.*

$ ✕ **Gar.** Lunch with in-the-know locals and expats at this inexpensive
but consistently good diner. Traditional Turkish cuisine, along with vegetarian variations and an inventive take on some international dishes,
makes this a welcome respite from kebabs. ⊠ *Horasan 2/B, Gazi
Osman Paşa,* ☎ *312/447–2996,* FAX *312/446–3162. MC, V.*

$$$$ ▥ **Ankara Hilton SA.** A luxurious 16-story hotel in a quiet hilly neigh-
★ borhood on Embassy Row, this Hilton provides many amenities and
a view to boot. Expect the standards of comfort and style that you've
come to expect from Hiltons the world over, but without many dis-
tinguishing characteristics to show that you're in Turkey. ⊠ *Tahran
Cad. 12, Kavaklıdere,* ☎ *312/468–2888,* FAX *312/468–0909. 324 rooms
with bath. 2 restaurants, 2 bars, minibars, no-smoking rooms, room
service, indoor pool, sauna, Turkish bath, health club, baby-sitting, dry
cleaning, laundry service, business services. AE, DC, MC, V.* ✍

$$$$ ▥ **Grand Hotel Ankara/Büyük Ankara.** This high-rise across from the
Grand National Assembly was long Ankara's poshest hotel. Now
competition from the international chains has relegated it to second
place. Then again, it's slightly less expensive than the Hilton or Sheraton and has more of a Turkish feel. ⊠ *Atatürk Bul. 183, Kavaklıdere,*
☎ *312/425–6655,* FAX *312/425–5070. 192 rooms with bath, 28 suites.
2 restaurants, bar, minibars, room service, pool, sauna, health club,
laundry service. AE, DC, MC, V.*

$$$$ ▥ **Sheraton Ankara.** The splashiest of Ankara's luxury hotels is hard
to miss; it's tall, white, and round. It is also well run, fashionable, and
thoroughly international in style. ⊠ *Noktalı Sok., Kavaklıdere,* ☎ *312/
468–5454,* FAX *312/467–1136. 307 rooms with bath, 12 suites. 2 restaurants, bar, café, pool, sauna, health club, squash, laundry service. AE,
DC, MC, V.* ✍

$$$ 🏨 **Dedeman Oteli.** The Dedeman is the best bargain among the upper-echelon hotels. It has two wings, one more modern and spacious (and expensive), the other with older, smaller rooms. ✉ *Büklüm Sok. 1, Küçükesat,* ☎ *312/417–6200,* ℻ *312/417–6214. 291 rooms with bath. 4 restaurants, 2 bars, indoor and outdoor pools, sauna, health club. AE, DC, MC, V.* 🍴

$$–$$$ 🏨 **Kent.** A pleasant, helpful staff distinguishes this hotel in the heart of the city, near the main shopping and business areas. Rooms are nice if nondescript. ✉ *Mithatpaşa Cad. 4, Sıhhiye,* ☎ *312/435–5050,* ℻ *312/434–4657. 117 rooms with bath. Restaurant, bar. AE, DC, MC, V.* 🍴

$$ 🏨 **King Hotel.** On a quiet street near the American Embassy and the
★ Turkish Grand National Assembly, the King Hotel is a favorite with perennial visitors to Ankara. The central location, the very helpful and friendly staff, the above-average restaurant, and the clean rooms all make it a great deal for the price (breakfast included). ✉ *Güvenlik Cad. 13, Aşağıayrancı,* ☎ *312/418–9099,* ℻ *312/417–0382. 36 rooms with bath, 3 suites. Restaurant, bar, room service, outdoor pool. AE, DC, MC, V.* 🍴

$$ 🏨 **Angora House Hotel.** A unique find in Ankara, this lovely small hotel
★ blends modern comforts and tradition. In a beautifully restored Ottoman house inside the Hisar presided over by its two gracious owners, Angora House offers a welcome break from modern Ankara's bustle. Room rates include breakfast. Guests may use the kitchen and laundry facilities. ✉ *Kale Kapısı Sk. 16, Kale İçi,* ☎ *312/309–8380 or 311–1609,* ℻ *312/309–8381. Email angorabazar@e-kolay.net.tr 6 rooms with bath. Bar, room service. DC, MC, V.*

$–$$ 🏨 **Hotel Almer.** Good hotels in Ulus are rare; this modern, clean place is one exception. With an ideal location in old Ankara, the Almer is an excellent choice. ✉ *Çankırı Cad. 17, Ulus,* ☎ *312/309–0435,* ℻ *312/311–5677. 81 rooms with shower. Restaurant, bar. DC, MC, V.*

### Shopping

Down the hill south of the Hisar is an area known as **Samanpazarı,** where you can find rugs, crafts, antiques, and copper for sale. The **Gesav Sanat Evi** (Gesav Art House, ✉ Kireçli Sok. 6, Kale İçi) offers fine handicrafts without the pressure of bargaining. In the pedestrian area of the district of **Kızılay,** look for books and Turkish music, especially on Konur Sokak.

---

# Hattuşaş

★ ⑯ *158 km (98 mi) from Ankara, east on Rte. E88 and northeast on Rte. 190 until past Sungurlu; then follow road signs.*

There is old, and then there is *old.* The Greek and Roman ruins elsewhere in the country are mere yearlings compared to Hattuşaş. The city dates from the Bronze Age and the sophisticated culture of a people called the Hatti, who were thriving here by 2300 BC. From about 2000 BC on, the Hatti princes ruling the main city-states of Hattuşaş, Kaneş, Kushara, and Zalpa were doing brisk trade with the great Mesopotamian towns, from which they derived considerable wealth. Around 1800 BC, Anitta, king of the lost city of Kushara, formed an Anatolian confederacy and took for himself the title *Rabum Rabum* (King of Kings). His glory was short-lived.

At about that time, a mysterious people known as the Hittites came to dominate the Hatti. The Hittites, of Indo-European origin, apparently entered Anatolia after crossing the Caucasus and the steppes beyond the Black Sea. They claimed Hattuşaş as their capital and soon built their own empire. Labarna, who ascended to the throne in 1680

BC, is considered the founder of the Old Kingdom. Royal intrigue and invasions by new tribes from the east sent the empire into decline, and the Old Kingdom was followed by the New Kingdom. A series of battles with the Egyptians in about 1296 BC appears to have favored the Hittites, but a pattern of family strife reemerged. In decline for a second time, the reign of the Hittites came to an end around 1200 BC, when Hattuşaş was sacked and burned by tribes from the north.

The first thing to notice about Hattuşaş is its location—an excellent defensive position in a valley framed on both sides by rivers. The second item of note is the city's incredible size. Its walls, made of brick on stone foundations, reinforced by large cut stones and surmounted by towers, were 7 km (4 mi) in circumference. Most structures at Hattuşaş can be clearly discerned because of the extensive use of stone at the site and a conscientious program by the German excavators of reconstructing and preserving building foundations. It is worth purchasing the guidebook to the site ($5), which contains a map and explanatory notes.

The site can be explored on foot or by car, with frequent stops along the way. Coming up the road into the site, turn right to the first ruins as you ascend, those of the **Temple of the Storm God** (Temple I). Hattuşaş had many temples, all patterned on the same model. They consisted of small rooms arranged around a paved courtyard that varied in size; this one is roughly 700 ft by 1,700 ft. Near the entrance to this temple complex are pieces of a ceremonial basin made from limestone and carved with trademark Hittite lions. Within the temple, you should be able to make out the main courtyard and two large rooms, which housed statues of the storm god and sun goddess. The long, narrow rooms opening out from the courtyard were administrative offices and archives.

Continuing on the road up the hill, you come to a series of gates in the city walls. Hattuşaş had seven gates, and it is worth stopping to admire those still present, both for their engineering and the often spectacular views. The first gate you pass is the **Aslanlıkapı** (Lion Gate); the lions themselves are reproductions. Next is the **Yerkapı** (Earth Gate). This gate was once flanked by sphinxes, now in the Istanbul and Berlin museums. Go through the tunnel under the gate to view the impressive human-made stone ridge on which the gate rests. After exiting the gate, look to your right, down the hill, to get a bird's-eye view of several temples on the plain. The final gate is the **Kral Kapısı** (Royal Gate), whose parabolic shape is fairly well preserved. The sculpture on the front of the gate is a reproduction; once thought to be a king, it is actually a god.

The last ruins are those of the **Büyükkale** (Great Fortress), reached by a modern stairway that has replaced the ancient ramp. On the terrace atop the sheer cliff stood the royal palace, probably two stories high. The citadel's outbuildings include the **State Archive**, where, in 1906, thousands of stone tablets were found, mute but eloquent survivors of the plundering Phrygians. Among them was a copy of the Treaty of Kadesh, signed in 1279 BC after the war with the Egyptian pharaoh Ramses II. . 🖼 *$1.75 (includes Yazılıkaya;* ☞ *below).* ☉ *Daily 8–noon and 1:30–5:30 (according to sunlight).* 🍴

## Boğazkale

⓱ *5 km (3 mi) north of Hattuşaş.*

The village of Boğazkale has little other than a few small restaurants and rug shops. It has a museum, the **Boğazkale Müzesi,** with finds from

Hattuşaş and Alacahöyük, but if you've been to the Museum of Anatolian Civilizations in Ankara, you've already seen the best finds from
the Hittite sites. *364/452–2006.* ☎ *$1.75.* ◷ *Daily 8–noon and 1:30–
5:30.*

## Yazılıkaya

⑱ *2 km (1 mi) northeast of Hattuşaş, 2 km (1 mi) east of Boğazkale.*

Yazılıkaya is thought to have served the capital city of Hattuşaş as a
religious sanctuary or temple complex. The name means "rock with
writing," a fitting title, as the natural rock walls here are covered with
the carvings of Hittite artists dating from about 1200 BC. At the site,
a large natural portal opens onto a crevice that forms a narrow passageway through the rocks and ends at a small, circular open space.
The rock walls of the passageway are decorated with bas-reliefs illustrating various Hittite gods, goddesses, and kings. Within the **main shrine,**
42 gods are depicted marching from the left to meet 21 goddesses coming from the right. At the spot they meet are the important weather
god **Teshub** (he's the fellow with the most horns in his cap), and his
consort, the goddess **Hepatu,** astride a leopard. They are accompanied
by their son **Sharruma,** also riding a leopard, and the king and queen.
Sharruma was the god who protected **Tudhaliya IV** (depicted in impressive scale on the opposite wall), the king who ordered the construction of Yazılıkaya.

Next to the main shrine, a second, smaller passageway leads to a small
gallery. Here again is King Tudhaliya IV, this time alongside a particularly fine and well-preserved image of Sharruma. The **frieze of the 12
gods** opposite is another exceptional work, as is the so-called **Sword
God,** a figure shown with the head of a god attached to a body made
up of four lions; he carries a sword with its point aimed downward.
Funeral rites for recently departed kings were probably held here.
There are no official guides, but pamphlets are available at the ticket
kiosk. ☎ *$1.75 (includes ruins at Hattuşaş).* ◷ *Daily 8–noon and 1:30–
5:30 (according to sunlight).*

## Alacahöyük

⑲ *28 km (17 mi) from Boğazkale, 20 km (12 mi) northeast of the Sungurlu–
Boğazkale road.*

The site of Alacahöyük was settled as early as 3500 BC but was not
discovered until the 19th century AD, by Englishman John Hamilton.
Continuing excavations have brought to light 15 levels on which are
relics from four cultures, beginning with 13 **rectangular burial chambers** belonging to Hatti kings. In the tombs were golden diadems,
belts, necklaces and other jewelry, silver combs, mirrors, drinking vessels, and other funerary artifacts, all now in the Museum of Anatolian
Civilizations in Ankara. A later Hittite temple was entered through the
Gate of Sphinxes, also now in Ankara; concrete replicas have replaced
them here. The double-headed eagle, an emblem of the Hittites as well
as many succeeding empires, appears on the inside wall. Concrete
casts of original bas-reliefs depict a royal couple before an altar with
a bull on it, the sun goddess Arima, two musicians playing odd instruments, and a procession of animals. Next to the site is a small **museum** with sketches of what the city once looked like and paintings from
the burial chambers. *364/422–7011.* ☎ *$1.75.* ◷ *Daily 8–noon and
1:30–5:30.*

# CAPPADOCIA AND KONYA
## Kaymaklı, Göreme, Ihlara, and Konya

The story of the incredible landscape of Cappadocia begins more than 10 million years ago, when the three peaks that dominate the region— Erciyes Dağı, Hasan Dağı, and Melendiz Dağı (Mts. Erciyes, Hasan, and Melendiz)—were active volcanoes. Aeons worth of eruptions dumped layers of mud, ash, and lava on the area. Eventually these layers compressed and turned into tufa, a soft, porous rock. Erosion by rain, snow, and wind created a fantastic relief of rock formations resembling chimneys, cones, needles, pillars, and pyramids, often topped by perfectly balanced gigantic slabs of rock. Then came earthquakes to add vast valleys, along with oxidation to give the area the final artistic touch: rocks "painted" yellow, pink, red, russet, and gray-violet.

No one is really sure when people came to inhabit Cappadocia. Although there are signs of Hittite occupation, by 600 BC there are references in ancient texts to the Kingdom of Cappadocia, a loose confederacy of neighboring states. Its first capital was Nissa (now referred to as Nevşehir); later it was moved to Mazaca (today called Kayseri). Alexander the Great never bothered with the region, and it wasn't annexed by Rome until Emperor Tiberius claimed it in AD 17 and changed the capital's name to Caesarea. Still a backwater, albeit now a Roman one, Cappadocia never gained much in the way of theaters and temples. It did, however, embrace Christianity with great zeal following a visit from St. Paul. In 370 a local son named Basilius became bishop of Caesarea. A believer in spiritual perfection through monasticism, he was also noted for his good works. His considerable inheritance was spent on the establishment of a charitable institution that cared for the poor and the sick. Though himself in bad health, he personally looked after the poorest of the poor—the lepers—and still found time to preach and write doctrinal treatises. The Eucharist Liturgy of the Greek Orthodox Church bears his name, and he is one of its Four Doctors. He died on January 1, 379, and, as St. Basil, entered Christian tradition as a bringer of joy and gifts. In the subsequent Byzantine era, the charitable institution he founded became the nucleus of Caesarea, and his rules for Orthodox monks are still followed today.

Long before the Arab raids forced local inhabitants into hiding, ascetics inspired by St. Basil carved cave dwellings into the soft tufa. This quickly led to the formation of religious colonies that combined the individuality of meditation with communal work on fertile volcanic soil wherever there was a patch of level ground. Rock chapels proliferated, especially in the Göreme Valley. Later, churches were designed in contemporary Byzantine architectural styles and decorated with geometric paintings and increasingly ambitious frescoes. Ironically, ecclesiastical art climaxed in the 11th century, just when the era of Christian rule in Turkey was drawing to a close. Yet scattered Christian communities persisted here, under tolerant Seljuk and Ottoman rulers, up until the exchange of Greek (Christian) and Turkish (Muslim) populations following World War I.

Cappadocia has changed little over the centuries—with the exception of the addition of a booming tourist industry. People travel between their farms and villages in donkey- and horse-drawn carts, women drape their houses with strings of apricots and paprika for drying in the sun, and nomads pitch their black tents beside sunflower fields and cook on tiny fires that send smoke billowing through the tent tops. In the distance, minarets pierce the sky. Recently, however, the spellbinding tufa rocks have been revealed to be no less dangerous to their inhabitants than the most ruthless invaders of old. For generations, villagers at Karain have suffered painful deaths, known throughout the area as "the Karain agony." This has finally been diagnosed as cancer, caused by prolonged exposure to the pale yellow rock. Karain and a similarly affected village nearby have been declared natural disaster areas, and the villagers have been evacuated, a fate that seems to them no less an evil than the disease. Only a few villages carved from the rocks are still inhabited, while the holes that riddle the nearby cliff bases shelter the occasional troglodyte.

Today Cappadocia forms a rough triangle between Nevşehir, Kayseri, and Niğde, starting about 272 km (169 mi) southeast of Ankara. The main sights are within an even smaller triangle, marked by Ürgüp, Göreme, and Avanos. Ürgüp is the center from which to explore the monastic villages of Cappadocia and the best place to shop; Göreme provides more small-town charm and excellent bargains on tours. Nevşehir, although marginally closer to the underground cities, is a significantly less pleasant base.

After visiting Cappadocia, you may want to continue on to Konya. As befits what was the capital of the Seljuk Empire for two centuries, Konya has Turkey's largest concentration of Seljuk architecture. The Seljuks chose their capital wisely; the combination of altitude and setting provides Konya with cool breezes from the surrounding mountain chains and a more moderate climate than in the rest of Anatolia.

## Kırşehir

**㉒** *203 km (126 mi) from Ankara, east on Rte. E88 and south on Rtes. 765 and 260; 166 km (103 mi) from Boğazkale, west on Rte. E88 and south on Rtes. 785 and 260.*

Kırşehir, an important agricultural center, has several Seljuk monuments. The Alaaddin Cami is one of many mosques in the region named after the great Seljuk sultan Alaaddin Keykubat (ruled 1219–1236). Caca Bey Cami was built in 1272 as an astronomical observatory. Ahi Evran Cami holds the *türbe* (tomb) of the founder of the Ahi brotherhood, a religious sect that exercised considerable influence in Anatolia for several centuries. Its precepts had much to do with hospitality and good fellowship, a likely reason for the group's popularity. Just before the junction with Route 260 stands the tomb of the poet Aşık Paşa, built during the Mongol occupation of the region.

## Hacıbektaş

**㉑** *44 km (27 mi) south of Kırşehir, Rte. 260 to Rte. 765.*

Hacı Bektaş Veli founded a religious sect in the 13th century in what is now Hacıbektaş (the town was named after him). An important order of the dervishes called the Bektaşi, it was based on teaching that was a synthesis of Sunnism and Shiism, two branches of Islam, blended with a touch of Christianity. Hacı Bektaş became the spiritual leader of the newly founded Janissary Corps, the fierce warriors of the Ottoman Empire, which gave him tremendous political as well as religious influence. The monastery that belonged to his disciples is now the **Hacıbektaş Müzesi** (Hacıbektaş Museum). Hacı Bektaş is buried in a tomb behind gilded door here. ✉ *In the center of town.* ▧ *$1.75.* ☉ *Tues.–Sun. 9–noon and 1–4:30.*

*En Route*    South of Hacıbektaş, on your way to Nevşehir, you'll pass through **Gülşehir,** where Grand Vizier Kara Mehmet Paşa constructed a rare Ottoman baroque complex with a mosque, *medrese* (mosque compound), *hamam* (Turkish bath), and six fountains next to some Byzantine ruins. Soon the scenery starts to change. Pink-and-white mushroom-shape rocks are scattered along the rest of the route to Nevşehir.

# Nevşehir

㉒ *49 km (30 mi) south of Hacıbektaş on Rte. 765.*

Known in ancient times as Nissa, Nevşehir is the region's largest town. It clings to the slopes below a ruined Seljuk fortress and has a 13th-century Seljuk mosque, the Kaya Cami. The town owes its prosperity to Grand Vizier Damat Ibrahim Paşa, who endowed his birthplace with the **Kurşunlu Cami** (Lead-Domed Mosque) and its medrese, hospice, and library in 1726.

## Dining and Lodging

$ ✕ **Aspava.** The centrally located Aspava serves good-quality *hazır yemek* (food prepared earlier and kept hot), kebabs, and *pide* (Turkish pizza). Men eat downstairs; upstairs is a section reserved for women and families. ⊠ *Atatürk Bul. 29,* ☎ *384/213–1051. No credit cards.*

$$$ 🏨 **Hotel Cappadocia Dedeman.** This modern high-rise is the closest thing to luxury near Nevşehir. It's about 2 km (1 mi) out of town along the road to Ürgüp. ⊠ *Ürgüp Yolu,* ☎ *384/213–9900,* ℻ *384/213–2158. 349 rooms with bath. 2 restaurants, 2 bars, indoor pool, pool, sauna, Turkish bath, tennis court, billiards, dance club. AE, MC, V.* ☙

$–$$ 🏨 **Hotel Orsan Kapadokya.** Quite chic by Turkish provincial standards, the Orsan has fine Turkish carpets in the public areas, a smart bar, and a pool. ⊠ *Yeni Kayseri Cad. 15,* ☎ *384/213–2115 or 384/213–5329,* ℻ *384/213–4223. 95 rooms with bath. Restaurant, bar, outdoor pool, dance club. MC, V.*

# Kaymaklı

★ ㉓ *21 km (13 mi) south of Nevşehir on Rte. 765.*

From the 7th through the 10th centuries, the Christian Cappadocians were under siege from Arab raiders. They took refuge in about 40 underground cities. These were cities in the truest sense, some stretching as deep as 20 stories below the surface and able to house as many as 20,000 people. Each had dormitories, dining halls, sewage disposal systems, and ventilation chimneys, as well as a cemetery and a prison. Large millstones sealed off the entrances from enemies. Who actually built these cities is a mystery. Some exhibit traces of Hittite settlements. The Greek historian Xenophon mentions Cappadocian underground dwellings as early as 401 BC. The Christians probably expanded what they found; certainly the cities took centuries to complete.

The narrow entrance to the ruins of Kaymaklı was only uncovered in the 1950s. A central air shaft assures perfect ventilation throughout the 394 ft that have been opened up so far, but if you have claustrophobic tendencies, you might want to skip this experience entirely. Sloping corridors and steps connect the floors, self-contained but for cemeteries and kitchens, which are spaced on every second level. The impermeable tufa kept the inside dry, and interior wells provided water. Smoke was not allowed to escape for fear of betraying the hideout. In some places a hole is cut above the doorway; through it defenders could pour boiling oil on their attackers. Little arrows enable you to take a self-guided tour; however, hiring a guide at the site who can explain what's what in the ruins will help you to better visualize daily life underground in chambers that otherwise look the same. A flashlight is helpful, and you'll want a sweater, even in summer. ☎ *384/ 218–2500.* 🚍 *$3.75.* ⊙ *Daily 8–5.* 🐾

# Derinkuyu

㉔ *30 km (19 mi) south of Nevşehir on Rte. 765, 9 km (6 mi) south of Kaymaklı on Rte. 765.*

Kaymaklı is believed to be connected by a 10-km (6-mi) tunnel to Derinkuyu, though it has not yet been unblocked. The layout here is similar to that of Kaymaklı, but there is an unusual Greek church about halfway down and several more levels to explore. Some carvings and paintings are visible, but they are fading fast. ☎ *384/381–3194.* 🚍 *$3.75.* ⊙ *Daily 8–5.*

# Ürgüp

㉕ *23 km (14 mi) east of Nevşehir.*

Ürgüp is a logical base for exploring the surrounding towns, but it's not necessarily the most pleasant, as its lodgings are often booked up by large tour groups. The town has some old, white Greek-style houses, converted into hotels and carpet shops. In summer its streets are filled with tourists haggling in myriad languages over "antique" copper and "old" kilims (you're unlikely to find real antiques), especially during the popular Saturday market. Hotel windows open on breathtaking scenery. A serrated white cliff is dotted with man-made holes. Some of the fragile walls have crumbled away, revealing the interiors of houses. These caves, as well as some giant cones and chimneys in nearby villages, are still inhabited by troglodytes, who simply remove any fallen walls and dig deeper into the rock.

## Dining and Lodging

**$–$$** ✕ **Han Çırağan.** In an old caravansary—an inn surrounding a courtyard where caravans rested at night—the Çırağan exudes charm. The menu usually includes *saç tava* (small pieces of fried beef, onion, pepper, tomato, and rice), *güveç* (a lamb or beef stew in a jealously guarded secret sauce), and *mantı* (Turkish ravioli). ⊠ *Cumhuriyet Meyd.,* ☎ *384/341–2566,* ℻ *383/341–4181. MC, V.*

**$** ✕ **Şömine.** In the center of Ürgüp, this restaurant serves traditional Turkish fare, including tile-baked *kebab.* Seats on the large terrace provide a view of the adjacent cave dwellings and the town below. ⊠ *On the main square, Cumhuriyet Meyd.,* ☎ *384/341–8442,* ℻ *384/341–8443. V.*

**$$$** ⌂ **Esbelli Evi.** One of the finest small inns in all of Turkey occupies sev-
★ eral old stone houses on the outskirts of town. Guests enjoy the sense of being in a private home, with use of a lovely Ottoman-style salon, a kitchen where snacks and beverages are complimentary, and even laundry facilities. Guest rooms are distinctive, with arches, stone walls and handsome, traditional furnishings, and many have fireplaces. Weather permitting, breakfast is served on one of several terraces. ⊠ *Esbelli Sokak 8.,* ☎ *384/341–3995,* ℻ *384/341–8814. 8 rooms with bath. MC, V.* 🐾

**$$** ⌂ **Perissia Hotel.** Probably the best in a string of good hotels along Kayseri Caddesi, the Perissia is clean and very comfortable. It has a large outdoor pool and other amenities, such as dry cleaning and a heliport, that you won't find elsewhere in the area. The marble lobby is impressive, and each room has a satellite TV system and a stereo. Room rates include breakfast and dinner. ⊠ *Kayseri Cad.,* ☎ *384/341–2930,* ℻ *384/341–4524. 230 rooms with bath. 2 restaurants, 3 bars, minibars, room service, pool, 2 tennis courts, dance club. AE, MC, V.* 🐾

$$ **⊞ Hotel Alfina.** If you really want to experience Cappadocia, why not lodge troglodyte style? In the Alfina, a hotel carved out of volcanic rock, you get the definite sensation of being in a cave. Rooms have simple furnishings; bathrooms are modern. The restaurant serves good Turkish fare. ⊠ *İstiklal Cad. 25,* ☎ *384/341–4822,* ℻ *384/341–2424 (Ankara representative* ☎ *312/417–8425,* ℻ *312/418–6207). 26 rooms with bath. Restaurant, bar. MC, V. Closed Nov.–Mar.*

$ **⊞ Kilim Hotel.** This small, pleasant hotel is centrally located. Friendly staff, clean rooms, spacious balconies on front-facing rooms, and a good breakfast make it a fine value. ⊠ *Dumlupinar Cad. 47,* ☎ *384/341–3131,* ℻ *384/341–5058. 15 with bath. No credit cards.*

*En Route* South of Ürgüp, on the Yeşilhisar road, there are several towns with cave churches, including **Mustafapaşa** and **Soğanlı.** The citadel of **Ortahisar** is hewn out of a gigantic serrated heap of stone; you can climb to the top for a panoramic view.

# Göreme

❷❻ *7 km (4 mi) northwest of Ürgüp.*

★ Though there's a small town catering to tourists, the main highlight of this vineyard-filled valley is the **Göreme Açık Hava Müzesi** (Göreme Open-Air Museum), containing a wealth of rock churches. Signs provide information about the site, but bring a flashlight—most churches are illuminated only by the natural light that seeps in. In summer arrive early to beat the heat and the crowds, who jam the fresco-filled spaces by midday.

The oldest rock church dates from the 4th century. Frescoes first appeared around the 8th century, when the geometric designs directly applied to the rock face gradually gave way to scenes from the New Testament and the lives of the more popular saints, all painted on plaster. The steep rock to the left of the site's entrance housed a six-story **convent,** which had a kitchen and refectory on the lower levels and a cruciform chapel on the third; large millstones lay ready to block the narrow passages in times of danger. Opposite is a **monastery** on the same plan, close to the **Elmalı Kilise** (Church with the Apple), which once had a fresco of Gabriel holding an apple. This church is relatively new—from the 12th century. Like those in other main churches, its polychrome pictures on a dark-blue background that depict scenes from the life of Christ have been restored under the auspices of UNESCO.

The **Barbara Kilise** (Church of St. Barbara) is decorated with early red designs from the Iconoclastic period (726–842) and 11th-century frescoes of St. Barbara above the baptistery font. The **Yılanı Kilise** (Serpent Church) is named for its fresco of St. George killing a snake. A bevy of saints adorns the two sections of this church, one barrel vaulted, the other flat roofed. In one mural, St. Thomas and St. Basil flank a rather unusual half-female, half-male figure—probably an ancient image of the Anatolian mother goddess, transformed under Christianity into a saint. The 11th-century **Karanlık Kilise** (Dark Church), extensively restored by UNESCO, provides a glimpse of how the frescos of this region looked in their prime, before vandals and the centuries took their toll. Entry to the church costs an additional $10 and is well worth the expense. The **Çarıklı Kilise** (Church of the Sandal) was named after the footprint below the Ascension fresco; some experts believe it to be a cast of Jesus's own footprint.

Just outside the confines of the fence surrounding the museum, along the path back to Göreme, is the largest of the churches, the 10th-century **Tokalı Kilise** (Church of the Buckle). With its scenes from the life of Christ and the sunlight streaming in from the barrel entry, turning the underground vaults golden, you might be in any Byzantine church. Continue following the path to the **Madonna Kilise** (Church of the Madonna) and the 11th-century **El Nazar Kilise** (Church of the Evil Eye). The price of Tokalı Kilise is included in the admission to the Göreme Open-Air Museum; the other churches are free but have irregular hours. ⊠ *Open-Air Museum: Ürgüp Yolu.* ☎ *$6.* ☉ *Daily 8–5.* ☙

The aptly named **Saklı Kilise** (Hidden Church) has fine 12th-century frescoes but is difficult to find. *1 km (½ mi) past Tokalı Kilise, on the left.*

If you haven't yet tired of rock churches, in the vicinity of the troglodyte village of **Avcılar,** a long walk or short drive away, there are five more. In **Çavuşin,** the church is flanked by frescoes of the angels Michael and Gabriel; inside are scenes from the life of Christ.

## Dining and Lodging

$$ ✕ **Harmandali.** This cavernous restaurant prides itself on serving more kinds of mezes (30) than any other place in the region. Popular with tour groups, Harmandali also prepares a variety of main dishes, all for one price. The house specialty is chicken güveç. But the real reason to come here is the folk and belly dancing that follow the meal. ⊠ *Üçhisar, near Göreme,* ☎ *384/219–2364,* ℻ *384/219–2394. Reservations essential. No credit cards.*

$$$$ 🏨 **Ataman.** Run by tourist guide Abbas and his wife, Şermin, this hotel partially built into the face of a rock invites wandering through its maze-like corridors. Rooms in the original section of the hotel are built into caves; all rooms are individually decorated with kilims and handicrafts, and some have fireplaces. The restaurant ($–$$) serves good Turkish and international cuisine. Room rates include breakfast and dinner. ⊠ *Uzundere Cad. 47,* ☎ *384/271–2310,* ℻ *384/271–2313. 26 rooms with bath. Restaurant, bar, minibars. No credit cards.* ☙

$ 🏨 **Cave Hotel Melek.** The Melek is special for one reason: It's partially carved out of the rock. Otherwise, rooms basically just have a bed and that's all. Proprietor Nico Leyssen is also responsible for the gorgeously restored Konak Türk Evi Restaurant ($–$$), only intermittently open. Room rates include breakfast. ⊠ *Up the hill behind bus station,* ☎ ℻ *384/271–2463. 20 rooms, 12 with bath. Restaurant. No credit cards.*

$ ✕🏨 **Ottoman House.** This charming and reasonably priced hotel is run
★ by an Australian and a Turk. It has a friendly staff and clean, simple rooms decorated with beautiful carpets and embroideries. The managers also have a high-end shop down the street at which they sell lovely but very expensive rugs. After a good dinner in the restaurant, head down to the cozy Harem Bar in the basement. ⊠ *Uzundere Cad. 21,* ☎ *384/271–2616,* ℻ *384/271–2351. 29 rooms with shower, 3 suites. Restaurant, bar, room service, laundry service. MC, V.* ☙

# Zelve

★ ㉗ *6 km (4 mi) northeast of the Göreme Open-Air Museum on the road to Avanos.*

Zelve is an open-air museum filled with fairy chimneys and churches. Rockfalls in the 1960s caused the town to be evacuated. If you prefer to explore on your own, you have the opportunity to discover tunnels, rooms, and churches in an atmosphere less restricted than that in the nearby Göreme Open-Air Museum (☞ *above*). The area also offers a more comprehensive experience of the local terrain. Note that venturing into the dwellings on your own requires a flashlight. At the far end of the left-hand valley is a narrow tunnel in the rocks; it leads to a canyon with a stream, a peaceful place to rest. ⊠ *$3.75.* ⊙ *Daily 8–5.*

# Avanos

**28** *8 km (5 mi) north of Zelve.*

Avanos, on the north bank of the Kızılırmak (Red River), is an attractive old town filled with shops selling onyx jewelry and pottery. The river is named for the local red clay, from which the pottery is made.

The latest of the region's underground cities has been discovered at **Özkonak,** off a dirt road 20 km (12 mi) north of Avanos. Potentially the largest of all, this hidden city may have been able to shelter up to 60,000 people, although as yet only a small portion of it has been excavated. Somewhat off the main circuit and still in need of cleaning up, it is omitted by most guided tours.

The **Sarı Han,** a 13th-century Seljuk caravansary from the time of Sultan Alaaddin Keykubat, is also nearby, about 5 km (3 mi) east of Avanos. Caravansaries were major outposts on trade routes. They had stables, sleeping quarters, a mosque, and baths, and within their sturdy walls, the goods carried by merchants were kept safe from highway robbers.

### Dining and Lodging

$ ✕🏨 **Sofa Motel.** The Sofa's manager estimates that the 10 restored old stone houses that form the motel are at least 200 years old. Be sure to ask for a room near the top of the hill so that you not only get an excellent view of the river and mountains but can also enjoy wandering through these old houses on your way up. Turkish fare is served in the restaurant. ⊠ *Orta Mah. 13,* ☎ 🖷 *384/511–4489. 36 rooms with shower. Restaurant, breakfast room. MC, V.*

# Kayseri

**29** *79 km (49 mi) from Avanos, south on Rte. 767 and north on Rte. 805.*

The last of the major cities of Cappadocia is Kayseri, a conservative, historic town that is unfortunately now being rebuilt in a style you could call international concrete modern. Still, there are some engaging Seljuk monuments here. On Cumhuriyet Meydanı, where Sivas Caddesi and Istanbul Caddesi meet at the center of town, are not one but two statues of Atatürk. The black-basalt walls of the **old citadel** still watch over the square; inside is a modern Turkish shopping mall. The citadel was built by the Byzantines in the 6th century and patched up by Sultan Alaaddin Keykubat in 1224 and again by the Ottomans after the conquest by Sultan Selim I in 1515. Two Seljuk lions guard the gate in the thick ramparts. The fortress walls, sufficiently intact for a trip around the catwalk, provide a fine view of the city.

Within **Atatürk Parkı** is the **Kurşunlu Cami,** which has a fine lead-covered cupola. It was completed in 1585 by Ahmet Paşa after a design by the 16th-century architect Sinan, who was born in a nearby village.

**Sahabiye Medrese** (Sahabiye Seminary) was established by the Seljuk vizier Sahipata in 1267. Around an open courtyard, the seminary has some of the finest carvings of the late Seljuk period. ⊠ *Cumhuriyet Meyd., facing the old citadel.*

In Mimar Sinan Parkı is the **Çifte Medrese** (Twin Seminaries), which houses the **Giyasiye Medrese,** the first medical school in Anatolia (and older than any in Europe). A passage joined it to the **Şifahiye Medrese,** a hospital. Both were built in 1206 from legacies left by the daughter of Sultan Giyassedin Keyhusrev I. Much restored, they are now museums of Islamic medicine. ✉ *Mimar Sinan Parkı,* ☎ *352/231–3565.* 🎟 *$1.25.* ⊙ *Wed.–Sun. 8–noon and 1–5.*

The architectural detail of the **Hacı Kılıç Cami and Medrese** (Hacı Kılıç Mosque and Seminary), built in 1249 by the Seljuk vizier Abdül Gazi, is quite nice, especially the handsomely wrought portals. ✉ *Off İstasyon Cad. north of the Çifte Medrese.*

The outstanding complex containing the **Hunat Hatun Cami, Medrese, and Türbe** (Hunat Hatun Mosque, Seminary, and Tomb) demonstrates the influence of Hunat Hatun, the wife of the greatest Seljuk sultan, Alaaddin Keykubat. The title *noble lady,* given to this Georgian princess refers clearly to birth rather than character, as it is suspected she poisoned the sultan when he was about to disinherit their son. In 1237, once the lad was safely enthroned, the queen mother had the medrese constructed, perhaps by way of atonement. The mosque has a finely decorated main gate and double arches. Re-opened after restoration work conducted in 1998, the complex now contains exhibits for the **Ethnographic Museum** (*see below*)). ✉ *Talas Cad. at Cumhuriyet Meyd.* 🎟 *Free. Daily 8–5.*

The centuries-old **Güpgüpoğlu Konağı** (Güpgüpoğlu Mansion) now houses part of Kayseri's **Ethnographic Museum**. This stone mansion is replete with a *haremlik* (women's living quarters) and *selamlık* (men's living quarters) restored to their original splendor. The museum also houses an array of regional costumes, ceramics, and weapons. ✉ *Across from Hunat Hatun complex,* ☎ *352/222–9516.* 🎟 *$1.75.* ⊙ *Tues.–Sun. 8–5:30.*

Kayseri's 15th-century **Bedestan** (covered bazaar) is noted, as you might expect, for its carpets—and there are plenty of exceptional pieces from which to choose. Other necessities of Turkish life are also stocked in this jumble. A word on Kayseri and its carpet salesmen: In Turkish folklore the people of Kayseri are renowned for being crafty dealers. So keep your wits about you during the many sales pitches and remember: If you don't want to shop or buy, make it absolutely clear from the outset. If all else fails, use the Turkish word *yok,* the ultimate, highly effective, don't-argue-with-me version of "no!" ✉ *West of citadel.*

The double-domed **Ulu Cami** (Great Mosque) was begun in 1135 and completed in 1205. It contains a finely carved wooden mimber. A tile mosaic is the outstanding feature of its cylindrical minaret. ✉ *Near Düvenönü Meyd. and the bazaar.*

Kayseri has several old **mausoleums.** By far the most interesting of these is the Seljuk **Döner Kümbet** (Turning Mausoleum) of Sultan Shah Cihan, which was built around 1276. The name is derived from the tomb's conical roof, which fits on the 12-sided structure so lightly that it might be turned by any breeze. All its panels are decorated with bas-reliefs, among others, the Tree of Life and a double-headed eagle above lions. The cylindrical **Sırçalı Kümbet** (Crystal Mausoleum), built in the 14th century, lies just south of Döner Kümbet and across Talas Caddesi. It was named for some decorative tiles that have since vanished. ✉ *Talas Cad., 1 km (½ mi) south of citadel.*

About 4 km (2½ mi) east of Kayseri is the **Çifte Kümbet** (Twin-Vaulted Mausoleum). This Seljuk octagonal tomb was built in 1243 for one of the wives of Keykubat I. ✉ *Take Sivas Cad. east out of Kayseri.*

The best pieces at the local **Arkeoloji Müzesi** (Archaeological Museum) are finds from Kültepe, site of the ancient Assyrian and Hittite city of Kaneş, including many cuneiform tablets. Greek and Roman artifacts are also exhibited. ⊠ *Kışla Cad. 2,* ☎ *352/222–2149.* ⌨ *$1.75.* ⊙ *Tues.–Sun. 8–5.*

### Dining and Lodging

$ ★ ✕ **Beyaz Saray.** If you want to eat with the locals, stop by this inexpensive restaurant where the specialty of the house is *oltu kebap,* a sandwichlike affair of spit-roasted meat. Also worth trying are the spicy chicken *pirzola* (finely ground, grilled meat), vegetable *köfte* (spicy meatballs), and divine chocolate baklava. ⊠ *Millet Cad. 16,* ☎ *352/222–3381. AE, MC, V.*

$ ✕ **Iskender Kebab Salonu.** You'll find a good range of standard Turkish fare at this place near the citadel. *Iskender kebab* (slices of lamb grilled on a spit and served with yogurt and a tomato sauce) is the specialty. ⊠ *Millet Cad. 5,* ☎ *352/231–2769,* FAX *352/232–7577. AE, DC, MC, V.*

$ ✕ **Mantı Restaurant.** The setting—inside a Toyota dealership—may be a little odd, but the food is unbeatable. Dime-size *mantı,* the Turkish version of ravioli, and a fresh salad bar are accompanied by live music on Saturday night. ⊠ *Toyota Plaza, Anbar Mah., Zafer Cad. 4,* ☎ *352/326–3075,* FAX *352/326–4404. MC, V.*

$$ ★ 🏨 **Hotel Almer.** This is the place to stay in Kayseri. It's modern and extremely clean and has a fine bar and restaurant serving local specialties. ⊠ *Osman Kavuncu Cad. 15, Düvenönü Meyd.,* ☎ *352/320–7970,* FAX *352/320–7974. 63 rooms with bath, 14 suites. Restaurant, bar, minibars, cable TV. AE, MC, V.*🍽

$ 🏨 **Hotel Turan.** This reliable old-fashioned hotel is right in the center of town. The place is a bit worn, but the charming staff makes up for its shortcomings. ⊠ *Turan Cad. 8,* ☎ *352/222–5537,* FAX *352/231–1153. 40 rooms with shower. V.*

*En Route* Past the archaeological museum in Kayseri, the boulevard narrows and climbs into the foothills of **Mt. Erciyes.** A suburb of villas has risen over the site of ancient Eusebeia, followed by barren slopes dotted with beehives, which supply the excellent honey sold along the roadside.

## Kültepe

③⓪ *20 km (12 mi) northeast of Kayseri, north of Rte. 300.*

Kültepe (Hill of Ashes) is the site of **Kaneş,** an important Hittite city. Inhabited from the 4th millennium BC, Kaneş became powerful around 2500 BC. Five hundred years later, Assyrian trade caravans passed through Anatolia, and the trade colony of Kaneş flourished behind its single wall, attached to the double fortifications of an upper town. Only the foundations are left, and most of the 15,000 cuneiform tablets, alabaster idols, statuettes, and painted pottery found here are now in Ankara and Kayseri museums.

OFF THE BEATEN PATH **SULTAN HANI –** Behind the thick, rectangular walls of this remarkable, handsome caravansary, built by Alaaddin Keykubat in 1236, travelers and their beasts found ample space for a rest. For a good view of the surroundings, take the stairway to the right of the main gate up to the roof. ⊠ *Rte. 260, about 30 km (18 mi) from Kültepe (head northeast on Rte. 300, then continue on Rte. 260 as Rte. 300 forks to southeast).* ☎ *$1.25.* ⊙ *Daily 9–1 and 2–5.*

## Niğde and Environs

③① *126 km (78 mi) southwest of Kayseri on Rte. 805.*

The quiet provincial town of Niğde has Hittite roots, though it really flourished in the 13th century when Sultan Keykubat built the **Alaaddin Cami**. The mosque proudly bears three domes, exquisitely pure in line. A century later the Mongol Sungur Bay constructed a mosque of his own, with portals distinguished by unusual Gothic features. The inevitable fortress looks down from the heights; dating from the end of the 11th century, it's the town's earliest Seljuk monument.

Subtle, lacy stone carvings adorn the Hüdavent Hatun Türbe (1312), the tomb, and the charming white **Ak Medrese** (1409), the seminary, which is now a small regional museum containing a Byzantine mummy that is something of a scene stealer. A 16th-century bedestan adds to the list of distinguished architecture here.

The 10th-century church of **Eski Gümüşler** (Old Silver) houses exceptionally well-preserved frescoes of Christ, the Virgin Mary, and the saints. The adjoining monastery is hollowed out of the rock. ⊠ *9 km (6 mi) northeast of Niğde, left off Rte. 805, in village of Gümüşler.* ☜ *$1.75.* ☉ *Daily 9–5; watchman will unlock bldg. for you.*

OFF THE
BEATEN PATH

**BOR AND KEMERHISAR –** Bor has another Alaaddin Cami, as well as a 16th-century covered bazaar and bath. The town is 14 km (9 mi) southwest of Niğde, along Route 330. Five kilometers (3 miles) farther, in Kemerhisar, are a Roman aqueduct, pool, and hot springs. The sites in Bor and Kemerhisar are free and are open during daylight hours.

# Aksaray

**㉜** *121 km (75 mi) from Niğde; take Rte. 330 west and E90 north.*

You might consider stopping in Aksaray, especially if you're heading to Konya. Thanks to the Melendiz Çayı (Melendiz River), Aksaray is surrounded by an oasis in the baked plain. The **Eğri Minare** (Crooked Minaret), a reddish brick structure, has leaned alarmingly over the low houses on the riverbanks since 1236. The **Ulu Cami,** one of the main monuments in Aksaray, dates from the 15th century. Also left over from Seljuk times is the **Zinciriye Medrese,** a restored seminary that is now home to the local museum.

Another old caravansary built under the aegis of Alaaddin Keykubat, **Ağzıkarahan,** 15 km (9 mi) northeast of Aksaray on Route 300, has been restored to a semblance of the splendor it had when it first opened, in 1239.

*En Route*   On your way back toward Aksaray from Ağzıkarahan, head east just after the Mamasın Rezervuar (Mamasın Reservoir) on the road leading south to Selime. Once again, you're back in the fairyland of Cappadocia.

# Ihlara Valley

★ **㉝** *42 km (26 mi) southeast of Aksaray (past Selime).*

At Ihlara, the Melendiz River has carved a rift into the sheer tufa cliffs, which rise up to 492 ft. They are pierced by thousands of churches, chapels, and caves. The best view can be obtained from the hilltop restaurant, from which 285 steps descend the wall-like rock to the bottom of the canyon, a green gash in the barren highland below Hasan Dağı (Mt. Hasan). Byzantine Peristrema, the ancient name for Ihlara, is still idyllic; poplars and wild olive trees shade the slow-moving water, along which the 20 main churches are slowly crumbling away. On a hot summer day, stroll through the valley with its breathtaking scenery and frescoed churches set in the cliffs.

*En Route*   Along Route 300 heading southwest to Konya is the **Sultan Hanı,** 95 km (59 mi) northeast of Konya, Anatolia's largest and best-preserved caravansary. Like the Sultan Hanı northeast of Kayseri (*see above*), this structure was built in the 1230s, and by the same ruler. During ancient times it was a resting place for travelers and their camels plying the trade routes. Hans were constructed every 30 km (19 mi) or so, so there are two others on this route: the **Ağızkara Han** (Dark-Mouthed Inn), near Aksaray (*see above*), dating from the 1230s, and the **Sarı Han** (Yellow Inn), dating from 1249, near Avanos (*see above*).

# Konya

**㉞** *258 km (160 mi) from Ankara, south on Rtes. E90 and 715; 142 km (88 mi) from Ihlara on Rte. 300, southwest from Aksaray.*

Konya, at an altitude of 3,336 ft in a large, well-watered oasis, is the home of the whirling dervishes. It's one of the fastest-growing cities in Turkey. When the Seljuks arrived in 1076, Konya was hardly new. Earlier there had been a Hittite settlement here and, later, an important Phrygian town. St. Paul and St. Barnabas delivered sermons here in the years 47, 50, and 53. Konya was prosperous under the Romans and hosted one of the first ecumenical councils, in 235. After being invaded by Arab raiders from the 7th to 10th centuries, the city flourished again in the early 13th century, during the reign of Alaaddin Keykubat. It was a golden era that would last until the city fell to Mongol invaders in the 13th century.

Although Konya is a big city, one of the fastest growing in Turkey, it remains fairly conservative. Alcohol is rarely consumed in public, and the majority of women wear head scarves. If you behave and dress in a manner that respects the local values (which means no shorts or short skirts and tank tops), you should enjoy your visit and avoid undesirable attention.

★   The most visited site in Konya is the **Mevlâna Müzesi and Türbesi** (Mevlâna Museum and Tomb of Mevlâna Celaleddin), dedicated to the 13th-century poet and philosopher who founded the mystic order of the Mevlevi dervishes. Born in present-day Afghanistan in 1207, Mevlâna Celaleddin was the son of a renowned theologian who fled with his family before Genghis Khan's hordes. Celaleddin came to Konya at the age of 22, during the reign of Sultan Alaaddin Keykubat. He studied philosophy and religion and, like his father, became famous as a teacher of canonical law. In 1244 he came under the influence of a Persian dervish named Mehmet Şemseddin Tebrizi (or Sems), abandoned his profession, and devoted himself to philosophical discussions with his new mentor. When Sems disappeared, most likely murdered by Celaleddin's jealous followers, Celaleddin in his grief turned to Sufi mysticism and to poetry. His greatest work, the *Mesnevi,* consists of 25,000 poems that were read and taught in the countless *tekkes* (monasteries) of the order he founded. The *Mesnevi* is the only philosophical system formulated in poetry. It ranks close to the Koran in Islamic literature. Mevlâna died in 1273 and was succeeded by Hüsamed-din Çelebi, followed in turn by Mevlâna's son, Sultan Veled.

Mevlâna was a firm believer in the virtues of music and dance as a means of abandoning oneself to God's love and freeing oneself from earthly bondage. He considered the whirling pattern of motion to be representative of the soul's state of agitation. In the early years of the republic all religious orders were banned and forced to go underground, although they have gradually been reemerging since the 1980s. Until recently very few Turks read Mevlâna's works, but the authorities did preserve the *sema*, the whirling dance of his order, as a folkloric spectacle. The sema is still held in Konya once a year, during the weeklong festival marking the anniversary of Mevlâna's death on December 17. When it came to communicating with God, Mevlâna made no distinction between social class, race, or even religion; the sema was open to all.

The dancers you see today are men of ordinary trades, and the sema retains all its religious symbolism. The dancers' accelerated turning and position—right arm pointing up and left down—suggest their openness to divine grace. Their conical hats represent tombstones, their jackets the tombs themselves, and their skirts the funerary shrouds. Removing their jackets signifies their shedding of earthly ties and their escape from their graves. As they whirl, they also rotate around the room, just as they believe the universe rotates in the presence of God. Thus, in whirling away his earthly ties, the dervish effects a union with God.

Several travel agencies operate tours to the Mevlâna festival; they are often fully booked weeks in advance. If you want to join a tour, book before you leave home. Konya's **Tourism Information Office** (☎ 332/351–1074, FAX 332/350–6461) can help you find tickets and make hotel reservations for the festival. Several of the staff speak English and are invariably delighted by foreign interest, but it is wise to call or fax several weeks in advance.

The monastery of Mevlâna became the Mevlâna Museum in 1927. Small, lead-top domes set over the dervishes' cubicles form an honor guard around the garden leading up to the entrance. Inside, vivid reconstructions illustrate the dervishes' way of life in their former cells. The square room that you enter first is the Koran reading room. On the walls hang framed examples of distinguished calligraphy, including one specimen executed by a great devotee of this art, Sultan Mahmut. The translation of the quotation above the silver door is "He who enters incomplete here will leave complete." One showcase contains the first 18 verses of the *Mesnevi*, written in Mevlâna's own hand. To the right and left of the reading room lie the tombs of the most illustrious disciples, 65 in all.

Continue on into the room where the enormous Tomb of Mevlâna rests on a pedestal. At its head are his black turban and the curious cylindrical headgear of the sect. Two silver steps lead up to the platform; they are the sacred stairway. Believers press their faces against it as a sign of devotion. A brocade cover, embroidered with gold thread and weighing almost 110 pounds, covers the biers of Mevlâna and his eldest son; it was a gift from the Ottoman sultan Mehmet II (1451–81). At the foot of the tomb, the coffin of Mevlâna's father stands vertically, his white funerary turban on top. Quotations from the Koran are embedded in the sarcophagus with the exquisite precision that characterizes Seljuk art at its best. The mausoleum dates from the 13th century; the rest of the monastery was built later. As this is an extremely important religious site, women are required to cover their heads; scarves may be borrowed at the entrance. ✉ *Mevlâna Meyd., at east end of Mevlâna Cad.,* ☎ *332/351–1215.* ✆ *$2.50.* ☉ *Daily 9–5.* ✎

The **Selimiye Cami** (Selim Mosque) was started by the heir to the throne in 1558, when he was governor of Konya, and finished after he had become Sultan Selim II. The style is reminiscent of that of the Fatih Cami in Istanbul, with soaring arches and windows surrounding the base of the dome. The surrounding streets, which contain some shops, are full of character. ✉ *Opposite Mevlâna Museum on Mevlâna Meyd.*

On the way to Konya's ancient acropolis, the **Üçler Mezarlığı,** heading west from Mevlâna Meydanı, are a few mosques on or just off Alaaddin Caddesi. **Şerefettin Cami,** built in 1636, was started by the Seljuks and completed by the Ottomans. The **Şemsi Tebrizi Cami and Türbe,** north of Şerefettin Cami, off Hükümet Alanı, is dedicated to Mevlâna's mentor and friend. Konya's oldest mosque, the **İplikçi Cami** (Thread Dealer Mosque), dates from 1202.

The beautiful **Alaaddin Cami,** completed in 1220 and recently restored, crowns the **Alaaddin Tepesi** (Alaaddin Hill). Designed by an architect from Damascus, the mosque is of the Syrian style, unusual for Anatolia. Its pulpit stands in a forest of 42 columns taken from Roman temples. Most of the hill is devoted to a park, which contains a café. Below are the scanty remains of a Seljuk palace—two venerable stumps of walls. The city has for some reason deemed it expedient to throw an unsightly concrete shelter over them.

The **Büyük Karatay Medrese,** a theological seminary, was founded by Emir Celaleddin Karatay in 1251. His tomb is in a small room to the left of the main hall. The medrese is now a ceramics museum, the **Karatay Müzesi** (Karatay Museum), and it is easy to understand why this particular building was selected for that purpose. Its dome is lined with tiles, blue predominating on white, and the effect is dazzling. The frieze beneath the dome is in excellent condition, and the hunting scenes on the rare figurative tiles from the Kubadabat Palace in Beyşehir show the influence of Persia on Seljuk art. The soothing sound of a fountain spilling into a basin in the middle of the main hall sets just the right mood for meditation and study. The spectacular ceramics collection includes figurines of humans and animals, with vine leaves highlighting them with shades of cobalt blue and turquoise. ⊠ *Alaaddin Bul., at intersection with Ankara Cad.* 🚌 *$1.75.* ☉ *Tues.–Sun. 8:30–noon and 1:30–5:30.*

At the 13th-century **İnce Minare Medrese** (Seminary of the Slender Minaret), the minaret is bejeweled with glazed blue tiles. Unfortunately, it is now only half its original size, thanks to a bolt of lightning. Now a museum, the İnce Minare has a fine collection of stone and wood carvings. Note the ornate decoration of the building's entry portal. Under restoration in 2000, the medrese is scheduled to reopen in spring 2001. ⊠ *Alaaddin Bul., west side of Alaaddin Tepesi.* 🚌 *$1.75.* ☉ *Daily 8:30–noon and 1:30–5:30.*

The **Sırçalı Medrese** (Crystalline Seminary) opened in 1242 as a school for Islamic jurisprudence. The seminary's lavish tile decoration provides a dignified home for the **Türbe Müzesi** (Museum of Funerary Monuments). The small Catholic Church of **St. Paul** next door proves that Konya has remained as tolerant as it was in its Seljuk heyday. On the opposite side of the Sırçalı are Roman catacombs and a mosaic. ⊠ *Mimar Muzaffer Cad., south of Alaaddin Bul.* 🚌 *$1.75.* ☉ *Daily 9–5.*

A magnificent portal marks the remains of the **Sahip Ata** complex, a group of structures dating from 1283. Mosque buildings here have been converted into an **Arkeoloji Müzesi** (Archaeological Museum). Though the collection begins with items from the Bronze Age, its most important artifacts are Greek and Roman; the 3rd-century BC marble depicting the Twelve Labors of Hercules is outstanding. ⊠ *Larende Cad.,* ☎ *332/351-3207.* 🚌 *$1.75.* ☉ *Tues.–Sun. 9–noon and 1:30–5:30.*

Next to the Sahip Ata complex is the **Etnoğrafya Müzesi** (Ethnographic Museum), containing Islamic art, embroidery, carpets, and weapons. ⊠ *Larende Cad.,* ☎ *332/351-8958.* 🚌 *$1.75.* ☉ *Tues.–Sun. 9–noon and 1:30–5:30.*

Konya's **bazaar** once was known for its rug shops, but these now are more likely to be found around Alaaddin Caddesi. Meanwhile, the bazaar features an amazing array of ordinary goods. It is flanked by the **Aziziye Cami** (Sultan Abdül Aziz Mosque), dating from 1676, which has two short minarets topped off by a kind of loggia with a Florentine flavor. ⊠ *Market district, near intersection of Selimiye Cad. and Karaman Cad.* ☉ *Mon.–Sat. during daylight hrs.*

OFF THE
BEATEN PATH

**HOROZLU HAN AND SILLE –** If you're heading out of Konya in the direction of Ankara, look for the fabulous Seljuk portal at the entrance to the ruined Horozlu Han, a former caravansary near the four-lane beginning of Route 715. At Sille, 8 km (5 mi) northwest, St. Helena, mother of Constantine the Great, built a small church in AD 327. Nearby, frescoed rock chapels overlook the shores of a tiny artificial lake.

## Dining and Lodging

$–$$  ✕ **Horozlu Han Kervansaray.** This restored 700-year-old Seljuk caravansary on the old Silk Road has a cavernous interior where the stone provides a cool refuge from the heat. There are often floor shows in the evening. Specialties include *ezo gelin* (lentil soup), *etli ekmek* (flat bread with ground lamb), and excellent fish, which vary according to the season. The menu is prix fixe. ⊠ *Konya–Ankara Yolu Üzeri, TNP Yanı,* ☎ *332/345–0538,* FAX *332/345–0541. No credit cards.*

$  ✕ **Konya Fuar.** The food at this outdoor dining spot is much the same as elsewhere: kebabs. Open only in the summer, the café tends to get very crowded. ⊠ *Luna Parkı,* ☎ *no phone. No credit cards.*

$  ✕ **Şifa 1.** This no-frills restaurant serves basic Turkish fare, including pide, kebabs, rice and beans, and roast chicken. No alcohol is served. ⊠ *Mevlâna Cad.,* ☎ *332/352–0519. AE, MC, V.*

$$  ☷ **Otel Selçuk.** The best in town, this hotel has many amenities, including air-conditioning, satellite TVs and bathroom phones in all rooms. ⊠ *Alaaddin Cad. 4,* ☎ *332/353–2525,* FAX *332/353–2529. 78 rooms with bath. 2 restaurants, minibars. MC, V.*

$–$$  ☷ **Konya Oteli.** The Konya is just a block from the Mevlâna Museum. Its staff is eager to please. Though older than other hotels here, the building is well kept; rooms are basic. ⊠ *Mevlâna Meyd. 8,* ☎ *332/351–6677,* FAX *332/352–1003. 32 rooms with shower. MC, V.*

$  ☷ **Şifa Otel.** This comfortable, modern hotel is only a few minutes' walk from the Mevlâna Museum. Rooms are simply decorated and clean. The hotel management also runs the Şifa 1 restaurant next door. ⊠ *Mevlâna Cad. 55,* ☎ *332/350–4290,* FAX *332/351–9251. 30 rooms with shower. AE, MC, V.*

# ANKARA AND CENTRAL ANATOLIA A TO Z

## Arriving and Departing

### By Bus

Few major towns or cities are not connected to Ankara by bus. The seven-hour trip from Istanbul costs about $22, the 14-hour trip to Trabzon around $36. There are many bus lines, and though there should always be seats available to major destinations, you may want to buy tickets in advance. The standard of buses is generally good, although some companies are better than others and cost a little more. The most comfortable and safest are **Varan Bus Company** (☎ 312/417–2525 for Ankara, 212/251–7474 for Istanbul) and **Ulusoy** (☎ 312/419–4080 for Ankara, 212/471–7100 for Istanbul). Ankara's *otogar* (bus station), called AŞTİ, is on Bahçelerarası Caddesi at Eskişehir Yolu. The Ankaray subway line from Kızılay district ends underneath the station (☎ 312/224–1000).

## By Car

Although most Turks and many tourists travel by bus, the independence provided by having a car in this region makes it a worthwhile expense. On the other hand, you may not want to deal with doing the driving yourself (☞ Car Travel *in* the Gold Guide for more information). There are good roads between Istanbul and the main cities of Anatolia: Ankara, Konya, and Kayseri. The highways are generally well maintained and lead to all the major sights, though truck traffic on the main highway from Istanbul to Ankara can be heavy. Two long stretches of toll road (*ücretli geçiş*) linking Istanbul and Ankara—E80 to beyond Düzçe and E89 south from Gerede—provide some relief from the rigors of the other highway. Minor roads are rough and full of potholes. On narrow, winding roads, look out for oncoming trucks—their drivers often don't seem to believe in staying on their side of the road. From Ankara, E90 (also known as Route 200) leads southwest toward Sivrihisar; continue southwest on E96 to Afyon, where you can pick up highways going south to Antalya or west to İzmir. Route E88/200 leads east out of Ankara and eventually connects with highways to the Black Sea Coast.

## By Plane

Central Turkey is well served by Ankara's **Esenboğa Airport,** 30 km (19 mi) north of the city. There are direct flights from Europe and New York, as well as many domestic flights. Carriers include **Delta Airlines** (☎ 312/468–7805; 800/241–4141 in the U.S.) and **THY Turkish Airlines** (☎ 312/419–2800). THY also has daily direct flights from Istanbul to the airport at Kayseri; the THY shuttle from there will take you to any hotel in Cappadocia for $7.

BETWEEN THE AIRPORT AND CENTER CITY

A **taxi** into Ankara can cost as much as $25. More affordable shuttle buses, operated by **Havaş,** cost $3.50. Board them in front of the terminal shortly after flight arrivals, and you will be delivered to the train station or bus station.

## By Train

Regular rail service connects Ankara to both Istanbul and İzmir. The **Ankara Express** runs between Ankara and Istanbul; it leaves both places at 10:30 PM and arrives the next morning at 8. The price is about $35 for the sleeper bed and is by far the most comfortable train. The **Anadolu (Anatolia) Express** also runs between Ankara and Istanbul, with simultaneous departures from both cities at 10 PM and with arrivals at 7 AM. There are no sleeper cars on this train, just regular seats that cost about $10. The final option between Istanbul and Ankara is the **Başkent Express,** which leaves Istanbul at 10 AM and arrives in Ankara at 4:50 PM, and leaves Ankara at 10:20 AM and arrives in Istanbul at 4:50 PM. The cost is about $13.

As for İzmir–Ankara train service, the **İzmir Express** leaves both cities at 7 PM and arrives at 10 the next morning; the cost is about $10 per person. Another option is the **İzmir Mavi,** or Blue Train, which departs both cities at 6 PM and arrives at 8:30 AM; the cost is about $11.

# Getting Around

## By Bus

Buses link most towns and cities, and fares are reasonable (less than $12 from Ankara to most anywhere in Central Anatolia, for instance).

## By Car

Ankara is a big city with chaotic traffic, so you'll save yourself a lot of grief if you park your car and get around by public transportation. The center of the city is relatively compact, and it is possible to walk to most places. A car is useful for excursions to the Hittite cities and to Cappadocia. Boğazkale and Hattuşaş are about 125 km (78 mi) east of Ankara, Konya is 261 km (162 mi) to the south, and Kayseri is 312 km (194 mi) southeast.

## By Taxi

The cost of traveling by taxi to historic sites outside Ankara is usually reasonable ($30–$60), but always agree on the fare in advance. Cabs can be hailed, or ask your hotel to call one.

## By Train

Though there is Blue Train service between the region's main cities— Ankara, Konya, and Kayseri—trains are almost nonexistent between small towns. The one route that may be of use to tourists is Ankara–Kayseri, but it's generally much quicker to take a bus. For information contact the **train station** (⊠ Talat Paşa Cad., at Cumhuriyet Bul., ☎ 312/311–0620 for information; 312/311–4994 for reservations).

# Contacts and Resources

## Car Rental

**Avis** (⊠ Esenboğa Airport, ☎ 312/398–0315; ⊠ Tunus Cad. 68, Kavaklıdere, ☎ 312/467–2313). **Budget** (⊠ Esenboğa Airport, ☎ 312/398–0372; ⊠ Tunus Cad. 39, Kavaklıdere, ☎ 312/417–5952). **Hertz** (⊠ Esenboğa Airport, ☎ 312/398–0535; ⊠ Atatürk Blv. 138/B, Kavaklıdere, 312/468–1029).

## Emergencies

**Ambulance** (☎ 112). **Police** (☎ 155). Your hotel is the best source of information on good hospitals, as well as on doctors and dentists.

## Guided Tours

If you are driving through Cappadocia, consider hiring a guide (about $25–$60 a day). Local tourist offices and hotels can make recommendations. Ankara travel agencies arrange bus tours to Cappadocia and Konya, as well as day trips within the city. In Ankara, try the following: **Setur Ankara** (⊠ Kavaklıdere Sok. 5/B, ☎ 312/467–1165, FAX 312/467–8775). **T & T Tourism and Travel** (⊠ Abdullah Cevdet Sok. 22/7, Çankaya, ☎ 312/440–9234, FAX 312/440–2234). **Türk Ekspres** (⊠ Cinnah Cad. 9, Çankaya, ☎ 312/467–7334, FAX 312/467–2920).

One of the best ways to appreciate the expansiveness and diversity of Cappadocia's landscape is from a hot-air balloon. Before or after exploring the area on foot, invest in a morning ride with **Kapadokya Balloons** (⊠ Nevşehir Yolu 14/A, Göreme, ☎ 384/271–2442, FAX 384/271–2586). Rides are offered from April through October and the cost is $230 per person.

## Visitor Information

**Ministry of Tourism** (⊠ Gazi Mustafa Kemal Bul. 121, ☎ 312/229–2631, FAX 312/229–3661; ⊠ Esenboğa Airport, ☎ 312/398–0348). **Kayseri** (⊠ Kağnı Pazarı 61, next to Hunat Hatun complex, ☎ 352/222–3903, FAX 352/222–0879). **Konya** (⊠ Mevlâna Cad. 21, by Mevlâna Museum, ☎ 332/351–1074, FAX 332/350–6461). **Nevşehir** (⊠ Atatürk Bul., next to hospital, ☎ 384/213–3659). **Ürgüp** (⊠ Kayseri Cad. 37, inside park, ☎ 384/341–4059).

# 6 THE BLACK SEA COAST

The Black Sea Coast harbors some of Turkey's wildest and most remote districts. In both physical distance and character, these undeveloped regions are far from the modern tourist resorts along the country's south and west coasts. In the tiny villages here, many of them unmarked on maps, alleys are filled with chickens and donkeys, and old Ottoman houses and spare-looking mosques stand proud as they have for centuries.

THE HISTORY OF THE BLACK SEA COAST, like the rest of Turkey's, is long and complicated. When Greek colonists first settled in the area during the 8th century BC, the interior was dominated by feudal Persian nobility. In 301 BC, following the War of Succession sparked by the death of Alexander the Great, octogenarian Mithridates II Ktistes (the Founder) established a dynasty in Amaseia, today's Amasya. During the next two centuries, his successors extended their rule over the petty Hellenistic and Anatolian states along the coast, making the kingdom of Pontus a power to reckon with in Asia Minor. Though superficially hellenized, the Pontic kingdom preserved a Persian religious and social structure, and the monarchs even claimed a spurious descent from Persia's great kings. Mithridates V's forces occupied the lands of Phrygia and Cappadocia to the southwest, and his son, known as Mithridates VI Eupator (132–63 BC), expelled the Roman armies from Asia Minor, advanced into Greece, and seriously contested Rome's influence. It took Rome's greatest generals—Sulla, Lucullus, and Pompey—30 years to drive Mithridates VI back to his homeland, where he committed suicide. Julius Caesar incorporated the kingdom into the Roman Empire in 63 BC.

*Revised and Updated by Eli Newell*

Things settled down for a long time, but the region had another brief moment of glory before all was said and done. In 1204, after the armies of the Fourth Crusade sacked Constantinople, a group of Byzantine aristocrats led by Alexius Comnene created the Trebizond Empire of the Grand Comneni. A lone Christian outpost in the Islamic East, the empire became a thriving city-state, with its capital, at what is now Trabzon, surviving for two centuries. Then came Sultan Mehmet II, who solidified the Ottoman position in the east by bringing Trabzon, the final Byzantine outpost on the Black Sea, under his control in 1461. During the Ottoman era, the importance of shipping routes made the Black Sea Coast a contested region coveted by czarist Russia. Intensifying the struggle was Russia's involvement in separatist movements waged by Christian populations along the Black Sea. The War of Independence settled these disputes, and today the Black Sea is both a scenic tourist destination and a thriving industrial and shipping region.

## Pleasures and Pastimes

### Beaches

Şile and Akçakoca are beach resorts popular with Istanbulites. A number of fine beaches lie between Amasra and İnebolu; Kapısuyu Beach, near Kurucaşile, is the nicest. Lovely Karakum Beach, at the tip of the Sinop Peninsula, is a good base for fishing trips or windsurfing. The Ünye Bay area also has several fine beaches, particularly the one at Çamlık.

### Dining

The Black Sea supplies the seafood restaurants along the coast with many varieties of fresh fish. The specialties are *palamut*—which tastes like a cross between tuna and mackerel—*alabalık*, stream trout, and *hamsi*, anchovies, prepared in countless ways. Delicious alternatives to fish include *pide*, a bread with meat or cheese that resembles Italian pizza, and *köfte*, tiny succulent meatballs. If these regional specialties don't appeal to you, there's always the standard kebab dish or rice and beans. For a chart that explains the cost of meals at the restaurants in this chapter, *see* Dining and Lodging Price Categories in Smart Travel Tips A to Z at the back of this book.

## Lodging

Rooms are simple, even in the few modern hotels in the bigger towns. If you're accustomed to satellite TVs and 24-hour room service, you may be disappointed with even some upscale hotels. Despite this, many hotels maintain fairly high standards; rooms are generally clean and hotel staffs are friendly, and the lack of luxury is a small price to pay for an unmediated glimpse of this part of the world. For a chart that explains the room rates at accommodations in this chapter, *see* Dining and Lodging Price Categories at the back of this book.

## Shopping

The best bazaars are in Trabzon, Amasya, and Kastamonu; each has a strong sense of history. In Ünye, hazelnuts are the thing to buy and are almost everywhere you look (the Black Sea region produces 80% of the world's hazelnuts). If you love chocolate, stop in Ordu to visit the Sagra Special chocolate factory store in the center of town, which also sells nuts, tea, and coffee. Safranbolu is named after the costly spice saffron, which you can buy in this region for considerably less than what you'd pay at home. Several smaller towns clustered around Trabzon hold weekly markets where you can see mountain villagers coming down to trade, as they have for centuries. And farther east, Rize is the undisputed tea-producing capital of Turkey.

# Exploring the Black Sea Coast

Driving the twisty roads along the Black Sea coastline is not easy, but the ride is always dramatic. On the one side lies a dark blue sea; on the other, surprisingly lush green hills slowly give way to snowy white peaks. The course rolls over steep forested hills, dips down to dry plains, scuttles over rocky outcrops, skims past wheat fields, and plunges back into forest. There aren't many towns along the way, the road is often in disrepair, and the going may be slow. Gas stations can be few and far between; try to keep the gas tank well topped off.

Gone is the guaranteed sunshine you find elsewhere in Turkey. Though the coastal climate is temperate, skies are often overcast. It may rain for days on end, even in summer—especially in the eastern parts below the Giresun Dağları and the Karadeniz Dağları, a pair of gently curved massifs that link into the mighty Pontic Mountains (now called the Kuzey Anadolu Sıradağları, or North Anatolian Mountain chain), rising nearly 13,000 ft. Each mountain and valley along the chain seems to shelter a distinct culture. In some villages you hear Greek spoken, while in others the locals speak Laz and a strong dialect of Turkish almost incomprehensible even to some other Turks.

## Great Itineraries

Since the distances between the major sites on the Black Sea are so vast, if you're pressed for time, you might do best by sticking to either the east or west end of the coast. If you think you'll be satisfied with just a glimpse of the sea, you can do as the Istanbulites do and take a relaxing weekend excursion to Şile or a more ambitious short trip to Lake Abant, Safranbolu, or Kastamonu. But if you want to experience the region fully, you'll need at least five days to make your way east—even just as far as Amasya. Roads are incredibly scenic but demanding, so don't try to cover too much ground at one time. Touring the Black Sea Coast is not only about getting from one must-see sight to another, but about adopting the laid-back lifestyle of the *Karadenizli* (Black Sea folk) and enjoying the ride and the scenery as it reveals itself along the way. If you're dead set on seeing the entire coast and have only a week, you're best off renting a car in Istanbul, driving east to Trabzon, and then flying back, or flying to Trabzon and driving west.

IF YOU HAVE 2 DAYS

*Numbers in the text correspond to numbers in the margin and on the Black Sea Coast map.*

If you're based in Istanbul and have only a couple days to sample the Black Sea, stick to the west end. Traveling on Route 20 from Istanbul, divert to Polonezköy for lunch in a Polish village, then continue to the beach resort of ⊞ **Şile** ①, dominated by a ruined Genoese castle. With its picturesque harbor and lighthouse, Şile makes an ideal short getaway.

IF YOU HAVE 5 DAYS

On day one, relax at the beach in ⊞ **Şile** ①. The next day, head inland on Route 20 until it meets Route 100E; follow it to Route 755N and to the historic town of ⊞ **Safranbolu** ③. Spend the afternoon viewing the town's Ottoman houses and mansions. On the morning of day three, visit Safranbolu's Arasta Bazaar. After visiting the bazaar, head 95 km (59 mi) east on Route 30, winding through the mountains until you reach the medieval city of **Kastamonu** ④; drive up to the town's castle past 19th-century Ottoman mansions. From Kastamonu, head south on Route 775 and then southeast on Route 100 until you arrive at ⊞ **Amasya** ⑥. View the provincial city from atop the town's citadel. On day four, stroll along Amasya's tree-lined river and explore the city's marketplace and climb up to the Pontic tombs. On your fifth day, visit the nearby town of **Tokat** ⑦.

IF YOU HAVE 7 DAYS

On day one, take Route 100E, then head north on Route 750 to ⊞ **Amasra** ②. Early on day two, view the sights of this small fishing port, then drive south on Route 755 to **Safranbolu** ③. Head next to ⊞ **Kastamonu** ④. On the morning of the third day, turn south toward ⊞ **Amasya** ⑥. On day four, after visiting **Tokat** ⑦, head north on Route 850, then east on Route 10, and spend the night in either **Ünye** ⑨ or **Ordu** ⑩. Continuing on Route 10, on the fifth day drive through **Giresun** ⑪ on the way to the ancient Byzantine city of ⊞ **Trabzon** ⑫ and pass the afternoon in the city's many museums. The next day, drive a short distance south of town and climb to the monastery at **Sumela** ⑬. On your last day, take a drive to the **Rize** ⑭ tea plantations and continue on to **Çamlıhemşin** ⑮.

## When to Tour the Black Sea Coast

The Black Sea Coast is mild and damp throughout the year. To capture the region at its lushest, greenest, and sunniest, you're best off visiting between late April and late October. Of this period, the nicest time to visit the Black Sea Coast is in late spring, when the blossoms are out and the tour groups have only started to arrive. It's not a problem traveling along the coast in winter, but many hotels and restaurants geared toward tourists are closed at this time. In winter (November–March), snow makes the climb to the Sumela Monastery difficult if not impossible.

# ŞILE TO SINOP

The 494 km (306 mi) stretch from the popular beach resort of Şile to Sinop, the oldest city on the Black Sea, was known in antiquity as Pamphlagonia. Beaches along this well-worn road are popular with cosmopolitan Turks because of their relative proximity to Istanbul and Ankara. Amasra, Safranbolu, and Kastamonu form a triumvirate of Ottoman towns that will tempt you to forsake the seaside.

## The Black Sea Coast

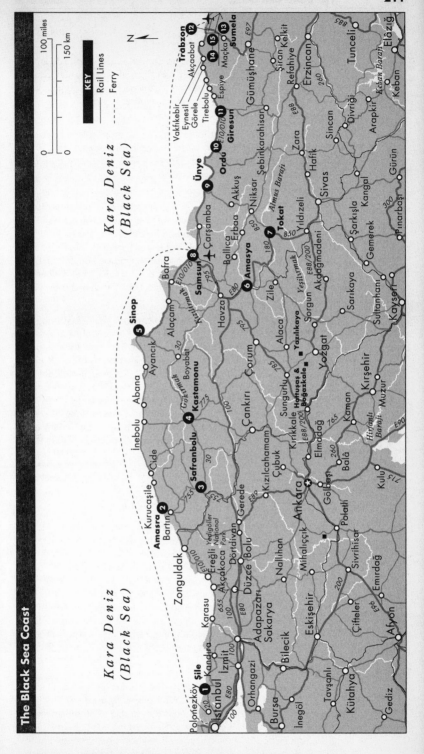

*Kara Deniz*
*(Black Sea)*

*Kara Deniz*
*(Black Sea)*

*Kara Deniz*
*(Black Sea)*

**KEY**
— Rail Lines
--- Ferry

100 miles

150 km

# Şile

**❶** *71 km (44 mi) northeast of Istanbul on Rte. 20.*

With its picturesque harbor, skyline dominated by a ruined Genoese castle on Ocaklı Island, and lively nightlife, Şile is a popular getaway for residents of Istanbul. Try to avoid the town's beach on summer weekends and holidays, when it gets very crowded.

### Lodging

**$–$$**   🏨 **Değirmen Hotel.** An old standby among vacationing Istanbulites, the Değirmen has a beach and a nightclub and a good sense of fun. ⊠ *Plaj Yolu 24,* ☎ *216/711–5048,* ℻ *216/711–5248. 73 rooms with bath. Restaurant, bar, pool, windsurfing. MC, V.*

OFF THE BEATEN PATH   **POLONEZKÖY –** Off Route 20 before Şile is Polonezköy (Polish Village). Founded in the mid-19th century by Polish nationals in exile from Russian-invaded Poland, Polonezköy operated as a semiautonomous colony. Now integrated into the Turkish Republic, residents of Polonezköy are citizens of Turkey, and few still speak Polish. Despite this integration, the town has retained much of its unique character and is now a popular country retreat filled with guest houses, small restaurants, and shops stocked with local produce. The local church and graveyard are well worth visiting.

**YEDİGÖLLER NATIONAL PARK AND LAKE ABANT –** If you're hankering for the great outdoors, Yedigöller National Park, southeast of Akçakoca and east of Şile (south on Route 655, east on Route E80, and north on a marked access road from Bolu), has seven lakes; forests of beech, oak, and elm; and wolves, deer, and brown bears. The magnificent Lake Abant resort area, southwest of Bolu, is renowned for its scenery and the best trout fishing in Turkey. The plush **Abant Palace Hotel** (☎ 374/224–5012, ℻ 374/224–5011), perched on a sliver of land between the lakeshore and pine-clad hills, is a favorite getaway for wealthy Istanbulites, who enjoy its many amenities (among them satellite TVs in every room).

# Amasra

**❷** *421 km (261 mi) east of Şile on Rte. 20 and Rte. 10.*

Amasra is named after Queen Amastris, a contemporary of Alexander the Great, who, after being wronged by her husband, retreated to this small fishing port, then called Sesamos. The walled city, between two harbors, remains a haven along this industrialized stretch of the coast. In the old quarter of town, on the Küçük Liman (Small Harbor), is the **Fatih Cami,** which was originally a cathedral and was later converted to a mosque. You'll also find **Kilise Mesciti,** a delightfully painted Byzantine church. Also perched over the Küçük Liman is the **Amasra Müzesi,** a museum containing classical sculptures and Ottoman wood carvings. The museum is open Tuesday–Sunday 9–5 and charges $1 admission.

OFF THE BEATEN PATH   **COASTLINE FROM AMASRA TO SİNOP –** The 166 km (103 mi) of Black Sea coastline leading up to İnebolu is a particularly untrammeled stretch, with ramshackle Mediterranean-style fishing villages and empty beaches. From İnebolu it's another 158 km (98 mi) to Sinop—a difficult drive, with the road perpetually under construction and few gas stations. The nearly deserted İnceburun Peninsula, extending into the Black Sea west of Sinop, has striking forests, sand dunes, and lagoons.

### Dining and Lodging

Like any seaside town, Amasra has its fair share of good fish restaurants. Two favorites are the **Çeşmi Cihan** (⊠ On main harbor) and **Mustafa Amca'nın Lokantası** (⊠ Küçük Liman Cad.).

$ 🏨 **Otel Timur.** This simple yet comfortable hotel is open year-round and is popular with repeat visitors. ⊠ *Çekiciler Cad. 57,* ☎ *378/315–2589,* FAX *378/315–3290. 18 rooms with shower. V.*

$ 🏨 **Nur Turistik Pansiyon.** Tucked away on small street, this decidedly basic pansiyon provides quiet rooms close to Amasra's sights. ⊠ *Çamlı Sok.,* ☎ *378/315–1015. 17 rooms, some with shower. No credit cards.*

*En Route* Some fine old villages punctuate Route 755 as it heads inland from Amasra toward Safranbolu. Along this route, note the traditional Ottoman houses: square, half-timbered buildings with tile roofs and overhanging second stories. You'll see the first of these in **Bartın,** just south of Amasra.

## Safranbolu

★ ❸ *97 km (60 mi) south of Amasra on Rte. 755.*

Tucked behind a modern town of the same name, old Safranbolu (Çarşı) has preserved a slice of the past and the historic center has been designated a UNESCO World Heritage site. Cars are banned, artisans ply their crafts in open storefronts, and many old Ottoman houses line the streets. Some buildings are open to the public, including the **Kaymakamlar Evi** (Governor's House), open Tuesday–Sunday 9–noon and 1:30–5 and charging 50¢ for entrance to the house, which has been restored with 200-year-old furnishings. Stop by the tourist information office in the **Arasta** (Ottoman Market Hall) to pick up a walking tour map of old Safranbolu.

### Lodging

$$ 🏨 **Havuzlu Asmazlar Konağı.** The hotel has been restored to resemble a typical affluent Safranbolu house in Ottoman times. Painstaking attention has been given to detail, from the embroidered floral motifs on the blinds to the *havuz* (pool) in the breakfast room from which the hotel takes its name. The excellent restaurant serves the Safranbolu kebab of grilled lamb, tomato sauce, and yogurt on pita bread, topped with cheese. On the same grounds is the Küçük Konak, a seven-room annex in which rooms share showers and toilets. ⊠ *Karabık Cad., Haci Halil Mah.,* ☎ *372/725–2883,* FAX *372/712–3824. Havuzlu Konak: 11 rooms with shower; Küçük Konak: 7 rooms, none with bath. Restaurant, outdoor café. MC, V.*

## Kastamonu

❹ *98 km (60 mi) east of Safranbolu on Rte. 30.*

The medieval city of Kastamonu was once the stronghold of Alexius Comnene, the founder of the Comnene dynasty in Constantinople (1081), who recaptured it from the Seljuk Turks during the First Crusade. The surviving *kale* (castle) is an amalgam of Byzantine, Seljuk, Mongol, and Ottoman reconstructions. For an incredible view of the countryside, drive up to the castle past splendid 19th-century Ottoman mansions.

The **Karanlık Bedestan,** a covered bazaar south of Nasrullah Meydanı, was built in the 1470s shortly after the Ottoman conquest of Kastamonu. It is still in use and bears few signs of change through the intervening centuries.

The **Kastamonu Müzesi,** the town museum, is housed in the building where Atatürk announced the abolition of the fez in 1925. Muslims wore the fez because, as a cap without a brim, it did not interfere with placing the forehead on the ground while saying the five daily prayers. The abolition of the fez was a symbolic break with Islam as well as with the Ottoman empire, with which the fez was identified, and was also a means of associating Turkey with the West. Unfortunately, much of the signage is in Turkish only. ⊠ *On Cumhuriyet Cad.,* ☎ *no phone.* ☎ *$1.* ☉ *Tues.–Sun. 9–5.*

OFF THE
BEATEN PATH
**MAHMUT BEY CAMI –** This 14th-century mosque with exquisite wood carvings is the chief attraction of the village of Kasaba, 15 km (9 mi) north of Kastamonu on the road to Daday, west of Route 765.

## Dining and Lodging

$ ✗ **Uludağ Pide ve Kebap Salonu.** One of the very few restaurants in town, Uludağ dishes up a typical array of ready-to-eat foods and kebabs. Come early—like most places in town, this spot is likely to close soon after dark. ⊠ *Corner of Belediye and Cumhuriyet Cads.,* ☎ *no phone. No credit cards.*

$ ✗▥ **Otel Mütevelli.** On the main road, this hotel is as close to comfort as you will find in Kastamonu. Catering to regional businesspeople, it exceeds expectations with clean bathrooms and comfortable beds. In a town with few restaurants, the one in the hotel is acceptable. ⊠ *Cumhuriyet Cad. 10,* ☎ *366/212–2020,* ℻ *366/212–2017. 55 rooms with shower. Restaurant, bar. V.*

*En Route* An old stone bridge with five arches, the **Taşköprü,** spans the Gökırmak River, northeast of Kastamonu on Route 30. Nearby, at **Ev Kaya,** is an interesting 6th-century BC rock tomb, with colonnades and a frieze. Just before the town of **Boyabat,** Route 785 branches northeast, rolling through tobacco fields and over the wild forests of the Damaz Pass, to return you to the coast at Sinop.

# Sinop

❺ *192 km (119 mi) northeast of Kastamonu on Rtes. 30, 785, and 10.*

Known in ancient times as Sinope, the oldest city on the Black Sea Coast was reputedly founded by the Amazon queen Sinova. Legend has it that Sinova attracted the interest of Zeus, who, to get on her good side, offered to grant her one wish. Sinova requested everlasting virginity, thus foiling the god's amorous intentions.

In the 7th century BC, the people of Miletus colonized this region and imported their Greek culture. In the town's museum, the **Sinop Müzesi,** don't miss the collection of Greek Orthodox icons, artifacts from nearby Kocagöz, and the statue of Sinope. ⊠ *In Municipal Park near intersection of Sakarya Cad. and Atatürk Cad.,* ☎ *no phone.* ☎ *$1.* ☉ *Mon. noon–5, Tues.–Sun. 9–5.*

In the courtyard of the town museum stands the 2nd-century BC **Temple of Serapis.** This spot also marks the birthplace of the Cynic philosopher Diogenes (about 400–325 BC), who reportedly lived in a large earthenware tub and preached a way of life that included the disregard of conventions, even suggesting that people should feel free to make love in public like dogs (*kyon* in Greek), hence the word *cynic.*

Some believe the first **citadel** at Sinop was built by the Hittites, though the present layout dates from the Pontic king Mithridates IV, who ordered its reconstruction in the 1st century BC. The **Alaaddin Cami** (⊠ Sakarya Cad.), a mosque named after the prominent Seljuk sultan, was

built following the Seljuk conquest of Sinop in 1214; its splendid original *mihrab* (prayer niche) is displayed in Istanbul's Museum of Islamic
Art. The **Alaiye Medrese** (⊠ Sakarya Cad.), once a seminary, now a
museum containing some interesting tombs, was built in 1262 by the
grand vizier of Keykubat, Süleyman Pervane, who also ordered the construction of the Alaaddin Cami.

A walk through Sinop reveals many other small mosques, tombs, and
fountains. The **Saray Cami and Fetih Baba Cami** were both built in 1339.
The **Çifte Hamam** (⊠ Sakarya Cad.) was built in 1332. The **Balat
Kilise** (⊠ Sami Paşa Cad.), standing on the grounds of a ruined palace,
is a Byzantine church dating from the 7th century. Though it retains
some frescoes, they are badly damaged; its fine icons are displayed now
in the city museum.

On a hilltop at the edge of town and seated on a narrow peninsula,
providing a good view of the town, is a mausoleum, the 14th-century
**Sayid Bilal Türbesi.**

### Lodging

$–$$  🏨 **Melia Kasım Hotel.** Though hardly memorable—rooms are very
plain—the Melia is on the water and is generally regarded as the best
lodging in Sinop. ⊠ *Gazi Cad. 49,* ☎ *368/261–4210,* 🅵🅰🆇 *368/261–1625.
57 rooms with bath. MC, V.*

$  🏨 **Karakum Holiday Village.** This hotel just outside town has a pri-
vate beach, but accommodations are uninspired, and the furnishings
are basic. Choose between private bungalows, a room in the hotel, or
the pansiyon. ⊠ *On the waterfront,* ☎ *368/261–2693,* 🅵🅰🆇 *368/261–
2694. 44 rooms with bath, 16 bungalows. Restaurant, bar. No credit
cards.*

*En Route*  The thermal springs in **Bafra,** near the mouth of the Kızılırmak (Red
River), 107 km (66 mi) from Sinop, on the way to Samsun, supply a
13th-century *hamam* (Turkish bath). Bafra is a good place to buy tobacco and caviar.

# AMASYA AND TOKAT

The terrain becomes more mountainous and less lush as you swing away
from the coast toward the ancient Pontic capital of Amasya, the ruined Seljuk fortress at Tokat, and the rural village and fortress at Zile.
The change is so great you may forget just how near you are to the
Black Sea.

## Amasya

★ ❻  *131 km (81 mi) south of Samsun on Rte. 795.*

According to its most famous son, the geographer-historian Strabo (circa
63 BC–AD 19), Amasya was founded by the Amazon queen Amasis. But
its epoch of glory was as the first capital of the kingdom of Pontus,
which lasted nearly 300 years, from the decline of Alexander the
Great's empire until the Romans took the town in 66 BC. The Seljuks
moved in after 1071, followed by the Mongols in the 13th century and
the Ottomans in the beginning of the 15th. During the Ottoman era,
Amasya was an important intellectual center—not only was it a training ground for Ottoman princes, but it was home to 18 *medreses*
(seminaries), earning the city the nickname "Baghdad of Anatolia." It
was in Amasya in 1919 that Atatürk rallied support for the War of Independence and outlined the basic tenets of the future state; the statue
of Atatürk and his compatriots in the central square commemorates
this 1919 meeting.

The historic center of Amasya is on the right (south) bank of the Yeşilırmak (Green River). Old Ottoman houses line the riverside, the two banks connected by several old and new bridges. The best way to immerse yourself in the history of this town and to feel the Ottoman presence is to wander along the river on Atatürk Caddesi (most of the sites below are on this street, unless otherwise noted) and through the neighborhoods of Dere Mahellesi, Helkis Mahellesi and İçeri Şehir.

As you walk along the river from the Atatürk statue into the main part of town, you will see a banner on a house on the north bank that marks the restored 19th-century **Hazeran Konağı** (Hazeran Mansion), where there's a small ethnology museum and art gallery. ⊠ *On the river; watch for signs.* 🖃 *Less than $1.* ☉ *Tues.–Sun. 9:30–11:45 and 2:30–5.*

Behind the Hazeran Mansion is a pathway up the steep cliff to the Pontic **Kral Kaya Mezarlığı** (King's Rock Tombs). On your way up you'll pass the misnamed **Kızlar Sarayı** (Palace of the Maidens), which was actually occupied by Pontic kings and later transformed into an Ottoman palace. Continue up to the 14 rock-cut tombs with impressive facades that loom over the city. During Pontic times the caves were used to worship the deified rulers; today they seem to be a favorite hangout of bored soldiers. To truly appreciate the enormousness of the tombs, drive up to the Çakallar Aile Gazinosu, a restaurant on the opposite side of the river, to drink tea, watch the sun set, and wait for the floodlights to come on.

Back on the south bank of the river is the 16th-century *bedestan* (covered bazaar). It anchors the marketplace that runs for several blocks between Ziya Paşa Bulvarı and Atatürk Caddesi, the two main roads through town running parallel to the Yeşilırmak. Behind the bazaar, away from the river, is the **Burmalı Minare Cami** (Mosque with the Twisted Minaret), built in 1242.

Farther upriver is the two-domed **Sultan Beyazıt II Cami,** along the river on a shady terrace. The mosque was begun by the former governor of Amasya and finished in 1486 by his son. The imposing mosque has a fine *mimber* (pulpit) and mihrab made of marble and blue tiles inscribed with quotations from the Koran.

The collection of the **Amasya Müzesi** (Amasya Museum) covers the nine civilizations that have ruled over the city. Wood carvings, astronomy instruments, old coins, and tombs make this a worthwhile stop; the **Tomb of Sultan Mesut** is on the museum grounds, alongside several mummies. ⊠ *Atatürk Cad. across from Sultan Beyazıt II Cami,* ☎ *358/ 218–6957.* 🖃 *$1.* ☉ *Tues.–Sun. 9:30–11:45 and 2:30–5:00.*

The **Gök Medrese Cami** (Mosque of the Blue Seminary), built in 1267, is named for the colorful tiles that once adorned the doorway. Next to it is the tomb of the founder of the seminary, Emir Torumtay, a man who started life as a slave and later became governor of Amasya.

Unless you're prepared for a big climb, Amasya's **kale,** high above the north bank of the Yeşilırmak, is only accessible by car (follow the small signs on the east side of the river). In the few bits of ruined tower and wall of the castle that remain upright, you can attempt to distinguish the different stones used by various builders, from the Greeks through the Romans to the Seljuks. The view from atop the citadel makes it the perfect spot for a picnic.

## Dining and Lodging

$  ✕ **Tadım Ocakbaşı.** Food is grilled on open coals at this simple restaurant on a market street near the square. Choose from the chicken *döner* (thinly sliced roasted meat), *iskender* kebab (thinly sliced meat on bread with tomato sauce and yogurt), pide, or the house specialty— the Ali Nazik kebab (lamb and vegetables). ⊠ *İğnecibaba Sok., behind Yampaş,* ☎ *358/218–1024. No credit cards.*

$–$$ 🏨 **Büyük Amasya Oteli.** Though seemingly no different from the army barracks next door and a bit overpriced, this hotel offers rooms overlooking the river and is one of few options if the pansiyons are full. ⊠ *Elmasiye Cad.,* ☎ *358/218–4054,* 🅵🅰🅇 *358/218–4056. 50 rooms with shower. MC, V.*

$ 🏨 **İlk Pansiyon.** An old Ottoman house painstakingly restored by
★ owner-architect Ali Kamil Yalçın, this pansiyon allows you to spend a night in Ottoman style while still enjoying such 20th-century comforts as private bathrooms. Enjoy breakfast in the courtyard. ⊠ *Gumuslu Mah. Hitit Sok. 1,* ☎ *358/218–1689,* 🅵🅰🅇 *358/218–6277. 6 rooms with shower. No credit cards.*

$ 🏨 **Emin Efendi Pansiyon.** Another traditional Ottoman house turned
★ pansiyon, this place overlooks the river and is quite charming. Make sure to request the only one of the five rooms with its own bathroom—otherwise, you will share with one other room. ⊠ *Elmasiye Cad. 73,* ☎ *358/212–0852,* 🅵🅰🅇 *358/212–1895. 5 rooms, 1 with bath. No credit cards.*

*En Route* Heading out of Amasya, south on Route 180, turn on Route 190 to reach Zile—a town famous for three words. It was from here that Julius Caesar, after defeating Mithridates VI's rebellious son Pharnaces, sent his pithy message to the Roman senate: *"Veni, vidi, vici"* ("I came, I saw, I conquered").

## Tokat

❼ *115 km (71 mi) southeast of Amasya on Rte. 180.*

Perhaps Tokat's most noted building, the **Gök Medrese** (Blue Seminary), built in 1275, is now a museum full of tiles and Byzantine frescoes. ⊠ *Gazi Osman Paşa Bul.,* ☎ *356/228–1509.* 🎟 *$1.* ☉ *8:30–12:30 and 1:30–5:30 (depending on mood of custodian).*

Also worth seeing while in Tokat is the **Latifoğlu Konağı** (Latifoğlu Mansion), a carefully restored 19th-century Ottoman mansion. This is one of the few places in Turkey where you can easily imagine how it would feel to live as a wealthy Ottoman during the declining years of the empire. *South of Cumhuriyet Alanı.* 🎟 *50¢.* ☉ *Tues.–Sun. 9–noon and 1:30–5.*

OFF THE **BALLICA MAĞARASI –** To escape the summer heat of the steppe, visit
BEATEN PATH Ballıca Mağarası (Ballıca Cave), an underground treasure, 45 km (28 mi) east of Amasya on Route 100. It was discovered in 1990 and only partially explored—2,200 ft of connecting cave galleries are currently open to the public. There is a veritable showcase of geological phenomena, from onion-shaped stalactites to gigantic stalagmites in a range of vibrant colors, and underground pools.

# EAST TO TRABZON AND SUMELA

As Route 10 heads east toward Trabzon and beyond, the landscape becomes dominated by lush green tea farms growing on seemingly uncultivatable, steep slopes. The twists and turns of the coastal road follow the terrain formed by centuries of waves crashing against the shore, hollowing out bays and inlets now harboring small towns and villages. Venturing off the main road provides unexpected glimpses into life along the Black Sea, which, while still Turkish, is more laid back than anywhere else in the country.

## Samsun

**❽** *168 km (104 mi) from Sinop on Rte. 10; 125 km (78 mi) north of Amasya on Rte. E80 to Rte. 795.*

Developed as a port under the Ottomans, Samsun is still a booming commercial harbor. It was here that Atatürk landed on May 19, 1919, after World War I, slipping away from the Allies occupying Constantinople to launch his campaign for Turkish independence. May 19 is now a national holiday commemorating this event. The monument opposite the government house is the largest dedicated to Atatürk outside Ankara.

The villa occupied by Atatürk is open to the public as a museum, the **Atatürk Müzesi,** where you can see his summer suit, silverware, pajamas, and shaving set. Next door is the **Arkeoloji Müzesi** (Archaeological Museum), where the highlight is a Roman mosaic from Karasamsun. ⊠ *Luna Parkı,* ☎ *362/431–6828.* ☞ *$1 for both museums.* ☉ *Tues.– Sun. 8:30–12:30 and 1:30–5:30.*

### Dining and Lodging

**$$** ✕ **Oskar Restaurant.** An upscale Black Sea eatery, this restaurant serves fresh fish and excellent marinated kebab. Be sure to ask for a seat away from the TV during soccer games. ⊠ *Belediye Meyd.,* ☎ *362/431–2040. MC, V.*

**$** ✕ **Cumhuriyet Restaurant.** Opened in 1934, the Cumhuriyet serves a range of cold mezes and grilled meats, but it prides itself on its *kuzu tandir* (baked lamb), and is open for breakfast. ⊠ *Saathane Meyd., Şeyhhamza Sok. 3,* ☎ *362/431–2165. MC, V.*

**$$$** ✕🏨 **Büyük Samsun Otel.** Possibly the largest hotel on the Black Sea, ★ the Büyk Samsun has amenities you'll be hard-pressed to find elsewhere on the coast. After taking in the sea view from the top-floor bar or your own balcony, dine in one of three fine restaurants or order up to your well-appointed room. ⊠ *Atatürk Bul. 629,* ☎ *362/432–4999,* ℻ *362/ 431–0740. 93 rooms with bath, 14 suites. 3 restaurants, 3 bars, café, in-room safes, ballroom, meeting room. DC, MC, V.*

**$–$$** 🏨 **Hotel Yafeya.** Right on the main square, this hotel has cheap, clean, and eminently acceptable rooms. From the rooftop terrace there's a clear view of the sea. Reasonably priced suites have minibars and TVs. ⊠ *Cumhuriyet Meyd.,* ☎ *362/435–1131,* ℻ *362/435–1135. 88 rooms with shower, 8 suites. Restaurant, café. V.*

## Ünye

**❾** *95 km (59 mi) east of Samsun on Rte. 10.*

The small port of Ünye, a popular weekend spot for Samsun's moneyed classes, has splendid beaches and campgrounds around its crescent-shaped bay. In the Middle Ages this was the western border of the Trebizond Empire, but in town the only notable architecture standing today is an 18th-century town hall. Trek 7 km (4½ mi) inland on the Niksar road to Çaleoğlu, where you can see a Byzantine castle flanked by Pontic rock-cut tombs.

### Lodging

**$$** 🏨 **Kumsal Hotel.** Five kilometers (3 miles) outside Ünye on the way to Samsun, the Kumsal is clean and simple, with whitewashed walls, wooden shutters, and balconies overlooking a lush garden. Spacious, affordable suites are well suited to large families. ⊠ *Gölevi Mahellesi,* *on the Samsun rd. (Rte. 10),* ☎ *452/323–1602,* FAX *452/323–4490. 32 rooms with shower. Restaurant, bar, sauna, beach. MC, V.*

**$** 🏨 **Belediye Çamlık Motel.** This little seaside motel in a pine forest has its own beach. Rooms are bare, with low wooden beds; nine have small kitchens, which aren't necessary since the hotel's restaurant serves good, inexpensive food. ⊠ *On Ünye's waterfront,* ☎ *452/323–1085. 13 rooms with bath. Restaurant, bar. No credit cards.*

# Ordu

🔟 *75 km (47 mi) east of Ünye on Rte. 10.*

Outside the town of Ordu, on the beach at Bozzukale, a few ruins from the 5th-century BC Greek settlement of Kotyora survive. Ordu itself is a port city dominated by an 8th-century basilica. Like many towns along the coast, Ordu has converted a local mansion into an ethnography museum. The second floor of the **Paşaoğlu Konağı** (Paşaoğlu Mansion) has restored rooms once filled with the ethnographic fare now displayed on the first floor.

### Lodging

**$$** 🏨 **Hotel Balıktaşı.** For the relatively undeveloped eastern Black Sea Coast, the newish (1995) Balıktaşı is considered a luxury resort. Though it has relatively standard hotel decor, the place is quite lovely, and its pool overlooks the sea. ⊠ *Sahil Cad. 13/1, Güzelyalı Mah.,* ☎ *452/223–0611,* FAX *452/223–0615. 48 rooms with shower. Restaurant, bar, pool, sauna, beach. MC, V.*

# Giresun

⓫ *45 km (28 mi) east of Ordu on Rte. 10.*

One of the best things to come out of Roman rule of this region was the introduction of the cherry to Europe from the orchards around Cerasus—the name by which Giresun was formerly known and the root of the word *cherry* (*kiraz* in Turkish). Today Giresun spreads over a cape below a ruined Byzantine fortress, where there is now a pretty city park. As the story goes, Jason and the Argonauts, on their search for the Golden Fleece, stopped at Büyük Ada (Big Island), off the coast of Giresun. There, they had a run-in with the Amazons on the island, where these fierce women had erected their temple to the war god Ares. Today women worship in a different manner on Büyük Ada, with a fertility festival every year in May.

*En Route* Follow Route 10 heading east from Giresun to get to **Tirebolu,** which was the ancient Tripolis, or Triple Town. The name refers to the three 14th-century Genoese fortresses in the area: Andos, near Espiye; St. John, atop Tirebolu itself; and Bedrama, 15 km (9 mi) inland on the Harşit River (with an exceptionally panoramic view). Between the pleasant fishing ports of Görele, Vakfıkebir, and Akçaabat, the road turns inland, up into densely wooded hills and narrow vales, before entering cosmopolitan Trabzon.

# Trabzon

⓬ *115 km (71 mi) east of Giresun on Rte. 10.*

Early in the 14th century a Venetian friar named Odoric described Trabzon, then known as Trebizond, as "a haven for the Persians, Medes, and all the people on the farther side of the sea." Built of golden towers and glittering mosaics—probably with family money diverted from the royal till before the fall of Constantinople—Trebizond was the capital of the empire founded in 1204 by Alexius Comnene, grandson of

Andronikos I, emperor of Byzantium. Alexius's successors continued to live well while playing their powerful Muslim neighbors against one another. Genoese and Venetian colonies at Trebizond ensured extensive cultural interaction with the West; Marco Polo, among others, came to visit, and Trebizond's own Cardinal Bessarion returned the favor by pursuing a successful career at the Medici court. The glory came to an end when the Turkish sultan Mehmet the Conqueror swept through the town in 1461.

At first glance the city may well disappoint you, with its squalid port area and far too much concrete. But if you push on up İskele Caddesi, you'll reach a pleasing central square atop the promontory, **Atatürk Alanı** (also called Taksim, or Parkı, Meydanı). Full of trees and tea gardens and surrounded by most of the city's hotels and restaurants, this is Trabzon's place to see and be seen. Women travelers should beware, however; due to the influx of Russian prostitutes here, you may get unwanted advances.

Maraş Caddesi leads west out of Trabzon's central square into the maze of the **covered bazaar** (⊠ Just past Cumhuriyet Cad.), which includes a 16th-century bedestan used by local jewelers. The city's largest mosque, the **Çarşi Cami** (built in 1839), is joined to the market by an archway. Trabzon's oldest church, the **Küçük Ayvasil** (⊠ Iskander Paşa quarter, off Hükümet Cad.), also known as St. Anne's, dates from the 9th century; unfortunately it is closed to visitors.

Trabzon's Comnene-built **citadel,** in between two ravines, is still imposing, though it's pretty much a ruin. Its ramparts were restored after the Turkish conquest in 1461 (an effective job of saber rattling by Sultan Mehmet), although the remains of the Byzantine palace are insignificant. No army ever took Trabzon by force, though many tried. Inside the citadel walls is the 10th-century Church of **Panaghia Chrysokephalos** (the Virgin of the Golden Head), which was the city's most important church for several centuries until the Aya Sofya was built. The Ottomans converted it into a mosque, the **Ortahisar Cami,** in the 15th century. ⊠ *Kale Cad.; from Hükümet Cad. (off Maraş Cad.), follow the Tabakhane Bridge over the gorge, turn left.*

You can get a good view of Trabzon from along **İç Kale Caddesi,** the street south of the citadel. You can also make out three other Byzantine monuments, all south of the Atatürk Alanı: the **Yeni Cuma Cami** (New Friday Mosque), built as the Church of St. Eugene in the early 13th century; the 13th-century **Teokephastos Convent,** on the other side of the hill; and the **Kudrettin Cami,** consecrated as the Church of St. Philip in the 14th century. Aya Sofya is visible about 3 km (2 mi) west of Atatürk Alanı.

★  Trabzon's best-known Byzantine monument, the 13th-century **Aya Sofya** (Church of the Holy Wisdom, or St. Sophia), sits on a green hill overlooking the Black Sea. The ruined church, known in Greek as Hagia Sofia, has some of the finest Byzantine frescoes and mosaics in existence. It was converted into a mosque in Ottoman times and first opened to the public as a museum in 1963. The west porch houses the real masterpieces: frescoes of Christ preaching in the Temple, the Annunciation, and the wedding at Cana, executed in a style that shows strong Italian influence. As at Istanbul's Aya Sofya, the artworks here were not destroyed by the Ottomans, only hidden under a hard layer of plaster. ⊠ *Kayakmeydan Cad.,* ☎ *no phone.* ☞ *$1.* ☉ *May–Sept., daily 8–6; Oct.–Apr., Tues.–Sun. 8–4.*

**Atatürk Köşkü,** Atatürk's summer villa (though he didn't actually spend much time here) is now a museum dedicated to the former leader. The attractive white gingerbread house, set in a small forest, is a pleasant place to visit. ⊠ *Soğuksu Cad., 7 km (4 mi) southwest of Trabzon's central square,* ☎ *no phone.* ☎ *$1.* ⊙ *May–Sept., daily 8–7; Oct.–Apr., daily 9–5.*

### Dining and Lodging

**$$** ✕ **Süleyman Restaurant.** This upscale restaurant has four prix-fixe menus that include between six and nine courses (if you count alcohol as a course) and a choice of à la carte Turkish dishes. A small indoor waterfall, a view of the Black Sea, musical performers in the evening, and good service make for a pleasant dining experience. ⊠ *100 Yil Parkı,* ☎ *462/325–0550. No credit cards.*

**$$** ✕☉ **Hotel Usta.** Off Atatürk Alanı, the Usta, although lacking character, has clean and well-furnished rooms. The above-par restaurant serves a substantial range of traditional Turkish fare. ⊠ *Telgrafhane Sok. 3, İskele Cad.,* ☎ *462/326–5700,* ☏ *462/322–3793. 86 rooms with bath. Restaurant. AE, DC, MC, V.*

**$–$$** ☉ **Horon Hotel.** One block off the main square, the Horon is the nicest
★ hotel in Trabzon. Rooms are impressive for their matched curtains, bedspreads, and wallpaper; bathrooms are spacious; and there are even English channels on TV. The professional staff is extremely helpful, and the parking and valet service are a blessing. On weekends be sure to ask for a room away from the rather loud bar. ⊠ *Sıramağazalar Cad. 125,* ☎ *462/326–6455,* ☏ *462/321–6628. www.otelhoron.com.tr. 44 rooms with shower. Restaurant, bar. DC, MC, V.*

**$–$$** ☉ **Hotel Özgür.** For years the best hotel in Trabzon, the Özgür has recently been renovated, but it is still a bit drab and down at the heels. In summer you can have tea in the garden or dine on the terrace, both in the back of the hotel. When booking, be aware that the hotel overlooks the main square, so rooms at the front tend to be noisy. ⊠ *Atatürk Alanı 29,* ☎ *462/326–4703,* ☏ *462/321–3952. 45 rooms with shower. 2 restaurants, bar. DC, MC, V.*

## Sumela/Mereyemana

⑬ *47 km (29 mi) south of Trabzon on Rte. 885 to Maçka, and then east on road to Altındere National Park.*

★ Sumela (Mereyemana in Turkish) is the site of the **Monastery of the Virgin.** The monks who founded the retreat in the 4th century carved their cells from sheer rock. Built to house a miraculous icon of the Virgin painted by St. Luke, this shrine was later rebuilt by Alexius III, who was crowned here in 1340—an event depicted in the frescoes of the main church in the grotto. Where chunks of the frescoes have fallen off—or been chipped away or scribbled over by overly enthusiastic souvenir hunters and graffiti artists—three layers of plaster from repaintings in the 14th and 18th centuries are clearly visible. Tolerant Ottoman sultans left the retreat alone, but after the Greeks were expelled from Turkey in 1922, the Turkish government permitted monks to transfer the Virgin icon to a new monastery in Greek Macedonia. The frescoes themselves are not as well preserved as those at Trabzon's Aya Sofya, but the setting—a labyrinth of courtyards, corridors, and chapels—is incredible. The monastery and its surrounding rooms are continually being renovated, but there's not much hope that the job will be finished soon. From the parking lot, pick up a well-worn trail for the rigorous 40-minute hike to the monastery, which clings to the cliff face more than 820 ft above the valley floor and disappears completely when the clouds come down. ⊠ *Altındere National Park,* ☎ *no phone.* ☎ *$3 per person, $4 for parking.* ⊙ *Apr.–Oct., daily 8–7; Nov.–Mar., daily 9–5.*

### Dining

$  ✕ **Sumela Ciftlik Restaurant.** Join families from Trabzon on their country outings as they congregate on the large stone patio on the banks of the river and enjoy the *canlı alabalık* (fresh trout) baked in butter, a popular regional dish. ⊠ *Just off the road between Sumela and Maçka,* ☎ *no phone. No credit cards. Closed Nov.–Mar.*

## Rize

⑭  *75 km (47 mi) east of Trabzon.*

Rize, the tea capital, sits above a small bay beneath the foothills of the Pontic Mountains. For an untrammeled view, head to **Zıraat Parkı,** near the town's western entrance. And don't miss Rize's ruined **Kale** (Genoese castle), which sits high on a slope above the sea.

### Lodging

$$$  ☷ **Dedeman Hotel.** One of the latest additions to this ever-growing chain of hotels, the Dedeman, 5 km (3 mi) outside of Rize, is what you'd expect from this reliable and upscale franchise. What makes this Dedeman exceptional is its restaurant, perched above the Black Sea, with picture windows on all sides. ⊠ *Ali PaşKöyü, on the road to Trabzon,* ☎ *464/223–5344,* ℻ *464/223–5348. www.dedemanhotels.com. 80 rooms with bath. 2 restaurants, 2 bars, sauna, health club. AE, MC, V.*

$  ☷ **Hotel Keleş.** Lodgings here are simple but acceptable, and the restaurant is good. ⊠ *Palandöken Cad. 2,* ☎ *464/217–4612,* ℻ *464/217–1895. 28 rooms with shower. MC, V.*

*En Route*  Perhaps the most scenic portions of the coastal Black Sea drive are the 189 km (117 mi) northeast from Trabzon to Hopa. Densely wooded slopes sometimes tumble straight into the sea but are more often broken by rice paddies and intensely green plantations where women in bright-striped aprons pick tea from early May to the end of October. One of the best places to venture off the coastal road and to see spectacular scenery is at **Ardeşen.** From there a 22-km (13-mi) drive inland brings you to Çamlıhemşin.

## Çamlıhemşin

⑮  *74 km (46 mi) northeast of Rize, 22 km (14 mi) south of Ardeşen.*

The small village of Çamlıhemşin is a good center for hiking and trout fishing. Another excellent reason to make this short detour is the food dished up at the Hoşdere Tesisleri, on the one (and only) road through town.

### Dining

$  ✕ **Hoşdere Tesisleri.** At this small restaurant you can taste *muhlama,* a fonduelike dish of melted cheese and butter into which you dip dense corn bread, and the ubiquitous regional *alabalık,* or river trout. ⊠ *On the main road through town,* ☎ *464/652–7107. No credit cards.*

*En Route*  From Çamlıhemşin, continue on Rte. 10 to **Hopa,** the last stop for Turkish Maritime Line boats, as well as all other travelers—the remaining 22 km (13 mi) to the Georgian border are under military control.

# THE BLACK SEA COAST A TO Z

## Arriving and Departing

### By Boat
**Turkish Maritime Lines** (⊠ Rıhtım Cad. 1, Karaköy, Istanbul, ☎ 212/293–7454; 212/249–9222 for reservations or ⊠ Trabzon Liman

Isletmesi, Trabzon, ☎ 462/321–2018 or 462/321–7096) operates two weekly ferries between Istanbul and the Black Sea ports of Giresun, Ordu, Samsun, Sinop, and Trabzon in summer. The trip from Istanbul to Trabzon takes a day and a half and costs from $30 for a Pullman seat and $95 for a private cabin; cars cost $50. Sleeper cabins and car spaces sell out quickly in summer, so reserve in advance.

### By Bus

You can get anywhere you want along the coast by bus. There is daily service from Istanbul (**Esenler bus terminal,** ☎ 212/658–0505) to the **Samsun bus terminal** (☎ 362/238–1706), which takes about 12 hours and costs around $10. From Istanbul to the **Trabzon bus terminal** (☎ 462/325–2397), the daily service takes 20 hours and costs $12. There is also daily service to these cities from Ankara (**AŞTİ bus terminal,** ☎ 312/224–1000).

### By Car

The quickest way to the east from Istanbul is to take the E80 toll road (Ücretli Geçiş) to Düzce, then cut up north along Route 655 to Akçakoca to join Route 10, which follows the coast the rest of the way east. The slower but more picturesque Route 20 passes through Şile to join up with Route 10 at Karasu. From Ankara you can take E89 north to Dörtdivan and then Route 750 to join Route 10 at Zonguldak; to explore only the eastern section of the coast, take E88 east through Kırıkkale, then head northeast along Route 190 toward Çorum to join Route 795 to Samsun, where you join Route 10.

### By Plane

The airports in Istanbul (☞ Istanbul A to Z *in* Chapter 2) and Ankara (☞ Ankara and Central Anatolia A to Z *in* Chapter 6) are the jumping-off points for the western half of the coast. There are also daily flights from both airports to Trabzon via **Turkish Airlines** (☎ 212/663–6300 in Istanbul) or **Istanbul Airlines** (☎ 212/231–7526 in Istanbul). Fares are about $50–$60 one way.

## Getting Around

### By Boat

*See* Arriving and Departing, *above.*

### By Bus

Bus service between towns runs frequently and is inexpensive. You can get schedules at the local tourist information office or directly from the bus station in each town: **Amasya** (☎ 358/218–1239); **Sinop** (☎ 368/261–5352); and **Trabzon** (☎ 462/325–2397).

### By Car

The coast road from Istanbul, Route 10, winds along cliffs, takes an occasional hairpin turn, and can be rough in spots. It is, however, passable, and once you get past Sinop, the road improves significantly.

#### RENTAL CARS

**Avis** has an office in downtown Trabzon(✉ Gazipaşa Cad. 20/B, ☎ 462/322–3740), as well as one at the airport (☎ 462/325–5582). There are also several local companies around Trabzon's main square (Atatürk Alanı). As elsewhere in Turkey, local companies may offer cheaper rates than international names, but not all companies include comprehensive insurance coverage in the price. Check the small print before agreeing on terms.

## Contacts and Resources

### Emergencies

**Police** (☏ 155). **Ambulance** (☏ 112).

### Guided Tours

For a first-class customized tour of the Black Sea with a local guide, consider **Tour Select,** an Istanbul-based company that works jointly with sister company Megatrails in New York (☞ Tour Operators *in* the Gold Guide); ☏ 212/232–4885, ᖴᐱᕽ 212/232–4889 in Istanbul; ☏ 800/547–1211 or 212/564–6642, ᖴᐱᕽ 212/564–3652, www.megatrails.com in New York.

### Visitor Information

Local tourist offices for towns in this chapter include the following: **Amasya** (✉ Ataturk Cad. 27, ☏ 358/218–5002); **Giresun** (✉ Gazi Cad. 72, ☏ 454/216–0161); **Ordu** (✉ Belediye Bldg., A Blok Kat [Floor] 1, ☏ 452/223–1607, ᖴᐱᕽ 452/223–2922); **Samsun** (✉ Talimhane Cad. off Cumhuriyet Cad., ☏ 362/431–2988); and **Trabzon** (✉ Atatürk Alanı, ☏ ᖴᐱᕽ 462/321–4659).

# 7 THE FAR EAST

The far east of Turkey is a harsh but beautiful region, with lonesome plains, sun-scorched desert, and imposing black mountains—the kind of countryside for adventuring on an epic scale.

Revised and
Updated by
Shoshanna
Matney and
Christine K.
Kimbrough

T HE POPULATION OF TURKEY'S eastern provinces is primarily Kurdish. In recent years, clashes between the Turkish armed forces and the PKK (Kurdistan Workers' Party), a Kurdish separatist group that wants to carve an independent state out of portions of Turkey, Iran, Syria, and Iraq, have restricted the movement of foreign visitors. Neither the Turkish army nor the PKK targets foreign travelers in the region (the horrendous civilian death toll since the full-scale rebellion began in 1984 is estimated at 30,000, mostly innocent Kurds caught in the crossfire and PKK members). Even so, the PKK has kidnapped several foreigners in the region to attract media attention.

At press time the State Department of the United States continues to advise Americans not to travel to certain places in the area unless the journey is essential, and a visit even to relatively safer areas is not without some risk. You can minimize that risk substantially by basing yourself in larger towns (there are direct flights from Istanbul and Ankara to Erzurum, Diyarbakır, Gaziantep, Kars, and Van); if you need to travel between them, do so only in daylight using a car or transportation provided by a reputable tour operator. The State Department discourages travel on public buses, especially at night, since these have been targets of attack.

It is possible to rent a car in Erzurum and Gaziantep, but the long distances and poor road conditions should make you think twice before tackling eastern Turkey in a private car. If you do drive, travel only in daylight and on major roads. Army roadblocks appear every few dozen miles, so keep your passport handy for inspection, roll down windows so soldiers can safely inspect the car, and do not make any sudden movements. Soldiers will give you an honest appraisal of the situation in their area; if a soldier warns you to avoid a particular road or region, follow his instructions. The State Department considers travel on foot or by bicycle to be especially hazardous, and you should avoid even a casual hike into remote areas. Camping is also dangerous.

Do not accept packages and letters from strangers, as the PKK has used foreigners to deliver them in past. Despite your innocence, you could be charged with aiding and abetting the PKK, a serious offense.

Up-to-date information about the situation in the eastern provinces can be obtained from the **U.S. Department of State** hot line (☎ 202/647–5225 in U.S.) or from the **American Consulate in Istanbul** (☎ 212/251–3602, ℻ 212/251–3218) and the **American Embassy** (☎ 312/468–6110, ℻ 312/467–0019).

## Pleasures and Pastimes

### Ancient Sites
The far east of Turkey has a staggering inventory of ancient sites, a few of which top many travelers' must-see lists despite the difficulties of travel in the region. Moving from the northeast to the southwest, you can visit the remarkable Armenian kingdom of Ani; Mt. Ararat (which, since it is off-limits as a military zone, you cannot ascend); the mighty black-basalt fortress at Diyarbakır; the birthplace of the patriarch Abraham in Şanlıurfa; and the awe-inspiring temple and sculptures atop Mt. Nimrod.

### Dining and Lodging
The draw of eastern Turkey isn't culinary experience or sumptuous lodgings. Restaurants serve standard Turkish cuisine, enlivened occasionally with such Kurdish specialties as *sac tava* (lamb and green peppers

lightly roasted in sunflower oil) and lamb stew served with fresh flat bread. Kurdish sheep and goat cheeses are deliciously pungent, and you'll have no trouble finding excellent baklava and *pasta* (pastries). Be vigilant about what you eat, however, as standards of cleanliness are lower here than in the rest of Turkey. Dysentery is a common complaint throughout the region, and recurring outbreaks of typhoid fever, meningitis, and other contagious diseases are common in Diyarbakır. Wherever you travel, drink only bottled water, eat plenty of fresh yogurt, avoid raw fruit and vegetables you do not peel and clean yourself, and make sure food is thoroughly cooked. As for accommodations, it's best to have humble expectations, although there are exceptions. For charts that explain meal and room rates at the establishments in this chapter, *see* Dining and Lodging Price Categories at the back of this book.

## Shopping

Erzurum has an authentic bazaar, with particularly talented metalworkers; Şanlıurfa's is marvelously medieval. Van is noted for its weavings, especially its kilims and traditional Kurdish fabrics.

# Exploring the Far East

Driving from Istanbul to Lake Van takes 25 grueling hours, and even if you fly directly to eastern Turkey, you still face long, hard outings from site to site within the region, with highways and facilities at best basic and often primitive. Whether you fly, drive, or arrive by bus, odds are that you will start your tour in the north at Erzurum (if you're coming from Ankara or the Black Sea Coast) or in the south at Diyarbakır (if you're coming from the Mediterranean); the region's two main airports are near these cities. Unless you rent a car in Erzurum or Gaziantep (☞ The Far East A to Z, *below*), the most efficient, and safest, way to visit the main sights is on a guided tour.

## Great Itineraries

Eastern Turkey is an unwieldy region, and without some sort of strategy you will spend too much time moving from one far-flung spot to another, fantasizing about a vacation from your vacation. To visit eastern Turkey's main sights, you'll need at least 10 days and plenty of patience. The following itineraries are designed for those with less time and a lower tolerance for crowded long-distance buses.

### IF YOU HAVE 3 DAYS

*Numbers in the text correspond to numbers in the margin and on the Lake Van and the East map.*

Begin your visit in ⊞ **Erzurum** ①. On day one, visit the Seminary of the Twin Minarets and the Great Mosque, and perhaps make an afternoon trip to the Çoruh River valley. On day two, travel to ⊞ **Kars** ② to view its old Georgian fort and to pick up the military permit that allows you entry to the ruins of the medieval Armenian town of **Ani** ③, which you will visit on day three.

### IF YOU HAVE 7 DAYS

Spend day one in ⊞ **Erzurum** ①. On day two, drive or take a bus east to ⊞ **Doğubeyazıt** ④, a sleepy agricultural town near the Iranian border. On day three, visit Doğubeyazıt's İshak Paşa Saray, followed by a drive around the base of **Mt. Ararat** ⑤. On day four, head south to ⊞ **Van** ⑦ and visit its castle above smooth **Lake Van** ⑥. On the fifth day, visit the island of **Akdamar** ⑧ and continue west to ⊞ **Diyarbakır** ⑩. On the morning of day six, visit Abraham's birthplace in **Şanlıurfa** ⑬, then head to the summit of ⊞ **Mt. Nimrod** ⑪ for one of the finest sunsets in Turkey. On the seventh day, enjoy the sunrise from Mt. Nimrod before heading to your next destination.

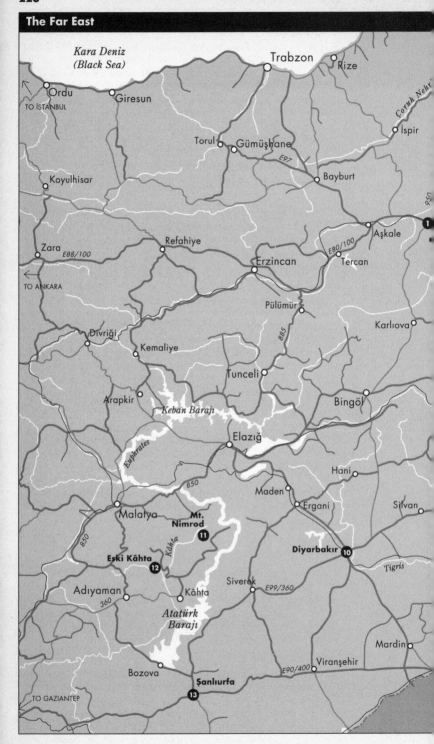

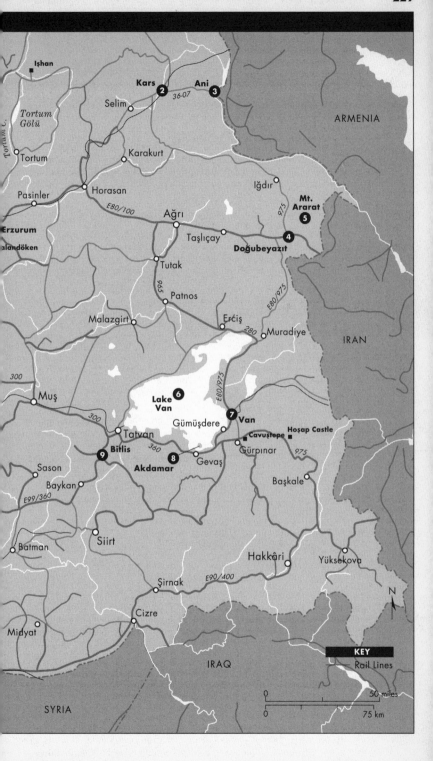

Işhan

*Tortum*
*Gölü*

Tortum

Pasinler

**Erzurum**
**alandöken**

Selim

Kars **2** 36-07 Ani **3**

Karakurt

Horasan

E80/100

Ağrı

Taşlıçay

Tutak

965

Patnos

Malazgirt

Iğdır

975

**Mt.**
**Ararat**
**5**

**Doğubeyazıt** **4**

Erciş

280

Muradiye

E80/975

300

Muş

300

Lake
Van **6**

E80/975

Gümüşdere **7** Van

Tatvan

360

**Bitlis** **9**

**8**

Gevaş

**Akdamar**

Sason

Baykan

E99/360

Siirt

Batman

Çavuştepe ■ **Hoşap Castle**

Gürpınar 975

Başkale

Hakkâri

Şırnak

E90/400

Cizre

Midyat

**IRAQ**

**SYRIA**

ARMENIA

IRAN

Yüksekova

N

**KEY**
Rail Lines

0             50 miles
0             75 km

**When to Tour the Far East**

Travel in eastern Turkey involves a lot of "don'ts"—don't travel alone, don't travel at night, and don't travel in areas where PKK guerrillas are active (contact your embassy for information and become an avid reader of the English-language *Turkish Daily News*). If possible, don't visit eastern Turkey in the height of summer—average daytime temperatures for August are 36°C (97°F) in Erzurum, 38°C (100°F) in Van, and 39°C (102°F) in Diyarbakır.

Winter is harsh but beautiful in eastern Turkey, and tourism is focused on the ski resorts of Palandöken (near Erzurum), Tekman, and Sarıkamış (near Kars). Spring and fall are the most temperate seasons, with occasional rainfall and breezy evenings. At higher elevations—particularly in Erzurum and Kars—nighttime temperatures are blissfully cool in May, June, September, and October.

In the wake of the continuing regional conflict, the number of tourists in eastern Turkey has dropped considerably; so, too, has the number of festivals and folk events in all but the smallest towns. In the last few years, however, organized events have begun to make a comeback: Van now hosts a music festival in mid-May, and there's a low-key music and food fair on Mt. Nimrod in mid-June. Contact local tourist offices for up-to-date information.

# NORTHEASTERN TURKEY

## Erzurum to Ani

One day is sufficient to see Erzurum's mosques and museum and to rent a car or arrange other transportation to Kars (where the only reason for stopping is to obtain the mandatory permit for visiting the sprawling 10th-century ruins at Ani). Depending on the season, the northeast's sparsely populated, high-altitude plains are either snowbound or baking hot; only as you approach Ani do dusty flatlands give way to rugged hills carpeted with wildflowers. In spring and summer Kurdish farmers set up isolated tent villages in the hills near Ani, both to graze sheep and to tame the wild horses that roam here in the hundreds.

### Erzurum

**❶** *880 km (546 mi) east of Ankara on Rte. E88 to E80, 300 km (186 mi) southeast of Trabzon on Rte. E97.*

Erzurum occupies a strategic spot along the old trade routes to Russia, India, and Persia—a fact quickly recognized by the Byzantines, who made it their eastern bastion. The city fell to the Seljuks in AD 1071, after the battle of Manzikert, and they built most of the sights that remain today. Erzurum was a secure outpost from the time of the Ottoman conquest in 1515, but beginning in 1828, the Russians occupied the city three times, finally leaving after being defeated by the Ottomans in 1918. The following year, Atatürk and his fellow nationalists arrived in town for the famed Erzurum Congress, where they drafted the National Pact defining Turkey's republican borders. Still a strategic spot (as you can see from the Turkish military barracks), Erzurum has developed into a sprawling, rather somber city, now the largest in eastern Anatolia, with factories and high-rise apartments that spread across an otherwise barren plateau at an elevation of 6,696 ft. You can ski in the surrounding mountains as late as mid-March. The most interesting sights are along Cumhuriyet Caddesi in the center of Erzurum; they are listed below from east to west.

Sultan Alaaddin Keykubat II sponsored the **Çifte Minareli Medrese** (Seminary of the Twin Minarets), which was built in 1253 at the height of the Seljuk Empire. The seminary, the largest in Anatolia, is renowned for its twin blue-tile minarets and for the elaborate interlocking spirals carved on the main portal. Inside at the far end of a courtyard sits the **Hatuniye Türbesi**, a 12-sided chamber that once held the tomb of the sultan's daughter. Today a teahouse occupies the courtyard. ⊠ *Cumhuriyet Cad., east end of street,* ☎ *no phone.* ☒ *Free.* ☉ *Daily 8:30–7.*

The **Ulu Cami** (Great Mosque) was built in 1179 with seven wide naves and a fine colonnaded courtyard. The exterior is plain, even severe. Inside are dozens of solemn columns and a small but dazzling pair of stained-glass windows. Visitors are not allowed to enter at prayer times, and women are asked to cover their heads. ⊠ *Cumhuriyet Cad., 1 block west of Çifte Minareli Medrese,* ☎ *no phone.* ☒ *Donation requested.* ☉ *Daily 9–noon and 1–8.*

Erzurum's **citadel,** notable for its precisely hewn blocks, was started in about AD 400. Today the poorly kept ruins attract more soccer-playing kids than tourists, but they do yield a sweeping view of Erzurum and beyond. Bring a flashlight if you want to climb the citadel's rickety clock tower. ⊠ *Tebriz Sok.; from Ulu Cami cross Cumhuriyet Cad. and walk 3 blocks up small alley.* ☒ *40¢.* ☉ *Open only in summer, generally dawn–sunset, though actual hrs vary at whim of caretaker.*

The classical 16th-century **Lala Mustafa Paşa Cami,** built by the grand vizier of the same name, looks rather similar to the other mosques designed by Sinan in Istanbul. The mosque faces the 17th-century Caferiye Cami. ⊠ *Cumhuriyet Cad. at Menderes Cad., 2 blocks west of Ulu Cami.* ☉ *Daily 9:30–sunset.*

★ The **Yakutiye Medrese** (Yakutiye Seminary), one of Erzurum's best sights, is a 14th-century seminary built by a Mongol emir. Mongol buildings are less refined than Seljuk ones, and many of Yakutiye's surviving embellishments—notably the stark portal, heavily carved with animal figures and floral patterns—were taken from contemporary Seljuk designs (the Mongols were usually more interested in conquering the next town than in building unique monuments). The ethnographic museum in the seminary's former prayer rooms displays Seljuk and Ottoman glasswork, jewelry, and armor. ⊠ *Cumhuriyet Cad., 2 blocks west of Lala Mustafa Paşa Cami,* ☎ *no phone.* ☒ *$1.* ☉ *Tues.–Sun. 8:30–noon and 1:30–5.*

The two-story **Rüstem Paşa Bazaar** is packed with brightly shining samovars, kilims and carpets, and Muslim prayer beads made from a lightweight, jet-black mineral called *oltutaş.* The bazaar itself is not especially photogenic, unless you're obsessed with plumbing fixtures and 14-karat jewelry. More appealing are the first-floor courtyard and tea garden. ⊠ *Menderes Cad., 3 blocks north of Cumhuriyet Cad.,* ☎ *no phone.* ☉ *Daily 9–7.*

At the **Erzurum Müzesi** (Erzurum Museum), Egyptian coins, Roman pottery, and Seljuk tile work are exhibited; the best pieces are the old Turkish kilims and carpets, home furnishings, and weapons. Items of greater antiquity, such as prehistoric fossils, as well as those from the more recent past, including an exhibit on the early 20th-century Armenian massacre of the local Muslim population, are also displayed. ⊠ *Yenipehir Cad. 11,* ☎ *442/218–1406.* ☒ *$1.* ☉ *Tues.–Sun. 9–noon and 1:30–5:30.*

## Dining and Lodging

Hotel dining rooms are your best bet, though there are acceptable inexpensive restaurants along the main street, **Cumhuriyet Caddesi.** The local specialties are kebabs served either with yogurt or *iskender* style (topped with a large helping of thin tomato sauce and yogurt).

$ ✕ **Salon Cağın.** This informal, friendly place is a reliable choice for sampling above-average Turkish cuisine. ⊠ *Cumhuriyet Cad. 20-C,* ☎ 442/218–9320. *No credit cards.*

$$$–$$$$ ⊞ **Palandöken Dedeman.** This popular ski lodge has a good restaurant and helpful staff, though it's only open from October to mid-May. Reservations are advised on winter weekends, when the hotel is inundated with wealthy students from Erzurum University and fugitive businessmen from Ankara. Ski equipment is available, and the hotel also provides airport transfers from Erzurum. ⊠ *Palandöken, 6 km (4 mi) south of Erzurum,* ☎ *442/316–2414,* ℻ *442/316–3607. 186 rooms, most with bath. Restaurant, bar, café, indoor pool, sauna, exercise room, dance club. V. Closed mid-May–Sept.*

$$ ⊞ **Dilaver.** Erzurum's plushest hotel is in the center of town and within walking distance of the main sights. Rooms are clean and modern, if somewhat lacking in character, and equipped with satellite TVs and direct-dial phones. ⊠ *Bakirü Mah., Petit Meyd.,* ☎ *442/235–0068,* ℻ *442/218–1148. 159 rooms with bath. Restaurant, 3 bars, air-conditioning, minibars. V.*

$–$$ ⊞ **Otel Oral.** Though this hotel has seen better days, it is clean and quiet. That said, it's still one of the better mid-range hotels in Erzurum. The major drawback is its location, on the outskirts of town. ⊠ *Terminal Cad. 6,* ☎ *442/218–9740,* ℻ *442/218–9749. 90 rooms with bath. MC, V.*

$ ⊞ **Otel Polat.** Inexpensive and central, the Polat is popular with budget travelers. Rooms are clean and have TVs and round-the-clock hot water. ⊠ *Kazım Karabekir Cad. 16-B,* ☎ *442/218–1623,* ℻ *442/234–4598. 60 rooms with shower. No credit cards.*

## Outdoor Activities and Sports

SKIING

The popular ski resort of **Palandöken** is only 6 km (4 mi) south of Erzurum, so expect crowds in peak season (December–March). The runs are good for beginning and intermediate skiers, but if you're an advanced skier, you may find yourself dreaming of the Alps. The snow is usually deep and powdery. You'll pay $15–$20 per day for a lift ticket and rental equipment. In winter there are daily buses (weather permitting) from Erzurum's bus station. In summer most everything on the mountain shuts down. Traveling by car from Erzurum, take Route E80 east toward Ağrı and look for a right-hand turnoff marked TEKMAN. Follow this road until it eventually branches right.

# Kars

➋ *211 km (131 mi) from Erzurum to Kars via Rte. E80 northeast through Pasinler, Horasan, and Karakurt, then north on Rte. 957.*

Kars looks like the frontier town it is: forbidding and grayish, set on a 5,740-ft plateau and forever at the mercy of the winds. Ever since the Seljuk sultan Alpaslan forced the last Armenian prince to abdicate in AD 1064, Kars has been besieged by various and sundry invaders: first the Akkoyun, then the Mongol warriors of Tamerlane, and finally three times in the 19th century by czarist armies from Russia. The Turks, under the leadership of Kazım Karabekir, retook the city in 1920, and Kars was formally ceded to Turkey after the war of independence in

1921. The Russian influence is still obvious in many buildings and in the rigid grid of streets that form the town's small, dusty center.

If you're traveling onward to Ani (☞ *below*), you must obtain a travel permit at the Kars **tourist office** (✉ On Atatürk Cad. next to Süleyman Demirel Parkı, on the 2nd floor of Milli Eğitim Bldg.; ☎ 474/ 223–2300). The tourist office is open daily 8:30–noon and 1:30–5, except weekdays only in winter. Take the free permit to police headquarters, farther west on Faik Bey Caddesi, to have it stamped. Finally, go to the Kars Museum (☞ *below*), on Cumhuriyet Caddesi, and buy tickets to the site (the caretaker at Ani does not sell them). If you hire a guide, he will take care of the paperwork for you.

**İç Kale** (Kars Castle) overhangs the town from a high, rocky vantage point. Though it dates from the 10th century, most surviving fortifications were commissioned by Lala Mustafa Paşa in 1579—in 1386 Tamerlane swept violently through the region and razed the original structure. Today the castle houses an army barracks and is of little interest; only the panoramic views of Kars merit the 20-minute walk uphill. ✉ *Kale Cad.,* ☎ *no phone.* 🎫 *Free.* ☉ *Daily 2 PM–sunset.*

The **Kümbet Cami** (Drum-Dome Mosque), at the foot of the hill by Kars River, is obviously not Turkish—originally the Armenian Church of the Twelve Apostles, it was built in the 10th century. You can still make out the Apostles on the exterior of the drum-shape cupola. The mosque is often locked, in which case the only view is through a rusty gate. Just to the northwest is the **Taşköprü**, a bridge of Seljuk origin dating from the 1400s. ✉ *Kale Cad., at foot of İç Kale,* ☎ *no phone.* 🎫 *Free.*

**Kars Müzesi** (Kars Museum), near the train station on the eastern edge of town, is very difficult to find—you need to take a taxi there—but it's well worth the trip. Two floors of displays cover Kars's many rulers—Roman, Greek, Seljuk, and Ottoman—and there are pieces of Armenian churches and a Russian church bell. You can buy tickets here for Ani, and the wall-size maps of the site will help you get your bearings. ✉ *Cumhuriyet Cad., on road to Ani,* ☎ *474/212–2387.* 🎫 *75¢.* ☉ *Daily 8–5:30.*

| | |
|---|---|
| NEED A BREAK? | Kars has two excellent *hamamı* (Turkish baths). Both are on the Taşköprü stone bridge near the foot of Kars Castle, and both are open daily 7 AM–11 PM. A bath and massage at either cost $7. The 16th-century **Mazlumağa Hamamı** is for men only. The 18th-century **İlbeyoğlu/Muradiye Hamamı** is exclusively for women. |

## Dining and Lodging

Kars is one of the few towns in the east where young men and women meet openly for a cup of coffee or a meal. Even so, there aren't many good places to eat. You can have a passable meal at kebab salons along Atatürk Caddesi and Kazım Paşa Caddesi, two parallel streets in the center of town. The local specialties are honey and Kaşar cheese, both displayed in copious quantities in nearly every shop window.

**$–$$** ✕🏨 **Hotel Karabağ.** Kars's most comfortable hotel is the central Karabağ. It primarily caters to Russian and Turkish businesspeople, for whom it provides direct-dial phones, room service, satellite TVs, and 24-hour hot water (a rarity in Kars). The adjoining restaurant serves above-average Turkish cuisine. ✉ *Faik Bey Cad. 42, at Atatürk Cad.,* ☎ *474/212–1633,* 📠 *474/223–3480. 50 rooms, most with bath or shower. Restaurant, bar, air-conditioning, room service. MC, V.*

**$**  🏨 **Hotel Temel.** The popular budget choice in Kars has fickle hot water, but the premises are clean and the management helpful. Ask for one of the rooms with small balconies. The sunny breakfast salon is an oasis of calm, but avoid the bleak smoke-filled restaurant. ⊠ *Kazım Paşa Cad. 39,* ☎ *474/223–1376. 28 rooms, some with bath. No credit cards.*

# Ani

❸  *42 km (26 mi) east of Kars on Rte. 36–07.*

Until the Mongol invasion of 1236, Ani (also called Ocaklı) was the chief town of a medieval Armenian kingdom, with 100,000 inhabitants and "a thousand and one churches," according to historical sources. Although it was occupied by the Mongols, Ani still had a large Armenian population well into the 14th century. In 1319 the city was struck by a terrible earthquake, after which the townspeople began to leave. The latest inscription to be found in the city is dated 1348. Scarcely a half-dozen churches remain today, and all are in shambles. Even so, the sprawling site is breathtaking, with hundreds of weather-beaten ruins on a triangular promontory bounded on two sides by steep river gorges. Equally majestic is the surrounding countryside, a mix of severe mountains, tiny Kurdish settlements, and fields of wildflowers fading to the horizon.

The ruins at Ani straddle the Alaçay River, which forms a natural border with Armenia. It's a sensitive military area—machine-gun towers keep a close watch on it—and to visit the site, you must obtain a permit and your entrance ticket in Kars (☞ Kars, *above,* for instructions). Soldiers at the entrance will hold your passport for the duration of your visit and, depending on their mood, may enforce the restriction on photography at the site, so be prepared to leave your camera at the gate.

Enter through the **Aslan Kapısı** (Lion's Gate), one of three principal portals in Ani's extensive city walls, which stretch for more than 8,200 ft. The 32-ft walls were raised in AD 972 by the Armenian king Smbat II, though the lion relief itself was added by the Seljuk sultan Menuçehr in 1064. A small trail makes a circle through Ani; following it clockwise the first major ruin you encounter is the **Keseli** (Church of the Redeemer), a huge quadrangular cathedral built in 1035. Its dome (1036) was hit by lightning in the 1950s, which cut the building neatly in half, leaving a surrealistic representation of an Armenian church with the rubble of its former half in the foreground. There are three churches in Ani dedicated to St. Gregory, the Armenian prince who converted his people to Christianity. The best preserved is the **Nakışlı,** built by an Armenian nobleman, Tigran Honentz, in 1215. Nakışlı is the most impressive ruin in Ani, not the least because it stands at the foot of a small ravine with a view over the Arpaçay River. Inside, note the remarkable cycle of murals depicting the Virgin Mary and St. Gregory. If you follow the path into the gorge, you will come to the striking **Kusanatz** (Convent of the Three Virgins), standing on a rocky outcrop.

The **Menüçehir Cami** (Menüçehir Mosque; 1072), which clings to the heights overlooking the Arpaçay River, was originally an Armenian building, perhaps even a palace. From here climb to the first citadel and continue to the second at the far edge of town, where the two gorges converge; you'll have a good view of the many cave dwellings in the walls of the western gorge, which once housed the city's poor. But the best view of Ani's ruins is from the **İç Kale** (Citadel), perched on a rocky plateau at the site's southeast end above a trail that cuts a steep path down to the river. Bring a flashlight for the climb inside the citadel's precarious tower and watch your footing. ☎ *no phone.* 🎫 *$2 for entire site.* ☉ *Daily 8:30–5.*

# MT. ARARAT AND LAKE VAN

Fighting between PKK militants and the Turkish government prevents travelers from trekking to the perpetually snowbound summit of Mt. Ararat—the mountain has been declared a military zone and access is prohibited. Instead, the region's few tourists (largely Turks and Iranians) console themselves with gazing upon the mountain from afar and with visiting only the İshak Paşa Saray, a striking mountain palace not far from sleepy Doğubeyazıt.

After the rough and rugged scenery of Mt. Ararat, the arid plains around Lake Van are a disappointment. Make a quick stop at the island of Akdamar, at the lake's south end, and do your best to enjoy the dusty six-hour drive west to Diyarbakır.

## Doğubeyazıt and Mt. Ararat

*286 km (177 mi) east of Erzurum on Rte. E80 to Doğubeyazıt.*

**❹** The rough frontier town of **Doğubeyazıt** (doh-*oo*-bay-yah-zuht) is a good base from which to enjoy views of Turkey's highest mountain, the majestic Mt. Ararat (Ağrı Dağı). You'll share the town with sheep, Iranian tourists, and smugglers. Because of the absence of carpet and kilim shops, you can wander the main street, Çarşı Caddesi, without being bothered too much.

**★** Doğubeyazıt's only sight, **İshak Paşa Saray** (İshak Paşa Palace), is in the mountains southeast of town. The fortified palace was built in the late 18th century by local potentate Çolak Abdi Paşa and his son İshak. The interior of the building is extremely ornate, a fantastic mixture of Georgian, Persian, and Ottoman styles, though the gold-plated doors were carted off by Russian troops in 1917. Late afternoon is the best time to visit, when the sun casts a deep orange glow over the palace and the ruins, carved into the opposite (and inaccessible) mountainside, of a citadel whose foundations are Urartian but which was rebuilt several times through the centuries. There is a teahouse immediately above the palace and a makeshift restaurant about 650 ft below the site. Otherwise, the only hints of civilization are a cluster of Kurdish mud-brick houses and the occasional Kurdish musician wandering from house to house in search of an audience. *6 km (4 mi) southeast of town on road to Göller,* 🕾 *no phone.* 🎫 *$1.* ⊙ *Mon.–Sat. 10–5.*

**❺** An extinct volcano, snow covered even in summer, **Mt. Ararat** (Ağrı Dağı) soars 16,850 ft, dominating an arid plateau. According to Genesis, after the Great Flood "the waters were dried up from off the earth; and Noah removed the covering of the ark, and looked, and behold, the face of the ground was dry." The survivors, as the story goes, had just landed on top of Mt. Ararat. Many other ancient sources—Chaldean, Babylonian, Chinese, Assyrian—also tell of an all-destroying flood and of one man who heroically escaped its consequences. Since medieval times the locals here have sold Christian pilgrims old planks reputedly from the ark; the modern ark hunt dates from 1876, when an Englishman named James Bryce discovered on the peaks "amid blocks of lava, a piece of wood about 4 feet long and 5 inches wide, which had obviously been shaped by means of a tool." Fragments of ancient timber, embedded in the ice, have been brought back by various ark-hunting expeditions since then, but radiocarbon dating tests have proved inconclusive. Satellite photos have shown a boat embedded in a glacier at 12,500 ft, but on-the-spot examination of one of these "boats" proved it to be nothing more than a freak formation in the strata. Even so, expeditions by Christian fundamentalist groups constantly make new claims, and a second Noah's Ark was "discovered" in the 1980s on a hillside 20 km (12 mi) southeast of Ararat. Tours from Doğubeyazıt (☞ Guided Tours *in* The Far East A to Z, *below*) visit the site, but don't get your hopes up: To the untrained eye, this ark is nothing more than a pile of rocks.

Because of ongoing PKK activity, Mt. Ararat has been declared a special military zone and is off-limits to visitors; you'll have to settle for viewing its sizable hulk from afar.

### Dining and Lodging

Hotels in Doğubeyazıt have the best restaurants, but don't overlook the family-run kebab and *pide* (Turkish pizza) salons that line Çarşı Caddesi. The local dessert specialty is *aşure,* a nut-and-raisin sweet nicknamed "Noah's Pudding."

$ ✕🏨 **Hotel Grand Derya.** Doğubeyazıt's most luxurious hotel was thor-
★ oughly refurbished a few years back, and all the fixtures—porcelain sinks, satellite TVs—are still shiny. The rooms themselves are comfortable, though clearly the management has put more effort into renovating the lobby and public spaces. The hotel restaurant is one of the best in town. ✉ *Çarşı Cad.,* ☎ *472/312–7531,* 🅵🅰🆇 *472/312–7833. 67 rooms with bath. Restaurant, bar. MC, V.*

$$ 🏨 **Hotel Nuh.** Clean and fairly attractive, the Nuh's greatest asset is its large terrace, perfect for taking in a view of Mt. Ararat and the fortress beyond. Although slightly pricier than other hotels in town, the Nuh is worth the few extra dollars. ✉ *Büyük Ağrı Cad. 65,* ☎ *472/312–7232,* 🅵🅰🆇 *472/312–6910. 57 rooms with bath. Restaurant. No credit cards.*

$ 🏨 **Hotel Kenan.** Reasonably priced and comfortable, this hotel is a good budget option. The cozy lobby and bar area makes a good place to relax. Rooms, however, are less than fancy, and some are poorly ventilated; ask to see a few before choosing. ✉ *Büyük Ağrı Cad. off Çarşı Cad.,* ☎ *472/312–7869,* 🅵🅰🆇 *472/312–7871. 28 rooms, most with shower. Restaurant, bar. No credit cards.*

## Lake Van and Environs

*171 km (106 mi) from Doğubeyazıt, west on Rte. E80 and south on Rte. E99/975, continuing past Muradiye to the town of Van.*

❻ The landscape at **Lake Van** (Van Gölü) is eerily barren and desolate, a result of winter flash floods and intense summertime heat—in August the average daytime temperature is 38°C (100°F). But it is Turkey's largest and most unusual lake, 3,738 square km (1,443 square mi) of brackish water surrounded by mighty volcanic cones. Lake Van was formed when a volcano blew its top and blocked the course of a river, leaving the newly formed lake no natural outlet; as a result the water is highly alkaline and full of sulfides and mineral salts, much like the Dead Sea. Lake Van's only marine life is a small member of the carp family, the *darekh,* which has somehow adapted to the saline environment. Recreational water sports are nonexistent, and beaches along the rocky shores are few and far between. Swimming in the soft, soapy water is pleasant, but try not to swallow any—it tastes horrible. The towns of Adilcevaz and Ahlat, on Lake Van's north shore, are worth visiting only if you're in the area; you probably want to head instead to Van and the nearby island of Akdamar, along the lake's south shore.

❼ **Van** first appears in history 3,000 years ago, when it was the site of the Urartian capital of Tushpa, whose formidable fortress—built on a steep cliff rising from the lakeshore—dominated the countryside. (The Urartians first appeared in this region in the 13th century BC and by the mid-8th century BC ruled an empire extending from the Black Sea to the Caspian Sea, only to be wiped out over the next 150 years by various rivals, primarily the Assyrians.) The old city, nestled below the southern cliff, was destroyed in battles with the Armenians and Russians during World War I. The melancholy jumble of foundations cannot be sorted out; only two vaguely restored mosques, one 13th century, the other 16th century, rise from the marshland. When it came time to rebuild the city after the war, the residents selected a higher, healthier spot, 5 km (3 mi) inland. Thus Van was robbed of a waterfront setting and, as a result, now looks like the tedious sun-scorched outpost it truly is. As the commercial center of southeastern Anatolia, Van has numerous banks, sleek European clothing shops, and a large university, but one afternoon is enough to cover the main sights.

Steps—considerably fewer than the 1,000 claimed in local tourist handouts—ascend to **Van Kalesi** (Van Castle), the sprawling Urartian fortress on the outskirts of town. A path branches right to Urartian tombs in the sheer south rock face; a cuneiform inscription here honors King Xerxes, whose Persian troops occupied the fortress early in the 5th century BC. The crumbling ramparts are still impressive, but as is true so often in these parts, it is the view from such a vantage point that makes the steep climb worthwhile. A taxi from the new town should cost no more than $4 one-way. Cheaper *dolmuşes* (shared taxis) depart regularly from Beş Yol, a large intersection two blocks west of the Büyük Urartu Hotel.

The new city has little to recommend it besides a large new mosque and the small but well-arranged archaeological and ethnographical **Van Müzesi** (Van Museum), which displays many Urartian artifacts: rich, golden jewelry; belts and plates engraved with lions, bulls, and sphinxes; and a carved relief of the god Teshup, for whom their capital was named. The small solarium has a varied collection, ranging from prehistoric rock art to Urartian inventory markers to Turkish sarcophagi, displayed in a haphazard manner. If you are interested in local history and archaeology, the books for sale (some in English) are a wonderful source of information—and a bargain to boot. ⊠ *1 block east of Cumhuriyet Cad.,* ☎ *432/216–1139.* 🎫 *$1.* ☉ *Daily 8–noon and 1:30–5:30.*

OFF THE
BEATEN PATH

**ÇAVUŞTEPE AND HOŞAP KALESI –** From Van drive 35 km (22 mi) south on the Hakkari road to Çavuştepe, where you can clamber around the stone foundations of a ruined 8th-century BC Urartian fortress-city, Sardurihinli. Nearby are temple ruins and a 6th-century BC sacrificial altar. Admission to the citadel is 50¢, though it's sometimes difficult to find the caretaker. Continue 15 km (9 mi) southeast on the same road to Hoşap Castle, a dramatic fortress looming over a river chasm. The 17th-century complex, which was used as a base to "protect" (i.e., ransack) caravans, included a palace, two mosques, three baths, and a dungeon. The great gate, with its carved lions and an inscription in Farsi, is quite a show of strength; a tunnel carved through bedrock leads inside from here. Bring a flashlight, as there are no lights in the castle, which is open daily 8–5. Admission is 75¢.

★ ⑧   On the tranquil, uninhabited islet of **Akdamar,** among wild olive trees, stand the scant remains of a monastery, including the truly splendid **Church of the Holy Cross.** Built in AD 921 by an Armenian king, Gagik Artzruni of Vaspurakan, it is very much a cousin to the Armenian churches at Ani in construction. Incredible high-relief carvings on the exterior make this church a work of art. Nearly the entire story of the Bible is told here, from Adam and Eve to David and Goliath. Along the top is a frieze of running animals; another frieze shows a vineyard where laborers work the fields and women dance with bears; and, of course, King Gagik is depicted, offering his church to Christ. To reach Akdamar from Van, follow Route 300 to Gevaş. Entering Gevaş you will spot ferries waiting at the landing to collect the required number of passengers—between 10 and 15—for the 20-minute ride. Depending on how many people board the ferry, the cost is $3–$5 per person. If other tourists don't turn up, you must pay $25–$40 to charter the entire boat, depending on your ability to bargain. ⊠ *Rte. 300, 56 km (35 mi) west of Van,* ☎ *no phone.* 🎫 *$1.25.* ☉ *Daily dawn–sunset.*

**❾ Bitlis,** west of Akdamar (and south of Tatvan), is a green oasis among towering mountains on a tributary of the Tigris. Its two principal landmarks are a sprawling castle built above the town on Byzantine foundations and the odd 12th-century **Ulu Cami** (Grand Mosque), with a noteworthy conical dome covering the *mihrab* (prayer niche). Bitlis is nearly halfway between Van and Diyarbakır, making it a convenient place to stop for lunch, but there's little reason to linger.

### Dining and Lodging

Although Van is not a culinary oasis, at least you're not limited to hotel restaurants—local businesspeople have created a demand for upscale eateries along Cumhuriyet Caddesi, Van's lively main street. Also note the cluster of breakfast-only restaurants—serving fresh bread, honey, herb-scented cheese, and olives—behind and immediately north of the large tea garden on Cumhuriyet Caddesi.

**$ ✕ Altınşiş.** Although the food here is not terribly different from what you find at any one of the restaurants along Cumhuriyet, the Altınşiş is worth mentioning for two reasons. It has cleverly dealt with the problem of non-Turkish-speaking tourists: a picture menu graces the wall as you enter, enabling you to simply point at the meal you want. And the spectacularly fancy *aile salonu* (family area) makes eating here a treat. ⊠ *Cumhuriyet Cad. 36,* ☎ *432/216–2265. No credit cards.*

**$$ 🏨 Büyük Urartu.** This well-run hotel, one of the town's best, is also ★ educational, since the manager is a professor of archaeology. Urartian motifs recur throughout. Guest rooms are small though still pleasant; some face the noisy street—so ask for one in the rear. The attached restaurant is quite acceptable (and one of the few places in town where you can get alcohol at dinner), though a bit overpriced. ⊠ *Cumhuriyet Cad. 32,* ☎ *432/212–0660,* 🖷 *432/212–1610. 75 rooms with shower. Restaurant, bar. AE, DC, MC, V.*

**$ 🏨 Hotel Bayram.** Renovated in the mid-1990s, the Bayram will never be a luxury choice. But it is a clean and extremely friendly spot right in the center of town. ⊠ *Cumhuriyet Cad. 1-A, entrance on Çakmak Cad.,* ☎ *432/216–1136,* 🖷 *432/214–2688. 60 rooms with shower. No credit cards.*

**$ 🏨 Hotel Şahin.** An outstanding choice for the price, this hotel has clean, modern rooms. Because it's on a side street, it is significantly quieter than any of the hotels lining Cumhuriyet Caddesi. The restaurant, replete with crisp white tablecloths, is better than you'd expect. ⊠ *İrfan Baştüg Cad. 30,* ☎ *432/216–3062,* 🖷 *432/216–3064. 36 rooms with shower. Restaurant, bar. No credit cards.*

# SOUTHEASTERN TURKEY

## Diyarbakır, Mt. Nimrod, and Şanlıurfa

The photo is famous: a series of decapitated stone heads rising out of the sand, framed against a hypnotic blue sky. The image appears on postcards and in tourist brochures throughout Turkey, seducing travelers by the hundreds to add Mt. Nimrod to their itineraries. It's an especially feasible detour if you're coming from Cappadocia, thanks to tour operators who run overnight trips from Nevşehir and Göreme. Traveling by car, it makes sense to include the bazaar and ruins at Şanlıurfa and perhaps the medieval citadel at Mardin. The region's largest city, Diyarbakır, has a few historic sights and is convenient if you're arriving from Van or Erzurum.

# Diyarbakır

★ ⑩ *357 km (221 mi) from Van on Rte. 300 to Rte. E99.*

Defended by a stretch of impregnable black-basalt walls, three layers thick in places, Diyarbakır commands the rough, dusty plain 195 km (121 mi) west of Bitlis. With its great walls, you would think the stronghold of Diyarbakır could survive any siege; in fact, it seems to have fallen to about every petty raider who passed this way. One of the oldest cities anywhere in the northernmost region of Mesopotamia (the area between the Tigris and Euphrates rivers), Diyarbakır has seen a lot of raiders in its 5,000 years. The Hurrians were probably the first, founding a city called Hurri-Mitanni. The Assyrians then absorbed it and used it as a trading post (*karum*). Next came Urartian domination, followed by the familiar succession of Medes, Persians, Macedonians, Romans (who named the city Amida), Sassanids, and Byzantines. In the 7th century several Arab Muslim groups battled with one another for possession of this strategic crossroads. They gave the city its present name, Diyarbakır, (City of the Bakr Tribes). Later came the Turkomans, the Artakids, the eastern and western Seljuks, and the Mongolian hordes. Finally, Selim I (known as Selim the Grim for his fierce style of conquering) took it and a significant portion of this region for the Ottomans in 1515, which was the beginning of a long and relatively calm period.

Diyarbakır's Roman influence is evident in the layout of the old town: a rough rectangle with two main streets connecting the four gates, one at each compass point. Connecting the four primary gates are the **city walls,** reconstructed by Emperor Constantius in AD 349 and further restored by the Seljuks in 1088 and again 120 years later by Artakid Turcoman emir al Malik al-Salih Mahmud. On the whole, the walls remain in good shape along their entire length of 5½ km (3 mi); indeed, if you feel like a bit of an adventure, the best way to appreciate this great wall is to wander along the top. Of the original 72 towers, 67 still stand, decorated with myriad inscriptions in the language of every conqueror and with Seljuk reliefs of animals and men; you can also explore their inner chambers and corridors. To make a circuit of the city walls on foot, start at the **Mardin Kapısı** (Mardin Gate), on the south side near the Otel Büyük Kervansaray and take the wall-top path west toward the **Urfa Kapısı** (Urfa Gate), also called the Bab er-Rum. About halfway you will come to the twin bastions, **Evli Beden Burcu** and **Yedi Kardeş Burcu** (Tower of Seven Brothers), added to the fortifications in 1209. From here you can see the old Ottoman bridge over the Tigris, called **Dicle Köprüsü** (Tigris Bridge). Continue clockwise along the city wall, and you'll eventually reach another gate, the **Dağ Kapısı** (Mountain Gate), which divides Diyarbakır's old and new towns. Farther east inside the ramparts are the sad remains of the **Artakid Saray** (Artasid Palace), surrounded by a dry, octagonal pool known as the **Lion's Fountain.** Not long ago there were two carved lions here; what happened to the second one is a mystery.

The ruins of the old town's **İç Kale** (Inner Fortress), a circular and heavily eroded section of the city walls, are notable for the 16th-century

Hazreti Süleymaniye Cami (Prophet Süleyman Mosque), which is also known as the Citadel Mosque. The mosque has a tall, graceful minaret and is striped with black basalt and pale sandstone, a favorite design of this city's medieval architects. Its courtyard fountain is fed by an underground spring that has probably supplied cold, clear water to the city for all its 5,000 years. ⊠ İzzet Paşa Cad., ☎ no phone. ☉ Daily dawn–sunset, except at prayer times.

In the center of the old city stands the **Ulu Cami** (Great Mosque), one of the oldest in Anatolia. Though its present form dates from the 12th century, in an older form it served as a Byzantine basilica; its colonnades and columns are made from bits and pieces of earlier Greek buildings. Note its Arabic courtyard plan, which contrasts with the covered and domed mosques common in Turkey. ⊠ Gazi Cad., opposite Yapı Kredi Bank, ☎ no phone. ☉ Daily 10–sunset.

Diyarbakır's **bazaar** encompasses the half-dozen streets surrounding Ulu Cami; most stalls are shrines to wrought metal, plumbing fixtures, and plastic shoes. Across the street from the mosque is the grand 16th-century **Hasan Paşa Hanı,** a photogenic caravansary now mostly used by carpet and souvenir dealers.

Zinciriye Medrese, a former seminary, now houses the local **Arkeoloji Müzesi** (Archaeological Museum), where the exhibits cover 4,000 years of history. ⊠ Gazi Cad., ☎ 412/221–2755. ☑ 50¢. ☉ Mon.–Sat. 8:30–noon and 1:30–5:30.

The old town's most recognizable mosque is the **Kasım Padişah Cami** (1512), famous for its Dört Ayaklı Minare (Four-Legged Minaret), which appears to be suspended in the air (the minaret balances on four basalt columns, a marvel of medieval engineering). Legend has it that your wish will come true if you pass under the minaret seven times. ⊠ Yenikapı Cad., ☎ no phone. ☉ Daily 10–sunset.

## Dining and Lodging

$  ✕ **Hevser Beyaz Köşk Ocakbaşı.** This mouthful of a name is hard to
★  spot in the clash of competing restaurant signs along İnönü Caddesi, but once you have found it, you'll be rewarded by some of the finest cooking in Diyarbakır. The airy courtyard garden is in the shadow of the city wall, the perfect atmosphere for sampling traditional Kurdish dishes. ⊠ İnönü Cad., ☎ 412/228–3950. No credit cards.

$  ✕ **Sarmaşık Sofra Salonu.** A newer and comparatively fancier dining spot (formerly known as the Güneydoğu), the Sarmaşık has decent Turkish entrées and air-conditioning, a blessing in the height of summer. ⊠ İnönü Cad. 31, ☎ 412/224–2597. No credit cards.

$$  ⊞ **Otel Büyük Kervansaray.** The Turkish concept of turning old car-
★  avansaries into fancy hotels seems particularly apt and, as is the case here, provides some pleasant lodgings. This attractive inn is in a 16th-century caravansary with sandstone walls and traditional furnishings. Rooms are comfortable enough, but what you're really paying for is the atmosphere and the location, next to the Mardin Kapısı, inside the city walls. ⊠ Gazi Cad., ☎ 412/228–9606, ⓕ𝔸𝕏 412/223–7731. 45 rooms with bath. Restaurant, bar, pool. MC, V.

$$  ⊞ **Turistik.** If you're feeling nostalgic for a 1950s-style hotel, try the Turistik. Guest rooms are larger than average and comfortable, and the garden restaurant, around a fountain, is appealing. Front rooms can be a bit noisy. ⊠ Ziya Gökalp Bul. 7, ☎ 412/224–7550, ⓕ𝔸𝕏 412/224–4274. 57 rooms with shower. Restaurant, bar. MC, V.

$–$$  ⊞ **D. Büyük Otel.** If it weren't in sun-baked eastern Turkey, the D. Büyük might be accused of having Art Deco tendencies. Rooms are high on style, with sleek bathroom fixtures and color-matched sheets and curtains—not to mention satellite TVs and direct-dial phones. ⊠ *İnönü Cad. 4,* ☎ *412/223–9111,* ℻ *412/221–2444. 62 rooms with shower. Restaurant, bar. AE, DC, MC, V.*

$ ⌆ **Otel Güler.** One of the best inexpensive hotels in town, the Güler is clean and quiet and has well-kept rooms. ⊠ *Kibris Cad. Yoğurtçu Sok. 7,* ☎ *412/224–0164.* ℻ *412/224–0294. 35 rooms with shower. Bar. No credit cards.*

## Mt. Nimrod and Environs

*169 km (105 mi) from Diyarbakır west on Rtes. E99 and 360 past Adıyaman to town of Kâhta; to reach mountain, take Rte. 02–03 north.*

★ ⑪ **Mt. Nimrod** (Nemrut Dağı) rises 7,052 ft above the Anatolian plain, a ruddy outcrop of rock and stunted trees overlooking a vast network of natural and man-made lakes, all part of Turkey's controversial GAP (Güneydoğu Anadolu Projesi, or Southeast Anatolia Project). In 1984, in an effort to harness the Tigris and Euphrates rivers, the Turkish government began damming and flooding valleys at the foot of Mt. Nimrod, forcing dozens of villages to relocate and causing a diplomatic stir from Damascus to Baghdad (neither Syria nor Iraq is pleased that water supplies can now be turned off at a moment's notice). Practically speaking, GAP has shortened travel times to Mt. Nimrod from Diyarbakır and Şanlıurfa, with car ferries making frequent daily trips year-round.

Approaching from the west, minibuses run to the peak from both Adıyaman and Kâhta ($40–$75, depending on the length of the tour); if you drive to the summit yourself, the trip from Kâhta takes a good two hours. Because of severe winter weather conditions, the trip should be undertaken only between May and October—even then, when it is baking down on the plain, there are strong winds and a stiff morning chill at the summit. Tour guides recommend setting out at 2 AM to reach the summit at sunrise. You can then return before the fierce midday heat. The sunrise is lovely, but if you start later, you'll avoid the sunrise tourist rush and the coldest part of the morning.

Cars must park ½ km (¼ mi) below the sepulchral mound that tops the ocher-pink, cone-shaped pinnacle of Mt. Nimrod. The hike up from here takes a good 20 minutes and can be tiring, given the altitude. When you finally reach the summit, though, you'll meet a stupendous spectacle. Temples stand on two terraces—one facing the rising sun, the other the setting sun—with a pyramid of small rocks, the **Tumulus of Antiochus,** between them. The man responsible for this fantastic project, King Antiochus I, is buried somewhere underneath (though they have tried, archaeologists have yet to find him—all attempts at excavation have caused cave-ins). From 64 BC to 32 BC, Antiochus was king of Commagene, a tiny Roman puppet state founded by his father, Mithridates the Great (it lasted until its annexation to Rome in AD 72). The kings of Commagene grandly claimed descent from Alexander the Great, and so young Antiochus reasoned that if Alexander was a god, he must be one, too. He set a veritable army of slaves to work building a suitable monument to himself. Enthroned on the two terraces are massive white statues of gods, Antiochus seated among them as an equal.

Originally 26 ft–30 ft high, the statues have been decapitated over the centuries by the forces of erosion and earthquakes; in 1926 a thunderstorm brought the last one—Tyche, goddess of fortune—crashing down. Their gigantic heads are nowadays set upright on the ground around the tumulus; note how they combine the Greek harmony of features with Asian-looking headgear and hairstyles. On the east terrace, left to right, they are: Apollo, Tyche/Fortuna, Zeus (at center, with his pointed cap and bushy whiskers), Antiochus, and Heracles. The west terrace is a mirror image of the east, with the addition of some fine relief carvings portraying Antiochus shaking hands with Apollo, Zeus, and Heracles, all with smiles and dignity. The inscriptions carved everywhere mostly describe the Commagenes and their religious practices; the message on the throne of Antiochus reads, "I, Antiochus, caused this monument to be erected in commemoration of my own glory and of that of the gods." Follow the path that runs behind the statues to view the particularly fine inscriptions on the backs of the figures. Given the severe temperatures and strong winds at the summit, and the overall isolation of the site, one wonders why Antiochus didn't choose a more inviting location—a question best discussed over a steaming cup of tea at the small visitor center or in the ramshackle tea shed on the summit itself. Bring your own food and water for the excursion up the mountain. ✉ *Nemrut Dağı,* ☎ *416/737–1231.* 🎫 *$1.* ☉ *May–late Oct., daily sunrise–sunset.*

⑫ Along the road back from Mt. Nimrod to Kâhta, you pass other remarkable relics of Commagene in the small village of **Eski Kâhta** (Old Kâhta). Cross the Kâhta River on the Seljuk Bridge to see Arsameia, now called **Eski Kale** (Old Castle), a former capital of the Commagene kingdom. Here, carved into the rock, is a stunning relief of Antiochus I's father, Mithridates, being greeted by Heracles. Higher up on the rock face are copious inscriptions proclaiming the glory of the Commagene dynasty; on the top of this peak stand the foundations of an ancient acropolis with colored floor mosaics. A short distance down the road, **Yeni Kale** (New Castle) was built by the Mameluks over a smaller Commagene fortress. Recross the Kâhta via the **Cendere Köprü,** a single-span bridge with two tall columns on one end and one on the other, built by the Roman emperor Septimus Severus in the early 3rd century AD. Ten kilometers (6 miles) before Kâhta is **Karakuş** (Black Bird), named for the black eagle that guards, from atop a large column, the tombs of the royal ladies of Commagene.

## Dining and Lodging

Few decent restaurants are to be found in Adıyaman or Kâhta; you're better off stopping for lunch or dinner just below the summit at the Otel Kervansaray Nemrut.

**$–$$** ✕🏨 **Otel Kervansaray Nemrut.** One of the few places to stop on Mt.
★ Nimrod itself, the caravansary is in a low stone building near a waterfall 8 km (5 mi) from Mt. Nimrod's summit. The location is stunning, and the rooms are clean and wonderfully quiet. The restaurant is one of the best for miles. ✉ *Nemrut Dağı, Karadut Köyü, 54 km (34 mi) from Kâhta,* ☎ *416/737–2190,* 🖷 *416/737–2085. 14 rooms with shower. Restaurant, pool, camping. MC, V.*

**$** 🏨 **Hotel Antiochos.** A lovely hotel in Adıyaman, the Antiochos has pleasant rooms and a pool to escape the summer heat. ✉ *Atatürk Bul. 148,* ☎ *416/225–0282,* 🖷 *416/225–0243. 21 rooms with shower. Restaurant, bar, pool. MC, V.*

**$** 🏨 **Hotel Kommagene.** Though it has pretensions of being a hotel, this place is really more of a guest house. Old kilims decorate the lobby, and a shady terrace makes a good place to rest. The restaurant is quite decent. ✉ *Rte. 360, Karakuş Yolu 3, Kâhta,* ☎ *416/715–1092,* 🖷 *416/725–5548. 21 rooms with shower. Restaurant. No credit cards.*

**$** 🏨 **Hotel Nemrut Tur.** Generally considered one of the better places to stay in Kâhta, this hotel is often booked solid by tour groups. Guest rooms are clean and comfortable, and the restaurant is on a shady terrace. ⊠ *Adıyaman Yolu, Kâhta,* ☎ *416/725–6881,* FAX *416/725–6880. 55 rooms with shower. Restaurant, pool. No credit cards.*

# Şanlıurfa

★ ⑬ *143 km (89 mi) southeast of Kâhta on Rte. E99, or 180 km (112 mi) southwest of Diyarbakır on Rte. E99.*

Şanlıurfa (more commonly called Urfa; *şanlı,* or "glorious," was added to the city's name in 1973) lies at the edge of the Syrian desert. Formerly a sleepy frontier town that experienced a huge boom due to GAP, Urfa is most famous as the birthplace of the biblical patriarch Abraham. A half-dozen mosques crowd around the cave where Abraham reputedly was born, and a pool near the cave is filled with sacred carp.

Urfa's old town, at the southern foot of Divan Caddesi, is a remarkable mix of Babylonian, Assyrian, Roman, Byzantine, and Ottoman architecture, albeit heavily eroded over the centuries. The **Urfa Kale** (Urfa Fortress) is a motley collection of pillars, upturned stones, and broken columns at the top of a wide staircase. It's impossible to detect any one architectural intent here, probably because the fortress has been razed and rebuilt at least a dozen times since the 2nd century BC. Climb to the summit for a fantastic view of the city. ⊠ *Kale Cad.,* ☎ *no phone.* 🎟 *50¢.* ⊙ *Daily 9–6.*

Legend has it that Abraham was born in the **Hazreti İbrahim Doğum Mağarası** (Prophet İbrahim's Birth Cave), a natural cave hidden behind the Hasan Paşa Mosque. Men and women enter through separate doorways. Most people huddled inside this small, dark cavern, darkened by 2,000 years of candle smoke, have come to pray, not to snap photos. ⊠ *Göl Cad.,* ☎ *no phone.* 🎟 *Free.* ⊙ *Daily sunrise–sunset.*

**Gölbaşı Parkı,** home of the famed carp pools, is a shady oasis on hot days. According to legend, King Nimrod, angry at Abraham's condemnation of the king's Assyrian polytheism, set about immolating the patriarch. God awakened natural springs, dousing the fire and saving Abraham. These springs remain in the form of these sacred pools, filled with carp—an incarnation, according to the myth, of the wood from Abraham's pyre.

A short walk east leads to Urfa's **bazaar,** where in summertime merchants wait patiently in the hot sun for the rare tour group. A few lucky families own stalls in the covered caravansary, where you'll find the best selection of dried fruits, gold jewelry, and miscellaneous plumbing fixtures. This is a good place to hunt for bargains, particularly on carpets and kilims.

## Dining and Lodging

$–$$ ✕🏨 **Harran Hotel.** Clean and modern rooms with televisions and minibars make the Harran the best bet in Urfa. The hotel is centrally located and staffed by a phalanx of friendly employees, and the manager speaks English. Be sure to try the restaurant on the top floor, where there's an unparalleled view of Urfa. ⊠ *Atatürk Bul.,* ☎ *414/313–2860,* FAX *414/ 313–4918. 82 rooms with shower. Restaurant, pool. AE, MC, V.*

---

OFF THE
BEATEN PATH

**MARDIN –** Mardin, only 30 km (19 mi) from the Syrian border, is a worthwhile day trip from Şanlıurfa or Diyarbakır. Mardin is defended by a medieval sandstone citadel—one so impregnable that neither the Seljuks in the 12th century nor the Mongols in the 13th managed to capture it. At the tail end of the 14th century, Tamerlane did conquer the city, but when he returned in 1401 to crush the revolt of his own brother, İsa, the citadel resisted even Tamerlane. Most of the other outstanding buildings in Mardin are Islamic: the Lâtifiye Cami (Lâtifiye Mosque, 1371); the Seljuk Ulu Cami (Seljuk Ulu Mosque), dating from the 12th century, disfigured in the 19th, and later restored; and the Sultan İsa Medrese (Sultan İsa Seminary, 1385), renowned for its exquisite stone carvings. Just 7 km (4 mi) southeast of Mardin is the Syrian Orthodox Dayrul Zafaran (Saffron Monastery). Dating to perhaps as early as the 6th century and partially restored in the 19th, the monastery is still in use. One of the brothers will give you a tour of the building and perhaps introduce you to one of the *rahip* (priests) who still speak and teach Aramaic, the language of Christ. Tour operators from Diyarbakır include Mardin on many itineraries, or you can drive there yourself in about two hours. *From Şanlıurfa take Route E90 east for 161 km (100 mi), or from Diyarbakır take Rte. 950 southeast for 94 km (58 mi).*

# THE FAR EAST A TO Z

## Arriving and Departing

### By Bus

Erzurum, the main hub of the regional transportation system, is about 15 hours from Ankara ($20), 20 hours from Istanbul ($26), and six hours from Trabzon ($10). The region's other main hub, Diyarbakır, is about 13 hours from Ankara ($15), 18 hours from Istanbul ($24), and 10 hours from Erzurum ($14). A half-dozen bus companies serve the region.

### By Car

From Trabzon a twisty, mountainous road (E97 to Aşkale, then E80) covers the 322 km (200 mi) to Erzurum. The drive from Ankara is a whopping 882 km (547 mi) across much of Anatolia, first on Route E88, then on E80. From Adana, on the Mediterranean Coast, take E90 to Şanlıurfa, then E99 to Diyarbakır, a total distance of 536 km (332 mi). Gas stations are plentiful, and roadside hotels and restaurants help break up the long, dusty, hot drives.

### By Plane

**Turkish Airlines** and **Istanbul Airlines** (☞ Air Travel *in* the Gold Guide for phone numbers) both have daily scheduled flights from Istanbul and Ankara to Erzurum, Diyarbakır, and Van, and from Ankara to Gaziantep, Kars, Malatya, and Batman. The fares, set by region, are about $75 one-way no matter where you're flying. There are less frequent flights from Istanbul to Gaziantep and from Ankara to Elazığ, Erzincan, Sivas, and Şanlıurfa.

### By Train

Not the best option, a train ride from Ankara to Erzurum (26 hours) and Van (38 hours or more) is brutally slow. Per-person fares range from $16 (first class) to $60 (sleeper bunk).

## Getting Around

### By Bus

Within the eastern region, buses take a long time—Erzurum is 10 hours from Diyarbakır, eight hours from Van, four hours from Kars—but you can get wherever you want to go without spending much money. There's an *otogar* (bus station) in each of the main towns.

### By Car

With fewer services and more heavy trucks than on the Mediterranean or Aegean coasts, these are not Turkey's best roads. To make matters worse, a series of dams under construction in the region can make existing highways impassable. Some sample distances: Erzurum to Kars, 212 km (131 mi); Erzurum to Van, 361 km (224 mi); Van to Diyarbakır, 408 km (253 mi).

**Avis** has an office in Gaziantep (☏ 342/336–1194, FAX 342/336–3058), near Şanlıurfa. Economy rates are $45–$55 per day with unlimited mileage; the drop-off fee is $100. In Erzurum there are two local options: **Evis Rent-a-Car** (☏ 422/234–4400), a small company opposite the Otel Oral, and **Best Rent-A-Car** (☏ 422/233–6144), down the street from the Otel Oral. Both require you to return the vehicle to Erzurum and charge $45–$100 per day, depending on the style of car.

## Contacts and Resources

### Emergencies
**Ambulance** (☏ 112). **Police** (☏ 155).

### Guided Tours
Tour offices in Doğubeyazıt tend to go in and out of business every week, so if you need a guide, it is best to ask at your hotel and or get recommendations from other travelers.

Diyarbakır is rife with guides, many of whom are dishonest and looking to make a quick buck. One exception is **Mehmet Nalbant** (☏ 412/235–0642), a fluent English speaker who arranges overnight trips to Mt. Nimrod ($25–$40 per person). The three-day grand tour—Mardin, Şanlıurfa, and Mt. Nimrod—costs $85–$100 per person.

**Dağcılı Federasyonu** (Turkish Mountaineering Club, B.T.G.M.; ✉ Ulus Işhanı, A Block, Ulus, Ankara) is a good source of information about guided mountain-climbing tours, including treks to the summit of Mt. Ararat.

### Precautions
Because of the unpredictable nature of conflicts in the Far East, be aware that a visit to this area is not without risk. *See* the introduction at the beginning of this chapter for a general idea of the risks that travel here presents and information on how to contact the U.S. State Department and American embassies for the most up-to-date travel information. Since the situation is extremely dynamic and volatile, it's also a good idea to read the local newspapers daily in order to keep up with the locations of current local disturbances.

### Visitor Information
Even before the current troubles, the number of tourists visiting eastern Turkey was relatively low. Usually someone in the visitor centers knows at least a few words of English, but you would be advised to have a Turkish speaker on hand to help with translation.

**Adıyaman** (✉ Atatürk Bul. 184, ☏ 416/216–1008, FAX 416/216–3840). **Ağrı** (✉ Özel İdare Binası Kat (Floor) 4, No. 11–12, ☏ 472/216–0450). **Diyarbakır** (✉ Dağkapi Bureu Giriş Bölmü, ☏ 412/221–2173, FAX 412/221–1189). **Erzurum** (✉ Cemal Gürsel Cad. 9, ☏ 442/218–5697, FAX 442/218–5443). **Kars** (✉ Atatürk Cad. next to Süleyman Demirel Parkı, in Milli Eğitim Bldg., ☏ 474/223–2300, FAX 474/223–8452). **Şanlıurfa** (✉ Asfalt Cad. 4-D, ☏ 414/215–2467, FAX 414/216–0170). **Van** (✉ Cumhuriyet Cad., ☏ 432/216–2018, FAX 432/216–3675).

# 8   BACKGROUND AND ESSENTIALS

Portraits of Turkey

Turkey at a Glance: A Chronology

Books and Videos

Smart Travel Tips

Turkish Vocabulary

# LAND OF CONTRASTS

To Western eyes, Turkey seems like a whole other world. Its domed mosques with minarets piercing the sky, the muezzin's call to prayer five times a day, its crowded bazaars gleaming with copper and gold and piled high with carpets, and its palaces and sultans' harems are the stuff of fables. Yet these legendary scenes also mask the reality that Turkey is a modern country, rapidly industrializing, constantly changing, growing quickly, and clamoring for recognition as a European power.

Istanbul is the world's only city to span two continents, which makes it something of a metaphor for the nation of which it is the largest city. The constant pull between East and West, between modern and traditional, creates an underlying tension that often erupts to confound Turkish society and politics. Although Turkey has been a secular democracy since 1923, Islam remains a strong force; 99% of the population is Muslim. Religious tradition prevails in rural areas and in the shanty towns that surround the major cities, where women wear head scarves and are sometimes completely veiled. In the centers of major Turkish cities, however, contrasting lifestyles are common, and you find religious tokenism and devotion side by side.

Urban Turkey is bursting at its seams as the countryside pours into the cities. The population of Istanbul soared from 700,000 inhabitants in 1923 to an estimated 12.5 million in 1999 and is still growing by several hundred thousand a year. At the same time, the population of İzmir, the Aegean port that's the nation's third-largest city, increased by nearly 40% a year in the 1980s, and though its growth has slowed down to 5%–10% per year, that's still very high for a city with a population already in the millions.

The immense effort of metropolitan areas to accommodate such staggering growth has resulted in crowding, overbuilding, and gridlock. Despite the increasingly widespread use of natural gas, air pollution is a real urban plague, especially in winter, because of the sooty lignite coal still used for heating. Electricity is expensive and at times unreliable, as is water. In Istanbul the water supply is sometimes cut off for short periods in summer. Better hotels now have their own water depots and electricity generators in readiness for cutoffs. Such private solutions to Istanbul's infrastructure problems have historical antecedents in the underground water cisterns of the old city. Among all of Istanbul's eerie wonders, the shadowy subterranean reservoir called Yerebatan Sarnıcı (Sunken Palace) may be the most unusual: Where else in the world can you descend into a dramatically illuminated 6th-century waterworks while listening to classical music?

Although the country has struggled with rapid industrialization, it has also benefited from it. Growth and prosperity have spurred the preservation of landmarks, the restoration of fine historic districts, and the creation of handsome new parks. Turkey has almost no Western-style drug problem and enforces stringent drug laws (these laws apply to visitors as well as Turks; it's foolhardy to transgress them).

What about the future? Turkey has a challenging agenda. It is determined to prosper and claim its place among the modern states of Europe. Although there were hopes of a decline in 2000, inflation has been running at 80%–90% per year since the early 1990s, and unemployment and underemployment have become widespread. More than half of

Portraits

Turkey's population of 70 million is under 20 years of age and readying to enter the crowded job market. Turkey's army temporarily siphons some of the excess job seekers; an 18-month military stint is compulsory for males.

In December 1999 Turkey was finally granted official candidate status for membership in the European Union (EU), 12 years after it first applied. The announcement was greeted with euphoria by Turks, most of whom initially assumed that membership was imminent. But in reality it is still several years, perhaps decades, away, not least because of concerns about the country's human rights record and continued objections from rival Greece (an EU member), which still blocks most of the EU aid designed to help Turkey prepare for membership. Turks, who have suffered from bad press in the West ever since the Crusades, argue that the EU has focused on Turkey's problems while ignoring the country's huge potential, its wide resources, and its astonishing progress. But even though it has now named Turkey as a candidate, the EU still insists that the country must undergo considerable change before discussions can begin on a final date for membership.

The liberalization of the economy in the early 1980s unquestionably brought huge material and technological benefits to many Turks. Stores that once stocked only a handful of shoddily made local goods now carry the very latest products, many of them either imported or manufactured locally under license. Turkish yuppies have MBAs from universities in the United States and Europe, carry credit cards and mobile telephones, and are Web savvy. But although some have become spectacularly rich, others, particularly those in lower income groups, have seen their standard of living fall. Traditionally close family structures have been strained and often broken by the stress of migration to Turkey's sprawling cities.

The result has been a rapid rise in support for extremist, particularly Islamist, political parties, which have flourished among the urban poor, particularly in the shanty towns that surround most of Turkey's major cities and where Islam has filled the ideological vacuum left by the collapse of communism. As one section of society has become increasingly integrated with the West, another is turning away from what it sees as the West's brash, amoral materialism and toward more traditional values and observance of Islam.

In December 1995 the Islamist Welfare Party emerged as the largest party in parliament and for 11 months in 1996–97 even headed a short-lived coalition government before being forced out of power by behind-the-scenes pressure from Turkey's powerful, rigorously secular military. The Islamists finished third in the next elections, in April 1999, when many of the Welfare Party's former supporters shifted to the National Movement Party (NMP), whose combination of a strong commitment to Islam and a hard-line anti-Western Turkish nationalism enabled it to more than double its vote compared with 1995 and to earn a place in the subsequent tripartite coalition government.

"Turkey is a man running West on a train heading East," goes a Turkish saying. Reconciling these divergent goals is just the latest challenge facing this fascinating nation, which has negotiated and survived other philosophical, cultural, and political evolutions over the centuries.

—By Rebecca Morris

# THE ART OF THE KILIM

What are kilims? The word *kilim* simply means a flat-woven rug, or a rug without a knotted pile. Different languages use variations on this word, including: *gelim* in Iran, *kelim* in Afghanistan, *palas* in the Caucasus, *bsath* in Syria and Lebanon, *chilim* in Romania, and kilim in Turkey, Poland, Hungary, and Serbia. Flat weaving is found in some form all over the world, from the Great Plains of North America to Scandinavia and Indonesia. At times there is only a structural similarity in what is produced, but the disciplines imposed by the materials and techniques often result in strikingly similar designs and compositions.

Until recently both collectors and traders have considered the kilim to be the poor relation of the Oriental knotted carpet. In the past two decades, however, there has been an explosion of interest in the decorative, utilitarian, and collectible qualities of these remarkable objects. Today kilims captivate an ever-widening audience throughout the Western world. And Anatolia, in Central Turkey, is leading the kilim-producing world in both quality and quantity for kilims created with modern production techniques.

Kilims have been an essential piece of decorative, practical, and portable furniture for the peoples of the Middle East and Asia for a very long time. Originally, they were made for use on the floors and walls of tents, houses, and mosques and as animal covers and bags. Most kilims were made for family and personal use, although some villages and towns became famous in the 17th and 18th centuries for their fine commercial production and remain so today. Family wealth was stored up in kilims, knotted rugs, precious metals, and animals, and at times of famine or crisis, any of these possessions could be bartered for grain or could be exchanged into local currency for use in the nearest market town.

Kilims have always played a central role in the family as part of the dowry or bride-price. The young girl, learning alongside her mother and other members of her family, made her own dowry of kilims and textiles as a labor of love. The position and status of a family were directly related to the quality and quantity of the bride's dowry, and this explains to some extent why the kilim has in the past had so much effort, craftsmanship, and creativity lavished upon it with no prospect of financial gain from the marketplace or bazaar.

The reasons for making kilims have changed greatly in recent years. Utility and religious and cultural significance have largely been replaced by profit and commerce. Present-day Turkey has become the center for the village and workshop production of kilims for export and trade; orders are placed by fax, and many designs and colors are inspired by Western interior designers. Chemical dyes are used, and yet it is interesting to see the reemergence of the rich, glowing colors of natural dyes, matched with ancient and often long-forgotten motifs and symbols, in order to satisfy an ever-growing demand for more-traditional kilims.

By looking at many different kilims, old and new, from many areas, you can begin to appreciate those that are original and not mass produced. These are the genuine article—kilims that retain their true ethnic identity, woven without compromise and with a craftsmanship that reflects love and heritage in their making.

Throughout central Asia the dominant source of yarn has always been the domesticated sheep. The quality of wool from various sheep depends entirely on climate and pasture, and the wool from the fat-tailed sheep is famous for its hard, coarse, and long staple, which gives a lustrous shine with excellent dye-taking qualities. Camels, goats, and horses also provide a source for yarn. Goat hair is used for its strength and its attractive high sheen. The warps of saddle and donkey bags, animal covers, and some of the kilims of central Asia are made of goat hair or of goat hair and sheep's wool combined. The sides of the kilims, the selvages, are often of goat hair. Camel hair is used for both the weft and warp in kilims to rich and subtle effect, especially when it is left undyed. Horse hair from the mane and tail is often tied in tassels on bags, and, like goat hair, it gives added strength in binding and finishing a kilim.

White cotton has always been used by certain tribes and is becoming increasingly popular as a material for highlighting designs and patterns. Unlike white wool, cotton does not turn cream or ivory in color with age. Its structural qualities are also much valued. Since the turn of the 20th century, cotton has tended to replace wool in the warps of Anatolian kilims. This is a good indication of how commercial zeal can influence traditional practice. Previously, there was no alternative to wool or local materials, and a weaver would never have parted with cash for cotton to weave into a kilim that she was not intending to sell for profit. Cotton-and-wool mixtures are found in 19th-century kilims, and the spinning of the materials together results in a fine yarn that is strong yet supple.

A distinctive feature of kilim weaving is that individual color sections are completed before the weaver moves on to other areas of the rug. This is in total contrast to knotted-pile carpets, where the weaver works straight across the carpet in horizontal lines of knots, using many colors in close succession. The kilim weaver will work on one block of color, laying perhaps 20 wefts before beating them down with a comb and moving on to the adjacent color.

Until the mid-19th century only colored dyes from animal, vegetable, and mineral sources were known, and there were thriving industries associated with the cropping and mining of the raw materials throughout Asia. In towns and villages yarn would be taken to professional dyers, and naturally dyed yarn could be bought in the markets. All kilims made before the 1850s were therefore naturally dyed, a process that has continued until very recently. The nomadic or seminomadic peoples, making kilims for their own use, sometimes had access to natural dyestuffs—substances that grew wild among their grazing animals—and so the women would collect herbs, flowers, and roots for their own special color recipes. The migratory life only allowed for the carriage of small quantities of dyed wool, made up a batch at a time, and this is one explanation for the natural variations in color found in the older kilims.

A whole spectrum of natural colors can be obtained from the flowers, fruit, vegetables, and insects—even the earth—in kilim-producing areas. All natural dyes (with the exception of yellow) retain their colors extraordinarily well, but they do begin to fade naturally after about 50 years and will run if not well fixed. The positive aspect of this is that a kilim will mellow beautifully over the years if traditionally made with natural dyes.

In the late 19th century weavers began experimenting with chemical dyes, at first achieving only occasional and limited success. However, with chemical dyes, weavers had a complete and relatively easy choice of colors. Vivid oranges and yellows that had been so difficult to fix in the past were now readily available. The use of chemical dyes spread rapidly, spawning village industries and reaching even the least accessible and most self-sufficient weavers of all, the nomadic tribeswomen.

Kilims produced in the first flush of this new craze display a rather startling use of many different, not always harmonious colors, and until recently, some chemical dyes, such as aniline and acid-base dyes, corroded the wool, faded quickly, and would not withstand washing with detergents. But chemical dyes do not always result in clashing color effects or poor durability. In the past 40 years chrome-mordanted colors have been developed that are indistinguishable from natural dyes when used well. Meanwhile, a price premium for kilims with vegetable dyes has ensured a contemporary revival in traditional techniques among the kilim producers of Anatolia.

In Islamic art, some figurative forms, human and animal, are permitted, but in many cases it is considered disrespectful to walk over them, thus precluding their use in knotted rugs and kilims. For the tribal weavers, however, connections with their natural environment, with their animals, and with their family groups are very strong and deeply rooted and will override religious taboo. The weaver will incorporate images from her own household, such as a kettle, teapot, ewer, comb, beater, or lamp, as well as, more recently, objects of Western influence, including cars and bikes and even helicopters and automatic rifles.

Perhaps the most familiar motif used on kilims is the Tree of Life, which to the weaver could represent equally well the presence of water in desert lands or the family, with the trunk as the father and the branches as the children. Another symbolic motif is the talismanic evil eye, or *nazarlık,* used to deflect evil and to balance the adverse effects on the kilim of other motifs, such as the spider or scorpion.

Until recently there were, generally speaking, three clear-cut categories from which to choose when buying a kilim: antique flat-weaves made more than 100 years ago, before the influences of export trade began to be felt; old kilims made in this century, some of whose compositions clearly display the blending of different tribal and regional traditions; and modern, largely commercially produced kilims, woven in village workshops, often to orders from retailers in the West and often much removed from the local traditional techniques and patterning.

A fourth category, however, has developed—the new facsimiles being produced in Anatolia. These are completely traditional in style and form and are made largely as a response to the increasing Western demand for authentic, quality weavings. Many have been specially commissioned by Western dealers, and most are made for export. Various grades are available, determined by the quality of the weaving—from coarse to very fine—and by the complexity of patterning in the overall composition. Most of these kilims are chemically dyed, and those that do make use of vegetable and natural dyes enjoy a considerable premium in price.

The safest purchase in terms of financial investment is without doubt an antique kilim. But it is dangerous to assume a kilim is rare or excellently designed and constructed simply because it is old; there have always been good weavers and bad weavers. Anyone interested in buying an antique kilim should take time to examine as many old and antique rugs as possible and should talk to a knowledgeable, trustworthy dealer to get a clear idea of which rugs are considered important and collectible.

Collectibility is not determined by the vagaries of fashion. A rug is collectible if it is rare or unusual and if it is very well woven; these are unchanging qualities, and you may assume that such a rug will increase in value as an investment. Antique kilims are invariably the most expensive to buy, both in the West and in their country of origin; ironically, there is often a much better choice in Europe and North America in terms of price and kilim type than there is in Anatolia or central Asia.

Very fine antique kilims are obviously too expensive for many people, but large numbers of old, traditional weavings can be found to suit most budgets. Of those made in modern production, it is safe to assume that the finest facsimiles of antique weaving and dyeing techniques will become the investments of the future, and the highest-quality naturally dyed Anatolian replicas will definitely improve and mellow with age and use.

In Anatolia, kilims can be recognized by their tribe and area of origin to within a group of villages or even a single village. Many distinctive kilims of the 19th century can be attributed to the area around Bergama and Balıkesir, in western Anatolia, now one of the last strongholds of the Yoruk peoples. Most of the antique Balıkesir kilims are patterned with an interlocking grid of blue on a red ground, with dazzling results. More recent Balıkesir kilims are varied in design, often decorated with medallions of different sizes on a plain ground, with simple side and end borders or skirts.

It is unusual to find kilims from Anatolia with any area left undecorated, and those from the Manastir region are therefore easy to recognize. The kilims have very strong and simple compositions, usually on a tomato red or black background with a plain central field decorated with very few designs. The mihrab, the ceremonial mosque archway, is represented in Manastir kilims by a distinct floating line rather than by a pattern.

The village of Mut lies south of the Taurus Mountains, another region of the seminomadic Yörük pastoralists. The kilims from this area are often found with dark warps of goat hair or brown wool. Brightly colored medallions are set against a red ground, usually a pair of designs in a mirror image.

Aydın, a town near the Aegean Coast, is a productive source of kilims, often woven in two halves and joined together. As with most western Anatolian kilims, the Aydın examples are brightly colored with small patterns.

The town of Konya lies at the south end of a most prolific weaving area, that of west-central Anatolia, once known as Karaman. Konya kilims are made wholly of wool and are often large, woven in two or three pieces, with a predominantly white or cream background color into which is woven a strong central series of oval medallions.

The kilims of the central area of Anatolia around Kayserı are very loosely woven, and the older examples have a silky and flat texture. Modern Kayserı kilims are generally red and black, fading to pinks and grays.

Malatya is in Kurdish country and gives its name to the numerous kilims produced in the area by both Kurdish and Turkic peoples. Woven in two pieces with warps of white wool, the kilims are usually long, relatively narrow, and difficult to make. Commonly, three central medallions are split by the central joint, at times in a most irregular way, and the white sections of the composition are given brilliance by the use of white cotton yarn. Some of the longest Anatolian kilims are found in the Malatya area. Known as band kilims, they can exceed 15 ft in length, and each of the two sections is often a complete composition in itself, a most unusual occurrence in Anatolia. They are sometimes cut and sold as runners. Predominant colors are red and blue, with striking white bands.

Woven by Kurds, most Sivas kilims, and indeed most kilims made anywhere east of here, are prayer mats in muted colors with a strong single and central mihrab motif. All are made in one piece, and the mihrab is bordered by three narrow bands full of floral designs.

Prayer rugs from around Bayburt and Erzurum are woven in predominantly yellow or ocher colors with tiered central mihrabs surrounded by stylized floral designs, especially carnations. Many times, the year of weaving will be woven directly into the design. Just east of this area is the village of Bardiz, where most of the Karabagh or modern Bessarabian kilims are made. The Kurdish weavers are excellent copyists and have been producing these large floral-pattern kilims since the 1920s, using European tapestry designs such as those from Aubusson and Savonnerie in France. Curiously, these were themselves derived from the original Ottoman floral kilims of the 17th century—a full circle of design ideas.

The remote and mountainous district of eastern Anatolia around Van has maintained many clans of seminomadic Kurds, largely undisturbed for thousands of years. The kilims are square, an unusual shape, and are generally in two pieces; many examples bear a resemblance to the kilims of northwest Persia and the Caucasus made by other Kurdish groups. Kilims from Van are well made with good-quality wool and will last for many years.

The kilims from the Kars area, close by the Russian border, are typical of most Kurdish work—either long narrow strips or small prayer rugs. Thick dark-wool warps give a ribbed effect, and the usual colors are browns, pinks, and oranges.

The area of European Turkey known as Thrace is thought to be the region of origin for many distinctive kilims. The typical composition is simple, often the Tree of Life in its many forms, surrounded by a floral border with animal and leaf motifs. Those from around the town of Sarkoy are of the finest quality.

When seeking out kilims, do not assume those bought in Turkey will be cheaper than those for sale in the West. A rug bought in an Istanbul bazaar may often be just as expensive as one purchased in London or New York, if not more so. And do beware of the hidden costs and regulations governing a sale for personal export. These include shipping, packing, and handling charges, as well as export and import tax. All these expenses add up and can mean that the overall cost is considerably more than you at first calculated. But for the memories and stories associated with the purchase of a kilim in a bazaar—the haggling, the playacting, and the gallons of sweet tea consumed before the deal is struck—there is no substitute.

— By Alastair Hull and Nicholas Barnard

Alastair Hull is a collector, expert, and dealer in kilims. Nicholas Barnard is a writer and organizer of original tribal-art exhibits.

# TURKEY AT A GLANCE

**ca. 9000 BC**  First agrarian settlements in the world are established in the area that is today southern Turkey and northern Iraq.

**6500–5650 BC**  Çatalhöyük, the largest early agricultural community yet discovered and the oldest known site with religious buildings, flourishes.

**2371–16 BC**  Reign of King Sargon of Akkad, whose empire reached from Mesopotamia to the southern parts of Anatolia (Asia Minor), the area that is now Turkey.

**ca. 2200–1200 BC**  Indo-European invaders include the Hittites, who establish an empire in Anatolia, pushing out the Mesopotamians.

**1296 BC**  Hittites defeat the Egyptian pharaoh Ramses II at the Battle of Kadesh, halting Egypt's northern advance and strengthening the Hittites' hold over Anatolia.

**ca. 1200 BC**  New waves of invaders break up the Hittite empire.

**1184 BC**  The traditional date for the end of the legendary Trojan War, the accounts of which are believed to be based on a real conflict.

**ca. 1000 BC**  West coast of Asia Minor settled by Aeolians, Dorians, and Ionians from Greece.

**ca. 657 BC**  Foundation of Byzantium by Megarian colonists from Greece, according to legend, led by Byzas, for whom the city was named.

**559–29 BC**  Reign of Cyrus the Great, the founder of the Persian empire, who subdues the Greek cities of Asia Minor, defeats the Lydian king, Croesus, reputedly the richest man in the world, and unifies Asia Minor under his rule.

**334 BC**  Alexander the Great conquers Asia Minor, ending Persian domination and extending his empire to the borders of India.

**323 BC**  Alexander the Great's sudden death creates a power vacuum, and his vast empire disintegrates into a number of petty kingdoms.

**190 BC**  The Seleucid monarch Antiochus III, defeated by the Romans at the battle of Magnesia, cedes his territory west of the Taurus Mountains to Rome.

**133 BC**  Rome consolidates its military and diplomatic gains in the region by creating the province of Asia Minor.

**AD 284–305**  Reign of the emperor Diocletian, who divides the Roman Empire into eastern and western administrative branches and shifts the focus of power eastward by establishing Nicomedia (İzmit) as a secondary, eastern capital.

**325**  The Ecumenical Council of Nicaea (İznik) meets in the first attempt to establish an orthodox Christian doctrine.

**330** The emperor Constantine establishes Christianity as the state religion and moves the capital of the Roman Empire from Rome to the town of Byzantium, which is greatly enlarged and renamed Constantinople (City of Constantine).

**527–63** Reign of Justinian I. The Byzantine empire reaches its military and cultural apogee. Aya Sofya, then known as Hagia Sophia, is rebuilt and rebuilt again.

**674–78** Arab invaders sweep through the Byzantine empire and lay siege to Constantinople before being repulsed.

**1037** The Seljuk Turks, nomadic tribes from central Asia recently converted to Islam, create their first state in the Middle East.

**1071** The Byzantine emperor Romanos IV is defeated by the Seljuk sultan Alp Arslan at the Battle of Manzikert (Malazgirt), opening Anatolia to Turkish settlement.

**1081–1118** Reign of Emperor Alexios I Commenus, who successfully deals with the threats of Venetians and crusaders. His daughter Anna chronicles the history of the time in the *Alexiad*.

**1204** Constantinople is sacked by the Fourth Crusade, the Byzantine emperor is expelled, and the Latin Empire of Constantinople is established.

**1243** The Seljuk sultan is defeated by Genghis Khan's Golden Horde at Kosedag, and the Seljuk Empire disintegrates into petty states.

**1261** The Byzantine emperor Michael Palaeologus is restored to a greatly weakened throne.

**1300** Traditional date of the foundation of the Ottoman Empire at Bursa under Osman I (1258–1326). Over the next century Osman and his sons conquer much of Anatolia and southeastern Europe.

**1402** The Mongol leader Tamerlane (Timur) defeats the Ottoman emperor Bayezit near Ankara, leading to a decade of civil war among his sons.

**1453** Constantinople, the remainder of the once mighty Byzantine Empire, falls to the Ottoman sultan Mehmet II.

**1462** Mehmet II begins building a new palace at Topkapı.

**1520–66** Reign of Süleyman the Magnificent, under whom the Ottoman Empire stretches from Iraq to Algeria. Ottoman culture reaches new heights, epitomized by the magnificent buildings of the architect Sinan.

**1571** The defeat of the Ottoman fleet at Lepanto by an alliance of European states dents the legend of Turkish invulnerability.

**1609** Work begins on the building of the Blue Mosque in Constantinople.

**1683** The failure of the Ottoman siege of Vienna means that the high point of Turkish expansion into Europe has already been reached and marks the beginning of a decline. Over the next century most of eastern Europe is detached from the empire.

**1774** The Treaty of Kuchuk Kainarji (Küçük Kaynarca) brings the Ottoman empire under the influence of Catherine the Great's Russia, and the Eastern question is posed for the first time: Who will get the Ottoman lands when the empire falls?

**1807** Sultan Selim II is overthrown by the Janissaries, the Ottoman praetorian guard, whose influence has grown to dominate the imperial court.

**1826** The sultan Mahmut II (1808–1839) massacres the Janissaries in the Hippodrome and attempts to introduce reforms, including compulsory male education; but the empire continues to disintegrate under the forces of nationalism.

**1853–55** The Crimean War. Britain and France support "the sick man of Europe" in a bid to prevent Russian expansion into the Mediterranean. Florence Nightingale nurses the sick and wounded at Scutari (Üsküdar).

**1876–1909** Reign of Sultan Abdül Hamid II, who begins as a constitutionally minded liberal and ends as a despot.

**1877–78** The Western powers come to the aid of the Ottomans after they are defeated in another Russo-Turkish war, but most of the empire's territory in Europe is lost.

**1889** Birth of Mustafa Kemal.

**1908** The revolution by the "Young Turks" compels Abdül Hamid to grant a new representative constitution.

**1909** Abdül Hamid reneges on his reforms and is deposed by the Young Turks, who replace him with his brother, Mehmet V, the first constitutional sultan.

**1911–13** The disastrous Balkan Wars discredit the liberal movement, and a military government takes power under Enver Pasha.

**914–18** Enver Pasha's decision to enter World War I on the side of the Central Powers precipitates the final collapse of the Ottoman empire. Despite repulsing an Allied landing at Gallipoli, the Turkish armed forces are resoundingly defeated, and the Ottomans are forced to accept humiliating peace terms, including the occupation of Constantinople.

**1919–22** Greek forces invade western Anatolia and are finally defeated by General Mustafa Kemal, the hero of the Turkish resistance at Gallipoli.

**1922** The Mudanya armistice recognizes the territorial integrity of Anatolia. Under the leadership of Mustafa Kemal, the sultanate is abolished, and Mehmet VI, the last sultan, goes into exile.

**1923** October 29: The Turkish Republic is proclaimed, with Ankara as its capital and Mustafa Kemal as its first president and leader of the sole political party, the Republican People's Party.

**1924–34** Mustafa Kemal, soon to be renamed Atatürk (Father of the Turks), introduces sweeping reforms, including the secularization of the legal system, the banning of the fez and the veil, the enfranchisement of women, the introduction of a Latin alphabet and calendar, and the introduction of surnames.

**1930** The name *Istanbul* is officially adopted.

**1938** Atatürk dies.

**1939–45** Turkey remains neutral throughout most of World War II, only declaring war on Germany in the final months in order to secure a seat at the new United Nations, of which the country becomes a founding member.

**1950** Other parties are allowed to stand in the general elections, and Adnan Menderes is elected prime minister as leader of the Justice Party. But the transition to multiparty democracy proves problematic as mounting civil unrest prompts three military coups over the next 30 years.

**1974** Turkey invades Cyprus in the wake of a failed, Greek-sponsored military coup, resulting in the island's partition.

**1980** The republic's third military coup brings Chief of Staff Kenan Evren to power. Turgut Özal, a U.S.-educated engineer, takes control of the economy and introduces radical, Western-oriented free-market reforms.

**1983** Turgut Özal is elected prime minister in the first postcoup elections.

**1987** Turkey applies for full membership in the European Union.

**1993** Tansu Çiller is appointed as Turkey's first female prime minister, succeeding Süleyman Demirel, who replaces the late Turgut Özal as president.

**1995** The pro-Islamic Welfare Party emerges as the largest party in December elections, but with only 21% of the vote, it is still far from a majority in parliament.

**1996** Turkey moves closer to economic integration with the European Union following a comprehensive free-trade agreement. The collapse of attempts by other parties to form a government allows the Welfare Party to take power at the head of a coalition with Tansu Çiller's True Path Party. Welfare Party chairman Necmettin Erbakan becomes Turkey's first avowedly Islamist prime minister, to the alarm of the country's staunchly secularist military.

**1997** The Welfare Party–led coalition is forced to resign following behind-the-scenes pressure from the military. It is replaced by a three-party minority coalition headed by Mesut Yılmaz, chairman of the center-right Motherland Party.

**1999** After being captured by Turkish agents on February 15, Abdullah Ocalan, head of the separatist Kurdistan Workers Party (PKK), announces an end to the PKK's 15 year-old armed struggle for Kurdish autonomy, raising hopes for a peaceful solution to a conflict that has cost an estimated 35,000 lives.

In the April 18 general elections the National Movement Party's (NMP) combination of ultranationalism and commitment to Islam enables it to more than double its votes by attracting former supporters of the Welfare Party and finish second behind the nationalist-left Democratic Left Party (DLP). The DLP and NMP subsequently form a coalition government with the conservative Motherland Party as a minority partner.

On August 17, an earthquake measuring 7.4 on the Richter scale hits the industrial town of İzmit just outside Istanbul, killing an estimated 25,000, leaving half a million homeless, and traumatizing the entire nation. On November 12, another earthquake, this time measuring 7.2 on the Richter scale, hits the northwestern provincial town of Düzce, killing another 1,000 people and leaving tens of thousands homeless.

On December 10, 1999, Turkey is finally included on the official list of candidates for EU membership.

# WHAT TO READ AND WATCH BEFORE YOU GO

Homer's *Iliad* is still the most evocative reading on the Trojan War and the key players of Turkish antiquity. The keenest insight into the ancient ruins that you may encounter on your trip comes from George Bean, author of *Aegean Turkey, Turkey Beyond the Meander, Lycian Turkey,* and *Turkey's Southern Shore.* John Julius Norwich's three-volume *Byzantium* chronicles the rise and fall of one of history's great empires.

Mary Lee Settle provides a vision of Turkey that is both panoramic and personal in *Turkish Reflections.* The book marks Settle's return to the country that was the setting for her novel *Blood Tie,* a 1978 National Book Award winner. Dame Freya Stark, one of the most remarkable travelers of our times, chronicles her visits to Turkey in *The Journey's Echo* and *Alexander's Path.* Only a piece of Mark Twain's *Innocents Abroad* is about Turkey, but it offers a witty glimpse of the country as it used to be. Hans Christian Andersen also wrote a memorable travelogue, *A Poet's Bazaar: A Journey to Greece, Turkey and Up the Danube.* Agatha Christie's *Murder on the Orient Express* provides the proper atmosphere for a trip to Istanbul. You can still visit Istanbul's Pera Palas Hotel, the terminus of the famous train, where Christie herself stayed. *The Letters and Works of Lady Mary Wortley Montagu* is a significant and entertaining book that delightfully documents life in 19th-century Ottoman Turkey—including its much-quoted passages about the harem—through the eyes of Lady Montagu, the wife of a consul. Good books on modern Turkey's history and politics are harder to find. One of the best is *Turkey: A Modern History,* by Erik J. Zürcher. For a more gossipy, journalistic account of republican Turkish politics, read *Turkey Unveiled,* by Nicole and Hugh Pope. Irfan Orga's exquisite *Portrait of a Turkish Family* provides an evocative true-life memoir of the impact of the upheavals of the early 20th century on his own family.

More books have been written about Istanbul than about the rest of Turkey. Two of the finest portraits of the city are the excellent *Constantinople: City of the World's Desire 1453–1924,* by Philip Mansel, and *Istanbul: The Imperial City,* by John Freely. *Istanbul: A Traveler's Companion,* by Laurence Kelly, contains a fascinating collection of contemporary writing about the city through the ages. If you love spy novels, *Istanbul Intrigues,* by Barry Rubin, paints a vivid picture of real cloak-and-dagger intrigues in the city during World War II.

For an introduction to Turkish literature, track down a copy of *An Anthology of Turkish Literature,* by Kemal Silay. Or if you want to plunge straight into a complete novel, look out for *Anatolian Tales* or *Mehmet, My Hawk,* by Yaşar Kemal, one of the country's most famous modern novelists. Orhan Pamuk's *White Castle* and *The New Life* are two examples of works by this contemporary writer, who has great talent and technical expertise.

Western movies tend to play up Turkey's exotic aspects. Director Joseph L. Mankiewicz's *Five Fingers* (1952), an Ankara-based spy thriller based on the book *Operation Cicero,* by C. L. Moyzisch, is noteworthy both for its action and for its clever dialogue ("Counter espionage is the highest form of gossip"). Peter Ustinov won an Academy Award for best supporting actor for his performance in the Jules Dassin–directed museum-heist film *Topkapi* (1964), which also stars Melina Mercouri and Maximilian Schell. Alan Parker directed the film version of *Midnight Express* (1978), about Billy Hayes's days in a Turkish prison following a drug conviction. The film's relentlessly horrific depiction of Hayes's experiences (some of which do not occur in his memoir) made the Turkish government exceedingly gun-shy about allowing Western moviemakers into the country. When *Midnight Express* was finally shown on Turkish TV in the mid-1990s, newscasters interviewed people in the street, who wept over the country's portrayal on-screen and the influence they feared the film may have had on perceptions of Turkey in the West. Peter Weir's *Gallipoli* (1981) follows the exploits of two Australian soldiers preparing for and fighting in the historic battles in the Dardanelles during World War I. Critics generally praise the film, though some have noted a lack of sensitivity to the Turks.

# Western Turkey and the Greek Isles

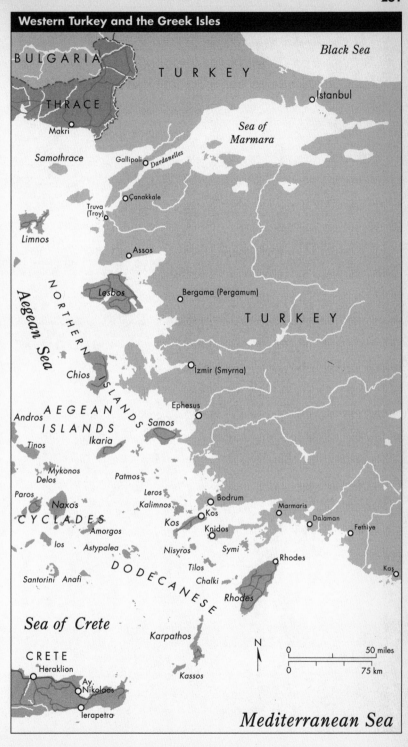

BULGARIA

THRACE

Makri

TURKEY

Black Sea

Istanbul

Sea of Marmara

Samothrace

Gallipoli

Dardanelles

Çanakkale

Truva (Troy)

Limnos

Assos

Lesbos

Bergama (Pergamum)

TURKEY

Aegean Sea

NORTHERN ISLANDS

Chios

Izmir (Smyrna)

AEGEAN ISLANDS

Andros

Samos

Ephesus

Tinos

Ikaria

Mykonos

Delos

Patmos

Paros

Leros

Bodrum

Marmaris

Naxos

Kalimnos

Kos

Dalaman

Fethiye

CYCLADES

Kos

Knidos

Ios

Amorgos

Nisyros

Symi

Astypalea

Rhodes

Kas

Santorini

Anafi

Tilos

Chalki

DODECANESE

Rhodes

Sea of Crete

Karpathos

N

CRETE

Heraklion

0        50 miles

Ay. Nikolaos

0        75 km

Ierapetra

Kassos

Mediterranean Sea

**Turkey**

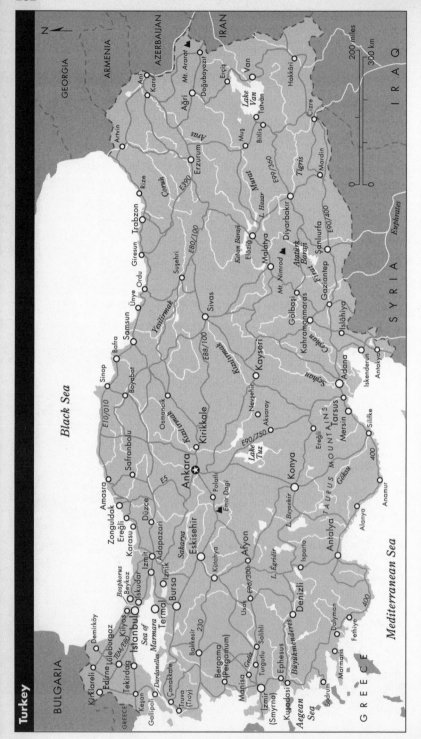

N

BULGARIA

GEORGIA

ARMENIA

AZERBAIJAN

IRAN

IRAQ

SYRIA

GREECE

Black Sea

Sea of Marmara

Aegean Sea

Mediterranean Sea

Bosphorus

200 miles
300 km

Kırklareli
Demirköy
Edirne
Lüleburgaz
Tekirdağ
Keşan
Gallipoli
GREECE
Çanakkale
Truva (Troy)
Dardanelles
Beykoz
Kilyos
Üsküdar
İstanbul
Termal
Bursa
İznik
İzmit
Adapazarı
Düzce
Karasu
Ereğli
Zonguldak
Amasra
Safranbolu
Sinop
Boyabat
Bafra
Samsun
Ünye
Ordu
Giresun
Trabzon
Rize
Arvin
Artvin
Ani
Kars
Ağrı
Mt. Ararat
Doğubayazıt
Erçiş
Van
Lake Van
Tatvan
Bitlis
Muş
Hakkâri
Cizre
Mardin
Şanlıurfa
Gaziantep
İslâhiye
Antakya
İskenderun
Adana
Tarsus
Mersin
Silifke
Anamur
Alanya
Antalya
Fethiye
Marmaris
Dalyan
Bodrum
Kuşadası
Ephesus
İzmir (Smyrna)
Manisa
Turgutlu
Salihli
Uşak
Denizli
Afyon
Kütahya
Eskişehir
Sakarya
Balıkesir
Bergama (Pergamum)
Büyükmenderes
Gediz
Isparta
L. Eğridir
L. Beyşehir
Konya
Ereğli
Emir Dağı
Polatlı
Ankara
Kırıkkale
Lake Tuz
Aksaray
Nevşehir
Kayseri
Kızılırmak
Sivas
Suşehri
Yeşilırmak
Osmancık
Çorum
Kızılırmak
Kahramanmaraş
Gölbaşı
Malatya
Mt. Nimrod
Elazığ
L. Hazar
Atatürk Barajı
Keban Barajı
Diyarbakır
Fırat
Tigris
Euphrates
Murat
Aras
Erzurum
Çoruh
Göksu
Seyhan
Ceyhan
TAURUS MOUNTAINS

E80/100
E90
E88/100
E90/750
E96/300
E5
E10/010
TEM/E80
E99/360
E97/100
230
400

✦ Ankara
▲ Mt. Ararat
▲ Mt. Nimrod
▲ Emir Dağı

# ESSENTIAL INFORMATION

## AIR TRAVEL

### BOOKING

When you book, **look for nonstop flights** and **remember that "direct" flights stop at least once.** Try to avoid connecting flights, which require a change of plane.

### CARRIERS

You will probably find that THY/Turkish Airlines, the national flag carrier of Turkey, offers the most nonstops, though an international carrier based in your home country is more likely to have better connections to your hometown and serve a greater number of gateway cities. Third-country carriers (a foreign carrier based in a country other than your own or Turkey) sometimes offer the lowest fares.

Turkish Airlines operates an extensive domestic network, with nine flights daily on weekdays between Istanbul and Ankara alone. In summer many flights to coastal resorts are added. Try to arrive at the airport at least an hour and a half before takeoff because security checks at the entrance to the terminal can be time consuming; **checked luggage must be identified by boarding passengers before it is put on the plane,** and all unidentified luggage is left behind and checked for bombs or firearms.

➤ MAJOR AIRLINES: From the U.S.: **Air Canada** (☎ 800/776–3000). **Air France** (☎ 800/237–2747). **British Airways** (☎ 800/247–9297). **Delta** (☎ 800/241–4141). **Lufthansa** (☎ 800/645–3880). **Northwest/ KLM** (☎ 800/447–4747). **Olympic Airlines** (☎ 800/223–1226). **Swissair** (☎ 800/221–4750). **TWA** (☎ 800/ 221–2000 in the U.S.; 800/892– 4141). **THY/Turkish Airlines** (☎ 212/339–9650; 800/874–8875; 212/ 252–1106 in Istanbul; 212/663– 6363 for reservations).

➤ FROM CANADA: **Air Canada** (☎ 800/776–3000). **British Airways** (☎ 800/247–9297). **Air France** (☎ 800/237–2747). **Alitalia** (☎ 800/223– 5730). **Finnair** (☎ 800/950–5000). **KLM** (☎ 800/374–7747). **Lufthansa** (☎ 800/645–3880). **Olympic Air** (☎ 800/223–1226). **SAS** (☎ 800/ 221–2350). **Swissair** (☎ 800/221– 4750). **TWA** (☎ 800/221–2000 or 800/892–4141).

➤ FROM THE U.K.: **British Airways** (☎ 020/8897–4000; 0345/222–111 outside London) and **Turkish Airlines** (✉ 11–12 Hanover St., London W1R 9HF, ☎ 020/7499–9249 or 020/ 7499–4499) fly to Istanbul. **Lufthansa** (☎ 0345/737–747) flies from London to Istanbul, Ankara, and İzmir, all via Frankfurt.

➤ WITHIN TURKEY: **Istanbul Airlines** (☎ 212/231–7526). **Turkish Airlines** (THY, ☎ 212/252–1106; 212/663– 6363 for reservations).

### CHECK-IN & BOARDING

Assuming that not everyone with a ticket will show up, airlines routinely overbook planes. When everyone does show up, airlines ask for volunteers to give up their seats. In return, these volunteers usually get a certificate for a free flight and are rebooked on the next flight out. If there are not enough volunteers, the airline must choose who will be denied boarding. The first to get bumped are passengers who checked in late and those flying on discounted tickets, so **get to the gate and check in as early as possible,** especially during peak periods.

At most airports you will be asked to **show your passport** before you are allowed to check in.

### CUTTING COSTS

The least-expensive airfares to Turkey must usually be purchased in advance and are nonrefundable. It's smart to call a number of airlines, and when you are quoted a good price, book it on the spot—the same fare may not be available the next day. Always check different routings and look into using different airports. Travel agents, especially low-fare specialists (☞ Discounts & Deals, *below*), are helpful.

Consolidators are another good source. They buy tickets for scheduled international flights at reduced rates from the airlines, then sell them at prices that beat the best fare available directly from the airlines, usually without restrictions. Sometimes you can even get your money back if you need to return the ticket. Carefully read the fine print detailing penalties for changes and cancellations, and confirm your consolidator reservation with the airline.

➤ CONSOLIDATORS: **Cheap Tickets** (☎ 800/377–1000). **Discount Airline Ticket Service** (☎ 800/576–1600). **Unitravel** (☎ 800/325–2222). **Up & Away Travel** (☎ 212/889–2345). **World Travel Network** (☎ 800/409–6753).

## ENJOYING THE FLIGHT

For more legroom request an emergency-aisle seat. Don't sit in the row in front of the emergency aisle or in front of a bulkhead, where seats may not recline. If you have dietary concerns, ask for special meals when booking. These can be vegetarian, low-cholesterol, or kosher, for example. On long flights try to maintain a normal routine to help fight jet lag. At night get some sleep. By day eat light meals, drink water (not alcohol), and move around the cabin to stretch your legs.

## FLYING TIMES

The flying time to Istanbul is 10 hours from New York, 13 hours from Chicago, and 15 hours from Los Angeles. The flight from Toronto to Istanbul takes 11½ hours. Flying time from London is 4 hours.

## HOW TO COMPLAIN

If your baggage goes astray or your flight goes awry, complain right away. Most carriers require that you file a claim immediately.

➤ AIRLINE COMPLAINTS: U.S. Department of Transportation **Aviation Consumer Protection Division** (✉ C-75, Room 4107, Washington, DC 20590, ☎ 202/366–2220, airconsumer@ost.dot.gov, www.dot.gov/airconsumer). **Federal Aviation Administration Consumer Hotline** (☎ 800/322–7873).

## AIRPORTS

Turkey's major airport is **Atatürk Airport,** about 18 km (12 mi) from Istanbul. Adana, Adıyaman, Ağrı, Ankara, Antalya, Batman, Çanakkale, Dalaman, Denizli, Diyarbakır, Edremit, Elazığ, Erzincan, Erzurum, Eskişehir, Gaziantep, İsparta, İzmir, Kars, Kayseri, Konya, Malatya, Muş, Nevşehir, Samsun, Siirt, Sinop, Sivas, Şanlırfa, Tokat, Trabzon, Uşak, and Van all have smaller domestic airports, although flights in and out of many are infrequent. A new, and much larger, international terminal was opened at Istanbul's Atatürk Airport in January 2000, replacing its overstrained and rather shabby predecessor, which was converted into the new domestic terminal.

## BIKE TRAVEL

Bicycling is very limited in Turkey. Some tourist areas have places where you can rent bikes; ask at the tourist office or your hotel. Bicycling in Istanbul and other major cities is not advised because of traffic, pollution, and poor road conditions.

## BIKES IN FLIGHT

Most airlines accommodate bikes as luggage, provided they are dismantled and boxed. For bike boxes, often free at bike shops, you'll pay about $5 at airlines (at least $100 for bike bags). International travelers can sometimes substitute a bike for a piece of checked luggage at no charge; otherwise, the cost is about $100.

## BOAT & FERRY TRAVEL

In some regions, particularly the Black Sea and greater Istanbul area, ferries are the most efficient means of getting around. On the Aegean and Mediterranean coasts, boats are used mostly for leisurely sightseeing and yachting.

Turkish Maritime Lines operates both car-ferry and cruise ships from Istanbul to various points in the country; cruises last from a day to a week, and ships are comfortable, rather like moderate-class Turkish hotels. Turkish Maritime's Black Sea ferry sails from June through September on Monday from the Karaköy dock in Istanbul to Samsun and Trabzon. The 40-hour one-way Istanbul–Trabzon trip costs about $30 for a reclining seat, $40 to $95 for a private cabin, plus $60 for a car. The Istanbul–İzmir car ferry down the Aegean Coast departs every Friday year-round. The 19-hour one-way trip costs from $50 for a Pullman seat to $90 for a cabin berth, plus $50 for a car. Both tourists and locals take these trips.

Yachting or sailing trips can be arranged in a number of ways: through tour operators with contacts and colleagues in Turkey (☞ Tour Operators, *below*); through tour operators in Turkey (☞ A to Z sections *in* individual chapters); or through private boat owners at the docks. No matter how you choose a sailing trip, make sure you have confidence in the people with whom you are working: The problem with simply finding someone at the dock is that you won't necessarily know anything about the crew, the boat, or the other passengers who will be on board. Yacht agencies are also listed with the Turkish Tourist Office (☞ Visitor Information, *below*). In addition, the Marmaris Tourist Office (☞ *below* and the Mediterranean Coast A to Z *in* Chapter 5) can be helpful.

➤ BOAT & FERRY INFORMATION: **Turkish Maritime Lines** (✉ Rıhtım Cad. 1, Karaköy, ☎ 212/249–9222 for reservations) or **Sunquest Holidays Ltd.** (✉ Alsine House, Alsine St., London W12 8AW, ☎ 020/8800–5455). Cruises are in great demand, so make your reservations well in advance.

➤ YACHT TOUR INFORMATION: **Marmaris Tourist Office** (☎ 252/412–1035). **Turkish Tourist Office** (☞ Visitor Information, *below*). *See also* Tour Operators, *below,* and A to Z sections *in* individual chapters.

## BUS TRAVEL

In Turkey, buses are much faster than most trains and provide inexpensive

service almost around the clock between all cities and towns; they're fairly comfortable and sometimes air-conditioned. All are run by private companies, each of which has its own fixed fares for different routes and, usually more significantly, standards of comfort. Most bus companies, such as Varan, Ulusoy, Koç, and Pamukkale, which go between major cities and resort areas, can be counted on for fairly comfortable air-conditioned service with snacks.

Note that express buses running between major cities are significantly faster and more comfortable than local buses; look for one of these if you're traveling long distances.

Most intercity buses, particularly those run by the larger companies, are supposedly nonsmoking, although the rule is sometimes ignored—even by the driver! For greater comfort on overnight trips, buy two seats and stretch out.

For very short trips or for getting around within a city, take a minibus or a *dolmuş* (shared taxi). Both are inexpensive and comfortable.

### FARES & SCHEDULES

The bus fare for Istanbul–Ankara costs about $10–$15 and for Istanbul–İzmir, from $12 to $18. Fares usually include *su* (bottled water) and/or tea, though you may want to bring your own water in case beverages are not available.

### PAYING

Tickets are sold at stands in a town's *otogar* (central bus terminal); the usual procedure is to go to the bus station and **shop around for the best bus.** All seats are reserved. When buying your ticket, tell the ticket agent that you would like to sit on the shady side of the bus; even on air-conditioned buses the sun can feel oppressive on a long trip.

## BUSINESS HOURS

### BANKS & OFFICES

Banks are normally open weekdays from 8:30 until noon or 12:30, depending on the bank, and from 1:30 until 5. However, selected branches of some Turkish banks now remain open during the middle of the day and for a few hours on Saturday. Many banks throughout Turkey, even those in small towns, provide 24-hour service from ATM machines.

## GAS STATIONS

Most gas stations are open from early morning until late evening, commonly from 6 AM to 10 PM, although there are no fixed rules and there can be considerable variation. In the larger cities and along major highways it is usually possible to find gas stations open 24 hours. Look for the sign 24 SAAT AÇIK.

## MUSEUMS & SIGHTS

Museums are generally open Tuesday through Sunday from 9:30 AM until 5 or 5:30 PM and closed on Monday. Palaces are open the same hours but are generally closed Thursday. Many museums stop selling tickets 30 minutes before the actual closing time. Sometimes this is explicitly stated in the official times, but very often, particularly away from the major sites, it is unofficial and just a way for museum staffers to make sure they get away on time. To be on the safe side, try to ensure that you arrive at least 45 minutes before closing time.

## SHOPS

Shops and bazaars are usually open Monday through Saturday from 9:30 to 7 and closed on Sunday. Smaller shops often close for lunch between 1 and 2, although all large stores and even most small shops in the major cities remain open throughout the day. However, in tourist areas, shops may stay open until 9 PM and all day Sunday.

## CAMERAS & PHOTOGRAPHY

Photography of what are deemed militarily sensitive sites is expressly forbidden in Turkey. Often you will see red signs with the silhouette of a soldier and a warning in Turkish, English, and German not to take photographs. But the definition of military sensitivity can be quite elastic. If in doubt, particularly when there are military personnel—such as guards—present, ask by gesturing with your camera before putting it to your eye. In rural areas, where children are usually falling over each other to have

their picture taken, women may be reluctant. Again, ask permission before taking a photograph.

➤ PHOTO HELP: **Kodak Information Center** (☎ 800/242–2424). *Kodak Guide to Shooting Great Travel Pictures,* available in bookstores or from Fodor's Travel Publications (☎ 800/533–6478; $18.00 plus $5.50 shipping).

## EQUIPMENT PRECAUTIONS

Always **keep your film and tape out of the sun.** Carry an extra supply of batteries, and **be prepared to turn on your camera or camcorder** to prove to security personnel that the device is real. Always **ask for hand inspection of film,** which becomes clouded after repeated exposure to airport X-ray machines, and **keep videotapes away from metal detectors.**

## VIDEOS

Most Turkish video players use VHS PAL. Most types of cassettes for camcorders (digital, VHS-C, 8 mm, etc.) are available in Turkey, but prices vary enormously.

## CAR RENTAL

Rates in Istanbul begin at $35 a day and $250 a week for an economy car with unlimited mileage. Gas costs about 75¢ per liter. The majority of rental cars are stick shift, though it is possible to get an automatic with advance arrangements. A wide variety of mostly European car makes are available, ranging from the locally manufactured Tofaş (a subsidiary of Fiat) to Renault and Mercedes.

In many places, such as Cappadocia and the Turquoise Coast, you may want to rent a car so you can go exploring on your own instead of having to be part of a guided tour. When traveling long distances, you may find it easier to take public transportation (either a bus or plane)—unless you plan on sightseeing en route, because a car will give you more scheduling freedom. For more information about driving in Turkey, *see* Car Travel, *below.*

➤ MAJOR AGENCIES: **Alamo** (☎ 800/ 522–9696; 020/8759–6200 in the U.K.). **Avis** (☎ 800/331–1084; 800/ 331–1084 in Canada; 02/9353–9000 in Australia; 09/525–1982 in New Zealand). **Budget** (☎ 800/527–0700;0870/607–5000 in the U.K., through affiliate Europcar). **Dollar** (☎ 800/800–6000; 0124/622–0111 in the U.K., through affiliate Sixt Kenning; 02/9223–1444 in Australia). **Hertz** (☎ 800/654–3001; 800/263–0600 in Canada; 020/8897–2072 in the U.K.; 02/9669–2444 in Australia; 09/256–8690 in New Zealand). **National Car Rental** (☎ 800/227–7368; 020/8680–4800 in the U.K., where it is known as National Europe).

## CUTTING COSTS

To get the best deal, **book through a travel agent who will shop around.**

Do **look into wholesalers,** companies that do not own fleets but rent in bulk from those that do and often offer better rates than traditional car-rental operations. Payment must be made before you leave home.

➤ WHOLESALERS: **Auto Europe** (☎ 207/842–2000 or 800/223–5555, FAX 800/235–6321, www.autoeurope. com). **Kemwel Holiday Autos** (☎ 800/678–0678, FAX 914/825–3160, www.kemwel.com).

## INSURANCE

When driving a rented car, you are generally responsible for any damage to or loss of the vehicle as well as for any property damage or personal injury that you may cause. Many agencies provide optional insurance for an extra charge; before you opt for such extra insurance, see what coverage your personal auto-insurance policy and credit cards already provide.

## REQUIREMENTS & RESTRICTIONS

In Turkey **a driver's license issued in most foreign countries is acceptable.**

## SURCHARGES

Before arranging to pick up a car in one city and leave it in another, **ask about drop-off charges or one-way service fees,** which can be substantial. Note, too, that some rental agencies charge extra if you return the car before the time specified in your contract. To avoid a hefty refueling fee, **fill the tank just before you turn in the car,** but be aware that gas stations near the rental outlet may overcharge.

## CAR TRAVEL

Turkey has one of the world's highest auto accident rates. That said, having a car allows you the freedom that traveling by bus, train, or plane does not. The country has 40,000 km (25,000 mi) of paved and generally well-maintained highways, but off the intercity highways, surfaces are often poor and potholes frequent. Most major highways are two lanes, and cars pass each other with some frequency. Sometimes roads will have a third lane meant for passing; although the lane is usually labeled with which direction of traffic it is meant to use it, drivers don't always follow this rule. So be extremely careful when passing. In general, always expect the unexpected. Don't, for example, always assume that one-way streets are one way in practice or that because you wouldn't do something, such as trying to pass in a dangerous situation, the other driver wouldn't either.

Driving in Istanbul and other major cities is best avoided. You should also avoid driving on highways after dusk because drivers often drive without turning their lights on. Vehicles may be stopped on the roads in complete darkness.

Highways are numbered or specified by direction (e.g., the route to Antalya). Trans-European highways have a European number as well as a Turkish number (E6 is the European number for Turkish Route D100, for example). Note that route numbers may be inconsistent from map to map.

Note that **archaeological and historic sites are indicated by yellow signposts.**

## AUTO CLUBS

➤ IN AUSTRALIA: **Australian Automobile Association** (☎ 02/6247–7311).

➤ IN CANADA: **Canadian Automobile Association** (CAA; ☎ 613/247–0117).

➤ IN NEW ZEALAND: **New Zealand Automobile Association** (☎ 09/377–4660).

➤ IN THE U.K.: **Automobile Association** (AA; ☎ 0990/500–600). **Royal Automobile Club** (RAC; ☎ 0990/722–722 for membership; 0345/121–345 for insurance).

➤ IN THE U.S.: **American Automobile Association** (☎ 800/564–6222).

## EMERGENCY SERVICES

A road rescue service is available on some highways; before you embark on a journey, ask your car rental agency or hotel how to contact it in case of an emergency. Most major car manufacturers in Turkey (for example, Renault, Fiat, and Opel/General Motors) also have roaming 24-hour services.

Turkish mechanics in the villages can usually manage to get you going again, at least until you reach a city, where you can have the car fully repaired. Most Turkish gas stations have at least one staff member with some knowledge of car mechanics who can diagnose problems and provide "first aid" or advice, such as directions to the nearest mechanic. If a gas station attendant fixes a minor problem, it is customary to give him a small tip of about $5–$10 depending on the time and effort expended.

In urban areas entire streets are given over to car-repair shops run by teams of experts—one specializes in radiators, another in electrical fittings, and another in steering columns. It's not expensive to have repairs done, but it's customary to give a small tip to the person who does the repairs. If you don't want to wait for the work to be done, **take all car documents with you when you leave the shop.**

## GASOLINE

Shell, British Petroleum, Total, Elf, and two Turkish oil companies, Petrol Ofisi and Türkpetrol, operate stations in Turkey. Many of those on the main highways stay open around the clock, others from 6 AM to 10 PM.

## ROAD CONDITIONS

Throughout Turkey signposts are few, lighting scarce, rural roads sometimes rough, and city traffic chaotic, and the country's accident rate is one of the highest in the world.

In the countryside watch out for drivers passing on a curve or on the top of a hill, and beware of carts, difficult to see at night, and motorcycles weaving in and out of traffic while carrying entire families.

Urban streets and highways are jammed with vehicles operated by high-speed lunatics and drivers who constantly honk their horns. In Istanbul avoid the many small one-way streets—you never know when someone is going to barrel down one of them in the wrong direction. Better yet, leave your car in a garage and use public transportation or take taxis. Parking is another problem in the cities and larger towns.

## RULES OF THE ROAD

In general, Turkish driving conforms to Mediterranean customs, with driving on the right and passing on the left. Be prepared for drivers to do anything. Seatbelts are required for front-seat passengers and a good idea for those in back seats. Using a cellular phone while driving is prohibited—but this law is seldom obeyed.

## CHILDREN IN TURKEY

Turkey is not the easiest place to travel with young children. There are long distances to cope with, lots of hiking around rock-strewn ruins, and few child-oriented facilities. Be sure to plan ahead and **involve your youngsters** as you outline your trip. When packing, include things to keep them busy en route. On sightseeing days try to schedule activities of special interest to your children.

However, Turks are traditionally very fond of children, and an eagerness to be of assistance often goes some way to offsetting frustrations at the absence of facilities. Restaurants are generally casual and accommodating to families, and diapers and baby food are easy to find in most towns. If you are renting a car, try to **arrange for a car seat** when you reserve, though it is not guaranteed that every agency will have one available.

## FLYING

If your children are two or older, **ask about children's airfares.** As a general rule, infants under two not occupying a separate seat fly at greatly reduced fares or even for free. When booking, **confirm carry-on allowances** if you're traveling with infants. In general, for babies charged 10% of the adult fare you are allowed one carry-on bag and a collapsible stroller; if the flight is full, the stroller may have to be checked, or you may be limited to less.

Experts agree it's a good idea to use safety seats aloft for children weighing less than 40 pounds. Airlines set their own policies: U.S. carriers usually require that a child with safety seat be ticketed, even if he or she is young enough to ride free, since the seats must be strapped into regular seats. Do **check your airline's policy about using safety seats during take-off and landing.** And since safety seats are not allowed everywhere in the plane, get your seat assignments early.

When reserving, **request children's meals or a freestanding bassinet** if you need them. But note that bulk-head seats, where you must sit to use the bassinet, may lack an overhead bin or storage space on the floor.

## LODGING

Most hotels in Turkey allow children under a certain age to stay in their parents' room at no extra charge, but others charge for them as extra adults; be sure to **find out the cutoff age for children's discounts.** In general, you can't count on Turkish hotels to have cribs or cots, so be sure to request them in advance.

## SIGHTS & ATTRACTIONS

Places that are especially appealing to children are indicated by a rubber duckie icon in the margin.

## COMPUTERS ON THE ROAD

Many of the better hotels have some means for guests to get on-line access, as does the youth hostel in Istanbul; ask when you make a reservation. In addition, larger post offices in major cities may have connection facilities. In an increasing number of places, especially larger cities and resorts, you may also be able to find a local Internet café. Make sure to **contact your Internet provider before you go** to find out if it has an access number in Turkey. If you have a GSM mobile,

you should be able to plug it into your computer and access the Internet while in Turkey.

Although it is possible to find spare batteries for laptops, it is not easy, particularly outside the major cities, and you're better off bringing one with you. If you have hardware problems with your computer while in Turkey, most major manufacturers have representatives in the major cities, although repair prices tend to be high.

Most important, remember that the Turkish electricity supply runs on 220 volts. Any equipment set up for U.S. voltage needs a good converter, and you are advised to bring one with you. Many laptops are equipped with built-in converters, but check with your computer dealer before you leave home to make sure you have what you need.

## CONSUMER PROTECTION

Whenever shopping or buying travel services in Turkey, **pay with a major credit card if you can** so you can cancel payment or get reimbursed if there's a problem. If you're doing business with a particular company for the first time, **contact your local Better Business Bureau and the attorney general's offices** in your own state and the company's home state, as well. Have any complaints been filed? Finally, if you're buying a package or tour, always **consider travel insurance** that includes default coverage (☞ Insurance, *below*).

➤ BBBs: **Council of Better Business Bureaus** (✉ 4200 Wilson Blvd., Suite 800, Arlington, VA 22203, ☎ 703/ 276–0100, FAX 703/525–8277 www.bbb.org).

## CUSTOMS & DUTIES

When shopping, **keep receipts** for all purchases. Upon reentering the country, **be ready to show customs officials what you've bought.** If you feel a duty is incorrect or object to the way your clearance was handled, note the inspector's badge number and ask to see a supervisor. If the problem isn't resolved, write to the appropriate authorities, beginning with the port director at your point of entry.

## IN TURKEY

Turkish customs officials rarely look through tourists' luggage on arrival. You are allowed to bring in 400 cigarettes, 50 cigars, 200 grams of tobacco, 1½ kilograms of instant coffee, 500 grams of tea, and 2½ liters of alcohol. Items in the duty-free shops in Turkish airports, for international arrivals, are usually less expensive than they are in European airports or in flight.

## IN AUSTRALIA

Australian residents who are 18 or older may bring home $A400 worth of souvenirs and gifts (including jewelry), 250 cigarettes or 250 grams of tobacco, and 1,125 milliliters of alcohol (including wine, beer, and spirits). Residents under 18 may bring back $A200 worth of goods. Prohibited items include meat products. Seeds, plants, and fruits need to be declared upon arrival.

➤ INFORMATION: **Australian Customs Service** (Regional Director, ✉ Box 8, Sydney, NSW 2001, ☎ 02/9213–2000, FAX 02/9213–4000, www.customs.gov.au).

## IN CANADA

Canadian residents who have been out of Canada for at least 7 days may bring home C$500 worth of goods duty-free. If you've been away less than 7 days but more than 48 hours, the duty-free allowance drops to C$200; if your trip lasts 24–48 hours, the allowance is C$50. You may not pool allowances with family members. Goods claimed under the C$500 exemption may follow you by mail; those claimed under the lesser exemptions must accompany you. Alcohol and tobacco products may be included in the 7-day and 48-hour exemptions but not in the 24-hour exemption. If you meet the age requirements of the province or territory through which you reenter Canada, you may bring in, duty-free, 1.14 liters (40 imperial ounces) of wine or liquor *or* 24 12-ounce cans or bottles of beer or ale. If you are 16 or older, you may bring in, duty-free, 200 cigarettes and 50 cigars. Check ahead of time with Revenue Canada or the Department of Agriculture for policies regarding meat products, seeds, plants, and fruits.

You may send an unlimited number of gifts worth up to C$60 each duty-free to Canada. Label the package UNSOLICITED GIFT—VALUE UNDER $60. Alcohol and tobacco are excluded.

➤ INFORMATION: **Revenue Canada** (✉ 2265 St. Laurent Blvd. S, Ottawa, Ontario K1G 4K3, ☎ 613/993–0534; 800/461–9999 in Canada, FAX 613/991–4126, www.ccra-adrc.gc.ca).

## IN NEW ZEALAND

Homeward-bound residents 17 or older may bring back $700 worth of souvenirs and gifts. Your duty-free allowance also includes 4.5 liters of wine or beer; one 1,125-milliliter bottle of spirits; and either 200 cigarettes, 250 grams of tobacco, 50 cigars, or a combination of the three up to 250 grams. Prohibited items include meat products, seeds, plants, and fruits.

➤ INFORMATION: **New Zealand Customs** (Custom House, ✉ 50 Anzac Ave., Box 29, Auckland,, ☎ 09/359–6655, FAX 09/359–6732).

## IN THE U.K.

From countries outside the EU, including Turkey, you may bring home, duty-free, 200 cigarettes or 50 cigars; 1 liter of spirits or 2 liters of fortified or sparkling wine or liqueurs; 2 liters of still table wine; 60 ml of perfume; 250 ml of toilet water; plus £136 worth of other goods, including gifts and souvenirs. If returning from outside the EU, prohibited items include meat products, seeds, plants, and fruits.

➤ INFORMATION: **HM Customs and Excise** (✉ Dorset House, Stamford St., Bromley, Kent BR1 1XX, ☎ 020/7202–4227, www.hmce.gov.uk).

## IN THE U.S.

U.S. residents who have been out of the country for at least 48 hours (and who have not used the $400 allowance or any part of it in the past 30 days) may bring home $400 worth of foreign goods duty-free.

U.S. residents 21 and older may bring back 1 liter of alcohol duty-free. In addition, regardless of your age, you are allowed 200 cigarettes and 100 non-Cuban cigars. Antiques, which the U.S. Customs Service defines as objects more than 100 years old, enter duty-free, as do original works of art done entirely by hand, including paintings, drawings, and sculptures.

You may also send packages home duty-free: up to $200 worth of goods for personal use, with a limit of one parcel per addressee per day (except alcohol or tobacco products or perfume worth more than $5); label the package PERSONAL USE and attach a list of its contents and their retail value. Do not label the package UNSOLICITED GIFT, or your duty-free exemption will drop to $100. Mailed items do not affect your duty-free allowance on your return.

➤ INFORMATION: **U.S. Customs Service** (✉ 1300 Pennsylvania Ave. NW, Washington, DC 20229, www. customs.gov; inquiries ☎ 202/354–1000; complaints c/o ✉ 1300 Pennsylvania Ave. NW, Room 5.4D, Washington, DC 20229; registration of equipment c/o ✉ Resource Management, ☎ 202/354–1000).

## DINING

Turkey is not just a geographic bridge between Europe, Asia, and the Middle East; it's a gastronomic one as well. Its cuisine reflects the long history of a people who emigrated from the borders of China to a land mass known as Asia Minor and built an empire that encompassed Arab, Asian, and European lands.

Turkish cuisine is full of vegetables, grains, fresh fish, and seemingly infinite varieties of lamb. Fish and meat are typically served grilled or roasted, although often with inordinate amounts of *yağ* (oil). The core group of seasonings and condiments is garlic, sage, oregano, cumin, mint, dill, lemon, and yogurt, always more yogurt. Turkish yogurt is among the tastiest in the world: Many travelers swear it helps keep their stomachs calm and stable while on the road.

The simplest establishments, Turkey's fast-food joints, are the *kebapcı*, the *dönerci*, and the *pideci*. The first specializes in kebabs—marinated cubes of meat (generally lamb), usually grilled and cooked with vegetables on a skewer. Dönercis provide a quick meal of spicy, spit-roasted sliced lamb, served either as a sandwich or with rice. At the pideci you'll find *pide*, a pizzalike snack made of flat bread topped with either butter, cheese, and egg or with ground lamb and baked in a wood-fired oven. Often these eateries are little more than counters at which you belly up to the bar for instant gratification; on occasion they attain luncheonette status.

*Lokantas* are unpretentious neighborhood spots that make up the vast majority of Turkish restaurants. In smaller cities there may well be three or four in a row, each with simple wooden chairs and tables and paper napkins. In towns, villages, and any city with a harbor, lokantas are often open-air, the better to take advantage of the waterfront and sky, or are surrounded by flower-filled trellises. Often you serve yourself cafeteria style from big display cases full of hot and cold dishes—a relief if you don't speak Turkish. If there is no menu, it is because the chef only serves what is fresh, and that changes from day to day.

In the more upscale *restorans* (restaurants), you can expect tablecloths, menus, even a wine list, and dishes drawn from the richer "palace" cuisine of Turkish royalty, often with Continental touches. The best restorans are in Istanbul and Ankara, though others are scattered throughout the country.

The restaurants we list are the cream of the crop in each price category. Properties indicated by an ✕🏨 are lodging establishments whose restaurant warrants a special trip.

Prices in the restaurant chart below are per person and include an appetizer, main course, and dessert but not drinks and gratuities. A service charge of 10% to 15% is added to the bill; waiters expect another 10%. If a restaurant's menu has no prices listed, ask before you order—you'll avoid a surprise when the bill comes.

The term *major cities* in the chart below refers to Istanbul and Ankara, as well as to such major resorts as Bodrum and Antalya. Prices tend to be lower in towns such as Izmir and Bursa that see less tourist traffic.

| CATEGORY | MAJOR CITIES* | OTHER AREAS* |
|---|---|---|
| $$$$ | over $40 | over $30 |
| $$$ | $25–$40 | $20–$30 |
| $$ | $12–$25 | $10–$20 |
| $ | under $12 | under $10 |

## MEALS & SPECIALTIES

Usually eaten at your hotel, breakfast typically consists of *beyaz peynir* (goat cheese), sliced tomatoes, cucumbers, and olives, with a side order of fresh bread; the menu varies little, whether you stay in a simple pansiyon or an upscale hotel. Yogurt with honey and fresh fruit is generally available as well, as are tea and coffee.

This guide makes frequent references to "traditional Turkish cuisine." Here's what to expect.

*Mezes* are appetizers; your selection is brought to your table with a basket of bread. Standard cold mezes include *patlıcan salatası* (roasted eggplant puree flavored with garlic and lemon), *haydari* (a thick yogurt dip made with garlic and dill), *dolma* (stuffed grape leaves, peppers, or mussels), *ezme* (a spicy paste of tomatoes, minced green pepper, onion, and parsley), *kızartma* (deep-fried eggplant, zucchini, or green pepper served with fresh yogurt), *cacık* (a garlicky cold yogurt "soup" with shredded cucumber, mint, or dill), *barbunya pilaki* (kidney beans, tomatoes, and onions cooked in olive oil), and *imam bayıldı* (slow-roasted baby eggplant topped with olive oil–fried onions and tomatoes and seasoned with garlic). One taste of this last meze, and you'll understand how it got its name—which means, "The imam fainted with delight." Inevitably there will be other dishes based on eggplant, *patlıcan* in Turkish. Hot appetizers, usually called *ara sıcak,* include *börek* (a deep-fried or oven-baked pastry filled with cheese or meat), *kalamar* (deep-fried calamari served with a special sauce), and *midye tava* (deep-fried mussels).

Available almost any place you stop to eat, kebabs (*kebaps* in Turkish) come in many guises. Although the

ingredient of choice for Turks is lamb, some kebabs are made with beef, chicken, or fish, usually grilled with vegetables on a skewer. *Adana kebaps* are spicy ground-lamb patties arranged on a layer of sautéed pita bread, topped with a zippy yogurt-and-garlic sauce. *İskender kebaps,* also known as *Bursa kebaps,* are sliced grilled lamb smothered in tomato sauce, hot butter, and yogurt. *Şiş kebaps* are the traditional skewered cubes of lamb, usually interspersed with peppers and onions. *Köfte kebaps* are meatballs made from minced lamb mixed with rice, bulgur, or bread crumbs, then threaded onto skewers.

Fresh fish, often a main course, is commonly served grilled and drizzled with olive oil and lemon. You will find *alabalık* (trout), *barbunya* (red mullet), *kalkan* (turbot), *kefal* (gray mullet), *kılıç* (swordfish, sometimes served as a kebab), *levrek* (sea bass), *lüfer* (bluefish), and *palamut* (bonito). In the meat department there is *mantı,* a sort of Turkish ravioli served with garlicky yogurt that has a touch of mint. Grilled quail is most common inland; it's often marinated in tomatoes, yogurt, olive oil, and cinnamon. *Karışık ızgara,* a mixed grill, usually combines tender chicken breast, beef, a lamb chop, and spicy lamb patties, all served with rice pilaf and vegetables. *Tandır kebap,* lamb cooked in a pit, is a typical Anatolian dish.

For dessert you'll encounter several varieties of *baklava* (phyllo pastry with honey and chopped nuts) and *burma kadayıf* (shredded wheat in honey or syrup). Also popular are puddings, made of yogurt and eggs, as well as sweet rice or milk and rice flour.

## MEALTIMES

Lunch is generally served from noon to 3, dinner from 7 to 10. You can find restaurants or cafés open almost any time of the day or night in cities; in villages getting a meal at odd hours can be a problem. Breakfast starts early, typically by 7. Most Turks fast during daylight hours during the Islamic holy month of Ramadan. During that time, many restaurants, particularly smaller ones outside the major cities, close during day and open at dusk.

Unless otherwise noted, the restaurants listed in this guide are open daily for lunch and dinner.

## RESERVATIONS & DRESS

Reservations are always a good idea: we mention them only when they're essential or not accepted. Book as far ahead as you can, and reconfirm as soon as you arrive. We mention dress only when men are required to wear a jacket or a jacket and tie.

## WINE, BEER & SPIRITS

Alcohol is readily available and widely consumed, despite Turkey's predominantly Muslim culture. However, restaurants are required to have a special license to serve alcohol, which many of the smaller eateries don't have. It is best to check first. Among the inexpensive, perfectly acceptable local wines, the best are Villa Doluca and Kavaklidere, available in *beyaz* (white) and *kırmızı* (red). The most popular local beer is Efes Pilsen, your basic American-type pilsner. In late 1997 Efes also started making a black beer called Efes Dark, and Tuborg pilsner is brewed under license in Turkey. In upscale bars and hotels it is also sometimes possible to find imported beers such as Budweiser. The national drink is rakı, a relative of the Greek ouzo, made from grapes and aniseed. Usually it's mixed with water or ice, though many connoisseurs insist it's best drunk neat, with each sip of rakı followed immediately by a sip of cold water. People drink it throughout their meal or as an aperitif.

## DISABILITIES & ACCESSIBILITY

Unfortunately, Turkey isn't on par with other parts of the world in terms of accessibility. However, many buses have special seats designated for passengers with disabilities, and some of those in larger cities "kneel" to make it easier for less-mobile travelers to board. Some museums and upscale hotels have ramps and elevators, but you are less likely to find these in older museums and small pansiyons. But locals are likely to be very helpful.

## RESERVATIONS

When discussing accessibility with an operator or reservations agent, **ask hard questions.** Are there any stairs, inside *or* out? Are there grab bars next to the toilet *and* in the shower/tub? How wide is the doorway to the room? To the bathroom? For the most extensive facilities meeting the latest legal specifications, **opt for newer accommodations.**

➤ COMPLAINTS: **Disability Rights Section** (✉ U.S. Department of Justice, Civil Rights Division, Box 66738, Washington, DC 20035-6738, ☎ 202/514–0301 or 800/514–0301; TTY 202/514–0383 or 800/514–0383, FAX 202/307–1198, www.usdoj.gov/crt/ada/adahom1.htm) for general complaints. **Aviation Consumer Protection Division** (☞ Air Travel, *above*) for airline-related problems. **Civil Rights Office** (✉ U.S. Department of Transportation, Departmental Office of Civil Rights, S-30, 400 7th St. SW, Room 10215, Washington, DC 20590, ☎ 202/366–4648, FAX 202/366–9371) for problems with surface transportation.

## TRAVEL AGENCIES

In the United States, the Americans with Disabilities Act requires that travel firms serve the needs of all travelers. Some agencies specialize in working with people with disabilities.

➤ TRAVELERS WITH MOBILITY PROBLEMS: **Access Adventures** (✉ 206 Chestnut Ridge Rd., Scottsville, NY 14624, ☎ 716/889–9096, dltravel@prodigy.net), run by a former physical-rehabilitation counselor. **Flying Wheels Travel** (✉ 143 W. Bridge St., Box 382, Owatonna, MN 55060, ☎ 507/451–5005 or 800/535–6790, FAX 507/451–1685, thq@ll.net, www.flyingwheels.com).

## DISCOUNTS & DEALS

Be a smart shopper and **compare all your options** before making decisions. A plane ticket bought with a promotional coupon from travel clubs, coupon books, and direct-mail offers may not be cheaper than the least-expensive fare from a discount ticket agency.

## DISCOUNT RESERVATIONS

To save money, **look into discount reservations services** with toll-free numbers, which use their buying power to get a better price on hotels, airline tickets, even car rentals. When booking a room, always **call the hotel's local toll-free number** (if one is available) rather than the central reservations number—you'll often get a better price. Always ask about special packages or corporate rates.

When shopping for the best deal on hotels and car rentals, **look for guaranteed exchange rates,** which protect you against a falling dollar. With your rate locked in, you won't pay more, even if the price goes up in the local currency. Many large agencies in the United States offer special prices if you prepay for a rental car in U.S. dollars.

## PACKAGE DEALS

Don't confuse packages and guided tours. When you buy a package, you travel on your own, just as though you had planned the trip yourself. Fly/drive packages, which combine airfare and car rental, are often a good deal.

## ELECTRICITY

To use your U.S.-purchased electric-powered equipment, **bring a converter and adapter.** The electrical current in Turkey is 220 volts, 50 cycles alternating current (AC); wall outlets take Continental-type plugs, with two or three round prongs.

If your appliances are dual-voltage, you'll need only an adapter. Don't use 110-volt outlets marked FOR SHAVERS ONLY for high-wattage appliances such as blow-dryers. Most laptops operate equally well on 110 and 220 volts and so require only an adapter.

## EMBASSIES & CONSULATES

➤ IN ANKARA: **Australia** (✉ 83 Nenehatun Cad., Gaziosmanpaşa, ☎ 312/446–1180). **Canada** (✉ 75 Nenehatun Cad., Gaziosmanpaşa, ☎ 312/436–1275). **New Zealand** (✉ 13/4 Iran Cad., Kavaklıdere, ☎ 312/467–9056). **U.K.** (✉ 46/A Şehit Ersan Cad., Çankaya, ☎ 312/468–6230). **U.S.** (✉ 110 Atatürk Bulv., Kavaklıdere, ☎ 312/468–6110).

➤ IN ISTANBUL: **Australian Consulate** (✉ 58 Tepecik Yolu, Etiler, ☎ 212/257–7050). **Canadian Consulate** (✉ 107/3 Büyükdere Cad., Gayrettepe, ☎ 212/272–5174). **U.K. Consulate** (✉ 34 Meşrutiyet Cad., Tepebaşı, ☎ 212/293–7540). **U.S. Consulate** (✉ 104 Meşrutiyet Cad., Tepebaşı, ☎ 212/251–3602).

## EMERGENCIES

If your passport is lost or stolen, contact the police and your embassy immediately (☞ Embassies and Consulates, *above*). For information about food and staying healthy, *see* Dining, *above*.

If you have an emergency, you're best off asking a Turk to call an emergency number for you because it's unlikely you'll find an English-speaking person. Even at the Tourism Police, the person answering the telephone is unlikely to speak English. So first, ask bystanders for help. They will almost invariably try their utmost to be of assistance and will usually know of nearby hospitals or doctors. The Turkish words for ambulance, doctor, and police—*ambulans, doktor,* and *polis,* respectively—all sound about the same as their English equivalents, as does *telefon* for telephone. Say whichever is appropriate, and you can feel fairly certain that you'll be understood when you using the words applicable to your emergency.

➤ CONTACTS: **Ambulance** (☎ 112). **Emergency (police, etc.)** (☎ 155). **Tourism Police (Istanbul)** (☎ 212/527–4503).

## ETIQUETTE & BEHAVIOR

Turks set great store in politeness. No one will expect you to have mastered the intricacies of polite speech in Turkish, but a respectful attitude and tone of voice, combined with a readiness to smile, will often work wonders.

Although Turks are a very tactile people, particularly with friends of the same sex, this physical contact is like a language, full of pitfalls for the unwary. Be very careful about initiating physical contact, as misunderstandings are easy. Overt public physical displays of affection between the sexes are still not widespread and are likely to offend, particularly outside the major cities.

Turks shake hands as a greeting, although this is more common between men than between women. It is quite acceptable, and often very appreciated, if a foreign male initiates a handshake with another male when, for example, leaving a carpet shop. For handshakes between the sexes, unless the Turkish woman is obviously highly Westernized, a foreign male should leave it up to her to initiate any physical contact. It is usually best for foreign women to allow a Turkish man to initiate the handshake rather than trying to judge whether it is advisable or not. Occasionally, very religious Turkish males will pointedly avoid shaking a woman's hand.

A combination of simultaneously shaking hands and kissing on both cheeks is the usual form of greeting between male friends, while women friends more often kiss without shaking hands. However, the kiss is stylized (a cheek-to-cheek "air-kiss"), and it is unusual for the lips to make contact with the skin. On occasion, a Turk will actually kiss the cheek, but such a kiss is considered very forward when given to members of the opposite sex, particularly those of little acquaintance, and if you are a recipient you should draw your conclusions accordingly. It is unusual for two people of the opposite sex to kiss cheeks at all, and you should be wary of kissing someone of the opposite sex in any manner unless you are confident it will not be misinterpreted.

Most Turks consider hospitality as both a duty and a source of pride. If you visit Turks in their homes, it is considered good manners to take off your shoes on entering. You will not be expected to bring gifts, particularly on a first visit, although a small token is always appreciated. Chances are the lady of the house will usually have gone to considerable trouble to prepare food if she has had prior knowledge of your arrival. So you, in turn, should go with an empty stomach and at least try the dishes that are offered to you. In appreciation, it is traditional to say *ellerinize sağlık* (ell-lair-in-izeh sah-luk), which translates

literally as, "May your hands be healthy." No offense will be taken if you don't manage to say it, but it will be much appreciated if you do.

## BUSINESS ETIQUETTE

Business etiquette is little different from everyday etiquette. In the major cities many managers of larger companies will have worked or trained abroad, particularly in the United States, and will be familiar with the ways in which Western companies do business. Punctuality is appreciated, but chronic traffic congestion in Istanbul and Ankara means most businesspeople are used to people arriving a little late for appointments. A telephone call to warn of a late arrival is appreciated.

Business negotiations are usually conducted in a relaxed atmosphere, and the business of the day may be padded with polite conversation and the ubiquitous cups of tea. Provided you eventually get down to business, it is usually a good idea not to force the pace, as the preliminaries are a way for the parties to assess each other and establish mutual trust.

If you are taken out to dinner or on a sightseeing tour, you will be treated more as a guest than a prospective business partner, and your Turkish counterpart will insist on paying for everything. Spouses will usually be more than welcome on such occasions, although it is always advisable to check with your Turkish counterpart first.

## MOSQUES

Turkey is comparatively lenient regarding the visiting of mosques—in many Muslim countries, non-Muslims are strictly forbidden to enter them at all. Most mosques in Turkey are open to the public during the day. Prayer sessions, called *namaz,* last from 30 to 40 minutes and are observed five times daily. These times are based on the position of the sun, so they vary throughout the seasons but are generally around sunrise (between 5 and 7), at lunchtime (around noon or 1, when the sun is directly overhead), in the afternoon (around 3 or 4), at sunset (usually between 5 and 7), and at bedtime (at 9 or 10)—a daily list of prayer times can be found in Turkish newspapers. During namaz it's best not to enter a mosque. Non-Muslims should especially **avoid visiting mosques midday on Friday,** when Muslims are required to congregate and worship.

For women, **bare arms and legs are not acceptable inside a mosque.** Men should avoid wearing shorts as well. Women should not enter a mosque without first covering their heads with a scarf, though some guardians will overlook it when a female tourist does not cover her head.

Before entering a mosque, **shoes must be removed.** There is usually an attendant, and shoes are generally safe. If you feel uncomfortable about leaving them, you can always carry them in your backpack or handbag. It is considered offensive for a non-Muslim to sit down in a mosque (many tourists do sit down despite the signs requesting them not to). It is also advisable to show respect for both the sanctity of the mosque and the piety of those who might be praying in it by talking only in whispers. On no account should you try to take photographs inside the mosque, particularly of people praying.

A small donation is usually requested for the upkeep of the mosque. The equivalent of approximately 50¢ to US$1 is appropriate. Some mosques heavily visited by tourists may also have a "shoe keeper," who will ask for a tip.

### GAY & LESBIAN TRAVEL

Openly gay men and women are still not generally accepted in Turkey, and the recent revival in conservative Islamic sentiment has made matters more difficult. Lesbians are virtually invisible in Turkey. Gay men are more visible (a few well-known singers are generally acknowledged to be gay), and there are gay bars in the major cities. There have been attempts to start a gay movement and to organize conferences on gay rights and other such events, but these have invariably been broken up by the police. Overt displays of affection between gay foreigners will undoubtedly attract stares at the very least and, particu-

larly in rural areas, are likely to generate considerable shock.

➤ GAY- & LESBIAN-FRIENDLY TRAVEL AGENCIES: **Different Roads Travel** (✉ 8383 Wilshire Blvd., Suite 902, Beverly Hills, CA 90211, ☎ 323/651–5557 or 800/429–8747, FAX 323/651–3678, leigh@west.tzell.com). **Kennedy Travel** (✉ 314 Jericho Turnpike, Floral Park, NY 11001, ☎ 516/352–4888 or 800/237–7433, FAX 516/354–8849, main@kennedytravel.com, www.kennedytravel.com). **Now Voyager** (✉ 4406 18th St., San Francisco, CA 94114, ☎ 415/626–1169 or 800/255–6951, FAX 415/626–8626, www.nowvoyager.com). **Skylink Travel and Tour** (✉ 1006 Mendocino Ave., Santa Rosa, CA 95401, ☎ 707/546–9888 or 800/225–5759, FAX 707/546–9891, skylinktvl@aol.com, www.skylinktravel.com), serving lesbian travelers.

### HEALTH

No serious health risks are associated with travel to Turkey, although you should take precautions against malaria if you visit the far southeast. No vaccinations are required for entry. However, to avoid problems at customs, diabetics carrying needles and syringes should have a letter from their physician confirming their need for insulin injections. Travelers are advised to have vaccinations for hepatitis, cholera, and typhoid for trips to the southeast. Rabies can be a problem in Turkey, occasionally even in the large cities. If bitten or scratched by a dog or cat about which you have suspicions, go to the nearest pharmacy and ask for assistance.

For minor problems, pharmacists can be helpful, and medical services are widely available. Doctors and dentists abound in major cities and can be found in all but the smallest towns; many are women. There are also *hastane* (hospitals) and *klinik* (clinics). Road signs marked with an H point the way to the nearest hospital.

### FOOD & DRINK

Tap water is heavily chlorinated and supposedly safe to drink in cities and resorts. It's best to play it safe, however, and stick to *şişe suyu* (bottled still water), *maden suyu* (bottled sparkling mineral water), or *maden sodası* (carbonated mineral water), which are better tasting and inexpensive. Otherwise, Turkish food is relatively safe, though you should still be careful, especially in more out-of-the-way areas.

## MEDICAL PLANS

No one plans to get sick while traveling, but it happens, so **consider signing up with a medical-assistance company.** Members get doctor referrals, emergency evacuation or repatriation, hot lines for medical consultation, cash for emergencies, and other assistance.

➤ MEDICAL-ASSISTANCE COMPANIES: **International SOS Assistance** (✉ 8 Neshaminy Interplex, Suite 207, Trevose, PA 19053, ☎ 215/245–4707 or 800/523–6586, ℻ 215/244–9617, www.internationalsos.com; ✉ 12 Chemin Riantbosson, 1217 Meyrin 1, Geneva, Switzerland, ☎ 4122/785–6464, ℻ 4122/785–6424; ✉ 331 N. Bridge Rd., 17–00, Odeon Towers, Singapore 188720, ☎ 65/338–7800, ℻ 65/338–7611).

## OVER-THE-COUNTER REMEDIES

Many over-the-counter remedies available in Western countries can also be found in Turkish pharmacies, which are usually well stocked. Even a Turkish pharmacist who doesn't speak English will often be able to recognize a specific remedy, particularly if you write the name down, and find an appropriate alternative if that medication is not available.

➤ HEALTH WARNINGS: **National Centers for Disease Control** (CDC; National Center for Infectious Diseases, Division of Quarantine, Travelers' Health Section, ✉ 1600 Clifton Rd. NE, M/S E-03, Atlanta, GA 30333, ☎ 888/232–3228 or 800/311–3435, ℻ 888/232–3299, www.cdc.gov).

## HOLIDAYS

January 1 (New Year's Day); March 5–8 (Kurban Bayramı, an important religious holiday, honoring Abraham's willingness to sacrifice his son to God); April 23 (National Independence Day); May 19 (Atatürk's Commemoration Day, celebrating his birthday and the day he landed in Samsun, starting the independence movement); August 30 (Zafer Bayramı, or Victory Day, commemorating Turkish victories over Greek forces in 1922, during Turkey's War of Independence); October 29 (Cumhuriyet Bayramı, or Republic Day, celebrating Atatürk's proclamation of the Turkish republic in 1923); November 10 (the anniversary of Atatürk's death, commemorated most notably by a nationwide moment of silence at 9:05 AM); December 16–18 (Şeker Bayramı, marking the end of Ramadan).

Please bear in mind that Muslim religious holidays are based on the lunar calendar and shift back about 10 days each year. The dates given here for the Şeker and Kurban holidays are for 2001. In 2002 the dates for the Kurban Bayramı and Şeker Bayramı will be February 22–25 and December 5–7, respectively.

Many businesses and government offices close at midday, usually either 12:30 or 1, on the day before major holidays such as the religious bayrams and Republic Day. If a religious holiday takes up three or four days of a working week, the government will often declare the rest of the week an official holiday as well. However, such decisions are usually made less than a month before the holiday actually begins. For example, in 2001, the government will probably make Friday, March 9, an official holiday, effectively extending the Kurban Bayramı from Saturday March 3 to Sunday March 11.

## INSURANCE

The most useful travel-insurance plan is a comprehensive policy that includes coverage for trip cancellation and interruption, default, trip-delay, and medical expenses (with a waiver for preexisting conditions).

Without insurance you will lose all or most of your money if you cancel your trip, regardless of the reason. Default insurance covers you if your tour operator, airline, or cruise line goes out of business. Trip-delay insurance covers expenses that arise because of bad weather or mechanical delays. Study the fine print when comparing policies.

If you're traveling internationally, a key component of travel insurance is coverage for medical bills incurred if you get sick on the road. Such expenses are not generally covered by Medicare or private policies. U.K. residents can buy a travel-insurance policy valid for most vacations taken during the year in which it's purchased (but check preexisting-condition restrictions). British and Australian citizens need extra medical coverage when traveling overseas.

Always **buy travel policies directly from the insurance company**; if you buy them from a cruise line, airline, or tour operator that goes out of business, you probably will not be covered for the agency or operator's default, a major risk. Before making any purchase, **review your existing health and home-owner's policies** to find what they cover away from home.

➤ TRAVEL INSURERS: In the U.S.: **Access America** (✉ 6600 W. Broad St., Richmond, VA 23230, ☎ 804/285–3300 or 800/284–8300, FAX 804/673–1583, www.previewtravel.com), **Travel Guard International** (✉ 1145 Clark St., Stevens Point, WI 54481, ☎ 715/345–0505 or 800/826–1300, FAX 800/955–8785, www.noelgroup.com).

➤ INSURANCE INFORMATION: In the U.K.: **Association of British Insurers** (✉ 51–55 Gresham St., London EC2V 7HQ, ☎ 0207/600–3333, FAX 0207/696–8999, info@abi.org.uk, www.abi.org.uk). In Australia: **Insurance Council of Australia** (☎ 03/9614–1077, FAX 03/9614–7924).

### LANGUAGE

In 1928, Atatürk launched sweeping language reforms that, over a period of six weeks, replaced Arabic script with the Latin-based alphabet and eliminated many Arabic and Persian words from the Turkish language.

English, German, and sometimes French are widely spoken in hotels, restaurants, and shops in cities and resorts. In villages and remote areas you may have a hard time finding anyone who speaks anything but Turkish, though rudimentary communications are still usually possible. Try

learning a few basic Turkish words; it will be appreciated.

### LODGING

Accommodations range from the international luxury chain hotels in Istanbul, Ankara, and İzmir to charming inns occupying historic Ottoman mansions and caravansaries to comfortable but basic family-run *pansiyons* (guest houses) in the countryside. It's advisable to **plan ahead for the peak season (April–October)**, when resort hotels are often booked by tour companies.

Note that **reservations should be confirmed more than once**, particularly at hotels in popular destinations. Phone reservations are not always honored, so it's a good idea to fax the hotel and get a written confirmation of your reservations, as well as to call again before you arrive. If you want air-conditioning, make sure to ask about it when you reserve.

Asking to see the room in advance is accepted practice. It will probably be much more basic than the well-decorated reception area. Check for noise, especially if the room faces a street or is anywhere near a nightclub or disco, and look for such amenities as window screens and mosquito coils—small, flat disks that, when lighted, emit an unscented vapor that keeps biting insects away.

The lodgings we list are the cream of the crop in each price category. We always list the facilities that are available—but we don't specify whether they cost extra: When pricing accommodations, always ask what's included and what costs extra. Properties indicated by an ✕☲ are lodging establishments whose restaurant warrants a special trip.

Prices in the lodging chart below are for two people in a double room, including VAT and service charge.

| CATEGORY | MAJOR CITIES* | OTHER AREAS* |
| --- | --- | --- |
| $$$$ | over $200 | over $150 |
| $$$ | $100–$200 | $100–$150 |
| $$ | $60–$100 | $50–$100 |
| $ | under $60 | under $50 |

Assume that hotels operate on the **European Plan** (EP, with no meals) unless we specify they use either the **Continental Plan** (CP, with a Continental breakfast), **Breakfast Plan** (BP, with a full breakfast) or the **Modified American Plan** (MAP, with breakfast and dinner) or are **all-inclusive** (including all meals and most activities).

## HOSTELS

No matter what your age, you can **save on lodging costs by staying at hostels.** In some 5,000 locations in more than 70 countries around the world, Hostelling International (HI), the umbrella group for a number of national youth-hostel associations, offers single-sex, dorm-style beds and, at many hostels, rooms for couples and family accommodations. Membership in any HI national hostel association, open to travelers of all ages, allows you to stay in HI-affiliated hostels at member rates; one-year membership is about $25 for adults (C$26.75 in Canada, £9.30 in the U.K., $30 in Australia, and $30 in New Zealand); hostels run about $10–$25 per night. Members have priority if the hostel is full; they're also eligible for discounts around the world, even on rail and bus travel in some countries. There are two youth hostels in Istanbul. Student residences in Ankara, Bolu, Bursa, Çanakkale, İzmir, and Istanbul also serve as youth hostels. Otherwise, you can usually find inexpensive lodging in pansiyons (☞ *below*).

➤ ORGANIZATIONS: **Hostelling International—American Youth Hostels** (✉ 733 15th St. NW, Suite 840, Washington, DC 20005, ☎ 202/783–6161, FAX 202/783–6171, hiayhserv@hiayh.org, www.hiayh.org). **Hostelling International—Canada** (✉ 400-205 Catherine St., Ottawa, Ontario K2P 1C3, ☎ 613/237–7884, FAX 613/237–7868, info@hostellingintl.ca, www.hostellingintl.ca). **Youth Hostel Association of England and Wales** (✉ Trevelyan House, 8 St. Stephen's Hill, St. Albans, Hertfordshire AL1 2DY, ☎ 01727/855215 or 01727/845047, FAX 01727/844126, customerservices@yha.org.uk, www.yha.org.uk). **Australian Youth Hostel Association** (✉ 10 Mallett St., Camperdown,

NSW 2050, ☎ 02/9565–1699, FAX 02/9565–1325, www.yha.com.au). **Youth Hostels Association of New Zealand** (✉ Box 436, Christchurch, New Zealand, ☎ 03/379–9970, FAX 03/365–4476, book@yha.org.nz, www.yha.org.nz).

## HOTELS

Hotels are officially classified in Turkey as HL (luxury), H1 to H5 (first- to fifth-class); motels, M1 to M2 (first- to second-class); and P (pansiyons—guest houses). However, these classifications can be misleading because they're based on the quantity of facilities rather than the quality of the service and decor, and the lack of restaurant or lounge automatically relegates the establishment to the bottom of the ratings. In practice, a lower-grade hotel may actually be far more charming and comfortable than one with a higher rating.

The major Western chains are represented by Hilton, Sheraton, and the occasional Ramada and Hyatt. All tend to be in the higher price ranges.

The standard Turkish hotel room, which you will encounter endlessly throughout the country, is clean, with bare walls, low wood-frame beds (usually a single bed, twin beds, or, less often, a double), and industrial carpeting or kilims on the floor. However, less expensive properties will probably have plumbing and furnishings that leave much to be desired. If you want a double bed, go to a more expensive property, either Turkish or Western style.

All hotels listed have private bath unless otherwise noted.

➤ TOLL-FREE NUMBERS: **Best Western** (☎ 800/528–1234, www.bestwestern.com). **Choice** (☎ 800/221–2222, www.hotelchoice.com). **Hilton** (☎ 800/445–8667, www.hiltons.com). **Holiday Inn** (☎ 800/465–4329, www.basshotels.com). **Hyatt Hotels & Resorts** (☎ 800/233–1234, www.hyatt.com). **Inter-Continental** (☎ 800/327–0200, www.interconti.com). **Renaissance Hotels & Resorts** (☎ 800/468–3571, www.marriott.com). **Sheraton** (☎ 800/325–3535, www.sheraton.com).

## PANSIYONS

Outside the cities and resort areas, these small, family-run places will be your most common option. They range from charming old homes decorated in antiques to tiny, utilitarian rooms done in basic modern. As a rule, they are inexpensive and scrupulously clean. Private baths are common, though they are rudimentary—stall showers, toilets with sensitive plumbing. A simple breakfast is typically included.

## MAIL & SHIPPING

Post offices are painted bright yellow and have PTT (Post, Telegraph, and Telephone) signs on the front. The central post offices in larger cities are open Monday through Saturday from 8 AM to 9 PM, Sunday from 9 to 7. Smaller ones are open Monday through Saturday between 8:30 and 5.

Mail sent from Turkey can take from 3 to 10 days to reach its destination. As a rule of thumb, expect mail to the United Kingdom to take around five days and seven or eight days to non-European destinations. But be warned that the mail service is erratic and that you may arrive home before your postcards are received by friends and family.

### OVERNIGHT SERVICES

There is no international overnight courier service to and from Turkey. The main couriers (DHL, Federal Express, etc.) have offices in Istanbul, but even they take three days from Turkey to the United States and United Kingdom.

### POSTAL RATES

Rates are frequently adjusted to keep pace with inflation, but the cost of sending a letter or postcard remains nominal. Shipping a 10-pound rug home via surface mail will cost about $25 and take from two to six months.

### RECEIVING MAIL

If you're uncertain where you'll be staying, have mail sent to Poste Restante, Merkez Posthanesi (Central Post Office), in the town of your choice.

## SHIPPING PARCELS

It is usually not only much quicker but also much safer to carry your purchases with you, even if you have to pay excess baggage, rather than entrusting them to the postal service. Most parcels from Turkey do eventually arrive at their destination, but be aware there is a risk they may become damaged or lost in transit. Other alternatives, such as courier services or shipping companies, are quicker and more reliable but often very expensive.

## MONEY MATTERS

Turkey is the least expensive of the Mediterranean countries. Although inflation hovers between 70% and 100%, frequent devaluations of the Turkish lira keep prices fairly stable against foreign currencies (which is why prices in this guide are listed in U.S. dollars). Only in Istanbul do costs approach those in Europe, and then only at top establishments. In the countryside, room and board are not likely to come to much more than $50 per person, per day.

Coffee can range from about 30¢ to $2.50 a cup, depending on whether it's the less expensive Turkish coffee or American-style coffee and whether it's served in a luxury hotel or a café; tea, 20¢–$2 a glass; local beer, $1–$3; soft drinks, $1–$3; lamb shish kebab, $1.50–$7; taxi, $1 for 1 km, about ½ mi (50% higher between midnight and 6 AM).

Prices throughout this guide are given for adults. Substantially reduced fees are almost always available for children, students, and senior citizens. For information on taxes see Taxes, below.

### ATMS

ATMs can be found even in some of the smallest Turkish towns. Many accept international credit cards or bank cards (a strip of logos is usually displayed above the ATM). Almost all ATMs have a language key that enables you to read the instructions in English. To use your card in Turkey, your PIN must be four digits long.

Using an ATM is one of the easiest ways to get money in Turkey. Generally the exchange rate is based on the Turkish Central Bank or the exchange rate according to your bank. The exchange rate is almost always better through an ATM than with traveler's checks, but not as good as when exchanging cash.

### CREDIT CARDS

Credit cards are accepted throughout the country (primarily Visa and MasterCard, and sometimes American Express or Diner's Club), especially in larger cities or towns. Note, however, that many budget-oriented restaurants or hotels do not accept credit cards.

If you're planning to get a cash advance on your credit card while in Turkey, it's a good idea to inform the credit company, as companies have been known to put freezes on credit cards because they assumed the transactions in Turkey were fraudulent.

Throughout this guide, the following abbreviations are used: **AE**, American Express; **DC**, Diner's Club; **MC**, Master Card; and **V**, Visa.

### CURRENCY

The monetary unit is the Turkish lira (TL), which comes in bank notes of 100,000; 500,000; 1,000,000; 5,000,000; and 10,000,000. Smaller denominations come in coins of 10,000; 25,000; 50,000; and 100,000. In fall 2000 the exchange rate was TL 687,800 to the U.S. dollar, TL 449,752 to the Canadian dollar, and TL 983,554 to the pound sterling.

Note that Turks often quote prices minus the last three zeros, or even the last five or six zeros. For 250,000,000 TL, for instance, a shopkeeper will say *ici bucuk* (two and a half) or will mark the price tag 250 TL.

In early 2000, the Turkish Central Bank announced plans to shave six zeros off the value of the Turkish lira and introduce a new Turkish lira worth around $2, probably in January 2002.

### CURRENCY EXCHANGE

Because Turkey constantly devalues its currency, wait to change money until you arrive. To avoid lines at airport exchange booths, however, **get a bit of local currency before you leave home.**

If you are staying for more than a few days, do not change all your money as soon as you arrive, as the exchange rate changes every day. Your best bet is to **shop around the exchange booths for the best rate and change enough only for the next few days.** A growing number of privately operated exchange booths offer significantly better rates than hotels or banks. Paying in American dollars, too, can sometimes lead to an extra discount on your purchase.

Although fees charged for ATM transactions may be higher abroad than at home, Cirrus and Plus exchange rates are excellent because they are based on wholesale rates offered only by major banks. You won't do as well at exchange booths in airports or rail and bus stations, in hotels, in restaurants, or in stores, although you may find their hours more convenient.

➤ EXCHANGE SERVICES: **International Currency Express** (☎ 888/278–6628 for orders, www.foreignmoney.com). **Thomas Cook Currency Services** (☎ 800/287–7362 for telephone orders and retail locations, www.us.thomascook.com).

### TRAVELER'S CHECKS

Many places in Turkey, even in Istanbul, do not take traveler's checks. And even those that do invariably offer better exchange rates for cash. Lost or stolen checks, however, can usually be replaced within 24 hours, so you may want the added security of traveler's checks even if they prove a little more expensive. To ensure a speedy refund, buy your own traveler's checks—don't let someone else pay for them: irregularities like this can cause delays. The person who bought the checks should make the call to request a refund.

## OUTDOORS & SPORTS

### BEACHES

Turkey's best beaches are on the Mediterranean Coast. From Bodrum, as you head east, top choices include the shores of Sedir Island; İztuzu Beach near Dalyan, a sweeping strand around a lagoon; the Gemiler Island beaches; the placid deep-blue bay of Ölü Deniz; Patara, with its endless stretch of dazzling white sand; the private coves along the Kekova Sound; the strand among the Roman ruins at Phaselis; and Ulas Beach, near Alanya. Beaches along the Aegean are pleasant enough if not as grand. The most popular are, from south to north, Altınkum, Samsun Dağı National Park, Sarımsaklı, near Ayvalık, and those along the Gulf of Edremit. Here the sand is still fine and white, but the beaches are shorter and more heavily used.

### BOATING AND SAILING

Boating the Aegean or Mediterranean coasts opens up otherwise inaccessible sights and bypasses the bumps and bustle of travel by road. You can choose from an array of boats, from sleek, modern yachts, which can be chartered bare or with crew, to traditional wooden boats, called *gulets,* always chartered with crew and often a knowledgeable guide.

### HIKING

Turkey has stunning national parks with sweeping vistas on high grassy plateaus: Uludağ, near Bursa; Kovada Gölü, near Isparta, off the E24 toward Konya; Güllük Dağı, at Termessos; the many trails throughout Cappadocia; and Yedigöller (Seven Lakes), north of Bolu. Even more exceptional for hikers are Turkey's ancient cities. Ruins lie up and down the Aegean and Mediterranean coasts; some (Termessos, Pergamum) are atop cliffs, some (Patara, Phaselis) along beaches. At many smaller sites you will find few—if any—other visitors. Yellow signs mark archaeological sites, both major and obscure.

### PACKING

Turkey is an informal country, so leave the fancy clothes at home. Men will find a jacket and tie appropriate only for top restaurants in Istanbul, Ankara, and İzmir; for more modest establishments a blazer will more than suffice. Women should avoid overly revealing outfits and short skirts. The general rule is: the smaller the town, the more casual and conservative the dress.

On the beaches along the Mediterranean, topless sunbathing is increasingly common—though it is still frowned upon. Shorts are acceptable for hiking through ruins but not for touring mosques. The importance of a sturdy, comfortable pair of shoes cannot be exaggerated. Istanbul's Topkapı Palace is incredibly large, and the ruins at Ephesus and elsewhere are both vast and dusty.

Light cottons are best for summer, particularly along the coast. If you're planning excursions into the interior or north of the country, you'll need sweaters in spring or fall and all-out cold-weather gear in winter. An umbrella is advisable on the Black Sea Coast.

Sunscreen and sunglasses will come in handy. It's a good idea to carry some toilet paper with you at all times, especially outside the bigger cities and resort areas. You'll need mosquito repellent for eating outside from March through October, a flashlight for exploring in Cappadocia, and soap if you're staying in more moderately priced hotels.

In your carry-on luggage **pack an extra pair of eyeglasses or contact lenses** and **enough of any medication you take** to last the entire trip. You may also ask your doctor to write a spare prescription using the drug's generic name, since brand names may vary from country to country. In luggage to be checked, **never pack prescription drugs or valuables.** To avoid customs delays, carry medications in their original packaging. And don't forget to carry with you the addresses of offices that handle refunds of lost traveler's checks.

### CHECKING LUGGAGE

How many carry-on bags you can bring with you is up to the airline. Most allow two, but not always, so make sure that everything you carry aboard will fit under your seat or in the overhead bin, and get to the gate early. Note that if you have a seat at the back of the plane, you'll probably board first, while the overhead bins are still empty.

If you are flying internationally, note that baggage allowances may be determined not by piece but by weight—generally 88 pounds (40 kilograms) in first class, 66 pounds (30 kilograms) in business class, and 44 pounds (20 kilograms) in economy.

Airline liability for baggage is limited to $1,250 per person on flights within the United States. On international flights it amounts to $9.07 per pound or $20 per kilogram for checked baggage (roughly $640 per 70-pound bag) and $400 per passenger for unchecked baggage. You can buy additional coverage at check-in for about $10 per $1,000 of coverage, but it excludes a rather extensive list of items, shown on your airline ticket.

Before departure, **itemize your bags' contents** and their worth, and label the bags with your name, address, and phone number (if you use your home address, cover it so potential thieves can't see it readily). Inside each bag, **pack a copy of your itinerary.** At check-in **make sure that each bag is correctly tagged** with the destination airport's three-letter code. If your bags arrive damaged or fail to arrive at all, file a written report with the airline before leaving the airport.

## PASSPORTS & VISAS

When traveling internationally, **carry your passport** even if you don't need one (it's always the best form of I.D.) and **make two photocopies of the data page** (one for someone at home and another for you, carried separately from your passport). If you lose your passport, promptly call the nearest embassy or consulate and the local police.

### ENTERING TURKEY

Citizens of Australia, Canada, and New Zealand need only a valid passport to enter Turkey for stays of up to 90 days. U.K. citizens need a valid passport and a visa for stays of up to 90 days. Visas can be issued at the Turkish embassy or consulate before you go, or at the point of entry; the cost is £10.

All U.S. citizens, even infants, need a valid passport and a visa to enter Turkey for stays of up to 90 days. Visas can be issued at the Turkish embassy or consulate before you go, or at the point of entry; the cost is

$45 and must be paid in American dollars.

Even though visas are multiple entry and usually valid for 90 days, they cannot be issued for periods longer than the validity of the passport you present. If your passport has less than a month to run, you may not be given a visa at all. Check the validity of your passport before applying for the visa. Turkish officials may impose stiff fines for an overstay on your visa.

### PASSPORT OFFICES

The best time to apply for a passport or to renew is in fall and winter. Before any trip check your passport's expiration date, and, if necessary, renew it as soon as possible.

➤ AUSTRALIAN CITIZENS: **Australian Passport Office** (☎ 131–232, www.dfat.gov.au/passports).

➤ CANADIAN CITIZENS: **Passport Office** (☎ 819/994–3500 or 800/567–6868, www.dfait-maeci.gc.ca/passport).

➤ NEW ZEALAND CITIZENS: **New Zealand Passport Office** (☎ 04/494–0700, www.passports.govt.nz).

➤ U.K. CITIZENS: **London Passport Office** (☎ 0990/210–410) for fees and documentation requirements and to request an emergency passport.

➤ U.S. CITIZENS: **National Passport Information Center** (☎ 900/225–5674; calls are 35¢ per min for automated service, $1.05 per min for operator service).

## REST ROOMS

Public facilities are common in the tourist areas of major cities and resorts and at archeological sites and other attractions; in most, a custodian will ask you to pay a small fee (100 TL or so). In virtually all public facilities, including those in all but the fanciest restaurants, toilets are Turkish style (squatters) and toilet paper is often not provided (to cleanse themselves, Turks use a pitcher of water set next to the toilet). Sometimes it is possible to purchase toilet paper from the custodian, but you are well advised to carry a supply with you as part of your travel gear. Alas, standards of rest room cleanliness tend to be a bit low compared to those in Western Europe and America.

## SAFETY

Violent crime against strangers is still very rare in Turkey. The streets of Turkey's major cities are considerably safer than their counterparts in the United States or Western Europe. You should nevertheless watch your valuables, as pickpockets, although not as common as in the United States or Europe, do operate in the major cities and tourist areas.

In late 2000, the 16-year-old low-level civil war in the southeast between the Turkish military and the separatist Kurdish nationalists, the Kurdistan Workers Party (PKK), appeared to be scaling down. However, it was still far from finished, and the possibility of another upsurge in violence meant that both the U.S. State Department and the British Embassy in Ankara still advised their citizens not to visit the area or, if they did go there, to remain within the major cities and to fly or travel only on main roads (the latter during daylight hours only). For an up-to-date report on the situation, check with the State Department hot line in Washington, D.C. (☞ Chapter 8).

### WOMEN IN TURKEY

Turkey is a generally safe destination for women traveling alone, though in heavily touristed areas such as Istanbul, Antalya, and Marmaris, women unaccompanied by men are likely to be approached and sometimes followed. In rural towns, where visits from foreigners are less frequent, men are more respectful toward women traveling on their own. However, **in the far east you should be particularly careful;** women traveling alone have been known to be harassed in this region.

Some Turkish men are genuinely curious about women from other lands and really do want only to "practice their English." Still, be forewarned that the willingness to converse can easily be misconstrued as something more meaningful.

As for clothing, Turkey is not the place for clothing that is short, tight, or bare, particularly away from the main tourist areas. Longer skirts and shirts and blouses with sleeves are what it takes here to look respectable. Though it may feel odd, covering your head with a scarf will make things easier on you (it's a good idea to have a scarf in your bag at all times). It also helps if you have the manager of the hotel where you are staying call ahead to the manager of your next hotel to announce your arrival—your next host will feel some responsibility to keep you out of harm's way.

As in any other country in the world, the best courses of action are simply to walk on if approached and to avoid potentially troublesome situations, such as deserted neighborhoods at night. Note that in Turkey many hotels, restaurants, and other eating spots identify themselves as being for an *aile* (family) clientele, and many restaurants have special sections for women and children. How comfortable you are with being alone will affect whether you like these areas, which are away from the action—and you may prefer to take your chances in the main room (though some establishments will resist seating you there).

When traveling alone by bus, you should request a seat next to another woman.

## SENIOR-CITIZEN TRAVEL

Although very few provisions are made for senior citizens in terms of the infrastructure in Turkey, you may find the Turks very helpful and courteous with older travelers.

To qualify for age-related discounts, **mention your senior-citizen status up front** when booking hotel reservations (not when checking out) and before you're seated in restaurants (not when paying the bill). When renting a car, ask about promotional car-rental discounts, which can be cheaper than senior-citizen rates.

➤ EDUCATIONAL PROGRAMS: **Elderhostel** (⊠ 75 Federal St., 3rd floor, Boston, MA 02110, ☎ 877/426–8056, FAX 877/426–2166, www.elderhostel.org). **Interhostel** (⊠ University of New Hampshire, 6 Garrison Ave., Durham, NH 03824, ☎ 603/862–1147 or 800/733–9753, FAX 603/862–

1113, learn.dce@unh.edu, www.
learn.unh.edu).

The bazaars, all brimming with copper
and brassware, hand-painted ceramics,
carved alabaster and onyx, fabrics,
richly colored carpets, and (truth be
told) tons of tourist junk, are the main
places to shop in Turkey. Whether
you're a serious shopper or are just
browsing, you won't roam the bazaars
too long before someone tries to lure
you in with a free glass of *çay* (tea).
Remember that bargaining is essential.

## ANTIQUES

Beware of antiques. When dealing
with pieces purported to be more
than 100 years old, chances are you
will end up with an expensive fake,
which is just as well since it's illegal
to export the real thing without a
government permit (and they are very
strict about this). If what you covet is
less than 100 years old, snap it up. If
your purchase looks old, it is advisable to have its date authenticated by
a local museum to avoid problems
when you leave the country.

Note, too, that Turkish antiquities
laws apply to every piece of detritus,
so **don't pick up anything off the
ground at archaeological sites.** You
may be offered *eski para* (old money)
and other "antiquities"; these are all
fake, and if they were not, they could-
n't be taken out of the country. You
are much better off buying high-
quality copies from museum gift
shops rather than from peddlers at
archaeological sites.

## BARGAINING

Outside the bazaars, prices are often
fixed, though in resort areas many
shopkeepers will bargain if you ask
for a better price. But in bazaars the
operative word is "bargain." As much
social ritual as a battle of wills, bargaining can be great fun once you get
the hang of it. There is no rule of
thumb for the difference between the
first price you are offered and how
much the seller will eventually accept.
If you are sure of how much the
article is worth, or how much you are
prepared to pay, then make an offer
15% to 25% under it. If not, don't
state a figure, even if the seller asks

you for one. Just smile, shake your
head sadly, and say the price he is
asking is too expensive. He will
invariably lower it. Express regret
that it is still expensive and ask for
the final price. The figure you are
then given won't, of course, be the
real final price. But the speed and
amount by which the seller changes
his supposed "final price" will give
you an idea of how close you are to
the lowest he will go—and where to
pitch your counteroffer.

Don't forget that you can always tell
the seller that, as much as you appreciate his time and admire the quality
of the item in question, it is still too
expensive, and then get up to leave.
The lowest price invariably comes
when the seller thinks he is about to
lose a customer; and you can always
double back into the store. Note,
however, that it's both bad manners
and bad business to bargain aggres-
sively or to decline to buy once the
seller has accepted your offer.

## RUGS

Persistent salesmen and affordable
prices make it hard to leave Turkey
without flat-woven kilims or other
rugs. No matter what you've planned,
sooner or later you'll end up in the
cool of a carpet shop listening to a
sales rap. Regardless of how many
cups of tea you drink and how persistent the salesmen may be, do not let
yourself be pressured into making a
purchase you do not want. Patterns
and colors vary by region. The best
prices and the best selection are in
smaller villages. You may pay twice
as much in Istanbul, particularly for
older rugs, and you won't find the
same selection or quality—shops here
cater to the package-tour crowd.
Salesmen will insist they can't lower
the price, but they almost always do.

If you buy a rug or kilim and can
manage to take it home on the plane,
do that. If you have purchased a
number of rugs, you might consider
shipping them yourself (or letting the
store do it for you if it has a good
reputation). Note, however, that you
are taking a risk by shipping your rug
and that it will probably take a while
to get to you (☞ The Art of the Kilim
*in* Chapter 8).

## SMART SOUVENIRS

Made of a light, porous stone found only in Turkey, meerschaum pipes are prized for their cool smoke; look for a centered hole and even walls. You can also buy tiles and porcelain, though modern work doesn't compare with older craftsmanship. Some spices, saffron foremost among them, can be purchased for a fraction of their cost back home. Another good deal is jewelry because you pay by weight and not for design—but watch out for tin and alloys masquerading as silver. Turkey is also known for its leather goods, but it's better to stick with merchandise off the rack and steer clear of made-to-order goods.

### STUDENTS IN TURKEY

Travelers 26 and under can purchase an Inter-Rail Pass, which allows unlimited second-class rail travel in Turkey and 19 other European countries. However, as most travel within Turkey is by bus, it is only worth buying a rail pass if you will also be using it outside the country.

It makes sense to **get an International Student Identification Card (ISIC)** or another form of international I.D., as university I.D. cards are rarely accepted; the card entitles you to discounts on airfare, lodging, and museum admission. Turkish Airlines, for instance, offers a 20% discount to all students under age 24 on domestic flights with a valid international student I.D. card. You can get an ISIC at student-oriented travel agencies (☞ Travel Agencies, *below*). Note that ISIC offers limited-coverage medical insurance.

➤ I.D.s & SERVICES: **Council Travel** (CIEE; ✉ 205 E. 42nd St., 14th floor, New York, NY 10017, ☎ 212/822–2700 or 888/268–6245, FAX 212/822–2699, info@councilexchanges.org, www.councilexchanges.org), for mail orders only, in the U.S. **Travel Cuts** (✉ 187 College St., Toronto, Ontario M5T 1P7, ☎ 416/979–2406 or 800/667–2887 in Canada, www.travel-cuts.com).

### TAXES

The value-added tax, in Turkey called Katma Değer Vergisi, or KDV, is 17% on most goods and services. Hotels typically combine it with a service charge of 10% to 15%, and restaurants usually add a 15% service charge.

Value-added tax is nearly always included in quoted prices. Certain shops are authorized to refund the tax (you must ask). Within a month of leaving Turkey, mail the stamped invoice back to the shop, and a check will be mailed to you—in theory if not always in practice.

### TAXIS

Taxis in Istanbul cost about $1 for 1 km, or about ½ mi (50% higher between midnight and 6 AM). Make sure the meter says *gündüz* (day rate); otherwise, you'll be overcharged. Be aware that taxi drivers in tourist areas sometimes doctor their meters to charge more. Don't ride in a taxi in which the meter doesn't work. If you have doubts, ask at your hotel about how much a ride should cost. Many larger hotels will also find cabs for you, usually drivers or companies they know and trust. Note that saying the word *direkt* after giving your destination helps prevent you from getting an unplanned grand tour of town. Tipping is not required, though many taxi drivers expect tourists to round up the price of the ride to the nearest hundred thousand lira (☞ Tipping, *below*).

### TELEPHONES

Telephone numbers in Turkey have seven-digit local numbers preceded by a three-digit city code. Intercity lines are reached by dialing 0 before the area code and number. In Istanbul, European and Asian Istanbul have separate area codes: The code for much of European Istanbul is 212 (making the number look like it's in New York City—but it's not), and the code for Asian Istanbul (numbers beginning with 3 or 4) is 216.

### AREA & COUNTRY CODES

The country code for Turkey is 90. When dialing a Turkish number from abroad, drop the initial 0 from the local area code. The country code for the United States is 1, 61 for Australia, 1 for Canada, 64 for New Zealand, and 44 for the U.K.

## DIRECTORY & OPERATOR ASSISTANCE

For international operator services, dial 115. Intercity telephone operators seldom speak English, although international operators usually have some basic English. If you need international dialing codes and assistance or phone books, you can also go to the nearest post office.

## INTERNATIONAL CALLS

To make an international call from a public phone in Turkey, dial 00, then dial the country code, area or city code, and the number. Expect to pay about $3–$5 per minute.

## LOCAL CALLS

Inside Istanbul you don't need to dial the code for other numbers with the same code, but you need to dial the code (0212 or 0216) when calling from the European to the Asian side of the city or vice versa. All local cellular calls are classed as long distance, and you need to dial the city code for every number.

## LONG-DISTANCE CALLS

To call long-distance within Turkey, dial 131 if you need operator assistance; otherwise dial 0, then dial the city code and number.

## LONG-DISTANCE SERVICES

AT&T, MCI, and Sprint access codes make calling long distance relatively convenient, but you may find the local access number blocked in many hotel rooms. First ask the hotel operator to connect you. If the hotel operator balks, ask for an international operator, or dial the international operator yourself. One way to improve your odds of getting connected to your long-distance carrier is to travel with more than one company's calling card (a hotel may block Sprint, for example, but not MCI). If all else fails, call from a pay phone.

➤ ACCESS CODES: **AT&T Direct** (☎ 00800/12277). **MCI WorldPhone** (☎ 00800/11177). **Sprint International Access** (☎ 00800/14477).

## PUBLIC PHONES

Most pay phones are blue push-button models, although a few older, operator-controlled telephones are still in use. Directions in English and other languages are often posted in phone booths.

Public phones either use phone cards (particularly in major cities) or *jetons* (tokens). Tokens are available in 7¢ and 30¢ denominations, while phone cards come in denominations of 30 ($2), 60 ($3.50), and 100 ($5) units; buy a 60 or 100 for long-distance calls within Turkey, a 30 for local usage. Both tokens and phone cards can be purchased at post offices and, for a small markup, at some corner stores, newspaper vendors, and street stalls. However, they can sometimes be difficult to find, so it's a good idea to buy one at the first opportunity.

To make a local call, insert your phone card or deposit a 7¢ token, wait until the light at the top of the phone goes off, and then dial the number.

### TIME

Istanbul is 2 hours ahead of London, 7 hours ahead of New York, 10 hours ahead of Los Angeles and Vancouver, 11 hours behind Auckland and 9 hours behind Sydney and Melbourne.

### TIPPING

In restaurants a 10%–15% charge is added to the bill in all but inexpensive fast-food spots. However, since this money does not necessarily find its way to your waiter, leave an additional 10% on the table. In top establishments waiters expect tips of 10%–15% in addition to the service charge. Although it's acceptable to include the tip on your bill in restaurants that accept credit cards, a small tip in cash is much appreciated.

Hotel porters expect about $2. Taxi drivers are becoming used to foreigners giving them something; round off the fare to the nearest 50,000 TL. At Turkish baths, staff members who attend to you expect to share a tip of 30%–35% of the bill. Don't worry about missing them—they'll be lined up expectantly on your departure.

Tour guides often expect a tip. Offer as much or (as little) as you feel the person deserves, usually $4–$5 per day if you were happy with the guide. If you've been with the guide for a number of days, tip more. Crews on chartered boats also expect tips.

## TOURS & PACKAGES

Because everything is prearranged on a prepackaged tour or independent vacation, you'll spend less time planning—and often get it all at a good price.

### BOOKING WITH AN AGENT

Travel agents are excellent resources. But it's a good idea to collect brochures from several agencies as some agents' suggestions may be influenced by relationships with tour and package firms that reward them for volume sales. If you have a special interest, **find an agent with expertise in that area**; ASTA (☞ Travel Agencies, *below*) has a database of specialists worldwide.

Make sure your travel agent knows the accommodations and other services of the place they're recommending. Ask about the hotel's location, room size, beds, and whether it has a pool, room service, or programs for children, if you care about these. Has your agent been there in person or sent others whom you can contact?

Do some homework on your own, too: local tourism boards can provide information about lesser-known and small-niche operators, some of which may sell only direct.

### BUYER BEWARE

Each year consumers are stranded or lose their money when tour operators—even large ones with excellent reputations—go out of business. So **check out the operator.** Ask several travel agents about its reputation, and **try to book with a company that has a consumer-protection program** (look for information in the company's brochure). In the United States, members of the National Tour Association and the United States Tour Operators Association are required to set aside funds to cover your payments and travel arrangements in the event the company defaults. It's also a good idea to choose a company that participates in the American Society of Travel Agents' Tour Operator Program (TOP); ASTA will act as media-

tor in any disputes between you and your tour operator.

Remember that the more your package or tour includes, the better you can predict the ultimate cost of your vacation. Make sure you know exactly what is covered, and **beware of hidden costs.** Are taxes, tips, and transfers included? Entertainment and excursions? These can add up.

➤ TOUR-OPERATOR RECOMMENDATIONS: **American Society of Travel Agents** (☞ Travel Agencies, *below*). **National Tour Association** (NTA; ✉ 546 E. Main St., Lexington, KY 40508, ☎ 606/226–4444 or 800/682–8886, www.ntaonline.com). **United States Tour Operators Association** (USTOA; ✉ 342 Madison Ave., Suite 1522, New York, NY 10173, ☎ 212/599–6599 or 800/468–7862, FAX 212/599–6744, ustoa@aol.com, www.ustoa.com).

## TRAIN TRAVEL

The term *express train* is a misnomer in Turkey. Although they exist, serving several long-distance routes, they tend to be slow. The overnight sleeper from Istanbul to Ankara (*Ankara Ekspres*) is the most comfortable and convenient of the trains, with private compartments, attentive service, and a candlelit dining car. There is also daytime service between Ankara and Istanbul (☞ Ankara and Central Anatolia A to Z *in* Chapter 6). In addition, trains run between Istanbul and Edirne and between Ankara and İzmir.

Dining cars on trains between major cities have waiter service and serve surprisingly good and inexpensive food. Overnight expresses have sleeping cars and bunk beds. Cost on the Istanbul–Ankara run is $35, including tips; though advance reservations are a must, cancellations are frequent, so you can often get a space at the last minute.

Fares are lower for trains than for buses (but trains are not as comfortable as buses), and round-trips cost less than two one-way tickets. Student discounts are 10% (30% from December through April). Ticket windows in railroad stations are marked GIŞELERI. Some post offices and authorized travel agencies also sell train tickets. It's advisable to **book in advance, in person, for seats on the best trains and for sleeping quarters.** *See* A to Z sections *in* individual chapters for more information on getting around the country by train.

### THE ORIENT EXPRESS

If you have the time—and money—consider the still-glamorous *Venice Simplon-Orient Express.* The route runs twice a year from Paris to Istanbul via Budapest and/or Bucharest.

➤ TRAIN INFORMATION: **Venice Simplon-Orient Express** (✉ Sea Containers House, 20 Upper Ground, London SE1 9PF, ☎ 020/7928–6000; 800/524–2420 in the U.S.).

### PAYING

Most train stations do not accept credit cards or foreign exchange, so be prepared to pay in Turkish lira.

### TRANSPORTATION AROUND TURKEY

How you get around Turkey depends on your time and budget. The most common way to get around the country for both Turks and tourists is to travel by bus (☞ Bus Travel, *above*). If you have less time or are traveling very long distances, you may want to fly (☞ Airline Travel, *above*). Once you have arrived at your destination, you can get around by taxi, minibus tour, or rented car. Renting a car gives you more freedom to explore on your own (☞ Car Rental *and* Car Travel, *above*) but is more costly and can be more stressful.

### TRAVEL AGENCIES

A good travel agent puts your needs first. Look for an agency that has been in business at least five years, emphasizes customer service, and has someone on staff who specializes in your destination. In addition, **make sure the agency belongs to a professional trade organization.** The American Society of Travel Agents (ASTA), with 27,000 agents in some 170 countries, is the largest and most influential in the field. Operating under the motto "Integrity in Travel," it maintains and enforces a strict code of ethics and will step in to help mediate any agent-

client disputes if necessary. ASTA also maintains a Web site that includes a directory of agents. (If a travel agency is also acting as your tour operator, *see* Buyer Beware *in* Tours & Packages, *above*.)

➤ LOCAL AGENT REFERRALS: **American Society of Travel Agents** (ASTA; ☎ 800/965–2782 24-hr hot line, FAX 703/684–8319, www.astanet.com). **Association of British Travel Agents** (✉ 68–71 Newman St., London W1P 4AH, ☎ 020/7637–2444, FAX 020/7637–0713, information£abta.co.uk, www.abtanet.com). **Association of Canadian Travel Agents** (✉ 1729 Bank St., Suite 201, Ottawa, Ontario K1V 7Z5, ☎ 613/237–3657, FAX 613/521–0805, acta.ntl@sympatico.ca). **Australian Federation of Travel Agents** (✉ Level 3, 309 Pitt St., Sydney 2000, ☎ 02/9264–3299, FAX 02/9264–1085, www.afta.com.au). **Travel Agents' Association of New Zealand** (✉ Box 1888, Wellington 10033, ☎ 04/499–0104, FAX 04/499–0827, taanz@tiasnet.co.nz).

### VISITOR INFORMATION

➤ TOURIST INFORMATION: Australia (✉ 280 George St., Suite 101, Sydney, NSW-2000, ☎ 02/9223–3055). Canada (✉ Constitution Sq., 360 Albert St., Suite 801, Ottawa, Ontario K1R 7X7, ☎ 613/230–8654, FAX 613/230–3683). U.K. (✉ 170–173 Piccadilly, 1st floor, London W1V 9DD, ☎ 020/7629–7771). U.S. (✉ 821 UN Plaza, New York, NY 10017, ☎ 212/687–2194, FAX 212/599–7568; ✉ 1717 Massachusetts Ave. NW, Suite 306, Washington, DC 20036, ☎ 202/429–9844, FAX 202/429–5649).

➤ U.S. GOVERNMENT ADVISORIES: **U.S. Department of State** (✉ Overseas Citizens Services Office, Room 4811 N.S., 2201 C St. NW, Washington, DC 20520, ☎ 202/647–5225 for interactive hot line, 301/946–4400 for computer bulletin board, FAX 202/647–3000 for interactive hot line); enclose a self-addressed, stamped business-size envelope.

### WEB SITES

Do check out the World Wide Web when you're planning your trip. You'll find everything from current weather forecasts to virtual tours of famous cities. Fodor's Web site, www.fodors.com, is a great place to start your online travels. When you see a ✍ in this book, go to www.fodors.com/urls for an up-to-date link to that destination's site.

➤ URLs: **Antalya** (www.antalya2000.com/; www.antalya-ws.com/). **Fethiye** (www.fethiye-net.com/). **Republic of Turkey** (www.turkey.org/). **Travel in Turkey** (www.mersina.com/; www.turkiye-online.com/; www.exploreturkey.com/). **Turkish Airlines** (www.turkishairlines.com/). **Turkish Tourist Office** (www.turizm.gov.tr/life.html).

## WHEN TO GO

### CLIMATE

Most tourists visit between April and the end of October. July and August are the busiest months (and the hottest). April through June and September and October offer more temperate weather, smaller crowds, and somewhat lower hotel prices.

Istanbul tends to be hot in summer, cold in winter. The Mediterranean and Aegean coasts have mild winters and hot summers; you can swim along either coast from late April into October. The Black Sea Coast is mild and damp, with a rainfall of 90 inches per year. Central and eastern Anatolia can be extremely cold in winter, and its roads and mountain passes closed by snow; summers bring hot, dry weather, with cool evenings.

➤ FORECASTS: **Weather Channel Connection** (☎ 900/932–8437), 95¢ per minute from a Touch-Tone phone.

**ANKARA**

| Jan. | 40F | 4C | May | 74F | 23C | Sept. | 79F | 26C |
|---|---|---|---|---|---|---|---|---|
| | 25 | – 4 | | 49 | 9 | | 52 | 11 |
| Feb. | 43F | 6C | June | 79F | 26C | Oct. | 70F | 21C |
| | 27 | – 3 | | 54 | 12 | | 45 | 7 |
| Mar. | 52F | 11C | July | 86F | 30C | Nov. | 58F | 14C |
| | 31 | – 1 | | 59 | 15 | | 38 | 3 |
| Apr. | 63F | 17C | Aug. | 88F | 31C | Dec. | 43F | 6C |
| | 40 | 4 | | 59 | 15 | | 29 | – 2 |

**ANTALYA**

| Jan. | 59F | 15C | May | 79F | 26C | Sept. | 88F | 31C |
|---|---|---|---|---|---|---|---|---|
| | 43 | 6 | | 61 | 16 | | 67 | 19 |
| Feb. | 61F | 16C | June | 86F | 30C | Oct. | 81F | 27C |
| | 45 | 7 | | 67 | 19 | | 59 | 15 |
| Mar. | 65F | 18C | July | 94F | 34C | Nov. | 72F | 22C |
| | 47 | 8 | | 74 | 23 | | 52 | 11 |
| Apr. | 70F | 21C | Aug. | 92F | 33C | Dec. | 63F | 17C |
| | 52 | 11 | | 72 | 22 | | 47 | 8 |

**ISTANBUL**

| Jan. | 46F | 8C | May | 69F | 21C | Sept. | 76F | 24C |
|---|---|---|---|---|---|---|---|---|
| | 37 | 3 | | 53 | 12 | | 61 | 16 |
| Feb. | 47F | 9C | June | 77F | 25C | Oct. | 68F | 20C |
| | 36 | 2 | | 60 | 16 | | 55 | 13 |
| Mar. | 51F | 11C | July | 82F | 28C | Nov. | 59F | 15C |
| | 38 | 3 | | 65 | 18 | | 48 | 9 |
| Apr. | 60F | 16C | Aug. | 82F | 28C | Dec. | 51F | 11C |
| | 45 | 7 | | 66 | 19 | | 41 | 5 |

**İZMIR**

| Jan. | 49F | 9C | May | 74F | 23C | Sept. | 81F | 27C |
|---|---|---|---|---|---|---|---|---|
| | 36 | 2 | | 54 | 12 | | 58 | 14 |
| Feb. | 50F | 10C | June | 83F | 28C | Oct. | 72F | 22C |
| | 36 | 2 | | 59 | 15 | | 52 | 11 |
| Mar. | 56F | 13C | July | 88F | 31C | Nov. | 63F | 17C |
| | 38 | 3 | | 63 | 17 | | 47 | 8 |
| Apr. | 67F | 19C | Aug. | 88F | 31C | Dec. | 52F | 11C |
| | 45 | 7 | | 63 | 17 | | 40 | 4 |

**TRABZON**

| Jan. | 50F | 10C | May | 67F | 19C | Sept. | 74F | 23C |
|---|---|---|---|---|---|---|---|---|
| | 40 | 4 | | 56 | 13 | | 63 | 17 |
| Feb. | 50F | 10C | June | 74F | 23C | Oct. | 70F | 21C |
| | 40 | 4 | | 63 | 17 | | 58 | 14 |
| Mar. | 52F | 11C | July | 79F | 26C | Nov. | 61F | 16C |
| | 40 | 4 | | 67 | 19 | | 52 | 11 |
| Apr. | 58F | 14C | Aug. | 79F | 26C | Dec. | 54F | 12C |
| | 47 | 8 | | 68 | 20 | | 43 | 6 |

## FESTIVALS AND SEASONAL EVENTS

➤ MAR. OR APR.: The **Mesir Festival in Manisa,** north of İzmir, celebrates *mesir macunu* (power gum), a healing paste made from 41 spices.

➤ APR.: Early April sees one of Istanbul's most popular events, the **Istanbul International Film Festival,** when the city's silver screens come alive with a multinational array of images. In late April the Istanbul suburb of Emirgan, full of gardens, stages its **Tulip Festival,** and the flower beds in its park become a riot of color.

➤ MAY: In Marmaris, the **Yacht Festival** attracts the international boating crowd, which gathers here before setting sail along the Aegean or Mediterranean. The **Ephesus Arts Festival,** held during the first full week of May, brings theater and music to the ancient city. At the end of May is the **Denizli-Pamukkale Festival,** notable for its setting amid calcified cliffs and natural hot springs.

➤ JUNE: The **Rose Festival** in Konya brings together gardeners from throughout the region for a floral competition. **Wrestling tournaments** are held in mid-June in villages throughout the country; the most famous is in Edirne, where burly, olive-oil-coated men have been facing off annually for more than 600 years. Mid-June also brings the monthlong **Istanbul Arts Festival,** Turkey's premier cultural event. Toward the end of June, the castle at İzmir's resort town Çesme becomes the site for the **Çesme International Song Contest.**

➤ JULY: **Folk Festivals** with ethnic dances, concerts, and crafts displays take place in both Kuşadası and Bursa toward the end of the month.

➤ AUG.: The **Assumption of the Virgin Mary** is celebrated on August 15 with a special mass at the House of the Virgin Mary near Ephesus. Also during August, the **Drama Festival in Troy** honors the work of Homer and culminates in the selection of a new Helen of Troy. From August 20 through September 10 the amusements and cultural and commercial displays of the **İzmir International Fair** fill the central Kültür Parkı.

➤ SEPT.: The **Cappadocian Wine Festival,** in Ürgüp, celebrates the grape harvest with midmonth tastings. Also in mid-September, special tours of archaeological sites are conducted as part of the **Hittite Festival,** centered in Çorum; crafts shows and concerts accompany the event. For four days in the middle of September, the **International Song Contest** in Antalya brings open-air concerts to the area around the marina.

➤ OCT.: For the first 10 days of the month, the "Oscars" (actually called the "Golden Oranges") of the Turkish film industry are presented at the **Antalya Film Festival.**

➤ DEC.: The **Festival of St. Nicholas** in Demre celebrates the original Santa Claus, who was a bishop here in the 4th century. The **Rites of the Whirling Dervishes,** which take place during December in Konya, are a rare and extremely popular display by this mystic order.

➤ JAN.: **Camel wrestling** takes place midmonth in Selçuk; there are beauty pageants for the camels, parties for their handlers, and a battle royal in the ancient theater at Ephesus.

# TURKISH VOCABULARY

## Words and Phrases

| English | Turkish | Pronunciation |
| --- | --- | --- |
| **Basics** | | |
| Yes/no | Evet/hayır | **eh**-vet/**hi**-yer |
| Please | Lütfen | **lewt**-fen |
| Thank you | Teşekkür ederim | tay-shake-**kur** eh-day-**reem** |
| You're welcome | Rica ederim Bir şey değil | ree-**jah** eh-day-**reem** beer shay **day**-eel |
| Sorry | Özür dilerim | oh-**zewr** deel-air-eem |
| Sorry | Pardon | **pahr**-dohn |
| Good morning | Günaydın | goon-eye-**den** |
| Good day | İyi günler | ee-yee gewn-**lair** |
| Good evening | İyi akşamlar | ee-yee ank-shahm-**lahr** |
| Goodbye | Allahaısmarladık | **allah**-aw-ees-mar-law-deck |
| | Güle güle | **gew**-leh-**gew**-leh |
| Mr. (Sir) | Bey | by, bay |
| Mrs. Miss | Hanım | ha-nem |
| Pleased to meet you | Memnun oldum | **mam**-noon ohl-doom |
| How are you? | Nasılsınız? | **nah**-suhl-suh-nuhz |

## Numbers

| | | |
| --- | --- | --- |
| one half | büçük | byoo-**chook** |
| one | bir | beer |
| two | iki | ee-**kee** |
| three | üc | ooch |
| four | dört | doort |
| five | beş | besh |
| six | altı | ahl-tuh |
| seven | yedi | yed-dee |
| eight | sekiz | sek-**keez** |
| nine | dokuz | doh-**kooz** |
| ten | on | **ohn** |
| eleven | onbir | **ohn**-beer |
| twelve | oniki | **ohn**-ee-kee |
| thirteen | onüç | **ohn**-ooch |

| | | |
|---|---|---|
| fourteen | ondört | **ohn-doort** |
| fifteen | onbeş | **ohn**-besh |
| sixteen | onaltı | **ohn**-ahl-tuh |
| seventeen | onyedi | **ohn**-yed-dy |
| eighteen | onsekiz | **ohn**-sek-**keez** |
| nineteen | ondokuz | **ohn**-doh-**kooz** |
| twenty | yirmi | yeer-mee |
| twenty-one | yirmibir | **yeer**-mee-beer |
| thirty | otuz | oh-**tooz** |
| forty | kırk | kerk |
| fifty | elli | ehl-lee |
| sixty | altmış | **alt**-muhsh |
| seventy | yetmiş | **yeht**-meesh |
| eighty | seksen | sehk-san |
| ninety | doksan | dohk-**san** |
| one hundred | yüz | yewz |
| one thousand | bin | bean |
| one million | milyon | **mill**-ee-on |

## Colors

| | | |
|---|---|---|
| black | siyah | **see**-yah |
| blue | mavi | **mah**-vee |
| brown | kahverengi | **kah**-vay-**rain**-gee |
| green | yeşil | yay-sheel |
| orange | portakal rengi | poor-tah-kahl rain-gee |
| red | kırmızı | ker-muz-uh |
| white | beyaz | **bay**-ahz |
| yellow | sarı | sah-**ruh** |

## Days of the Week

| | | |
|---|---|---|
| Sunday | Pazar | pahz-**ahr** |
| Monday | Pazartesi | pahz-**ahr**-teh-see |
| Tuesday | Salı | sahl-luhl |
| Wednesday | Çarşamba | char-shahm-**bah** |
| Thursday | Perşembe | pair-shem-**beh** |
| Friday | Cuma | **joom**-ahz |
| Saturday | Cumartesi | joom-**ahr**-teh-see |

## Months

| | | |
|---|---|---|
| January | Ocak | oh-**jahk** |
| February | Şubat | shoo-**baht** |
| March | Mart | mart |
| April | Nisan | nee-**sahn** |
| May | Mayıs | my-us |
| June | Haziran | hah-zee-**rahn** |
| July | Temmuz | **tehm**-mooz |
| August | Ağustos | ah-oos-tohs |
| September | Eylül | ey-**lewl** |
| October | Ekim | eh-**keem** |
| November | Kasım | kah-suhm |
| December | Aralık | ah-rah-**luhk** |

# Useful Phrases

| English | Turkish | Pronunciation |
|---|---|---|
| Do you speak English? | ingilizce biliyor musunuz? | in-**gee-leez**-jay bee-lee-**yohr**-moo-soo-nooz |
| I don't speak Turkish | Türkçe bilmiyorum | **tewrk**-cheh **beel**-mee-yohr-um |
| I don't understand | Anlamıyorum | ahn-**lah**-muh-yohr-um |
| I understand | Anlıyorum | ahn-**luh**-yohr-um |
| I don't know | Bilmiyorum | **beel**-meeh-yohr-um |
| I'm American/ | Amerikalıyım | ahm-ay-**ree**-kah-luh-yuhm |
| I'm British | İngilizim | **een**-gee-leez-eem |
| What's your name? | İsminiz nedir? | ees-mee-niz nay-deer |
| My name is . . . | Benim adım . . . | bay-**neem** ah-duhm |
| What time is it? | Saat kaç? | sah-aht **kahch** |
| How? | Nasıl? | **nah**-suhl |
| When? | Ne zaman? | **nay** zah-mahn |
| Yesterday | Dün | dewn |
| Today | Bugün | **boo**-goon |
| Tomorrow | Yarın | **yah**-ruhn |
| This morning/ afternoon | Bu sabah/ ögleden sonra | **boo** sah-bah/ **ol-lay**-den sohn-rah |
| Tonight | Bu gece | **boo** ge-jeh |
| What? | Efendim?/Ne? | **eh**-fan-deem/neh |
| What is it? | Nedir? | **neh**-deer |
| Why? | Neden/Niçin? | **neh**-den/**nee**-chin |
| Who? | Kim? | keem |
| Where is . . . | Nerede . . . | **nayr**-deh |
| . . . the train station? | . . . tren istasyonu? | tee-**rehn** ees-**tah**-syohn-oo |
| . . . the subway station? | . . . metro durağı? | metro doo-**raw**-uh |
| . . . the bus stop? | . . . otobüs durağı? | oh-toh-**bewse** dor-**ah**-uh |
| . . . the terminal? (airport) | . . . hava alanı? | hah-**vah** **ah**-lah-nuh |
| . . . the post office? | . . . postane? | post-**ahn**-eh |
| . . . the bank? | . . . banka? | **bahn**-kah |
| . . . the hotel? | . . . oteli? | oh-**tel-lee** |
| . . . the museum? | . . . müzesi? | mew-zay-**see** |
| . . . the hospital? | . . . hastane? | hahs-**tah**-neh |
| . . . the elevator? | . . . asansör? | ah-**sewr** |
| . . . the telephone? | . . . telefon? | teh-leh-**fohn** |

| | | |
|---|---|---|
| Where are the restrooms? | Tuvalet nerede? | twah-**let** nayr-deh |
| Here/there | Burası/Orası | **boo**-rah-suh/ **ohr**-rah-suh |
| Left/right | sağ/sol | sah-ah/sohl |
| Is it near/ far? | Yakın mı?/ Uzak mı? | yah-**kuhn** muh/ ooz-**ahk**muh |
| I'd like . . . | . . . istiyorum | **ees**-tee-yohr-ruhm |
| . . . a room | . . . bir oda | beer oh-**dah** |
| . . . the key | . . . anahtarı | **ahn**-ah-tahr-uh |
| . . . a newspaper | . . . bir gazete | beer **gahz**-teh |
| . . . a stamp | . . . pul | pool |
| I'd like to buy . . . | . . . almak istiyorum | ahl-**mahk** ees-tee-your-ruhm |
| . . . cigarettes | . . . sigara | see-**gahr**-rah |
| . . . matches | . . . kibrit | **keeb**-reet |
| . . . city map | . . . şehir planı | shay-**heer plah**-nuh |
| . . . road map | . . . karayolları haritası | **kah**-rah-yoh-lahr-**uh** hah-ree-tah-**suh** |
| . . . magazine | . . . dergi | dair-gee |
| . . . envelopes | . . . zarf | zahrf |
| . . . writing paper | . . . mektup kağıdı | **make**-toop **kah**-uh-duh |
| . . . postcard | . . . kartpostal | cart-poh-stahl |
| How much is it? | Fiyatı ne kadar? | fee-yaht-uh **neh** kah-dahr |
| It's expensive/cheap | pahalı/ucuz | pah-hah-**luh**/ oo-**jooz** |
| A little/a lot | Az/çok | ahz/choke |
| More/less | daha çok/daha az | da-ha choke/ da-ha ahz |
| Enough/too (much) | Yeter/çok fazla | **yay**-tehr/**choke** fahz-lah |
| I am ill/sick | Hastayım | **hahs**-tah-yum |
| Call a doctor | Doktor çağırın | dohk-toor **chah**-uh-run |
| Help! | İmdat! | eem-**daht** |
| Stop! | Durun! | doo-**roon** |

## Dining Out

| | | |
|---|---|---|
| A bottle of . . . | bir şişe . . . | **beer** shee-shay |
| A cup of . . . | bir fincan . . . | beer **feen**-jahn |
| A glass of . . . | bir bardak . . . | beer **bar**-dahk |
| Ashtray | kül tablası | kewl tah-blah-**suh** |
| Bill/check | hesap | heh-**sahp** |
| Bread | ekmek | ekmek |
| Breakfast | kahvaltı | **kah**-vahl-tuh |
| Butter | tereyağı | tay-**reh**-yah-uh |

| | | |
|---|---|---|
| Cocktail/aperitif | kokteyl, içki | cocktail, **each**-key |
| Dinner | aksam yemeği | **ahk**-shahm yee-may-ee |
| Fixed-price menu | fiks menü | feex menu |
| Fork | çatal | **chah**-tahl |
| I am a vegetarian/ I don't eat meat | vejeteryenim/ et yemem | vegeterian-**eem**/ eht yeh-**mem** |
| I cannot eat . . . | . . . yiyemem | **yee**-yay-mem |
| I'd like to order . . . | . . . ısmarlamak isterim | us-mahr-lah-**mahk** ee-stair-eem |
| I'd like . . . | . . . isterim | ee-stair-**em** |
| I'm hungry/ thirsty | acıktım/ susadım | ah-**juck**-tum/ soo-sah-**dum** |
| Is service/the tip included? | servis fiyatı dahil mi? | sehr-rees **fee**-yah-tah dah-heel-**mee** |
| It's good/bad | güzel/güzel değil | gew-**zell**/gew-**zell day**-eel |
| It's hot/cold | sıcak/soğuk | suh-**jack**/soh-**uk** |
| Knife | bıçak | buh-**chahk** |
| Lunch | öğle yemeği | **oi**-leh **yeh**-may-ee |
| Menu | menü | meh-**noo** |
| Napkin | peçete | **peh**-cheh-teh |
| Pepper | karabiber | kah-**rah**-bee-behr |
| Plate | tabak | tah-**bahk** |
| Please give me . . . | lutfen bana . . . verirmisiniz | **loot**-fan bah-nah vair-**eer**-mee-see-niz |
| Salt | tuz | tooz |
| Spoon | kaşık | kah-**shuhk** |

# INDEX

1

# NOTES

# NOTES

# NOTES

# NOTES

# NOTES

# NOTES

# NOTES

# NOTES

# NOTES

# NOTES

# NOTES

# NOTES

# NOTES

# NOTES

# NOTES

# FODOR'S TURKEY 2001

**EDITOR:** Stephen Brewer

**Editorial Contributors:** Linda Cabasin, Gareth Jenkins, Margaret Lynch, Eli Newell, Nancy Van Itallie

**Editorial Production:** Tom Holton

**Maps:** David Lindroth, *cartographer*; Rebecca Baer and Bob Blake, *map editors*

**Design:** Fabrizio La Rocca, *creative director*; Guido Caroti, *art director*; Jolie Novak, *photo editor*; Melanie Marin, *photo researcher*

**Cover Design:** Pentagram

**Production/Manufacturing:** Yexenia Markland

Fifth Edition

ISBN 0–679–00673–7

ISSN 0071–6618

## SPECIAL SALES

Fodor's Travel Publications are available at special discounts for bulk purchases for sales promotions or premiums. Special editions, including personalized covers, excerpts of existing guides, and corporate imprints, can be created in large quantities for special needs. For more information contact your local bookseller or write to Special Markets, Fodor's Travel Publications, 280 Park Avenue, New York, NY 10017. Inquiries from Canada should be directed to your local Canadian bookseller or sent to Random House of Canada, Ltd., Marketing Department, 2775 Matheson Boulevard East, Mississauga, Ontario L4W 4P7. Inquiries from the United Kingdom should be sent to Fodor's Travel Publications, 20 Vauxhall Bridge Road, London, England SW1V 2SA.

PRINTED IN THE UNITED STATES OF AMERICA

10 9 8 7 6 5 4 3 2 1

## IMPORTANT TIP

Although all prices, opening times, and other details in this book are based on information supplied to us at press time, changes occur all the time in the travel world, and Fodors cannot accept responsibility for facts that become outdated or for inadvertent errors or omissions. So always confirm information when it matters, especially if you're making a detour to visit a specific place.

## PHOTOGRAPHY

Corbis: *Adam Woolfitt, cover (Ortahisar's Castle, Cappadocia).*

Kindra Clineff, *4–5, 6A, 30B.*

Coral Planet, *10A, 10B, 11D, 14E, 15G, 15H, 19D, 20 top, 22A, 22C, 23D, 25E.*

Corbis: *Archivo Iconografico, S.A., 12B. Gian Berto Vanni, 11C.*

Dennis Cox, *7C, 7E, 9J, 12A, 13C, 16C, 17E, 18A, 18B, 19C, 21H, 21I, 24B, 25D, 25F, 30C.*

DIAF: *Bruno Morandi, 17D. Yvan Travert, 6B, 9 center.*

Four Seasons Istanbul, *30I.*

Owen Franken, *8G, 17F.*

Hotel Empress Zoë, *30J.*

The Image Bank: *Grant V. Faint, 1. Stefano Scata, 32.*

Len Kaufman, *7D, 9I.*

Izzet Keribar, *8H, 11E, 16A, 16B, 22B, 23E, 23F, 24A, 24C.*

Ministry of Tourism, Turkey, *2 top left, 2 top right, 2 bottom left, 2 bottom center, 2 bottom right, 3 top left, 3 top right, 3 bottom left, 3 bottom right, 13D, 19E, 20F, 20G.*

Richard Nowitz, *14 top.*

Turkish Tourist Office, *30A, 30D, 30E, 30F, 30G, 30H.*

Nik Wheeler, *8F.*

Tim Thompson, *15F.*

# ABOUT OUR WRITERS

Every trip is a significant trip. Acutely aware of that fact, we've pulled out all stops in preparing *Fodor's Turkey 5th Edition*. To help you zero in on what to see in Turkey, we've gathered some great color photos of the key sights in every region. To show you how to put it all together, we've created great itineraries and neighborhood walks. And to direct you to the places that are truly worth your time and money, we've rallied the team of endearingly picky know-it-alls we're pleased to call our writers. Having seen all corners of the regions they cover for us, they're real experts. If you knew them, you'd poll them for tips yourself.

British-born **Gareth Jenkins** is a writer and journalist who has lived in Istanbul since 1989 and describes his fascination with Turkey as being almost an addiction. He has written three books on Turkish history and culture and is currently researching a fourth. Gareth updated the Istanbul, Southern Marmara region, Aegean Coast, Portraits, and Smart Travel Tips chapters.

**Margaret Lynch** is a doctoral student in geography. She began visiting Turkey in 1986 and has traveled there extensively: from Istanbul to Kars, the Mediterranean coast to Erzurum. Most of her time, however, has been spent in Ankara, where for

three out of the last four years she has done research on that city's modern development. Margaret updated the Ankara and Central Anatolia chapter as well as the A to Z section of the Far East chapter.

**Eli Newell,** who updated the Mediterranean Coast and Black Sea Coast chapters, grew up in Portland, Oregon, and received his BA from Wesleyan University. In addition to traveling throughout Turkey and the rest of Europe and Asia as a tourist, Eliís time abroad has included a year in France as an exchange student and a year in Central Asia working for Mercy Corps International.

## Don't Forget to Write

Keeping a travel guide fresh and up-to-date is a big job. So we love your feedback—positive and negative—and follow up on all suggestions. Contact the Turkey editor at editors@fodors.com or c/o Fodor's, 280 Park Avenue, New York, New York 10017. And have a wonderful trip!

Karen Cure
*Editorial Director*